THE BISHOP OF ROME IN LATE ANTIQUITY

The Bishop of Rome in Late Antiquity

Edited by

GEOFFREY D. DUNN
Australian Catholic University, Australia

LONDON AND NEW YORK

First published 2015 by Ashgate Publishing

Published 2016 by Routledge
2 Park Square, Milton Park, Abingdon, Oxon OX14 4RN
711 Third Avenue, New York, NY 10017, USA

Routledge is an imprint of the Taylor & Francis Group, an informa business

© Geoffrey D. Dunn 2015

All rights reserved. No part of this publication may be reproduced, stored in a retrieval system or transmitted in any form or by any means, electronic, mechanical, photocopying, recording or otherwise without the prior permission of the publisher.

Geoffrey D. Dunn has asserted his right under the Copyright, Designs and Patents Act, 1988, to be identified as the editor of this work.

Notice:

Product or corporate names may be trademarks or registered trademarks, and are used only for identification and explanation without intent to infringe.

British Library Cataloguing in Publication Data
A catalogue record for this book is available from the British Library

The Library of Congress has cataloged the printed edition as follows:
The Bishop of Rome in Late Antiquity / edited by Geoffrey D. Dunn.
    pages   cm
Includes bibliographical references and index.
1. Popes – Primacy – History of doctrines – Early church, ca. 30-600. 2. Church history – Primitive and early church, ca. 30-600. I. Dunn, Geoffrey D., 1962- editor.
BX1805.B55 2015
262'.1309021–dc23   2014035205

ISBN   9781472455512 (hbk)

Contents

List of Contributors vii
List of Abbreviations ix

Introduction 1
Geoffrey D. Dunn

PART I: THE FOURTH CENTURY

1 The *Pax Constantiniana* and the Roman Episcopate 17
  Glen L. Thompson

2 The Bishop of Rome and the Martyrs 37
  Marianne Sághy

3 Siricius and the Rise of the Papacy 57
  Christian Hornung

4 Pope Siricius and Himerius of Tarragona (385): Provincial Papal
  Intervention in the Fourth Century 73
  Alberto Ferreiro

PART II: THE FIFTH CENTURY

5 Innocent I and the First Synod of Toledo 89
  Geoffrey D. Dunn

6 Reconsidering a Relationship: Pope Leo of Rome and Prosper of
  Aquitaine 109
  Michele Renee Salzman

7 Narrating Papal Authority (440–530): The Adaptation of *Liber
  Pontificalis* to the Apostolic See's Developing Claims 127
  Philippe Blaudeau

| 8 | Are All Universalist Politics Local? Pope Gelasius I's International Ambition as a Tonic for Local Humiliation
George Demacopoulos | 141 |

| 9 | Crisis in the Letters of Gelasius I (492–96): A New Model of Crisis Management?
Bronwen Neil | 155 |

PART III: THE SIXTH CENTURY

| 10 | *Ipsis diebus Bonifatius, zelo et dolo ductus*: The Root Causes of the Double Papal Election of 22 September 530
Dominic Moreau | 177 |

| 11 | Gregory the Great and Sicily: An Example of Continuity and Change in the Late Sixth Century
Christopher Hanlon | 197 |

Bibliography — *217*
Index — *257*

List of Contributors

Philippe Blaudeau is Professor of Roman History at Université d'Angers and member of the Institut Universitaire de France. He is the author of *Alexandrie et Constantinople (451–491). De l'histoire à la géo-ecclésiologie* (Rome, 2006) and *Le Siège de Rome et l'Orient (448–536). Etude géo-ecclésiologique* (Rome, 2012). His research interests include the history of early Christianity (particularly ecumenical councils and the papacy) and the later Roman empire.

George Demacopolous is Professor of Theology and Director of the Orthodox Christian Studies Center at Fordham University, New York. He is the author or editor of multiple books, including *The Invention of Peter: Apostolic Discourse and Papal Authority in Late Antiquity*.

Geoffrey D. Dunn is Senior Research Fellow at the Centre for Early Christian Studies, Australian Catholic University and a research associate at the Department of Ancient Languages, University of Pretoria. He is currently the editor of *Journal of the Australian Early Medieval Association* and associate editor of *Journal of Early Christian Studies* and the author of many books and articles. His research interests include North African Christianity and fifth-century Roman bishops.

Alberto Ferreiro is Professor of European History at Seattle Pacific University. He is the author of 9 books, among them *Simon Magus in Patristic, Medieval, and Early Modern Traditions*. He has also published 80 articles in patristic and medieval studies. His research interests are Visigothic Hispania, late antique Gallia, New Testament apocrypha, St Vincent Ferrer, medieval pilgrimage, and Iberian patristics.

Christopher Hanlon is an Honorary Research Fellow at the Centre for Early Christian Studies, Australian Catholic University. He is a presbyter of the Catholic Archdiocese of Brisbane.

Christian Hornung is Deputy Director of the Franz Joseph Dölger-Institut zur Erforschung der Spätantike, University of Bonn, Germany. He studied classical philology, theology and German philology at the Universities of Bonn and Vienna. His research interests are the development of ecclesiastical offices and asceticism.

Dominic Moreau is Associate Professor in Late Antiquity at Université de Lille 3 – Sciences humaines et sociales. His research interests include the ancient and early medieval papacy and canonical collections, as well as the ecclesiastical organisation and Christian topography of Italy and the Balkans from the fifth to the sixth centuries.

Bronwen Neil is the Burke Associate Professor in Ecclesiastical Latin at Australian Catholic University and Assistant Director of the Centre for Early Christian Studies, Australian Catholic University. She is immediate past President of the Australian Association for Byzantine Studies and a Fellow of the Australian Humanities Academy. She has published widely on Maximus the Confessor, Pope Martin I, Anastasius Bibliotecarius, and Pope Leo I, as well as poverty and welfare in late antiquity.

Marianne Sághy is Associate Professor in the Department of Medieval Studies, Central European University.

Michele Renee Salzman is Professor of History at University of California at Riverside. She has published extensively on the history and religion of late antiquity, including Leo the Great and the Codex-Calendar of 354. Her most recent publication is *The Letters of Symmachus. Book 1: Introduction, Commentary, Translation* with Michael Roberts. She was the General Editor of the Cambridge History of Religions in the Ancient World.

Glen L. Thompson is Academic Dean and Professor of New Testament and Historical Theology at Asia Lutheran Seminary, Hong Kong. He is the author of *The Correspondence of Pope Julius I* in the Library of Early Christianity series. His research interests include mapping the Roman road system in Anatolia, Christianity in Tang dynasty China, the interplay between church and empire in the fourth century (www.fourthcentury.com) and the early papacy.

List of Abbreviations

ACO	*Acta Conciliorum Oecumenicorum*
AHC	*Annuarium Historiae Conciliorum*
AKG	Arbeiten zur Kirchengeschichte
AntTard	*Antiquité Tardive*
Aug	*Augustinianum*
AugSt	*Augustinian Studies*
BEFAR	Bibliothèque des Écoles françaises d'Athènes et de Rome
BETL	Bibliotheca Ephemeridum Theologicarum Lovaniensium
BJRL	*Bulletin of the John Rylands Library*
BLE	*Bulletin de littérature ecclésiastique*
ByzZ	*Byzantinische Zeitschrift*
CBCR	R. Krautheimer, *Corpus Basilicarum Christianarum Romae*, 5 vols (Vatican City, 1937–77)
CCCOGD	G. Alberigo et al., *The Ecumenical Councils from Nicaea I to Nicaea II (325–787)*, Corpus Christianorum Conciliorum Oecumenicorum Generaliumque Decreta, vol. 1 (Turnhout, 2006)
CCH	G. Martínez Díez and F. Rodríguez, *La colección canónica Hispana*, 6 vols, Monumenta Hispaniae Sacra, serie Canónica (Madrid, 1966–2002)
CCL	Corpus Christianorum, series Latina
CCM	Corpus Christianorum, continuatio Mediaevalis
CEFR	Collection de l'École française de Rome
CH	*Church History*
CHR	*Catholic Historical Review*
CIL	Berlin-Brandenburg Academy of Sciences and Humanities (ed.), *Corpus Inscriptionum Latinarum*, 17 vols (Berlin, 1893–986)
CISAM	Centro italiano di studi sull'Alto Medioevo
CSCO	Corpus Scriptorum Christianorum Orientalium

CSEL	Corpus Scriptorum Ecclesiasticorum Latinorum
CTh	*Codex Theodosianus*
EAA	Collection des Etudes Augustiniennes: Antiquité
ECS	Early Christian Studies
EME	*Early Medieval Europe*
ETL	*Ephemerides Theologicae Lovanienses*
GCS	Die griechischen christlichen Schriftsteller
ICUR	G.B. de Rossi, rev. A. Silvagni, A. Ferrua, D. Mazzoleni and K. Carletti (eds), *Inscriptiones Christianae Urbis Romae Septimo Saeculo Antiquiores*, 10 vols n.s. (Rome, 1922–92), 2 vols orig. series (Rome, 1857–88).
ILCV	E. Diehl (ed.), *Inscriptiones Latinae Christianae Veteres*, 3 vols (Berlin, 1925–31)
ILS	H. Dessau (ed.), *Inscriptiones Latinae Selecta* (Berlin, 1892–1916)
JAEMA	*Journal of the Australian Early Medieval Association*
JbAC	*Jahrbuch für Antike und Christentum*
JE	P. Ewald, 'Ab anno DXC usque ad annum DCCCLXXXII', in P. Jaffé, *Regesta Pontificum Romanorum ab condita ecclesia ad annum post Christum natum MCXCVIII*, Bd. 1: *A S. Petro ad a. MCXLIII*, rev. W. Wattenbach (Leipzig, 1885 [rev. edn]), pp. 143–422.
JK	F. Kaltenbrunner, 'Ab condita Ecclesia ad annum DXC', in P. Jaffé, *Regesta Pontificum Romanorum ab condita ecclesia ad annum post Christum natum MCXCVIII*, Bd. 1: *A S. Petro ad a. MCXLIII*, rev. W. Wattenbach (Leipzig, 1885 [rev. edn]), pp. 1–140.
JRH	*Journal of Religious History*
JRS	*Journal of Roman Studies*
JThS	*Journal of Theological Studies*
MEFRA	*Mélanges de l'école française de Rome. Antiquité*
MGH.AA	Monumenta Germaniae Historica Auctores Antiquissimi
MGH.GPR	Monumenta Germaniae Historica Gesta Pontificum Romanorum
MGH.SRM	Monumenta Germaniae Historica Scriptorum Rerum Merovingicarum

NA	*Neues Archiv der Gesellschaft für ältere deutsche Geschichtskunde zur Beförderung einer Gesamtausgabe der Quellenschriften deutscher Geschichten des Mittelalters*
NBA	Nuova Biblioteca Agostiniana
OCM	Oxford Classical Monographs
OCP	*Orientalia Christiana Periodica*
OECS	Oxford Early Christian Studies
OECT	Oxford Early Christian Texts
OHM	Oxford Historical Monographs
OTM	Oxford Theological Monographs
PBSR	*Papers of the British School at Rome*
PCBE	C. and L. Pietri (eds), *Prosopographie chrétienne du Bas-Empire*, 2 vols (Rome, 1999–2000).
PG	Patrologia Graeca
PL	Patrologia Latina
PLRE	A.H.M. Jones [vol. 1], J.R. Martindale [vols 1–3] and J. Morris [vol. 1], *The Prosopography of the Later Roman Empire*, 3 vols (Cambridge, 1971–92).
RB	*Revue bénédictine*
REAug	*Revue des Études Augustiniennes [et patristiques]*
RSR	*Revue des sciences religieuses*
RTAM	*Recherches de théologie ancienne et médiévale*
SAC	Studi di Antichità Cristiana
SC	Sources Chrétiennes
SEAug	Studia Ephemeridis Augustinianum
TCH	The Transformation of the Classical Heritage
TTH	Translated Texts for Historians
TU	Texte und Untersuchungen zur Geschichte der altchristlichen Literatur
VChr	*Vigiliae Christianae*
WUNT	Wissenschaftliche Untersuchungen zum Neuen Testament
ZKG	*Zeitschrift für Kirchengeschichte*
ZPE	*Zeitschrift für Papyrologie und Epigraphik*

Introduction

Geoffrey D. Dunn

The bishop of Rome is one of the most recognisable religious figures in the world. The office is one of the oldest in continuous existence for the past two millennia. In the popular media there is fascination with the incumbent – his personality and activity – with a particular interest, as with all tarred with the brush of celebrity, on any scandal surrounding the institution, as well as him personally. This fascination reached something of a frenzy in 2005, with the death of John Paul II and the election of Benedict XVI and was repeated in 2013 with the abdication of Benedict and the election of Francis. For some the interest broadens to include the role the Roman bishop plays within the Catholic church, where stories about the interventions of Rome into the lives of individual local churches are well reported, whether favourably or not, and between Christian churches, where the activities of Roman bishops throughout history are seen as having contributed to the fracturing of Christianity into its current various denominations. The reasons behind such fracturing were the Roman bishops' claims to a universal primacy of jurisdiction (the authority to intervene in all other churches). Such claims have existed for quite some time and contributed to the division of the church into Catholic and Orthodox in 1054 and to the Protestant Reformation in the sixteenth century. So entrenched in the popular mind are these notions of Rome's authority within the Catholic church (or at least claims to such authority) that many find it difficult to entertain the notion that it could ever have been different.

Every student of religious history knows that the amount of power, whether sacred or secular, a Roman bishop has been able to exercise in practice has varied considerably over the centuries. The less frequently asked question has been about the amount of power they have claimed in theory (and others were prepared to recognise) and whether this has varied or not over time. Of course, theoretical and practical claims are not unrelated. The question to be asked is about how long Roman bishops have claimed a universal primacy of jurisdiction. Of interest to the contributors to this volume is the question of such claims in the church of late antiquity. When it has been asked, the answer has depended upon the perspective of the person asking the question. As Kristina Sessa has pointed out, in an admirable survey of late antique papal authority, scholarship did turn to this question in the years after papal infallibility was defined at the First Vatican Council in 1870 to see how the Roman bishop was perceived and how he operated in late antiquity.[1] She notes how both Protestant and Catholic scholars, at least until the 1960s, read the evidence in light of later history, seeing in embryonic form in late antiquity realities that would develop fully later. Their approach suggested that the Roman bishops always claimed a universal primacy even if not always able to put that into effect.

Is it possible for us to read the late antique evidence from the Roman bishops themselves in its own context, without the influence of later history? Can one avoid prochronism? Can any scholar turn to the letters of these individuals without a predisposition to interpret the evidence one way or the other? The contributors to this volume believe that one can. Even though some of us may find that Roman bishops did always claim a universal primacy and others may not find that, we would all assert that our findings come from the evidence itself and not from later considerations. As an example of the influence of later perspectives upon reading the evidence from late antiquity, even the very term 'pope' creates problems. Certainly during these centuries the term was used sometimes for the Roman bishop but, since it was used of a number of other bishops as well, it could not mean what it has come to mean in the minds of most people today. The term, like others related to it (patriarch and primate for example), tends to be applied prochronistically, whereby modern ideas are projected back into the literary evidence. Those who are conscious to avoid this (and refer simply to the office holder as bishop of Rome as we do in the title of this volume) tend to suggest that Roman bishops did not have a sense of universal primacy in late antiquity, not even in embryonic form.

It is not disputed that the church of Rome was highly regarded in antiquity. The evidence from the Councils of Nicaea I and Constantinople I attest to this. Rome was an apostolically founded church and was no doubt the founding church of many other Christian communities in the West. It was also a church that could lay claim to the burial sites of two apostles. Even more perhaps than any Petrine claim that involved ranking Peter above the other apostles, it probably was one of the largest churches in the ancient world, given that Rome was by far the largest city of the empire, and the city was still at the empire's centre as its spiritual home, even when the only real Roman capital was Constantinople.

---

[1] K. Sessa, 'Exceptionality and Invention: Silvester and the Late Antique "Papacy" at Rome', in J. Baun, A. Cameron, M. Edwards and M. Vinzent (eds), *Studia Patristica*, vol. 46, papers presented at the Fifteenth International Conference on Patristic Studies held in Oxford 2007 (Leuven, 2010), pp. 77–94, at pp. 77–8

Even if emperors no longer resided there permanently (and in the West there was no emperor at all after 476), the Senate, bureaucratic machinery, and aristocratic families remained and Rome's significance was undiminished. While the church of Milan certainly came to prominence at the time emperors lived there late in the fourth century, this was probably more related to the personality of Ambrose as its bishop than it was to the presence of the imperial court there. Certainly Ravenna, when it became the dominant imperial residence from early in the fifth century, did not emerge as one of Italy's leading churches. To what degree the Roman church's exceptional status translated into power or authority is what is debated, as well as what was the basis for that authority.

Of course, the primary source evidence is itself not unbiased and adds to the difficulty in addressing this question. Sessa points to the invention of Sylvester, bishop in Rome during the time of Constantine I, by which she means not his existence but the later fifth- and sixth-century creations of fictitious accounts of his life (*Liber Siluestri* and *Liber pontificalis*). She suggests that these accounts assisted squabbling Roman factions in times of schism to assert their legitimacy over rivals, helped explain or cover up embarrassing truths about early Roman bishops and, by creating him in ways that would appeal to local Roman aristocrats, contributed to definitions of the powers of the Roman bishop in terms of management of the local church and relationship with secular authority.[2] If evidence about a fourth-century bishop is available to us only through the prism of fifth- and sixth-century interpretations, which had their own agenda and perspectives, it is little wonder that scholars cannot agree on the realities behind these interpretations of the Roman episcopacy and its claims to power during this period.

My own contention is that while the Roman bishops of this period, particularly early in the fifth century, did refer to Peter and to their own church as the apostolic see, the real basis for their authority over other bishops was the hierarchy of the Roman provincial system. Since the reforms of Emperor Diocletian, Roman provinces, now smaller than ever before, had been grouped together to form civil dioceses, and civil dioceses grouped together to form praetorian prefectures. While the idea of a metropolitan bishop within a province was firmly in place by the time of the Council of Nicaea in 325 (although not uniformly applied it would seem), the idea of the bishops of the capitals of civil dioceses and, over above them, the bishops of the capitals of praetorian prefectures, having even greater prestige and authority only gradually asserted itself, and not uniformly. As the fortunes waxed and waned of these

---

[2] Sessa, 'Exceptionality and Invention', pp. 83–94.

cities in which governors, vicars and prefects lived, due in no small part to the migration/invasion of waves of outsiders like the Goths and Vandals from the end of the fourth century onwards, tensions arose within the churches. Should a metropolitan bishop cease enjoying that responsibility and prestige if the governor of the province or vicar of a civil diocese or prefect of a praetorian prefecture was forced to move to another city? What of the place of traditional practice? We see this most clearly in the troubles experienced in the churches in the south of Gaul during the time of Zosimus in Rome (417–18), where the earlier move of the praetorian prefect from Trier to Arles and of the governor from Vienne to Arles triggered squabbling among the local bishops about who was the leading bishop among them, a squabble into which Rome allowed itself to become embroiled.[3]

This imitation of the political framework for the hierarchy of churches certainly placed the bishop of Rome at the pinnacle in the West. While the authority of a metropolitan received some canonical attention in late antiquity and included judicial appeals, confirmation of episcopal elections and presiding over provincial synods, that of other leading bishops is less clear. Just what authority did such leading bishops in capitals of civil dioceses and praetorian prefectures have? The evidence suggests that initially it was related (or perhaps restricted is the more appropriate term here) to judicial appeals: a bishop judged at the provincial level could appeal up the ladder as it were. This was a specific and narrow band of authority. I would argue that early in the fifth century the Roman bishop had what we could call not a universal primacy of jurisdiction but a western primacy of judicial appeals. In terms of other aspects of his authority beyond judicial appeals the Roman bishop had what I would consider a geographically differentiated degree of impact: for those bishops within the area over which he was metropolitan (and this seems to have included all of the provinces of Italy, depending upon when Milan came to be accepted as a metropolitan), the Roman bishop had a very direct say in the appointment of bishops and in directing them in the management of their local churches (as did other metropolitans within their own provinces); for those further afield, like Illyricum Occidentale and even Illyricum Orientale, there seems to have been a less direct say, for those in Africa, where there was a very organised system in place with the bishop of Carthage long recognised as primate over the whole of western Africa, the impact of Roman directives would have been less again,

---

[3] G.D. Dunn, 'Zosimus and the Gallic Churches', in W. Mayer and B. Neil (eds), *Religious Conflict from Early Christianity to the Rise of Islam*, AKG, Bd 121 (Berlin, 2013), pp. 169–85.

and for bishops in the other western prefecture (in Spain, Gaul and Britain) it was even less again, and it was almost negligible over the East. Of course, this did not stop some Roman bishops from offering advice as though they had been asked to make a ruling. They all would have expected their opinions to be followed. The question of authority is one of the ability to ensure compliance – the further from Rome a bishop was the less ability the Roman bishop had to make that happen.

With the disappearance of the Roman provincial system in the West over the course of the fifth century and with perhaps what might best be described as the natural inclination to augment one's authority, the position of the Roman bishop changed over the course of the centuries of late antiquity. The way Damasus operated in the fourth century was different from the way Gregory operated 200 years later both in terms of his relationship with Italian bishops and with those further afield, whether they were other bishops or civic officials. While from a modern perspective this may seem to have been an inevitable development, good scholarship should avoid looking at events in one period through the prism of later developments. The 'rise of the papacy' school casts its shadow over scholarship into the Roman bishops of late antiquity. The chapters of this volume challenge that to a considerable extent by being more attuned to geographical and chronological differences.

This shifting reality of political power from the fifth to the sixth centuries resulted in Roman bishops engaging more and more with civil authority, becoming part of a triangular interplay involving the Byzantine empire in Constantinople and the Ostrogoths in Ravenna, which complicated or even created some of the theological tensions between East and West at this time.

Interest in Roman bishops in late antiquity has been growing recently as the bibliography to this volume shows. Yet, with the exception of Gregory I,[4] most of the letters of the late antique Roman bishops have not been edited critically or translated into modern languages (while many of Leo I's letters are translated into English there are some that are not and many still awaiting a more critical Latin edition), thereby restricting their utility to contemporary scholarship. There are some large comprehensive historical surveys, most notably by Caspar, Ullmann and Pietri,[5] as well as numerous studies of individuals, but limited

---

[4] Gregory I, *Epistulae* (D. Norberg [ed.], *S. Gregorii Magni Registrum Epistularum libri I–XIV*, CCL, vols 140 and 140A [Turnhout, 1982]).

[5] E. Caspar, *Geschichte des Papsttums von den Anfängen bis zur Höhe der Weltherrschaft*, 2 vols (Tübingen, 1930–33); W. Ullmann, *A Short History of the Papacy in the Middle Ages* (London, 2003 [2nd edn]); and Ch. Pietri, *Roma Christiana. Recherches sur l'Église de Rome*,

mainly to Leo and Gregory.[6] It is all a bit hit and miss. Perhaps the topic had been too much of a hot potato, best avoided in an ecumenical gesture of not dragging up the past. Is there nothing more to be said about these early Roman bishops? Is the evidence too scant to make it a worthwhile topic? Are the other Roman bishops of late antiquity of less interest or significance? Are scholars now simply redressing the imbalance by turning their attention to other late antique churches and exploring the role of their bishops? Perhaps the answer involves all of this and more.

The idea for this volume grew out of two workshop sessions held at the 2011 International Conference on Patristic Studies at Oxford University. Some of the chapters originally were presented as papers there, others have been written especially for this volume. All the contributions have been revised by the authors, reviewed by the editor, by anonymous readers chosen by the editor and by an anonymous reviewer chosen by the publisher, and have therefore undergone substantial revision from their original forms for inclusion in this volume to ensure that they cohere to the specific theme.

The chapters of this volume are indeed concerned with the Roman episcopacy in late antiquity, from the end of the fourth century to the beginning of the seventh. This was a turbulent time in world history, recognised now as epoch changing, as antiquity gave way to the middle ages, yet close enough to the origins of the office to see something of its original limited scope in the wider world. It was a time of dramatic transformation. The Roman empire, the largest the world had seen, disappeared, at least in the West, and new peoples swept across the European stage, destroying and imitating what they found in equal (or unequal) measure. Every institution reinvented itself as it responded to the numerous challenges a new age presented. These chapters will illustrate, in episodic fashion, that gradual reinvention of the role and function of the Roman bishop over these centuries. Not every chapter deals with the question of papal primacy, but each one is interested in questions of authority to some extent.

The focus of this volume will be on how the bishop of Rome operated in three spheres: within his own church in Rome, in relationship with other bishops and in relationship with civil authorities. It will also chart how such operations

---

son organisation, sa politique, son idéologie de Miltiade à Sixte III (311–440), BEFAR, vol. 224 (Rome, 1976).

[6] E.g.: B. Green, *The Soteriology of Leo the Great*, OTM (Oxford, 2008); S. Wessel, *Leo the Great and the Spiritual Rebuilding of Rome*, Supplements to Vigiliae Christianae, vol. 93 (Leiden, 2008); J. Richards, *Consul of God: The Life and Times of Pope Gregory the Great* (London, 1980); G.R. Evans, *The Thought of Gregory the Great* (Cambridge, 1986); R.A. Markus, *Gregory the Great and his World* (Cambridge, 1997).

changed over these few centuries. Not every essay will deal with all three topics. This may reflect the fact that some bishops themselves concentrated on one or another of them, or that those who preserved the source material were concerned with differing topics, depending on the collection into which that material was placed. It may reflect the differing scholarly interests of the contributors who were not required to cover all three topics in each chapter.

Glen Thompson, Marianne Sàghy and Michele Salzman look at the Roman bishop within his own church, the first interested to some extent in the way in which imperially sponsored Christian building programmes had an impact upon episcopally sponsored building programmes and the last with a relationship between Rome and Gaul. Christopher Hanlon considers Gregory the Great and the churches of Sicily. The chapters by Christian Hornung, Alberto Ferreiro and Geoffrey D. Dunn, with their focus on Spain, consider the Roman bishop in relation to other bishops, although the last has something to say about other bishops and imperial authority. George Demacopoulos and Bronwen Neil both look at Gelasius I within the local church of Rome and in relation both to other bishops and to civil power. Philippe Blaudeau looks at how the narrative of the Roman bishops was shaped by local and regional factors, at both an ecclesiastical and civic level through the interplay of politics and theology. Dominic Moreau also looks at the impact of political factors both local and in the East on the Roman bishop with regard to the election of Boniface II in the first half of the sixth century.

The contributors to this volume represent some of the spectrum of opinion about the degree to which the Roman bishop claimed a universal primacy in late antiquity. Some of us would disagree politely with each other on a number of the interpretations we offer about the question of primacy. The advantage of a collection of chapters by different authors is that it exposes readers to this range of thinking and allows them to evaluate the evidence for themselves. Having two chapters in this volume on Siricius and two on Gelasius I, for example, makes this point all the more clearly: there is no single, definitive way of understanding late antique Roman bishops.

Glen Thompson looks at the material remains of Christianity in Rome itself during the fourth century. In this chapter we see how Roman bishops in the earliest phase of late antiquity operated within their own church. This has been a topic of some popularity recently. He argues for the Roman bishops being much more actively involved in a building programme than Sessa or Kim Bowes would support, seeing the bishops as complementary rather than competitive with aristocratic foundations.[7] The increased sophistication in the training of clergy and the construction of large basilicas provided the means by which the Roman bishop gained more control over the life of his own church.

Marianne Sághy also looks at the local Roman church, specifically under Damasus (366–84). Her attention is turned to the catacomb inscriptions and the way Damasus used them to claim the martyrs for his faction of Christianity in the city during a time of noticeable division, particularly against Arians. The epigrams to be found not only in martyr catacombs but in those of others as well, including members of Damasus' own family, record Damasus' struggles to control the local church and the ways in which he associated the saints in any victories he had. This kept the focus on the suburbs and on small local communities, maximising his exposure, in contrast to the monumentalising building programmes of Constantine's family. Celebrating the lives of other Christians helped promote the communion of saints and the loyalty and unity of the local community to its bishop.

Both Christian Hornung and Alberto Ferreiro look at Siricius (384–99) and his relationship with the Spanish churches and, from their differing perspectives, both reach the conclusion that Siricius, in his letter *Directa*, was claiming an extensive authority. Hornung considers the similarities with Roman legal language and, in the episcopal adoption of the civil language of legislating, sees Siricius legislating for the regulation of church, especially clerical, life in the Spanish churches, partly in response to questions asked by Himerius but partly on his own initiative. He sees a universal character in the rules promulgated by Siricius. Ferreiro looks more at the relationship between Spain and Rome and finds that there is a mixture of both pastoral and authoritative language in Siricius' letter, that it was not targeted at Priscillianists and that it was intended only for the churches of Spain and Gaul. He sees it as contributing to the development of Rome's Petrine authority. While these two scholars mention Innocent, they evaluate him in continuity with Siricius as issuing universal legislation; I do not consider Innocent's letters to be legislative. Indeed, I would dispute the contention that Siricius developed the decretal as a new genre. I would contend that this reflects more of the mind of those who, in later centuries, would come to collect and transmit these letters in canonical collections, again in an attempt to find their own experience of papal authority reflected in the past.[8] This is not the

---

[7] K. Bowes, *Private Worship, Public Values, and Religious Change in Late Antiquity* (Cambridge, 2008).

[8] G.D. Dunn, 'The Emergence of Papal Decretals: The Evidence of Zosimus of Rome', in G. Greatrex and H. Elton with L. McMahon (eds), *Shifting Genres in Late Antiquity* (Farnham: Ashgate, 2015), 81–92.

place to debate these points and perhaps it is a little unfair that as editor I get the last word, but it is worth noting the differing interpretations we hold. The reader is left to decide whether bishops at the start of the fifth century consulted Rome looking for advice or sought directives from their superior bishop and how the Roman bishop saw his own role.

In contrast with Hornung and Ferreiro, I assert that early in the fifth century a bishop such as Innocent I (402–17) did not even make such claims to a universal authority. He had, I believe, a geographically differentiated sense of his level of authority or his ability to achieve compliance, shaped to a great extent by the imperial provincial structures of late antiquity, as I outlined earlier in this introduction. Over those bishops he met regularly in synod as metropolitan, his ability to get them to do what he wanted, to put it crudely, was strongest. Over bishops who resided within the prefecture of Italy (a region that had often included Africa and Illyricum), for whom he was a court of appeal for matters first judged at a local level, his influence was still considerable. For bishops in the remainder of the West (Gaul, Spain and Britain) we know that Innocent encouraged them to turn to Rome for advice (advice which he presumed they would accept) and as a court of appeal. Bishops from those regions were happy to turn to Rome when they were confident that his opinion would match their own locally contested opinion and add support to them against local opponents. For the East, however, the Roman bishop could be a source of support or an ally in the religious politics that involved Constantinople, Antioch and Alexandria in unceasing rivalry, but he was not an arbitrator or superior. In my chapter (Chapter 5) I have outlined how the Spanish bishops, rent by division in light of the Priscillianist crisis, looked to Rome for guidance and encouragement but not for decision-making, even though Innocent's letter might have been preserved in the following centuries by those who did read it as an example of extensive papal authority in the West.

Michele Salzman questions the accepted view that Prosper of Aquitaine came to Rome and remained there working as secretary or theological adviser to Leo I (440–61). The argument advanced here is that a re-reading of the evidence from Gennadius, Ado of Vienne and Photius that has been taken as suggesting that he was, in fact shows that he was not. Even the greater detail about Rome in Prosper's *Epitoma chronicon* after 433 is not evidence of his being there, just evidence of an increased awareness and interest in what was going on there. Tied to that is a consideration of Leo's administrative outlook, which is seen as not as organised as is sometimes believed, with the Roman bishop depending upon limited assistance. This chapter also helps retain Prosper as a Gallic aristocrat and Leo as working to establish relationships with such individuals. We are told that Leo was an advocate of papal primacy but did not have the resources to pursue it effectively.

George Demacopoulos argues that whatever claims Gelasius (492–96) might have made at the end of the fifth century about his authority, especially its superiority to civic authority (and those claims bore no resemblance to the realities), in the city of Rome itself he was a weak figure, unable to stop the annual celebration of *Lupercalia* because within the local church his authority was in competition with that of aristocratic families who established, endowed and controlled what we would call today private chapels. Rome remained, in part, a collection of household churches outside episcopal control.[9] Demacopoulos has elsewhere examined Gregory I (590–604) and argued for much the same position, this time with regard to his assertion of a Petrine authority: it was employed when he was most unlikely to succeed with what he wanted to achieve.[10] The point about the importance of language is well made. It is all well and good for a Roman bishop to make sweeping claims to their own extensive authority, if and when they did, but quite another thing entirely as to whether anyone believed these claims.

The second chapter on Gelasius is by Bronwen Neil. By way of contrast, she argues that in the ways Gelasius responded to the local crises that beset his time as bishop he was following an African model distinct from that followed previously in Rome. This is discussed in terms of care for the poor, almsgiving, legal defence and advocacy, the maintenance of societal *status quo* in the prevention of slaves being ordained, the management of refugees, the administration of church property, the repudiation of violence and interventions on behalf of those in need and responding to social abuses. Gelasius is seen as the first Roman bishop to have such an extensive interest in such topics.

At first sight these two chapters appears to reach very different conclusions, with Demacopoulos painting a bleak picture of Gelasius' impotence and Neil one of his endless activity. The two are not irreconcilable or utterly discrepant. The first deals with the thorny issue of Gelasius' authority, particularly in relation

---

[9] Sessa, 'Exceptionality and Invention', p. 83: '... during the fourth, fifth, and even sixth centuries, I would contend that Rome's bishops and their supporters were acutely conscious of their relative weaknesses and hindrances. They recognized that even the mighty power of Peter would not be enough when it came to the exercise of authority within a city where a resolutely traditional elite still largely controlled the rules of competition'.

[10] G. Demacopoulos, 'Gregory the Great and the Appeal to Petrine Authority', in J. Baun, A. Cameron, M. Edwards and M. Vinzent (eds), *Studia Patristica*, vol. 48, papers presented at the Fifteenth International Conference on Patristic Studies held in Oxford 2007 (Leuven, 2010), pp. 333–46.

to non-Christians on the local level and to Christian civic leaders in the East. Demacopoulos's point is to show that there was a difference about what one could claim in theory and exercise in practice (similar to the contrast perhaps between *auctoritas* and *potestas*). Episcopal authority, no different no doubt from any other sort, was effective only to the extent that those under that authority were compliant. With regard to *Lupercalia* and the reconciliation of Misenus, which indeed are issues relating to Gelasius within Rome, it would seem that Gelasius did not always get his own way even within his own city. While Neil gives the impression of a Roman bishop wielding considerable authority, not only within Italy, where one would presume his authority to be most respected, but elsewhere as well, what she has not considered, because the evidence is lacking, is the extent to which any of Gelasius' instructions, recommendations, urgings and orders were obeyed. That Theodoric sent back two clerics from Nola when requested indicates that he achieved success at least some of the time. In addition, the fact that there are not follow-up letters suggests that, more often than not, what Gelasius asked for was done. However, addressing the question of just how widespread Gelasius' authority was and just how compliant the recipients of his letters were is not the issue for Neil's findings here and there is little discussion about Gelasius and the East, as there is in Demacopoulos. Her point is to reveal a bishop who involved himself far more than his predecessors did in a variety of local crises, which we do not find them doing. It is not surprising to find him trying to find new ways of cementing his authority when other means failed him. Perhaps one could make the argument that, by surveying more of the evidence in Gelasius, Neil gives us a more complete and balanced picture of Gelasius' degree of authority locally than Demacopoulos does, but that is a decision best left to the readers.

Philippe Blaudeau seeks to look at the original purpose of the earliest versions of *Liber pontificalis*, that amazing and constantly rewritten record of the lives of Rome's bishops. Locating its genesis in the Laurentian schism at the beginning of the sixth century, Blaudeau surveys recent scholarship on the evolution of versions of the text to show how the composition of the lives and their subsequent modifications by later editors served a variety of purposes in drawing attention to the activities of contemporary Roman bishops, particularly Symmachus, to overcome eastern controversies. Earlier bishops back to Leo I were recast positively or negatively in this light to portray an unbroken tradition of Rome's primacy.

Dominic Moreau considers the election of Boniface II. His appointment by his predecessor sparked a schism involving Dioscorus as a rival bishop. This is located in the context of rivalries related back to the Laurentian schism, and the relationship between Rome, Constantinople and the Ostrogoths in Ravenna in light of the Acacian schism over the place of Chalcedonian theology. It is also within the context of one Roman bishop (Felix IV [III]) appointing his own successor (Boniface II). The argument is advanced that the 530 electoral schism involving Boniface and Dioscorus was not the result of a conflict between Ostrogoths and Byzantines but a more overtly religious one where the political overlords wanted a bishop who would not get involved in the Theopaschite controversy while Dioscorus wanted to oppose it more actively (to say nothing of those who supported the formula). Although chosen as a non-interventionist, Boniface's conflict with Constantinople over the deposition of Stephen of Larissa, which is chronicled in the *Collectio Thessalonicensis*, shows him to be a defender of Rome's prerogatives.

What we discover in the chapters by Blaudeau, Demacopoulos, Neil and Moreau is just how much competition between the Ostrogoths and the Byzantines for political or religious control in Italy blended with and made use of divisions within the Roman church and of theologically contentious issues to create a complex reality that is difficult to unfold and narrate but points in the direction of a weakening of the prestige of the Roman church on the global stage.

The final chapter looks at Gregory the Great and the church in Sicily. Christopher Hanlon also has the opportunity to examine Gregory's dealings with Byzantine officials on the island. He notes the ways in which Gregory respected the individuals who held public office in Sicily, working with them to ensure justice within the church, yet criticised them when they interfered in the life of the church, which seemed to have been too frequent for Gregory's liking. In terms of the local churches Gregory was very involved early in his episcopate with revitalising the Sicilian episcopacy through installing hand-picked candidates in vacant churches (including Maximian, his friend from Rome, into the key position in Syracuse) and in using a Roman subdeacon for administering Roman lands there (about which there are a substantial number of letters) and communicating Gregory's will to the local bishops. Those in the monastic life also did not escape Gregory's attention. He was a very interventionist bishop in Sicilian affairs.

Can we notice any changes from the late fourth to the late sixth centuries in the way the Roman bishops thought of their own position, or dealt with other bishops or civic authorities? Were they more or less effective in having their instructions obeyed over the course of these centuries? Do we witness the growth of papal power or just the ebbs and flows of stronger and weaker personalities? We certainly notice the growing complexity of life as the old imperial system was replaced by the new dispensation of what was becoming the early medieval world, where the empire in the East related to various 'barbarian' kingdoms in the West, and we notice the increasing claims to Roman primacy during these centuries. Personality must also have played its part. Some of these individuals were more skilled and experienced at negotiation and persuasion. Yet, changing circumstances over time must also have played its part. Claims to a Petrine authority had a cumulative effect, but just as much as time was a factor so too was geography. We do witness, over time, various Roman bishops seeking to apply the authority they exercised over churches closest to them to churches further and further away from them. Thus, in a sense, although Hanlon shows Gregory as a very interventionist bishop it must be remembered that he is examining Gregory's relationship only with Sicilian bishops, not with those further afield. I for one would assert that, within Italy, we see Innocent I, some two hundred years earlier, operating with just as much intervention as we see in Gregory.[11] It is on this basis that I would contend that geography is often an even more important factor than time when one attempts to analyse these letters. A true indication of the changes from the late fourth to the late sixth centuries would come from considering the relationship between the Roman bishops of those times with other bishops and political leaders further afield. The relationship with civic leaders, whether they were Ostrogoths in Ravenna or emperors in Constantinople did ebb and flow depending upon changes in the triangular power plays between those three centres and the theology expressed by them. With regard to Gregory the Great this has been examined by other scholars to some extent, although there is more work to be done on this. While there certainly was a rise of the papacy by the middle ages, it was geographically differentiated and did not chart a smooth trajectory over time. A variety of factors ensured that it was never going to be inevitable.

It is my hope that this volume will contribute to an increased understanding and appreciation of the role of the bishop of Rome and the importance of the late antique world. The world of early Christianity is an important one for exploring alternative possibilities for the ways in which Roman bishops today conceive of their own position within the Christian community (both local and at a distance) and in the wider world.

---

[11] G.D. Dunn, 'Innocent I and the Suburbicarian Churches: The Letter to Florentinus of Tivoli', *JAEMA*, 6 (2010): pp. 9–23; and G.D. Dunn, 'Innocent I's Letter to the Bishops of Apulia', *JECS*, 21 (2013): pp. 27–41.

PART I
The Fourth Century

Chapter 1

The *Pax Constantiniana* and the Roman Episcopate[*]

Glen L. Thompson

After his victory over Maxentius, Constantine entered Rome, but he remained only 10 weeks. Within days, not only had he made contact with the church but had made a large donation of imperial property, and the planning of the Lateran church was begun.[1] This involved input from the local church, so Constantine's people must have met with Bishop Miltiades' people and worked out the details. Miltiades' staff was probably led by the future bishop, Mark, for the imperial letter of the following year calling for an ecclesiastical court to meet in Rome to examine the accusations of the North African Donatists was addressed 'to Miltiades, bishop of the Romans, and to Mark'.[2] In October 313 Miltiades presided over the hearing. When the Donatists appealed the verdict, Constantine arranged for a second hearing in the autumn of 314, this one at Arles where the emperor was then residing. Its decisions were forwarded to Rome, specifically addressed to Sylvester, who had in the meantime succeeded Miltiades.[3]

---

[*] An earlier version of this chapter was presented at the sixteenth International Conference on Patristic Studies, Oxford University, 8–12 August 2011.

[1] He entered the city on 29 October 312 and was in Milan by mid-January 313. See *CBCR* 5.10 and 90; and J. Curran, *Pagan City and Christian Capital: Rome in the Fourth Century*, OCM (Oxford, 2000), pp. 93–5. Others have argued that a *dedicatio* – a ceding of the land for the purposes of constructing the Christian basilica – took place on 9 November 312, just two weeks after Constantine's entry into Rome. In essence, this was an *ex uoto* or thankoffering for his victory.

[2] Eusebius, *Hist. eccl.* 10.5.18–19 (SC 55.108): '... ἐπισκόπῳ Ῥωμαίων καὶ Μάρκῳ' (my own translation).

[3] Two versions (or a preliminary report and a full version) have survived; see Synod of Arles (CCL 148.3–25). On Sylvester see Kristina Sessa, 'Exceptionality and Invention: Silvester and the Late Antique "Papacy" at Rome', in J. Baun, A. Cameron, M. Edwards and M. Vinzent (eds), *Studia Patristica*, vol. 46, papers presented at the Fifteenth International Conference on Patristic Studies held in Oxford 2007 (Leuven, 2010), pp. 77–94.

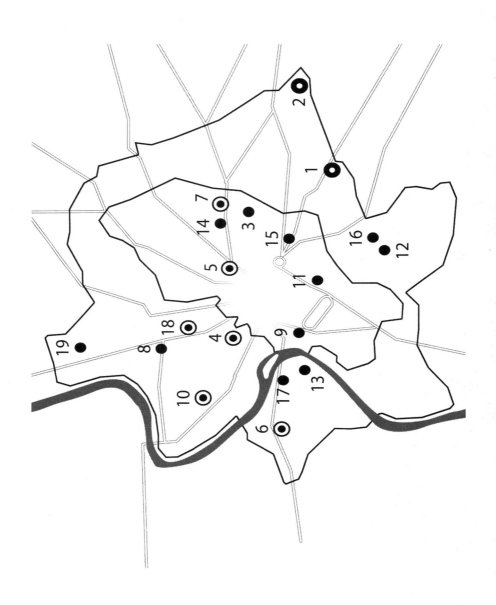

Fourth-Century Church Buildings

The map shows the approximate locations of known fourth-century parishes inside the city walls.

- ◯ Imperial foundations
- ◉ Episcopal foundations
- • Other foundations

Before 337:
- 1. Basilica Salvatoris in Laterano
- 2. Basilica Sessoriana
- 3. Ecclesia Equitii
- 4. S. Marco

Before 352:
- 5. Basilica Julii (iuxta Forum Traiani)
- 6. Basilica Julii (iuxta Callistum)

Before 366:
- 7. Basilica Liberiana
- 8. Ecclesia in Lucina

Before 384:
- 9. S. Anastasia
- 10. Titulus Damasi
- 11. Pammachius et Vizantis
- 12. Titulus Fasciolae
- 13. S. Caecilia
- 14. S. Pudenziana

Before 401:
- 15. Ecclesia Clementis
- 16. Ecclesia Crescentiana

Sometime in fourth century:
- 17. S. Crisogono
- 18. Ecclesia Marcelli
- 19. Ecclesia Felicis

All of these events, like the surviving correspondence of Julius, Liberius, Damasus and Siricius over the following half-century, indicate a clear spiritual and administrative authority for the bishop of Rome within the city and region. Clearly a single bishop of Rome was accepted in the broader Christian community and by the emperors and imperial officials as the leader of the Christian community in Rome. Letters from the bishops of Antioch,

Alexandria, Macedonia and Asia, as well as various parts of the western church, from numerous councils and occasionally from the emperor himself, sought the Roman bishop's solidarity on various doctrinal, disciplinary and practical issues, and in so doing recognised him as the formal representative of the Roman church.[4] In fact, many of these letters concern the episcopal divisions and controversies present in Antioch and Alexandria, and were directed to Rome precisely because there was more stability there.

Rome did experience its own divided episcopacy in the time of Liberius (352–66) and Felix II, and again in the early years of Damasus (366–84) and Ursinus. As a result, for a decade or more the Roman bishop lost much of his regional pre-eminence; but Damasus was able to re-group quite quickly and for a century or more there were no major internal problems within the Roman clergy, except for the dispute between Boniface I (418–22) and Eulalius in 418 and 419 over who was legitimate bishop. These bishops had a ready supply of priests and deacons to carry their correspondence around the Mediterranean. They oversaw a rudimentary bureaucracy and archives, allowing them to access and cite previous correspondence. So while it is prudent not to *assume* a highly developed and consolidated monarchic episcopate during the fourth century, as nearly everyone has done until recently, the evidence in favour should also not be minimised. Normally a single individual was viewed throughout the Roman world – and in Rome itself – by both government and church authorities, as the leader of the Roman church, even by those who were in total disagreement with him and had every reason to find and recognise alternative claimants. This essay will sketch how the construction of Christian basilicas across the city and the concomitant move to more public worship affects our picture of the Roman bishop during the first half-century of the Constantinian peace.

---

[4] First Council of Nicaea, can. 6 (CCCOGD 1.23), gave the bishop of Alexandria jurisdiction over the surrounding areas: ' ... ἐπειδὴ καὶ τῷ ἐν τῇ Ῥώμῃ ἐπισκόπῳ τὸ τοιοῦτον σύνηθές ἐστιν'. (' ... since for the bishop of Rome there is a similar practice ... ') (English translation in P. L'Huillier, *The Church of the Ancient Councils: The Disciplinary Work of the First Four Ecumenical Councils* [New York, 1996], p. 45). Earlier, in the mid-third century, Eusebius, *Hist. eccl.* 6.43.2–3 (SC 41.153–4), mentioned a synod held at Rome attended by some 60 bishops and many more presbyters and deacons.

The Growth of Christianity and Church Building in Rome

A famous comment of Cyprian provides evidence for the size of the Roman church in the mid-third century. He says that the church had only one bishop, but it also had:

> ... forty-six presbyters, seven deacons, seven sub-deacons, forty-two acolytes, fifty-two exorcists, readers, and doorkeepers, and over fifteen hundred widows and persons in distress, all of whom are nourished by the Master's grace and kindness.[5]

The presence of 46 presbyters, almost as many acolytes and only slightly more lower clergy, would point in the direction of some 45 to 50 house-churches or worship groups at the time, each with its presiding presbyter/priest and acolyte.[6] Furthermore, the church's ability to feed some 1,500 widows, orphans and other marginalised members of society would indicate a total membership of perhaps 10,000 to 20,000 adults.[7]

Our lack of specifics during the following century has led to a wide divergence in opinion about the rate of Christianisation in Rome. Ramsay McMullen's estimate that a mere 5 per cent of the city's population was Christian in 300 and 7 per cent a century later is at one extreme, and Christie's approximation of

---

[5] Eusebius, *Hist. eccl.* 6.43.11 (SC 41.156): ' ... πρεσβυτέρους εἶναι τεσσαράκοντα ἕξ, διακόνους ἑπτά, ὑποδιακόνους ἑπτά, ἀκολούθους δύο καὶ τεσσαράκοντα, ἐξορκιστὰς δὲ καὶ ἀναγνώστας ἅμα πυλωροῖς δύο καὶ πεντήκοντα, χήρας σὺν θλιβομένοις ὑπὲρ τὰς χιλίας πεντακοσίας, οὓς πάντας ἡ τοῦ δεσπότου χάρις καὶ φιλανθρωπία διατρέφει ... '.

[6] Sozomen, *Hist. eccl.* 1.15.11 (GCS n.F. 4.34–5), reports that a Palestinian council of ca. 321/22 stated that 'in Alexandria it was and still is the custom that all the churches should be under one bishop, but that each priest should have his own church in which to assemble the people' (my own translation). *Lib. pont.* repeatedly claims that there were 25 *tituli* in Rome long before Constantine: Cletus had ordained 25 priests to whom Evaristus then gave the 25 parishes or *tituli* (3.2 [L. Duchesne and C. Vogel (eds), *Le* Liber pontificalis*; Texte, introduction et commentaire*, BEFAR, vol. 1 (Paris, 1955 [2nd edn]), p. 122]; and 6.2 [Duchesne and Vogel, *Le* Liber pontificalis, p. 126]); Urban donated sacred vases and 25 silver patens for them (18.2 [Duchesne and Vogel, *Le* Liber pontificalis, p. 143]); and Marcellus ordained 25 priests and authorised them to administer baptism, penance and burials in the 25 *tituli* (31.2 [Duchesne and Vogel, *Le* Liber pontificalis, p. 164]). While these are all certainly later additions, they do show the fifth-century belief that from early on the church was organised around 25 *tituli* in the city.

[7] Note we are speaking here of adults, and the addition of children and youthful dependents would raise the total considerably.

50 per cent by the year 400 is at the other.[8] Rodney Stark postulated a growth rate of 3.4 per cent per year (or 40 per cent per decade) across the empire.[9] Yet the periodic persecutions, the opposition of the old pagan aristocracy and the transiency found in the empire's metropolis must have led to a somewhat slower growth rate for the city of Rome itself, perhaps in the 2 per cent range, or some 25 per cent per decade. For the latter half of our period Rome also had a rapidly declining population, and Christians would have been among those emigrating from the city. And while usually it is assumed that there was more rapid growth in the fourth century when it might have become advantageous from a political point of view to become a Christian, in the latter half of the century the pool of potential converts was also declining, since a substantial part of the population was already Christian. All in all, we may envisage the congregation in Rome starting the century with some 20,000 members and ending it with 100,000 or more.

So where did so many Christians gather for worship? In Rome, as elsewhere, the first groups were so-called house-churches, i.e., comparatively small assemblies, which met in the homes of Christians or in rented facilities.[10] By our period, however, Christians in Rome could worship in larger buildings, usually referred to as basilicas in the sources. By the fifth century more than two dozen of these structures were further designated as *tituli*. According to the traditional theory, as such groups out-grew the limited space in houses they remodelled them to allow for larger worship assemblies. These larger spaces, often termed *domus ecclesiae* in the modern literature, were in turn eventually replaced by structures built specifically for Christian meetings, usually in the form of the traditional Roman basilica, many of which were designated by the name of the group's founding leader or benefactor, together with the term *titulus*.

---

[8] R. MacMullen, *The Second Church: Popular Christianity A.D. 200–400* (Atlanta, 2009), p. 170, n. 61; and N. Christie, *From Constantine to Charlemagne: An Archaeology of Italy, AD 300–800* (Aldershot and Burlington, VT, 2006), pp. 98 and 321.

[9] R. Stark, *The Rise of Christianity: A Sociologist Reconsiders History* (Princeton, 1996), p. 6.

[10] For convenience I use the traditional term 'house-churches' to refer to the original small groups of Christians and the locations in which they met for worship and fellowship. This is not meant to imply that the meetings were always held in private dwellings, either unaltered or altered for Christian purposes, but simply to denote those meetings that were not held in purpose-built larger structures more visible to the public. K. Sessa, '*Domus Ecclesiae*: Rethinking a Category of *Ante-Pacem* Christian Space', *JThS*, n.s. 60 (2009): pp. 90–108, has shown that there was no common term used by Christians for such gathering places and that a term such as *domus ecclesiae* is both later and broader in meaning. She does not, however, question that such meeting places must have existed, nor does she suggest a better term by which to denote them.

More recent scholarship has shown that such *tituli* were the results of some sort of benefactory foundation by which local elites provided land, paid for the construction of a worship structure and provided an endowment for permanent clergy and other ongoing maintenance of the structure and its ministry. Thus, the word originally referred to the legal and financial status associated with the basilica's construction or transfer to the church. Pietri argued that the foundation was designed to protect the intentions of the donor, but Julia Hillner has convincingly argued that instead

> ... the term *titulus* must refer to the wish of the bishop's church to show that it had acquired the church in question by just means. It does not provide any clues regarding the origin of the patrimony of a titular church from the honoured founder of the titular church, or indeed any conditions the founder had laid down'.[11]

Hillner admits that the exact meaning of its earliest Christian usage in the fourth century is still vague. She does argue, however, for the clear involvement of the bishop in the establishment of the *tituli*.

The theory of a house-church being architecturally modified and expanded to form a *domus ecclesiae*, which in turn gave way to a basilica, has also now disintegrated. Excavations have routinely found pre-Constantinian structures beneath the early basilicas and *tituli*, but there is almost no evidence that these structures were used for Christian worship. On the other hand, this evidence does not preclude some continuity from earlier groups. We should still expect that in many cases early Christian house churches did eventually turn into neighbourhood congregations that did have their own specific-purpose structures, often with one or more intermediary steps. We should further expect that these groups periodically would have been forced to move locations within a neighbourhood. The density of housing, the fragility of lease-arrangements, fires, floods and building collapses – all of these could have prevented expansion on the original site. There were also frequent expropriations of land for imperial and civic building projects. Even though the size and scope of such projects declined during the economic crisis of the third century, the list of projects from

---

[11] Ch. Pietri, *Roma Christiana. Recherches sur l'Église de Rome, son organisation, sa politique, son idéologie de Miltiade à Sixte III (311–440)*, BEFAR, vol. 224 (Rome, 1976), pp. 95–6; and J. Hillner, 'Families, Patronage, and the Titular Churches of Rome, c. 300–c. 600', in K. Cooper and J. Hillner (eds), *Religion, Dynasty, and Patronage in Early Christian Rome, 300–900* (Cambridge, 2007), pp. 225–61, at pp. 236–7.

that period is still impressive.[12] Thus, a group might need to change locations within an immediate neighbourhood numerous times during the first centuries of its existence.

The preservation of groups, often but not always under the same names, the occasional amalgamation of two groups and the disappearance of others, is exactly what we find in our evidence for the city of Rome. For example, we are told in *Liber pontificalis* that Bishop Mark (whose brief bishopric was in 336) built a basilica *iuxta Pallicinis*. Although the earliest brick-work under the current S. Marco dates only to the fifth century, we can be confident that an early congregation did exist in that neighbourhood on the evidence of a mid-fourth-century inscription, which mentions a *lector de Pallicine*.[13] Geertman's studies have shown that much can be learned about the post-third-century church from *Liber pontificalis* when its entries are used cautiously, and its record of fourth-century basilica construction appears to be both sober and quite accurate.[14]

---

[12] The major imperial building projects within the walls of Rome during the third century include the following: Septimius Severus (193–211) constructed a new camp for the cavalry of the praetorians (*equites singulares*), erected an impressive Septizodium on the south-eastern end of the Palatine and built new baths in Regio I; Caracalla (211–17) enlarged the baths built by Severus, added a new approach called Via Nova and on end of the Quirinal built an enormous temple to Isis and Serapis, modelled on the Serapeum in Alexandria; Elegabalus (218–22) built a new temple to himself as a god on the Palatine, added a circus and amphitheatre for public games while renovating the imperial estate called *ad Spem Veterem*, including a second temple to himself, and also built a temple on the Capitoline or Arx to the African goddess Venus Caelestis; Severus Alexander (222–35) rededicated the temple of Elagabalus on the Palatine to Jupiter Ultor, added a portico and then overhauled the Neronian baths in the Campus Martius to create the new Thermae Alexandrinae, and also seems to have constructed a new *horrea publica* for the *cura annonae*; Decius (249–51) is known to have built a 35 x 70 m bath complex on the Aventine; and Aurelian (270–75) built a temple of Sol in the Campus Martius, redid the camp for the urban cohorts on Via Lata and finally built an expanded wall to enclose 1,372 hectares of city. See Curran, *Pagan City and Christian Capital*, pp. 5–25.

[13] Other references which identify clergy by regions include *lector r(egionis) sec(undae)* (*ICUR* n.s. 3.8719) and *de Belabru* (*ICUR* n.s. 4.12476). Ch. Pietri, 'Régions ecclésiastiques et paroisses romaines', *Actes du XI*ᵉ *Congrès international d'archéologie chrétienne (1986)*, SAC, vol. 41/2 (Rome, 1989), pp. 1035–62, at pp. 1047–8, dated the formation of the seven ecclesiastical regions to this period, further ingraining topographical continuity into the Christian landscape.

[14] See the collected essays of H. Geertman in *Hic fecit basilicam: Studi sul* Liber Pontificalis *e gli edifici ecclesiastici di Roma da Silvestro a Silverio* (Leuven, 2004). The notice on the basilica of Mark on Via Ardeatina is one example (see below).

Mapping Christian Rome in the Fourth Century

With the Christian population numbering 25,000 or more by our period, we would expect Christian parish groups, based on the size limitations of worship sites, to have numbered in the dozens if not a hundred or more. Christians everywhere were expected to attend services on the Lord's Day, so both the number and size of worship locations would have had to increase rapidly as the church's growth accelerated. This would have been the case despite the fact that after legalisation, the church would have attracted more nominal members and therefore the percentage of total adherents attending weekly worship would have begun to decrease. Synodal canons bear this out, warning about the importance of regular attendance.[15] Secondly, in such a large and densely populated metropolitan area as Rome, where land was scarce and expensive, we should expect that church groups from early on had to hold multiple services at one location merely to accommodate the number of worshippers.[16] There is some evidence for this practice in the early church in general, including services on Saturday. So while the fifth- and sixth-century sources make it clear that the *tituli* churches, together with churches designated as deaconries, became the primary *loci* of parish life and the episcopal structure of the city, we should expect that, as these systems began to develop in the fourth century, there was already a much larger number and variety of other locations in and around Rome where Christian worship continued to be held.

Two pieces of literary evidence provide some control for our study. The first comes from the North African bishop, Optatus, in a passage composed

---

[15] Synod of Elvira, can. 21 (*CCH* 4.249): 'Si quis in ciuitate positus tres dominicas ad ecclesiam non accesserit, pauco tempore abstineatur, ut correptus esse uideatur'. ('Anyone living within a city who does not attend church for three Sundays must abstain from communion for a short period, so that he is seen to have been reprimanded'.) (my own translation). Can. 46 (*CCH* 4.257) (can. 22 onwards are probably from a later period) decreed a 10-year probation period before one could again receive communion if there had been an extended absence from worship. In 343, can. 21 (or a similar decision of another synod) was remembered with approval in canon 14 of the Synod of Serdica (H. Hess, *The Early Development of Canon Law and the Council of Serdica*, OECT [Oxford, 2002], p. 221) (Latin version) or can. xi (Hess, *Early Development*, p. 235) (Greek version) or can. T15 (Hess, *Early Development*, p. 251) (Theodosian version).

[16] In the later fifth centuries from 58 to 82 priests were in attendance at various Roman synods, probably already past the peak number. With declining populations, the number continued to drop substantially through the following century. See Ch. Pietri, 'Clercs et serviteurs laïcs de l'Église romaine au temps de Grégoire le Grand', in *Grégoire le Grand: Colloque international du Centre National de la Recherche Scientifique, Chantilly, 15–19 septembre 1982* (Paris, 1986), pp. 107–22.

between the mid-360s and the mid-380s. When ridiculing the Donatist claim to be the 'original' church of Christ, he asks why the Donatist congregation in Rome meets in a cave outside the city, and not in a single one of the forty-odd Christian basilicas within Rome itself (*qui inter quadraginta et quod excurrit basilicas locum*).[17] Secondly, in the mid-380s the Luciferians mocked the size and beauty of Rome's churches – 'basilicas glittering with gold and ostentatiously decorated with expensive marble, held up by splendid columns' and built on 'extensive property' while the Luciferians still worshipped 'in the meanest and most abject hovels', more in line with the stable where Christ was born.[18]

In her study of the Roman church Kimberly Bowes speaks of 'the slow pace of fourth-century church building'.[19] Some Christian buildings must have existed before the great persecution in the early years of the fourth century and would have been restored to the church in accord with the so-called Edict of Milan, but unfortunately we cannot identify these.[20] Yet Optatus tells us that scarcely half a century later, there were some 40 Christian basilicas in the city. And while the accidents of literary, epigraphic and archaeological information have preserved information on only a fraction of the existing Christian groups, we can still name some 20 public worship sites inside the walls of Rome in the fourth century – and only two of these were imperial donations. We will now review how the church of Rome became visible during the course of the fourth century (see Map on p. 18).

We can name four churches which existed in Rome before 337: the *ecclesia Equitii* (in the *praedium*/garden of the priest Equitius *iuxta termas Domitiani*, later known as S. Silvestro, then S. Martino al Monte),[21] the *basilica Salvatoris*

---

[17] Optatus, *De schis.* 2.4.5 (SC 412.248).

[18] Faustinus and Marcellinus, *Liber precum* 121 (*Collectio Avellana, Ep.* 2) (CSEL 35.43): ' ... basilicas auro coruscantes pretiosorumque marmorum ambitione uestitas uel erectas magnificentia columnarum ... in longum possessiones ... uilissima et abiecta praesepia ... '. (my own translation).

[19] K. Bowes, *Private Worship, Public Values, and Religious Change in Late Antiquity* (Cambridge, 2008), p. 62.

[20] The edict ordered all confiscated Christian *loca* and *topoi* be restored. The text is reproduced by both Lactantius, *De mort.* 48.2–12 (SC 39.132–5) and Eusebius, *Hist. eccl.* 10.5.9–12 (SC 55.106–7). A rescript from Constantine to the African proconsul Anulinus also ordered the restitution of church property: ' ... εἴτε κῆποι εἴτε οἰκίοι εἴθ' ὁτιουνδήποτε τῷ δικαίῳ τῶν αὐτῶν ἐκκλησιῶν διέφερον ... ' (Eusebius, *Hist. eccl.* 10.5.17 [SC 55.107–8]). Augustine, *Breu. conl.* 3.18.34 (NBA 16/2.188), informs us that such restitution also occurred in Rome, stating that in 311 Galerius restored to Miltiades through the prefect of Rome the *loca ecclesiastica* confiscated over the previous eight years.

[21] *Lib. pont.* 34.3 (Duchesne and Vogel, *Le* Liber pontificalis, pp. 170–71). See *CBCR* 3.87–125, especially 122–3; M.L. Accorsi, 'Il complesso dei SS Silvestro e Martino ai Monti

*in Laterano*²² and the *basilica Sessoriana*²³ (both funded by Constantine), and the already mentioned church of S. Marco *iuxta Pallacinis*, probably begun by Bishop Mark (March–October 336), and perhaps completed and named for him by his successor, Julius (337–52).²⁴ During his 15-year reign, the latter constructed two churches, a *basilica Iulii iuxta Forum Traiani*²⁵ and a second in Trastevere, described in *Catalogus Liberianus* of *Chronographus anni CCCLIIII* as *iuxta Callistum*.²⁶ In addition, we hear of a church served by the presbyter Vito where Julius held a synod.²⁷ During the episcopate of Liberius, two additional

---

dal III al IX secolo. Appunti di studio', in F. Guidobaldi and A.G. Guidobaldi (eds), *Ecclesiae Urbis*, Atti del congresso internazionale di studi sulle chiese di Roma (IV–X Secolo), Roma, 4–10 Settembre 2000, SAC, vol. 59, 3 vols (Vatican City, 2002), vol. 1, pp. 533–63, at pp.537–41; E.M. Steinby, *Lexicon Topographicum Urbis Romae*, 6 vols (Rome, 1993–2000), vol. 4, pp. 325–8; and H. Brandenburg, *Ancient Churches of Rome from the Fourth to the Seventh Century: The Dawn of Christian Architecture in the West*, trans. A. Kropp, Bibliothèque l'Antiquité Tardive, vol. 8 (Turnhout, 2005 [Eng. edn]), p. 111.

²² *Lib. pont.* 34.9–15 (Duchesne and Vogel, *Le* Liber pontificalis, pp. 172–5); *Sylloge Laureshamensis* 17 (*ICUR* 2, pp. 149–50); *CBCR* 5.1–96, especially pp. 93–4; and Brandenburg, *Ancient Churches of Rome*, pp. 20–37.

²³ Later S. Croce in Gerusalemme; *Lib. pont.* 34.22 (Duchesne and Vogel, *Le* Liber pontificalis, pp. 179–80); *CIL* 6.1134; *CBCR* 1.165–94, especially 167–8 and 191–2; and Brandenburg, *Ancient Churches of Rome*, pp. 103–8.

²⁴ *Lib. pont.* 35.3 (Duchesne and Vogel, *Le* Liber pontificalis, p. 202); *ICUR* n.s. 1.97; *CBCR* 2.218–49, especially 219 and 249; and Brandenburg, *Ancient Churches of Rome*, pp. 111–12.

²⁵ *Lib. pont.* 36.2 (Duchesne and Vogel, *Le* Liber pontificalis, p. 205). See H. Geertman, 'Forze centrifughe e centripete nella Roma cristiana: Il Laterano, la Basilica Iulia e la Basilica Liberiana', *Rendiconti della Pontificia Accademia Romana di Archeologia*, 59 (1986–7): pp. 63–91.

²⁶ *Chronographus anni CCCLIIII Episcopi Romani Iulius* (MGH.AA 9.76). See also *CBCR* 3.65–71. It might well have been 'near' another meeting place or even basilica built by or associated with the third-century bishop, Calixtus (217–22), as mentioned in *Lib. pont.* 17.3 (Duchesne and C. Vogel, *Le* Liber pontificalis, p. 141). See P. Guerrini, 'Le chiese e i monasteri del trastevere', in F. Guidobaldi and A.G. Guidobaldi (eds), *Ecclesiae Urbis*, Atti del congresso internazionale di studi sulle chiese di Roma (IV-X Secolo), Roma, 4–10 Settembre 2000, SAC, vol. 59, 3 vols (Vatican City, 2002), vol. 1, pp. 377–96, at pp. 379–80); and Brandenburg, *Ancient Churches of Rome*, pp. 112–13. This might be a case of two nearby groups merging when a new larger basilica was erected.

²⁷ Athanasius, *Apol. sec.* 20.3 (H.G. Opitz [ed.], *Athanasius Werke*, vol. 2/1 [Berlin, 1938], p. 102). Curran, *Pagan City and Christian Capital*, p. 123, thinks this is the little church of S. Vito on the Esquiline, which is said to have fourth-century ruins beneath it, citing F. Coarelli, *Guida Archeologica di Roma* (Rome, 1995 [3rd edn]), p. 220. He further comments on p. 124, that this was likely a private dwelling, but that after the council met it received ' ... enhanced status that eventually made the site's transformation into a church

churches are attested in the almost contemporary *Liber precum* found at the beginning of the *Collectio Avellana*: a *basilica Liberiana iuxta macellum Liuiae* (at or near the present S. Maria Maggiore), and an *ecclesia in Lucina*, the later S. Lorenzo in Lucina.[28] During the time of Damasus, famous for his elaboration of martyr shrines, another half-dozen buildings come to light: S. Anastasia at the western foot of the Palatine,[29] the *titulus Damasi* (the later S. Lorenzo in Damaso),[30] the church of Pammachius and/or *Vizantis* (either two groups, or one group known by two different names, which eventually merged to become SS Giovanni e Paolo),[31] the *titulus Fasciolae* (the first church to be specifically

---

both possible and desirable'. The size of the council, in fact, makes it unlikely that this was a private dwelling rather than a church. However, the entire identification with the later S. Vito on the Esquiline is highly speculative. See Brandenburg, *Ancient Churches of Rome*, p. 113.

[28] *CBCR* 2.161–86. See also H.O. Maier, 'The Topography of Heresy and Dissent in Late Fourth-Century Rome', *Historia: Zeitschrift für alte Geschichte*, 44 (1995): pp. 232–49, at pp. 244–5; and Brandenburg, *Ancient Churches of Rome*, pp. 113 and 166–7.

[29] *CBCR* 1.43–63. Two medieval collections preserve the text of an apse inscription from Pope Hilary which begins: 'Antistetes Damasus picturae ornarat honore tecta quibus nunc dat pulchra metalla decus ... ' See *Sylloge Einsiedlensis* 25 (*ICUR* 2, p. 24) and *Sylloge Laureshamensis* 18 (*ICUR* 2, p. 150). Cf. 2.28–31 (cf. also the edition of G. Walser, *Die Einsiedler Inschriftensammlung und der Pilgerführer durch Rom [Codex Einsidlensis 326]*, Historia, Einzelschriften vol. 53 [Stuttgart, 1987], pp. 28–31 [for his text, numbered as 23] and pp. 82–3, where he translates as: 'Antistes Damasus hatte die Gewölbe mit der Zier der Bemalung geschmückt, denen nun schöne Metalle ihren Schmuck geben'.); and Brandenburg, *Ancient Church of Rome*, pp. 134–5.

[30] Damasus, *Epigr*. 57 (A. Ferrua [ed.], *Epigrammata Damasiana: Recensuit et adnotauit*, Sussidi allo studio delle antichità cristiana, vol. 2 [Vatican City, 1942], pp. 210–12); *CBCR* 2.147–53. If K. Blair-Dixon, 'Damasus and the Fiction of Unity', in F. Guidobaldi and A.G. Guidobaldi (eds), *Ecclesiae Urbis*, Atti del congresso internazionale di studi sulle chiese di Roma (IV-X Secolo), Roma, 4–10 Settembre 2000, SAC, vol. 59, 3 vols (Vatican City, 2002), vol. 1, pp. 331–52, is correct that this church was built to strengthen Damasus' position vis-à-vis Ursinus, then it probably dates to the early part of his episcopate. She further notes that this was the first basilica within the city walls given the name of a saint (p. 350). See Brandenburg, *Ancient Churches of Rome*, pp. 135–6.

[31] *ICUR* n.s. 5.13122 mentions two priests of a *titulus Byzanti*; [Damasus], *Epigr*. 61 (Ferrua, *Epigrammata Damasiana*, pp. 229–30) is in honour of SS Giovanni e Paolo; *Sylloge Laureshamensis* 20 (*ICUR* 2.150), records an apse mosaic from this church and concludes with ' ... si quaeris cultor Pammachius fidei'. See *CBCR* 1.265–300, especially 268 and 297–8; and Brandenburg, *Ancient Churches of Rome*, pp. 155–62.

attested as a *titulus* and which later became SS Nereo ed Achilleo),[32] the church of S. Cecilia;[33] and the church of S. Pudenziana.[34]

By the time of Siricius (384–99) the *ecclesia Clementis* is mentioned,[35] and during the episcopate of Anastasius I (399–402) an *ecclesia Crescentiana* (later S. Sisto Vecchio) is attested.[36] Three additional worship places probably also date to this century: S. Crisogono in Trastevere,[37] the *ecclesia Marcelli* (on Via Lata)[38] and a church of St Felix of Nola somewhere on the Pincian Hill.[39] These churches provide us with at least an outline map of some of the important Roman urban churches which existed by 400 – and, as said earlier, it does not indicate a lack of church construction.

What else does this map tell us? First of all, that there is no need to continue to speak of early churches avoiding the monumental centre of Rome in deference (or fear?) of the pagans. Churches were built in virtually all parts of the ancient city where land was available and where there was residential housing. The fact that we have no confirmed sites on the Aventine is probably an accident

---

[32] *ICUR* n.s. 2.4815: 'Cinnamius Opas lector tituli Fasciole amicus pauperum / qui vixit ann. XLVI. Mens VII. D. VIIII deposit in pace. kal. Mart. / Gratiano IIII et Merobaude conss'. (AD 377). See also *CBCR* 3.29–135; G.B. de Rossi, 'Dei marmi trovata entro l'area della basilica. Sue relazioni col titolo urbano appellato *Fasciolae*', *Bullettino di'archeologia cristiana*, ser. 2, vol. 6 (1875): pp. 49–56; G.B. de Rossi, 'Scavi nelle catacombe romane, specialmente nel cimitero di Domitilla", *Bullettino di'archeologia cristiana*, ser. 3, vol. 4 (1879), pp. 91–6; and Brandenburg, *Ancient Churches of Rome*, pp. 136–7.

[33] *Martyrologium Hieronynianum* 15 kal. Dec. (17 Nov) (G.B. de Rossi and L. Duchesne [eds], *Acta Sanctorum Novembris*, t. 2/1 [Brussels, 1894], p. 144). See also *ICUR* n.s. 1.816; *CBCR* 1.95–112; and Brandenburg, *Ancient Churches of Rome*, pp. 193–4.

[34] *ICUR* n.s. 1.347; *CBCR* 3.280–305, especially 282–3 and 302; and Brandenburg, *Ancient Churches of Rome*, pp. 137–42.

[35] Jerome, *De uir. illust.* 15.4 (E.C. Richardson, *Hieronymus. Liber de uiris inlustribus; Gennadius. Liber de uiris inlustribus*, TU, 14 [Leipzig, 1896], p. 17): ' ... nominis eius [i.e. Clement] memoriam usque hodie Romae exstructa ecclesia custodit'. See also *CBCR* 1.118–36; and Brandenburg, *Ancient Churches of Rome*, pp. 142–52.

[36] *Lib. pont.* 41.2 (Duchesne and Vogel, *Le* Liber pontificalis, p. 218); *CBCR* 4.157–70, especially 167; and Brandenburg, *Ancient Churches of Rome*, pp. 152–3.

[37] *CBCR* 1.144–64, especially 144 and 160; and Brandenburg, *Ancient Churches of Rome*, pp. 163–4.

[38] *CBCR* 2.207–17, especially 216–17; and Brandenburg, *Ancient Churches of Rome*, pp. 164–5.

[39] C. Sotinel, 'Chronologie, topographie, histoire: Quelques hypothèses sur S. Felix in Pincis, église disparue', in F. Guidobaldi and A.G. Guidobaldi (eds), *Ecclesiae Urbis*, Atti del congresso internazionale di studi sulle chiese di Roma (IV–X Secolo), Roma, 4–10 Settembre 2000, SAC, vol. 59, 3 vols (Vatican City, 2002), vol. 1, pp. 449–71, especially pp. 466–71. See also Bowes, *Private Worship*, pp. 84–96.

of preservation, since we have Lampe's evidence of earlier communities and fifth-century evidence for several churches in this region. Secondly, the imperial building programme, while it provided the bishop of Rome with the very large Lateran church, did not dominate, or even shape, the early Christian landscape of Rome. Instead we see a variety of other foundations, including episcopal churches and titular churches in virtually every residential area of the city. If anything, it was the episcopal building programme of Julius, Liberius and Damasus that provided the infrastructure for Christian Rome and an example for the Christian elite to imitate. It was not until well into the fifth century that the first Roman aristocrat is elected bishop, and so the fourth-century basilicas credited to bishops were not constructed from the bishops' own private wealth, but rather from church funds and might have been more modest in size and decoration. If some basilicas were as ornamented as the Jovinianists claimed, these would have been decorated by the elite, perhaps in imitation of the emperor's benefactions. But in any case, the bishops were not sitting idly on the sidelines, but were key players in ecclesiastical building throughout the century.

Private Worship and the Episcopacy

Did the bishop's prominent role in public building, however, necessarily mean that he had no competitors? Bowes also argues correctly that long after 312 many Christian groups continued to worship in more private locations. This was often corporate worship, yet it remained private in location and sponsorship. We can point to a few specific archaeological sites and literary notices of such worship in fourth-century Rome – the household chapel under the present SS Giovanni e Paolo,[40] a small Christian sanctuary in the *hortus* of Domitia Lucilla from the Liberian period[41] and a domestic space in Trastevere where Ambrose celebrated a mass,[42] as well as the patrician homes where some of Jerome's ascetic

---

[40] This chapel probably dates to Julius' reign. See Bowes, *Private Worship*, pp. 88–92.

[41] On the space in the *hortus* of Domitia Lucilla see Bowes, *Private Worship*, pp. 83–4. On the domestic spaces in Rome which have been identified as Christian see A. Cerrito, 'Oratori ed edifici di culto minori di Roma tra il IV secolo ed I primi decenni del V', in F. Guidobaldi and A.G. Guidobaldi (eds), *Ecclesiae Urbis*, Atti del congresso internazionale di studi sulle chiese di Roma (IV–X Secolo), Roma, 4–10 Settembre 2000, SAC, vol. 59, 3 vols (Vatican City, 2002), vol. 1, pp. 397–418.

[42] According to Paulinus of Milan, *Vita Ambr.* 10.1 (G. Banterle [ed.], *Le fonti latine su Sant'Ambrogio*, Opera Omnia di Sant'Ambrogio, vol. 24/2 [Milan, 1991], p. 38): ' ... cum trans Tiberim apud quandam clarissimam inuitatus sacrificium in domo offerret ... '. See

students lived and worshipped.[43] But what was the function of and relationship between private and public worship in this period? Was it location, sectarian preferences, kinship or patronage issues, loyalty to some leader figure (Christian patron, presbyter or bishop) or some other factor that influenced where Christians worshipped?[44]

In the early fifth century, the Roman church still practised a decentralised celebration of the eucharist. After it was blessed by the bishop, the *fermentum* (the leavened bread used in the sacrament) could be taken by the priests to the people scattered throughout the city, and the faithful might have reserved part of what they received from the priest for later consumption in private during the week.[45] It appears that baptism was also not totally centralised even after the construction of the Lateran baptistery, since other early baptisteries have been excavated across the city.[46] Yet there seems no doubt that the sacramental life of the church was still primarily centred in the public facilities of the church. On the other hand, prayer and praise could very well have taken place regularly in domestic or private settings. Was then the increasing centralisation of worship in public spaces – venues approved and overseen by the bishop – merely a matter of order or also of control? Were public and private worship 'competing

---

Bowes, *Private Worship*, pp. 81–2; and also Guerrini, 'Le chiese e i monasteri del trastevere', p. 381. This event probably took place in the later years of the episcopate of Damasus.

[43] Although Bowes, *Private Worship*, p. 74, has suggested we have not found more private cult areas because we have been digging/looking in the wrong places, I would suggest that we have not found them because there is little to help us identify them when we do find them. On early attempts to place some strictures on domestic worship see Synod of Laodicea (320), can. 58 (C.H. Turner [ed.], *Ecclesiae Occidentalis Monumenta Iuris Antiquissima*, t. 2 [Oxford, 1907], p. 388); Synod of Gangra (328), can. 6 (Turner, *Ecclesiae Occidentalis*, t. 2.190); Synod of Carthage (390), can. 9 (CCL 149.16–17); and the Council of Chalcedon (451), can. 4 (CCCOGD 1.139–40).

[44] Pietri, 'Régions ecclésiastiques', p. 1036, claims that the construction of larger basilicas in the fourth-century resulted in the clergy of the smaller *conuenticlula* being more rigorously integrated into an episcopal church (citing Ambrosiaster, *In Ep. ad Ephes.* 4.11.3 [CSEL 81/3. 99]).

[45] Basil, *Ep.* 93 (Y. Courtonne [ed.] *Saint Basile. Lettres*, Collection des Universités de France, vol. 1 [Paris, 1957], pp. 203–4), states this was practised in Asia Minor and in Egypt.

[46] A. Cosentino, 'Il battesimo a Roma: edifici e liturgia', in F. Guidobaldi and A.G. Guidobaldi (eds), *Ecclesiae Urbis,* Atti del congresso internazionale di studi sulle chiese di Roma (IV–X Secolo), Roma, 4–10 Settembre 2000, SAC, vol. 59, 3 vols (Vatican City, 2002), vol. 1, pp. 128–37, lists the following post-Constantinian baptisteries that have been archaeologically attested: S. Crisogono, S. Clemente, S. Cecilia, S. Marcello, S. Lorenzo in Lucina, S. Marco, S. Anastasia, S. Sabina, S. Maria Maggiore, S. Pietro, S. Stefano on Via Latina and S. Croce. See also G. Bartolozzi Casti, 'Battisteri presbiteriali in Roma. Un nuovo intervento di Sisto III?', *Studi Romani*, 48 (1999): pp. 270–88.

elements' (as Bowes reads the evidence) or rather complementary elements, or a combination of the two? Did they provide choices or reflect allegiances?[47]

At least one answer lies in the centrality of exhortation and instruction. A clerical *cursus honorum* had already developed in part to provide the necessary on-the-job training for clergy. Ordination gave witness within the community to its successful completion.[48] Such training also required literacy. Lectors were given that name because the mastery of literacy and public reading was part of their training for higher office.[49] Did such trained and ordained clergy preach and teach in domestic settings? While this was certainly the case during the early days, as public worship settings developed, especially ones that could contain larger groups of worshippers, the attention and duties of most presbyters would naturally have shifted to such settings.[50] In this period of rapid growth, as throughout the church's history, there must have been a shortage of trained clergy.[51] Thus, groups that met in domestic settings and wished to continue Sunday and festival liturgical worship and preaching would have had to compete

---

[47] The Roman Synod of 378 successfully convinced the emperors to crack down on public worship by heretical sects. This probably led to even more underground/private activities by these groups. See Maier, 'Topography of Heresy', p. 238.

[48] Synod of Serdica, can. 13 (Hess, *Early Development*, p. 220) (Latin version) or can. x (Hess, *Early Development*, pp. 232–4) (Greek version) or can. T13 (Hess, *Early Development*, p. 248) (Theodosian version), indicates the *cursus* also helped ensure that men were tested properly before gaining the higher offices of the church: ' ... if it happens that either a rich man or a jurist from the forum, or an administrator, shall have been asked for as bishop, he shall not be ordained before he has discharged the function of lector and the office of deacon and the ministry of presbyter, that he may ascend [by these] grades one by one (if he is suitable) to the summit of the episcopate'. (English translation in Hess). See G.D. Dunn, 'The Clerical *cursus honorum* in Late Antique Rome', *Scrinium*, 9 (2013): 132–45.

[49] Note that both the *cursus* that continues to the diaconate and that which continues to the priesthood normally both start with the office of lector. See Pietri, 'Régions ecclésiastiques', pp. 1046–7.

[50] There is limited evidence for presbyters continuing to perform priestly functions in private settings. Besides the example of Ambrose presiding over a private eucharistic service in Trastevere mentioned above in n. 41, Basil, *Epp.* 199.17 and 27 (Y. Courtonne [ed.], *Saint Basile. Lettres*, Collection des Universités de France, vol. 2 [Paris, 1961], pp. 155 and 159), refers to a certain Bianor who, because of an oath, is excluded from presiding over public but not private worship.

[51] Council of Nicaea, can. 2 (CCCOGD 1.20–1), warns against ordaining recent converts 'whether this has been done because of a lack of ministers or simply from impatience'. Canons 8–10 (CCCOGD 1.24–5) deal further with the proper use of priests who had lapsed, had joined the *cathari* or had been improperly examined before ordination, attesting further to a concern for upholding necessary qualifications while still maximising the number of priests.

to gain or hold on to qualified clergy, clergy who could only be properly ordained by the local bishop.[52] Even if they had elite patronage, such groups would have had trouble providing for the regular homiletical and catechetical functions, which public services could increasingly provide. Thus, the larger basilicas paved the way not only for the monumentalisation and formalisation of the liturgy, but equally for the formalisation of preaching and catechesis.

These developments therefore affected the functions more than either the frequency or importance of domestic worship.[53] House groups continued to function as more personal prayer and fellowship gatherings as the basilicas grew larger and their worship more formal, but they also became the earliest centres in Rome for both monastic practices and the cult of martyrs, as Bowes has argued in her study.[54] Clergy serving the now basilica-centric parishes might have taken part in the leadership of such gatherings outside of their regularly scheduled public duties without such activity being viewed as competing with public worship.

The situation seems to have been a bit different in suburban Rome. The construction of the Aurelian Wall in the late third century drew new and very precise boundaries delimiting urban and suburban spaces. That this distinction was real can be seen from the cemeterial building programme of Constantine. Even if Logan is correct in attributing the basilica of St Peter on the Vatican and St Paul on Via Ostiensis to Constans rather than his father, Constantine was still responsible for an additional four cemeterial basilicas, each with a distinctive horseshoe or *circus* design, and each with an associated circular mausoleum for a martyr or member of the imperial family. Nearly a dozen additional basilicas were built in suburban cemeteries by the end of the fourth century. Although

---

[52] Conversely, the shortage would make the 'free-agents' mentioned by Bowes, *Private Worship*, p. 80, all the more marketable. As for numbers of priests in Rome, we know 82 took part in a council in 487, 58 in 495, and 66 in 499; hence some have seen a diminution of titular clergy in the sixth century. See Pietri, 'Clercs et serviteurs', pp. 108–10. This may merely be a reflection of population decline. A further question involves the diaconate and its separate *cursus*, which often culminated in election as bishop. By Gregory I the number of deacons had risen to 12, with an additional 12 subdeacons.

[53] Domestic worship had other problems as well. Synod of Elvira, can. 41 (CCH 4.255), warns against household idols, but allows them to remain if their removal might cause violence among the household slaves.

[54] It is no accident that by 386 Gratian, Valentinian II and Theodosius I found it necessary to issue a mandate against trafficking in martyrs' relics or transferring them to new locations while allowing their veneration in purpose-built structures that were to be called *martyria* (*CTh* 9.17.7 [Th. Mommsen and P. Krüger [eds], *Codex Theodosianus*, vol. 1: *Theodosiani Libri XVI cum constitutionibus Sirmondinis* (Hildesheim, 1990), p. 466]).

not the product of imperial patronage, they were all similar in function and location, and often as large as or larger than urban basilicas.[55] Again, the bishops played a role in perhaps half or more of these. The recently excavated basilica of Mark on Via Ardeatina confirms the location noted in *Liber pontificalis*. The *Catalogus Liberianus* of *Chronographus anni CCCLIIII* states that Julius added three more, one each on Via Portuensis, Via Flaminia and Via Aurelia.[56] *Liber pontificalis* also credits both Felix I and Damasus as building basilicas in the cemeteries where each was buried, the former on Via Aurelia, the latter on Via Ardeatina.

There is also the likelihood that domestic habitation for the city, not only in the form of rural villas, but the ancient equivalent of modern shanty towns, continued to sprawl outside the walls throughout our period, even with the declining population. If this were so, the rural basilicas might have been constructed not just to serve as funerary basilicas, but also as focal points for weekly worship for the suburban population, i.e., as the *foci* of suburban parishes. Like the Donatists and Jovinianists mentioned earlier, the followers of Ursinus met for worship in the *coemeteria* of the martyrs after being dispossessed of the basilicas inside the city.[57] But although the sectarians found locations to use for worship beyond the walls, even here we have no reason to believe

---

[55] A list of fourth-century suburban basilicas would include: St Lawrence, Sts Marcellinus and Paul and the *basilica Apostolorum* (all built by Constantine); St Peter, St Paul, and St Agnes (all erected under the patronage of the Constantinian dynasty); one on Via Ardeatina by Mark (where he was buried, *Lib. pont.* 35.1 [Duchesne and Vogel, *Le* Liber pontificalis, p. 202]); three by Julius – a basilica of St Valentine at mile 2 on Via Flaminia, one *ad Callistum* at mile 3 on Via Aurelia, and one at mile 3 on Via Portuensis (*Lib. pont.* 36.1 [Duchesne and Vogel, *Le* Liber pontificalis, p. 205]); one by Felix on Via Aurelia (*Lib. pont.* 38.2 [Duchesne and Vogel, *Le* Liber pontificalis, p. 211]); and one by Damasus on Via Ardeatina (*Lib. pont.* 39.2 [Duchesne and Vogel, *Le* Liber pontificalis, p. 212]). There were probably additional structures, associated with other catacombs, of which we are as yet unaware. One should take special note of the monumental enlargement of the basilica of St Paul on Via Ostiense carried out under the patronage of Valentinian II, Theodosius I and Arcadius, and for which we have the original imperial order and details as issued to the urban prefect Sallust in 386 (*Collectio Avellana, Ep.* 3 [CSEL 35.46–7]). A. Logan, 'Constantine, the *Liber Pontificalis*, and the Christian Basilicas of Rome' in A. Brent and M. Vizent (eds), *Studia Patristica*, vol. 50, papers presented at the National Conference on Patristic Studies, Cambridge 2009 (Leuven, 2011), pp. 31–53, at pp. 43–9, has recently argued that St Peter's, St Paul's, and St Agnes' did not owe their patronage to Constantine directly.

[56] *Chronographus anni CCCLIIII Episcopi Romani Iulius* (MGH.AA, 9.76).

[57] *Quae gesta sunt inter Liberium et Felicem episcopos* 12 (*Collectio Avellana, Ep.* 1 [CSEL 35.4]): ' ... per coemeteria martyrum stationes sine clericis celebrabat'. See Maier, 'Topography of Heresy', p. 245.

that the episcopal structure was not dominant. The early fifth-century letter of Innocent I to Decentius, which mentions the *fermentum*, states that it did not have to be sent 'to priests situated at the various cemeteries, for those priests have the right and privilege of preparing it themselves'.[58] It would be the bishop who assigned priests to these cemeterial basilicas, and there they carried on their normal sacramental functions. One would assume they also led Sunday and other normal parish services. Therefore, our picture of the fourth-century Roman church should include not only some 50 or more urban parishes but also several dozen suburban ones. And although our knowledge of parish life in such extra-mural communities is minimal, the bishop's administration was also in evidence there.[59]

Conclusion

Already by the mid-fourth century the Roman church centred on some 50-plus urban parishes, with another one to two dozen suburban parishes – each served and overseen by a presbyter approved and ordained by the bishop of Rome. Some groups might have continued to worship in private settings, but increasingly church life was centred in the basilicas that provided new and more spacious homes in the fourth and fifth centuries. Purpose-built structures were visible reminders of the growing status of the church within the community, and perhaps assisted in attracting new adherents to Christianity. The bishop served as the spokesman and administrator for the church and its resources. Constantine himself boosted the church's image not only by donating the property, but also by funding the construction and decoration of several urban basilicas, as well as providing liturgical items for those churches, and lands whose income would

---

[58] Innocent I, *Ep.* 25.V.8 (Robert Cabié [ed.], *Le letter du pape Innocent I à Décentius de Gubbio [19 mars 416]: Texte critique, traduction et commentaire*, Bibliothèque de la Revue d'Historie Ecclésiastique, vol. 58 [Louvain: Publications Universitaires de Louvain, 1973], pp. 26–8): ' ... nec nos per cimeteria diuersa constitutis presbiteris destinamus et presbiteri eorum conficiendorum ius habeant atque licentiam'.

[59] Maier, 'Topography of Heresy', p. 246, postulates that ' ... Damasus and his successors endeavored to make the presence of the official church increasingly felt in the more public cemeteries, by assigning their oversight to the resident clergy of extra-mural parish churches and by decorating martyrs' tombs with papal inscriptions ... ' thus forcing heretical and schismatic groups to retreat ' ... to more private cemeteries near the sites of martyrs'. While Damasus' use of inscriptions to reclaim the suburban graves of the martyrs is well documented, even the existence of extra-mural parish churches beyond the cemeterial basilicas can only be inferred from our current archaeological evidence.

support their clergy and maintain the structures themselves. However, the Roman bishops not only oversaw this work, but were seen as responsible for the construction of numerous basilicas which provided public worship venues across the city. This framework was further expanded by additional buildings, the funding for which came, at least partially, from the local Christian elite. While the imperial gifts of land for long-term income might have served as models for such *tituli*, the structures built by the bishops were probably more practical models for imitation. By the end of the century basilicas were to be found throughout all residential areas within the Aurelian Walls, including the so-called pagan centre. In addition, suburban basilicas constructed by Constantine, the bishops and the elite served the worship needs of the extensive suburban population, as well as serving as appropriate sites for burial and memorial services, family tombs for the emperors' and bishops' brothers and sisters in the faith.

Meanwhile private worship continued, often in the houses of elite patrons. At times this was done because of lack of access to a larger public structure, but as the fourth century progressed, such groups increasingly became archaic holdouts against the new reality, and perhaps as attempts by some elite to maintain their influence in the face of the growing episcopal organisational structure. Yet the turbulence associated with the return of Liberius and the later election of Damasus was neither caused by a reaction against the episcopal structure nor its increasingly elaborate bureaucracy. Whether urban or suburban, the new Christian basilicas and their operation were evidence of a stable and increasingly comprehensive episcopal structure in Rome.

Chapter 2
The Bishop of Rome and the Martyrs[*]

Marianne Sághy

Bishops and martyrs formed an unbeatable tandem in late ancient Christian Rome and produced one of the greatest success stories in world history. Theirs is a complex relationship, which cannot be constrained into an evolutionary pattern from pre-Constantinian illegality to post-Constantinian public triumph. While the fourth-century 'rise of the bishop' is closely connected with the rise of the martyr, their alliance increasingly appears as an unforeseen, yet patiently engineered, by-product of the Constantinian revolution. Bishop and martyr both changed profile after the 'peace of the church' and their partnership also altered significantly. The supervision of the cult of the martyrs did not figure in the early Christian bishop's job description; it developed, rather, as a series of innovative responses to religious conflict and to the appearance of potent and purposeful public patrons within the church. Not the weight of some immemorial tradition, but the heavy pressures brought by Constantine's new *Religionspolitik* compelled the bishop of Rome to reinvent himself as the 'impresario' of the saints.[1]

Scholarship on the sacred nexus between the bishop of Rome and the martyrs is inversely proportional to the significance of the topic. While the cult of the saints became a historical growth industry in past decades, and the (re)organisation of martyr veneration was studied as a means of conflict management and consensus building[2] – from Ambrose of Milan's street-smart exploitation of

---

[*] An earlier version of this chapter was presented at the sixteenth International Conference on Patristic Studies, Oxford University, 8–12 August, 2011. I wish to thank Geoff Dunn for organising the 'Bishop of Rome in Late Antiquity' session at the conference and for inviting me to participate in it. I am grateful to my colleagues on the panel for inspiring questions and comments.

[1] P.R.L. Brown, *The Cult of the Saints: Its Rise and Function in Latin Christianity*, The Haskell Lectures on History of Religions, new series, vol. 2 (Chicago, 1981).

[2] J. Howard-Johnston and P.A. Hayward (eds), *The Cult of the Saints in Late Antiquity and the Early Middle Ages. Essays on the Contribution of Peter Brown* (Oxford, 1999); C. Rapp, *Holy Bishops in Late Antiquity: The Nature of Christian Leadership in an Age of*

martyr power to Paulinus of Nola's poetry[3] – the bishop of Rome, despite his pioneering role in the episcopal appropriation of martyr cult, somehow was slow to catch the revisionist train.[4] Yet it was the model set by Damasus of Rome (366–84) that came to be copied by colleagues from Nola to Rouen. Rich in martyrs and in racy pontifical ambition, Rome created a robust combination of episcopal authority and martyr power that stood the test of time in the intensely agonistic world of late ancient Christianity – and beyond.

Instead of surveying the Roman saga of a martyr made bishop (St Peter), or the rather lacunose documentation of the relationship between bishops and martyrs in the earlier Christian period, this paper focuses on Damasus' enterprise in the catacombs as it illustrates the best way episcopal authority was grafted onto martyr charisma.[5] I argue that the discourse on the martyrs in Rome was part of a larger polemic about the church, an acute debate in the aftermath of the Arian

---

Transition, TCH, vol. 37 (Berkeley, 2005); K. Cooper, 'Ventriloquism and the Miraculous: Conversion, Preaching and the Martyr Exemplum in Late Antiquity', in K. Cooper and J. Gregory (eds), *Signs, Wonders, Miracles: Representations of Divine Power in the Life of the Church*, Studies in Church History, vol. 41 (Chippenham, 2005), pp. 22–45; K. Cooper and J. Hillner (eds), *Religion, Dynasty, and Patronage in Early Christian Rome, 300–900* (Cambridge, 2007); and K. Bowes, *Private Worship, Public Values, and Religious Change in Late Antiquity* (Cambridge, 2008.)

[3] N.B. McLynn, *Ambrose of Milan: Church and Court in a Christian Capital*, TCH, vol. 22 (Berkeley and Los Angeles, 1994); D.E. Trout, *Paulinus of Nola: Life, Letters and Poems*, TCH, vol. 27 (Berkeley and Los Angeles, 1999); and G. Luongo, 'Paolino testimone del culto dei santi', in G. Luongo (ed.), *Anchora vitae*, Atti del II convegno paoliniano nel XVI centenario del ritiro di Paolino a Nola (Nola 18–20 maggio 1995) (Naples and Rome, 1998), pp. 295–347.

[4] No monograph exists on the relationship of episcopal power and martyr cult in Rome. For a synthetic survey see Ch. Pietri, *Roma Christiana. Recherches sur l'Église de Rome, son organisation, sa politique, son idéologie de Miltiade à Sixte III (311–440)*, BEFAR, vol. 224 (Rome, 1976). For a feminist interpretation see N. Denzey, *The Bone Gatherers: The Lost Worlds of Early Christian Women* (Boston, 2007). See also A. Thacker, 'Rome of the Martyrs: Saints, Cults and Relics, Fourth to Seventh Centuries', in É. Ó'Carragain and C. Neuman de Vegvar (eds), *Roma felix: Formation and Reflections of Medieval Rome*, Church Faith and Culture in the Medieval West (Aldershot, 2007), pp. 13–49; K. Cooper, 'The Martyr, the Matrona and the Bishop: The Matron Lucina and the Politics of Martyr Cult in Fifth-and Sixth-Century Rome', *EME*, 8 (1999): pp. 297–317; S. Diefenbach, *Römische Erinnerungsräume: Heiligenmemoria und kollektive Identitäten im Rom des 3. bis 5. Jahrhunderts n. Chr.* Millennium-Studien, vol. 11 (Berlin and New York, 2007).

[5] U. Reutter, *Damasus, Bischof von Rom (366–384): Leben und Werk*, Studien und Texte zu Antike und Christentum, vol. 55 (Tübingen, 2009); and *Saecularia Damasiana*, Atti del convegno internazionale per il XVI centenario della morte di Papa Damaso I, 11-12-384, 10–12 dicembre 1984, SAC, vol. 39 (Vatican City, 1986).

crisis when opposing Christian factions cast themselves as 'the church of the saints'. Damasus' martyr inscriptions were polemical and propagandistic works directed against rival pieties.[6] The cult of the martyrs divided and united the various congregations at the same time. It is a *cultor martyrum* that the Catholic bishop of Rome was able to emerge as an authority in a city of heterogeneous and fractured Christian communities.

Bishop and Martyr: A New Alliance

The first bishop of Rome to launch an ambitious programme to revive and reform martyr cults in Rome, Damasus localised and reconstructed the holy tombs of the martyrs in the suburban catacombs, constructed underground basilicas and decorated the subterranean shrines with mosaics, reliefs and inscriptions.

Catacombs in Rome seem today such an obvious choice for martyr veneration that we tend to forget that they almost fell out of use in the fourth century. Nothing predetermined the transformation of catacombs into cult centres after 312, when emperors and bishops displayed a great deal of creativity in enhancing the *praesentia* of the martyrs in the cities of the Roman empire – from the construction of basilicas to the translations of bodies into town, and from the revision of earlier cults to the denunciation of fake martyrs.[7] The trend was to leave suburban cemeteries and bring the holy relics closer to the city or to the home. Not so in Rome. Instead of shepherding pilgrims towards downtown basilicas, Damasus singled out the catacombs to be the headquarters of martyr cult. Creating a physical link with the martyrs' bodies, Damasus linked directly

---

[6] M. Sághy, 'Martyr Cult and Collective Identity in Fourth-Century Rome', in A. Marinković and T. Vedriš (eds), *Identity and Alterity in Hagiography and the Cult of Saints* (Zagreb, 2010), pp. 17–35; and M. Sághy, 'Martyr Bishops and the Bishop's Martyrs in Fourth-Century Rome', in T. Vedriš and J. Ott (eds), *Saintly Bishops and Bishops' Saints* (Zagreb, 2012), pp. 31–45.

[7] *Translationes* and commerce in relics were popular in the East: E.A. Clark, 'Claims on the Bones of Saint Stephen: The Partisans of Melania and Eudocia', *CH*, 51 (1982): pp. 141–56; K.G. Holum and G. Vikan, 'The Trier Ivory, *Adventus* Ceremonial and the Relics of Saint Stephen', *Dumbarton Oaks Papers*, 33 (1979): pp. 113–33; and D. Woods, 'The Date of the *Translation* of the *Relics* of SS. Luke and *Andrew* to Constantinople', *VChr*, 45 (1991): pp. 286–92. In Italy martyrs were transferred from Lodi to Milan (Paulinus of Nola, *Carmen* 19.322-7 [CSEL 30.129]), and several martyrs were brought to Rome from Pannonia: St Anastasia, St Quirinus, the Four Crowned Saints [J. Guyon, "Les Quatre Couronnés et l'histoire de leur culte des origines à la fin du IXe siècle", *MEFRA*, 87 [1975]: pp. 505–61).

his faction to the 'church of the martyrs' and put the Roman *suburbia* onto the Christian map of the city.[8] Corporeal cults, without the removal or disturbance of relics, would be the rule observed by the church of Rome for centuries to come.

Damasus' guiding principle in inaugurating the catacombs as centres of worship was communal: instead of constructing a single 'super-memorial', he roamed dozens of underground cemeteries, endowing each of them with holy shrines. Integration, rather than exclusivity, was the leading idea in the creation of these 'halls of fame'. Directing attention to the 'crowds of saints' buried in the *suburbia*, the bishop emphasised the equal holiness among the followers of Christ. This is particularly obvious in comparison with the imperial building projects over sacred Christian sites. As opposed to the Constantinian monumentalisation of the holy tombs, which highlighted the emperor's pious *largitas* towards, and connection with, the martyr, and appropriated the saint for the imperial family (St Peter – Constantine; Sts Peter and Marcellinus – Helena; and St Agnes – Constantina),[9] Damasus put the sign of his church in several dozens of catacombs. His purpose was less to compete with imperial and private sponsors,[10] but also to maximise the effect of the collective sanctity of the martyrs.

Damasus' signature is best seen in the Vergilian-style epitaphs (*carmina* or *epigrammata*), which he composed mainly for the martyrs, decorating the large marble plaques above the tombs.[11] Fifty-nine such metrical epigrams survived: two dedicated to martyr apostles, six to martyr bishops, twenty-three to martyrs and four to Damasus' family:

1. The apostles Peter and Paul (*Epigramma* 20 – *basilica apostolorum*, catacomb of San Sebastiano);
2. Roman bishops (*Epigrammata* 17 – Sixtus II; 18 – Eusebius; 19 – Cornelius [fragmentary]; 40 – Marcellus; and 50 – Mark [fragmentary]);
3. Bishop (*Epigramma* 59 – Felix of Nola);
4. Martyrs (*Epigrammata* 4/1 – Anastasia; 6 – Simplicius, Faustinus, Viatrix and Rufus; 7 – Felix and Adauctus; 8 – Nereus and Achilleus; 16 – the

---

[8] P.R.L. Brown, *Through the Eye of a Needle: Wealth, the Fall of Rome and the making of Christianity in the West, 350–550 AD* (Princeton, 2012), pp. 250–54.

[9] H. Brandenburg, *Die frühchristlichen Kirchen in Rom vom 4. bis zum 7. Jahrhundert: Der Beginn der abendländischen Kirchenbaukunst* (Regensburg, 2005).

[10] J. Guyon, *Le cimetière aux deux lauriers. Recherches sur les catacombes romaines*, BEFAR, vol. 264 (Rome, 1987); and Denzey, *The Bone Gatherers*.

[11] A. Ferrua (ed.), *Epigrammata Damasiana*, Sussidi allo studio delle antichità cristiana, vol. 2 (Rome, 1942).

saints buried near the popes; 24 – Ianuarius; 25 – Felicissimus and Agapitus; 28 – Marcellinus and Peter; 31 – Tiburtius; 32 – Gorgonius; 33 – Lawrence; 34 – Ireneus and Abundius [?] 35 – Hippolytus; 37 – Agnes; 39 – Felix and Philip; 41 – Vitalis, Martialis and Alexander; 42 – group of unknown martyrs; 43 – 62 martyrs; 44 – Maurus; 45 – Chrysanthius and Daria; 46 – Saturninus; 47 – Protus and Hyacinthus; and 48 – Hermes);

5. Non-martyrs (family, friends, colleagues) (*Epigrammata* 2 – Tityrus diaconus; 57 – Damasus' father; 10 – Damasus' mother Laurentia; 11 – Damasus' sister Irene; 12 – Damasus' own epitaph; and 51 – Proiecta); and

6. Buildings or monuments (*Epigrammata* 1 – the Pauline epistles; 3 – the waters of St Peter; 4 – the Vatican baptistery; 57 – the papal archives; and 58 – the church of S. Lorenzo in Damaso).

The epigrams reveal that the promotion of martyr bishops was important for Damasus, without being his chief concern. He did honour his episcopal forebears, yet only six epigrams are dedicated to the bishops of Rome. Most of the *elogia* are dedicated to non-episcopal, still mostly clerical martyrs. Damasus' bishop list is shorter, his martyr list is longer than the Roman church's official calendar of saints, the so-called *Catalogus Liberianus*. Damasus provided Rome with 13 new martyrs (Anastasia, Simplicius, Faustinus, Viatrix and Rufus, Felix and Adauctus, Nereus and Achilleus, Ireneus and Abundius, and Chrysanthius and Daria) and three large groups of anonymous saints.

The main questions concerning Damasus' monumentalisation of the martyrs is its relation to cultic and textual traditions. Archaeological evidence attests the unbroken continuity of martyr cults in Rome from the second century, textual evidence, however, is meagre about the saints of Rome before Damasus. Written sources about the cult of the martyrs are disconcertingly leaky: thousands of Christians were martyred in Rome, but only three authentic martyr acts survive and the relationship between martyr act and the bishop of Rome is very unclear.[12] The church of Rome had a festal calendar made up of martyr lists (*depositio episcoporum* and *depositio martyrum*, also called *Catalogus Liberianus*). Paradoxically, the church's official martyr lists were preserved in a compilation made for the private use of a Christian aristocrat in 354.[13] There seems to have

---

[12] H. Musurillo, *The Acts of the Christian Martyrs* (Oxford, 1972), pp. 38–41 (Ptolomeus and Lucius); 42–61 (Justin and his companions); and 90–105 (Apollonius).

[13] *Chronographus anni CCCCLIIII* (Th. Mommsen [ed.], *Chronica Minora saec. IV. V. VI. VII*, vol. 1, MGH.AA, vol. 9 [Berlin, 1892], pp. 13–148; and M.R. Salzman, *On*

been no connection between the martyr acts and *Catalogus Liberianus*: the martyrs mentioned by the acts do not figure in the calendar.

Did Damasus rely on tradition or did he invent new martyrs? Given the paucity of information about martyr cults before Damasus, scholars tend to accept his claim that the martyrs of Rome had been forgotten by the mid-fourth century.[14] Some argue that earlier martyr cults were blotted out by Damasus, others claim that so little had been known about the martyrs of Rome that Damasus literally had to reinvent them.[15] It is hard to believe that a bishop simply could ignore local traditions about the martyrs of his city. Damasus did rely on clerical and private martyr lore, but by acknowledging this tradition, he too created a tradition. Above all, he cemented the bishop's place in martyr veneration, as he was *ex officio* chief supervisor and caretaker of the cult. The martyr lists of *Catalogus Liberianus* were copied for *Chronographus anni CCCCLIIII* by Furius Dionysius Filocalus, 'friend and admirer of Pope Damasus', the same artist who engraved Damasus' epigrams in marble. The connection between these lists and the Damasian epigrams cannot be ignored. Damasus used the *depositiones*-lists, but he revised them in the light of Roman devotional practice and his own research, adding personal memories and oral tradition about the local saints. Remarkably for a collection celebrating martyrs, the Damasian epigrams are not dedicated exclusively to martyrs, but also family members and friends. The presence of the private is a telling feature in a series publicising martyr virtue, for it reveals the context that informed the bishop's project and spurred Damasus to expand episcopal control over the martyrs.

The Challenge of Heresy and Schism

Rome in the fourth century teemed with heretical and schismatic Christian congregations. Half a dozen bishops stood at the helm of various, often imperially recognised, churches – Novatianist, Donatist, Melitian, Apollinarian and Sabellianist. The Nicene faction was just one of these. Arianism still represented a threat for Nicene orthodoxy. Throughout the Arian struggle in the first half of the

---

Roman Time. The Codex-Calendar of 354 and the Rhythms of Urban Life in Late Antiquity, TCH, vol. 17 (Berkeley, 1990).

[14] M. Sághy, '*Renovatio memoriae*: Pope Damasus and the Martyrs of Rome', in R. Behrwald and C. Witschel (eds), *Rome in der Spätantike: Historisch Erinnerung im städtischen Raum* (Stuttgart, 2012), pp. 251–67.

[15] L. Duchesne, *Histoire ancienne de l'Église* (Paris: De Boccard, 1910), pp. 482–3; and Thacker, 'Rome of the Martyrs', p. 36.

fourth century, Nicene Catholic ecclesiology emphasised that the bishop derived his authority from Christ. Hard pressed by Arianising emperors, Catholic bishops took strength from the faith that the Christ in their midst was the Lord of all, while 'the Arians could at best derive their apostolic authority from a demigod'.[16] Arianism did not develop martyr veneration and was critical towards the saints' cults and their promoters.[17] Nowhere is the *communio sanctorum*, the eucharistic fellowship of all believers and their participation in the resurrection body, made more tangible than in Damasus' great martyr memorials in subterranean Rome. Directing a poetic polemics against the Arians, Damasus brought home with extraordinary confidence and purposefulness the Nicene conviction that the church was the Body of Christ.

Christ is the epicentre of the Damasian epigrams: he is 'the safe cover'[18] under which the bishop can sing the praise of the Saviour and his followers, the martyrs. Damasus conveys the central tenet of Nicene orthodoxy – Christ's divinity – in his own epitaph.[19] Christ's life-giving and miracle-working power is the bishop's key poetic theme: 'Have faith, through Damasus, in the power of Christ's glory'.[20] The persecuting power rages against Christ, compelling the martyr to renounce him, but 'He could not force you, oh saint, to deny Christ'.[21] Christ strengthens the martyrs' resolve: 'Eutychius the martyr proved that Christ's glory could defeat the cruel orders of a tyrant and the thousand means of torture his executioners

---

[16] G.H. Williams, 'Christology and Church-State Relations in the Fourth Century', *Church History*, 20.3 (1951): pp. 3–33 and 20.4 (1951): pp. 3–26, at p. 5.

[17] Damasus was rebuked by his Arian opponents for appropriating Peter and Paul for Rome: *Maximini contra Ambrosium dissertatio* (PLS 1.722). See also Ch. Pietri, 'Concordia apostolorum et renovatio urbis (Culte des martyrs et propagande pontificale)', *Mélanges d'archéologie et d'histoire*, 73 (1961): pp. 275–322, at p. 305, n. 4.

[18] Damasus, *Epigr.* 2 (Ferrua, *Epigrammata Damasiana*, p. 87): ' ... fido recubans sub tegmine Christi'.

[19] Ibid., 12 (Ferrua, *Epigrammata Damasiana*, p. 112): 'He who grants earth's dying seeds to live, He who could loosen the fatal bounds of death when its darkness had fallen, And could restore a brother to his sister Martha, Among the living again after the third shining of the sun, That He will make Damasus rise after death, believe'. (English translation by W.L Watson, 'The Epigrams of St Damasus: A Translation and Commentary', (MA diss., University of Texas, Austin, 1958).

[20] Damasus, *Epigr.* 8 (Ferrua, *Epigrammata Damasiana*, p. 103): 'Credite per Damasum, possit quid gloria Christi ... '

[21] Ibid., 46 (Ferrua, *Epigrammata Damasiana*, p. 189): ' ... cogere non potuit Christum te, sancte, negare'.

devised'.[22] The martyrs 'follow Christ through the stars'[23] to his heavenly court: 'the inner court of heaven lies open for the holy martyrs, if he seeks the rewards of Christ'.[24] Christ vouchsafes the bishop's orthodoxy: 'Christ, who bestows the rewards of life, showed the pastor's worth'.[25] The martyrs intercede with Christ to grant the prayers of the living: 'Know that Damasus the Pope adorned their grave, In glorious commemoration of his clergy – thanks be to Christ. To the holy martyrs this priest returns his vows'.[26]

Apart from the Arian heresy, schism was another target of Damasus' martyr propaganda. A crime against the Body of Christ, disunion and fragmentation threatened the Christian community as a whole. Damasus came to power after a double election in 366, and his opponent Ursinus, possibly supported by influential aristocrats,[27] presented a stark opposition throughout his pontificate. The Ursinians rioted in the city and organised sit-ins in the catacomb of St Agnes to resist Damasus. Cemeteries were crowded, competitive hubs in antiquity, figuring prominently in the *Vrbs*' 'topography of dissent'. Damasus' supporters attacked the Ursinians in the catacomb, made famous by imperial and episcopal patronage. Constantine's daughter, Constantina, constructed the basilica of St Agnes and her own mausoleum next to the saint. Constantine composed an exquisite hexameter about 'victorious Agnes', and Bishop Liberius offered two marble slabs as an *ex uoto* to the martyr. The Damasian epigram dedicated to Agnes begs the martyr to listen favourably to *his* prayers – instead of those of his rivals: 'Oh gentle object of my veneration, holy heroine/ of chastity, I beg you to favour the prayers of Damasus,/ oh glorious martyr'.[28]

---

[22] Ibid., 21 (Ferrua, *Epigrammata Damasiana*, p. 146): 'Martyr Eutychius crudelia iussa tyranni/ carnificumque vias pariter tunc mille nocendi/ vincere quod potuit monstravit gloria Christi'.

[23] Ibid., 20 (Ferrua, *Epigrammata Damasiana*, p. 142): ' ... sanguinis ob meritum Christumque per astra secuti'.

[24] Ibid., 39 (Ferrua, *Epigrammata Damasiana*, p. 179): ' ... martyribus sanctis pateat quod regia caeli/ respicit interior, sequitur si praemia Christi'.

[25] Ibid., 17 (Ferrua, *Epigrammata Damasiana*, p. 124): 'Ostendit Christus, reddit qui praemia vitae/ pastoris meritum'.

[26] Ibid., 42 (Ferrua, *Epigrammata Damasiana*, p. 184): 'Ornavit Damasus tumulum, cognoscite, rector/ pro reditu cleri Christo prestante triumphans/ Martyribus sanctis reddit sua vota sacerdos'.

[27] R. Lizzi Testa, *Senatori, popolo, papi: il governo di Roma al tempo dei Valentiniani* (Bari, 2004), p. 195.

[28] Damasus, *Epigr.* 37 (Ferrua, *Epigrammata Damasiana*, p. 176): 'O ueneranda mihi, sanctum decus, alma, pudoris,/ ut Damasi precibus faueas, precor, inclycta martyr'.

The bishop casts himself as a supplicant, as a client to the martyrs, avidly seeking their intercession. Damasus spurs the heavenly 'lobbying' of the martyrs on his behalf, as opposed to Constantine and Constantina, who emphasise their own *liberalitas* and donations to the saints rather than the spiritual or practical benefactions received from them. The bishop as client is accentuated in an epigram from 367 that commemorates the end of the schism. Damasus gives thanks to a group of unknown, unremembered martyrs who, despite their obscurity, successfully intervened with Christ for 'the return of his clergy', and thus re-established the unity of the church of Rome.[29] Yet again a supplicant appears in the epigram dedicated to St Felix. In 378, the Ursinians hired Isaac, a converted Jew, to accuse Damasus of adultery. Damasus convoked a synod to clear himself. The emperor acquitted Damasus and granted judicial powers (*priuilegium fori*) to the bishop. Damasus attributed the miracle to Felix:

> Oh Felix, equally felicitous in body, in mind
> and in soul as well as in name
> an associate of the triumph of Christ,
> Among the number of the saints
> who solicitously grant all
> Requests to those who come to you
> and never allow any pilgrim
> To depart in sadness
> I have been spared, by your guidance,
> And have broken death's chains;
> my lying enemies have been destroyed;
> I, Damasus, your supplicant, pay with these verses my vow.[30]

Damasus' three epigrams connected with the Ursinian schism celebrate the miracle-working power of the martyrs, their practical help in re-establishing the unity of the church and their heavenly intercession in saving Damasus' life.

The Ursinians were not the only schismatic group active around holy tombs. The Novatianists and the Donatists also developed their own martyr cults. The rigorist Novatianists condemned the moral laxity of other churches, did not

---

[29] Ibid., 42 (Ferrua, *Epigrammata Damasiana*, p. 184).
[30] Ibid., 59 (Ferrua, *Epigrammata Damasiana*, p. 214): 'Corpore, mente, animo pariterque et nomine Felix,/ sanctorum in numero Christi sociate triumphis,/ qui ad te sollicite uenientibus omnia prestas,/ nec quemquam tristem pateris repedare uiantem;/ te duce seruatus mortis quod uincula rupi,/ hostibus extinctis, fuerant qui falsa locuti,/ uersibus hic Damasus supplex tibi uota repondo'.

consider worthy of participation in the sacraments those who had committed a sin unto death, and advocated rebaptism. The Novatianists held their meetings at the tomb of their founder in the catacomb of Cyriaca on Via Tiburtina in Rome. A deacon decorated Novatian's grave with an inscription in the fourth century: 'Nouatiano beatissimo martyri Gaudentius diac(onus) fecit'.[31] Damasus answered the challenge of schism at the holy grave. He placed an epigram at the strategic position, opposite Novatian's tomb, on the other side of the road, on the tomb of Hippolytus. A three-bayed, underground basilica was built above the tomb decorated with mural paintings. Hippolytus, antipope (?), was banished in 235 together with Bishop Pontian to the lead mines of Sardinia, where the two men reconciled. Damasus' poem casts Hippolytus anachronistically as a Novatianist schismatic, and the faith to which he converted, the 'Catholic' faith:

> Hippolytus the priest is said to have remained in the schism of Novatian
> During all the time of pressure under a tyrant's orders.
> When the sword cut the holy bowels of Mother Church,
> While he was on his way to the Realms of the Blessed, devoted to Christ,
> the people asked him which way they should turn,
> He said that all should follow the Catholic faith.
> So professed, he deserved to be our martyr.
> Damasus relates these things on hearsay; Christ judges all.[32]

The story of a division healed, the example of the converted schismatic overcome with the grace of martyrdom was an appeal to the Novatianists, encouraging them to leave their error and join Damasus' church.

Family Traditions and Private Patrons

Damasus brought martyr cults under episcopal control by wrapping them in the traditional family commemoration of the dead. Damasus' mausoleum next

---

[31] R. Giordani, '*Novatiano beatissimo martyri Gaudentius diaconus fecit*: Contributo all'identificazione del martire Novaziano della catacomba anonima sulla Via Tiburtina', *Rivista di Archeologia Cristiana*, 68 (1992): pp. 240–51.

[32] Damasus, *Epigr.* 35 (Ferrua, *Epigrammata Damasiana*, p. 171): 'Hippolytus fertur, premeret cum iussa tyranni/ presbiter in schisma semper mansisse Nouati/ Tempore quo gladius secuit pia uiscera matris/ deuotus Christo peteret cum regna piorum/ quaesisset populos, ubinam procedere posset/catholicam dixisse fidem sequentur ut omnes,/ sic noster meruit confessus, martyr ut esset./ Haec audita refert Damasus, probat omnia Christus'.

to the martyrs Marcus and Marcellinus in the cemetery of San Callisto between Via Appia and Via Ardeatina testifies to lived Christian virtue and staunch Nicene belief in a clerical family. Known as *coemeterium Sanctorum Marci et Marcelliani Damasique*, the exact location of the mausoleum has been forgotten. The cemetery complex of San Callisto–San Sebastiano is the oldest funerary area of the church of Rome, housing the common memorial of the apostles Peter and Paul (*memoria apostolorum*). Damasus sought the proximity of the apostles and popes, but did not want to 'disturb the holy ashes'.[33]

The 'coupling' of ordinary believers and martyrs expressed a new spiritual trend in the fourth century: Christians sought to associate themselves with the martyrs not only in the grave, but also in their lives so that in heaven they could participate in the glory of the 'friends of God'. The faithful patronised the saints, striving to imitate the martyrs' virtue and share their friendship in heaven. The attraction of the martyrs was shown by burials 'next to the saints' (*depositio ad sanctos*). Christians gave other expressions to their wish to be considered 'partners' of the martyrs sharing heavenly bliss. Ascetics declared themselves 'heirs of the martyrs', their lifestyle a 'bloodless martyrdom'. Bishop Liberius of Rome called the exiled Latin bishops 'martyrs'.[34] The family of Crescentius, a deacon in Thabarka, called their beloved one a 'companion of the martyrs'.[35] The 'martyrisation' of the ordinary dead swelled martyr lists and caused considerable confusion in the fourth century. Damasus' family crypt on Via Ardeatina offers a precious example of an individualistic episcopal burial. As opposed to the communal traditions of the third century, when the tombs of bishops were grouped in a 'crypt of the popes', the fourth century saw the resurgence of individual family mausolea.[36] Damasus chose a burial near the saints, but not next to the bishops.

Damasus' epitaph dedicated to his mother Laurentia attests that she lived for 60 years as a widow, and was more than 90 years old when she died. Widows enjoyed a special status in the church. Prototype of the unprotected and underprivileged, the widow was the image of the person who depended on God alone. The church took particular care of the practical and spiritual

---

[33] Ibid., *Epigr.* 16 (Ferrua, *Epigrammata Damasiana*, p. 120): ' ... cineres timui sanctos vexare piorum'.

[34] Liberius, *Ep. ad Eusebium, Dionysium et Luciferum* (CSEL 65.164–6) = JK 216.

[35] Y. Duval, Loca sanctorum Africae: *Le culte des martyrs en Afrique du IVe au VIIe siècle*, Collection de l'École française de Rome, vol. 58 (Rome, 1982), p. 431, nos 208–9.

[36] J.-C. Picard, *Évêques, saints et cités en Italie et en Gaule: Études d'archéologie et d'histoire*, Collection de l'École française de Rome, vol. 242 (Rome: École Française de Rome, 1998), p. 46.

accompaniment of widows. Models of piety and poverty, the paradigm of the soul in need of God, widows were symbols of the Kingdom. They expected a sixty-fold harvest in heaven for their pious dedication.

Surpassing even widows, virgins represented on earth the Kingdom to come. Icons of integrity, virgins stood for the wholeness of the Christian doctrine and of the Catholic church. Virgins became the 'icons' of Catholicism in post-Arian Rome. In times of adversity, they advertised best the integrity of the church. The fourth-century ascetic revolution was largely brought to success by virgin sisters of continent bishops. Not only did bishops elevate on a pedestal their widowed mothers, they also paid a respectful tribute to their virginal sisters, ascribing to them their ascetic conversion. Macrina, Marcellina and Irene stand out as inspirations and companions of their episcopal brothers' conversion to the ascetic life.

Damasus' poem to his sister Irene, who 'had consecrated herself to Christ while life remained', lived a life of 'outstanding virtue' and died at the age of 20 'when the better court of heaven snatched her to itself',[37] was an act of devotion with a purpose. Remembering Irene in the 370s was a respectful salute towards the ascetic ladies of the Aventine who raised their daughters as virgin 'brides of Christ', or towards Ambrose's sister Marcellina, the trusted *confidente* of her powerful brother. The epigram thus denotes a network of clerical and ascetic families rising to power after the Arian conflict. While the Cappadocian theologians, Basil the Great and Gregory of Nyssa, emphasised their sister Macrina's ascetic initiative and philosophical influence on their lives, Damasus presents Irene as a psychopomp angel. The virgin illuminates Damasus' journey beyond the grave: 'Now when God shall come, remember us, virgin;/ So that your torch, by the Lord, may give me light'.[38]

Damasus' confidence in Irene's heavenly status is unique. At a time when John Chrysostom warns in a homily on Lazarus that the soul cannot cross the border of the other world all by itself and needs a sure guide to show the way to the heavenly city,[39] Damasus finds his guide in the person of his sister Irene who will light his way with her torch. No angel is required in the dangerous journey after death: Irene herself assumes this role. This shows firm belief in Irene's salvation and her prominence in the other world. Irene is not presented as a 'star', like the apostles Peter and Paul and the young Christian lady, Proiecta,

---

[37] Damasus, *Epigr.* 11 (Ferrua, *Epigrammata Damasiana*, pp. 108–9): ' ... quem sibi cum raperet melior tunc regia caeli'.

[38] Ibid. (Ferrua, *Epigrammata Damasiana*, p. 109): 'Nunc ueniente Deo nostri reminiscere, uirgo,/ ut tua per Dominum prestet mihi facula lumen'.

[39] John Chrysostom, *De Lazaro conciones* 2.2 (PG 48.984).

also mourned by Damasus. Instead of an astral afterlife, Damasus attributes an angelic existence to Irene.

Damasus referenced a scriptural rather than martyrial paradigm when commemorating his family. Despite the key role that he played in the revival of the cult of the martyrs and the prestige that martyr ancestors gave to any family, Damasus did not appropriate the martyr discourse for his mother and sister. As opposed to Macrina, there is no 'martyrisation' of Laurentia and Irene. The differentiation between martyr and family is maintained down to the level of the script: the family epitaphs, as far as we can tell from the fragments, were written in an ordinary script, not in the beautiful Filocalian font. The martyrs Marcus and Marcellinus go unmentioned in the epigrams. Instead of the martyr discourse, Damasus uses a biblical language: the memorial of the episcopal family is characterised by a theology firmly anchored in the Scriptures.

Damasus views the defunct members of his family as partakers of the *communio sanctorum*. The theology of the martyr cult is based on the belief that both dead and living Christians form a solid community in Christ. Damasus' epigrams testify to this *communio* as well as to the triumph of Christ. Surrounded by believers in a paradisiacal setting, Christ's centrality is visible from catacomb representations to church iconography. Invited to partake in the life of Christ, the church participates in the earthly adventure of exile and in the heavenly history of salvation. Martyrs are protagonists of the story, but so are ordinary Christian believers. The two-dimensional life of the Christian draws both on the past lives of the saints recorded in the Gospels and on the hope in the life to come.

An obtrusive feature of Damasus' pontificate is the lack of evidence testifying connections between the bishop and the great aristocratic families of Rome.[40] The bishop was politely ignored at the funerals of the clarissimate. The only example of Damasus being involved in an upper-class burial is the epitaph of Proiecta, daughter of the imperial servant Florus, a careerist who 'was most likely to feel the need for a papal imprimatur'.[41] Damasus strikes a drastically different tone from his martyr poetry when lamenting Proiecta's death. Remarkably, the bishop strikes a sentimental, bombastic chord, but draws from the classical, rather than Christian, legacy in describing Proiecta's rise to the stars, as she 'went

---

[40] Brown, *Through the Eye*, p. 252; and N.B. McLynn, 'Damasus of Rome: A Fourth-Century Pope in Context', in T. Führer (ed.), *Rom und Mailand in der Spätantike: Repräsentationen städtischer Räume in Literatur, Architektur und Kunst*, Topoi Berlin Studies of the Ancient World, vol. 4 (Berlin, 2012), pp. 305–20.

[41] McLynn, 'Damasus of Rome', p. 319.

away eagerly to mount to the light above'.[42] No allusions to Christ, to heaven, to salvation: without a trace of Christian faith, this epigram is indistinguishable from the great Vergilian lore of Roman funerary epitaphs.[43]

Private patrons of the martyrs do appear in the Damasian epigrams, even if only allusively.[44] Thus, we hear of the parents of the young girl, Agnes, the first caretakers of their daughter's story and tomb:

> It is said that her holy parents told the story of how,
> When the trumpet sounded its mournful call,
> The girl Agnes quickly left her nurse's lap and,
> On her own impulse trampled the grim tyrant's threats and rage.[45]

The pious Lucilla makes a cameo appearance as a visionary and pioneer bone gatherer:

> Later on, Lucilla was informed of this by your [i.e., the martyrs'] goodness,
> And she decided it was better to entomb your most holy members here.[46]

Nevertheless, Damasus cuts a singularly solitary figure as a religious entrepreneur in the vast labyrinth of vested private – family – interests that were the catacombs. Hardly any trace of earthly, secular networking transpires from his monuments, as opposed to a heavy dose of clerical networking.

---

[42] Damasus, *Epigr.* 51 (Ferrua, *Epigrammata Damasiana*, p. 202): '... aetheriam cupiens caeli conscendere lucem'. See J. Guyon, '*Cunctis solacia fletus* ou le testament-épigraphe du pape Damase', in Quaeritur inventus colitur: *Miscellanea in onore di Padre Umberto Maria Fasola*, SAC, vol. 40/2, (Vatican City, 1989), pp. 423–38; and P. Santorelli, 'L'epigramma a Proiecta di Damaso (51 F.)', in S. Pricoco, F. Rizzo Nervo and T. Sardella (eds), Sicilia e Italia suburbicaria tra IV e VIII secolo, Atti del convegno di Studi, Catania, 24–27 ottobre 1989 (Catania, 1991), pp. 327–36.

[43] R.P. Hoogma, *Der Einfluss Vergils auf die Carmina Latina Epigraphica* (Amsterdam, 1959).

[44] L. Spera, 'Interventi di papa Damaso nei santuari delle catacombe romane: il ruolo della committenza privata', *Bessarione*, 11 (1994): pp. 111–27.

[45] Damasus, *Epigr.* 37 (Ferrua, *Epigrammata Damasiana*, p. 176): 'Fama refert sanctos dudum retulisse parentes Agnen cum lugubres cantus tuba concrepuisset/ nutricis gremium subito liquisse puellam/ sponte trucis calcasse minas rabiemque tyranni'.

[46] Ibid., 28 (Ferrua, *Epigrammata Damasiana*, p. 161): 'Postea commonitam vestra pietate Lucillam/ Hic placuisse magis sanctissima condere membra'.

Communio sanctorum and the Unity of the Church

The reconstruction of martyr monuments served, above all, to create a united front of heavenly patrons for the city. Damasus' revamping of the Crypt of the Popes in San Callisto testifies his efforts towards concord and unity. This cemetery was the first communal funerary space sponsored by the church of Rome: Bishop Zephyrinus (199–217) charged the deacon Calixtus to purchase burial grounds for Christian believers and bishops alike in this graveyard.[47] In 258, Sixtus II was slaughtered here together with his seven deacons. The tradition of communal burial and papal enhancement of the site influenced Damasus' choice when he reconstructed the Crypt of the Popes as a small underground church, decorating the walls with marbles, two skylights, an altar, and two spiral columns on high bases supporting an architrave from which hung lamps, crosses and ornamental wreaths.[48] On the lower part of the wall, Damasus placed an epigram commemorating the martyrs and confessors buried in the crypt:

> Here, if you ask, lies gathered a group of devout men.
> The venerable graves still hold the saints' bodies,
> but the court of heaven has seized aloft to itself their souls.
> Here are the companions of Sixtus, who carry off the trophy from their foes.
> Here is the throng of prelates that keeps the altars of Christ.
> Here is laid the priest who lived during the long time of peace.
> Here are the holy confessors whom Greece has sent.
> Here are young men and boys, old men and their chaste grandsons,
> whose preference it was to keep a virginal purity.
> Here I, Damasus – I admit it – wished to bury my own body,
> but I was afraid of disturbing the holy ashes of the saints.[49]

---

[47] J. Guyon, 'La vente des tombes à travers l'épigraphie de la Rome chrétienne (IIIe, VIIe siècles): le rôle des fossores, mansionarii, parepositi et prêtres', *MEFRA*, 86 (1974): pp. 540–96; É. Rebillard, 'L'Église de Rome et le développement des catacombes: à propos de l'origine des cimetières chrétiens', *MEFRA*, 109 (1997): pp. 741–63.

[48] L. Reekmans, 'Recherches récentes dans les cryptes des martyrs romains', in M. Lamberigts and P. Van Deun (eds), *Martyrium in Multidisciplinary Perspective: Memorial Louis Reekmans*, BETL, vol. 117 (Leuven, 1995), pp. 32–70; and L. Reekmans, 'L'œuvre du pape Damase dans le complexe de Gaius à la catacombe de S. Callixte', in *Saecularia Damasiana*, Atti del convegno internazionale per il XVI centenario della morte di Papa Damaso I, 11-12-384, 10–12 dicembre 1984, SAC, vol. 39 (Vatican City, 1986), pp. 261–81.

[49] Damasus, *Epigr.* 16 (Ferrua, *Epigrammata Damasiana*, p. 120): 'Hic congesta iacet quaeris is turba piorum,/ corpora sanctorum retinent ueneranda sepulcra,/ sublimes

Instead of naming the bishops of Rome and evoking individually their martyrdom, Damasus monumentalises the group of leaders as a single body. The nameless individuals melt into a pious crowd (*turba piorum*), united by office, purpose and commitment. The epigram conveys the idea of unity: the bishops of Rome (*numerus procerum*) form a single tradition. It is left to the visitors to the crypt to reconstruct mentally the list of the bishops buried here: 'the throng of prelates that keeps the altars of Christ' are Pontian (230–35), Antherus (235–36), Fabian (236–50); Lucius I (253–54), Stephen I (254–57), Sixtus II (257–58), Dionysius (259–68), Felix I (269–74) and Eutychian (275–83). 'The companions of Sixtus' are the four deacons: Gennarius, Magnus, Vincent and Stephen. Two other deacons, Felicissimus and Agapitus, as well as Sixtus' archdeacon, Lawrence, are commemorated elsewhere. 'The bishop who lived through the long peace' probably refers to Fabian (or Dionysius or Eutychian). 'The holy confessors from Greece' are a group of martyrs buried elsewhere in the catacomb: Martia, Neon, Hippolytus, Adria, Paulina, Martha, Valeria, Eusebius and Marcellus. Heir to this army of saints, who defended heroically their faith and their flock, Damasus inscribes himself in the list of bishops, but refuses to enter their tomb; out of respect for the inviolability of the grave, he refrains from disturbing the peace of the holy ashes.

This epigram makes the *communio sanctorum* a reality as the community of believers remembers her heavenly patrons. Not even the epigram commemorating Sixtus II in the same crypt dispels the communal spirit of the place. Damasus stresses that Sixtus sacrificed himself for his congregation:

> At the time when the sword cut the holy bowels of mother church,
> the pope here buried was teaching the commandments of heaven.
> Those suddenly rush in who seize him as he sits there by chance.
> The people than began to offer their necks to the soldiers who had been sent.
> Then, when the old man saw that someone wished to steal his palm,
> he was the first to offer himself and his head,
> before their reckless brutality could harm anyone.
> Christ, who bestows the rewards of Life, showed the pastor's worth.

---

animas rapuit sibi regia caeli./ Hic comites Xysti, portant qui ex hoste tropaea,/ hic numerus procerum, seruat qui altaria Christi,/ hic positus, longa uixit qui in pace sacerdos;/ hic confessores sancti, quos Graecia misit;/ hic iuuenes puerique, senes castique nepotes,/ quis mage uirgineum placuit retinere pudorem./ Hic, fateor, Damasus uolui mea condere membra,/ sed cineres timui sanctos uexare piorum'.

In his own person, he guards each member of the flock.⁵⁰

The most powerful epigram of collective commemoration, however, is that dedicated to the apostles Peter and Paul. Instead of individual *elogia* at the apostolic shrines on the Vatican and on Via Ostiensis, Damasus chose to locate his epigram at the venerated cult place of the *basilica apostolorum* on Via Appia.⁵¹ This time Damasus selected a surrogate memorial, a cult place without corporeal relics. The dual veneration of Peter and Paul at Rome had a long tradition; the congregation took great pride in possessing the bodies of two apostles, for among the Christian churches, only Rome could boast a double apostolic foundation. According to the apocryphal acts (if not according to the Bible) the apostles worked together in perfect concord and remained united even in death, for they died on the same day. The twin apostles symbolised Christian unity and gave a noble example of political harmony and unanimity (*concordia*). The memorial in the *basilica apostolorum* demonstrated the spiritual brotherhood of Peter and Paul in Christ. At the Roman synod of 382, Damasus declared that Peter and Paul 'together sanctified the Roman church to our Lord Jesus Christ'.⁵² Gaudentius of Brescia was spellbound by the fraternity and concord of the apostles.⁵³ Ambrose of Milan declared the twin apostles the true founders of Rome, capital of mankind.⁵⁴

Peter and Paul became the chief architects of Roman Catholic unity in the papal propaganda.⁵⁵ Instead of expanding on the theme of spiritual brotherhood, or on the unity of the church,⁵⁶ Damasus gives a remarkable twist to the twins and conjures the apostles into Rome's national heroes:

---

⁵⁰ Ibid., 17 (Ferrua, *Epigrammata Damasiana*, p. 124): 'Tempore quo gladius secuit pia uiscera matris,/ hic positus rector caelestia iussua docebat./ Adueniunt subito, rapiunt qui forte sedentem:/ militibus missis populi tunc colla dedere./ Mox ubi cognouit senior, quis tollere uellet/ palmam, seque suumque caput prior optulit ipse,/ inpatiens feritas posset ne laedere quemquam./ Ostendit Christus, reddit qui praemia uitae,/ pastoris meritum, numerum gregis ipse tuetur'.

⁵¹ H. Chadwick, 'St. Peter and St. Paul in Rome: The Problem of the Memoria Apostolorum ad catacumbas', *JThS*, n.s. 8 (1957): pp. 39–51; and J. Kjaergaard, 'From Memoria Apostolorum to Basilica Apostolorum. On the Early Christian Cult Centre on the Via Appia', *Analecta Romana Instituti Danici*, 13 (1984): pp. 59–76.

⁵² Damasus, *De explanatione fidei* (PL 13.374): ' ... et pariter supradictam Romanam ecclesiam Christo Domino consecrarunt ... '.

⁵³ Gaudentius of Brescia, *Tract*. 20.9–10 (CSEL 68.183).

⁵⁴ Ambrose, *Hymnus* 12 (J. Fontaine [ed.], *Ambroise de Milan. Hymnes* [Paris, 1992], pp. 515–45).

⁵⁵ J.M. Huskinson, *Concordia Apostolorum. Christian Propaganda at Rome in the Fourth and Fifth Century: A Study in Early Christian Iconography and Iconology* (London, 1984).

⁵⁶ Pietri, '*Concordia apostolorum et renovatio urbis*, pp. 275–322.

> Here you should know that the saints dwelt at one time
> You who seek the names of both Peter and Paul.
> We freely acknowledge that the East sent them as disciples
> For Christ's sake and the merit of his blood
> They followed Him across the stars
> And sought heavenly regions, kingdom of pious souls
> Rome has merited to claim them as citizens.
> Damasus wished to proclaim these things, O new stars,
> to your praise. [57]

Peter and Paul bought heaven *and* Roman citizenship by the effusion of their blood (*ius sanguinis*). Ascent to Paradise is linked with a quick process of 'naturalisation'. In the course of a life journey leading from the East to the stars, Peter and Paul honoured Rome with their deaths. As new stars (*noua sidera*), they protect Rome, substituting for earlier twins, Romulus and Remus, or Castor and Pollux.[58] Theirs is the winning constellation: their blood exorcises pagan gods and founds Rome anew as a Christian city.[59] The relationship between the apostles and Rome is reciprocal: mother-city to the empire, no other city can rival the prestige of Rome, just as no other martyr can compete with the prestige of the princes of the apostles in the Roman empire. When Damasus affirms the primacy of Rome against that vindicated for the East as the glory of Peter and Paul, Damasus also reacts to the recent *translatio* of the apostles Andrew and Timothy to Constantinople.

Conclusion

Damasus tied the martyrs to Rome and the bishop of Rome to the martyrs. The Damasian programme is a unique example of how the alliance between bishop

---

[57] Damasus, *Epigr.* 20 (Ferrua, *Epigrammata Damasiana*, p. x): 'Hic habitasse prius sanctos cognoscere debes,/ nomina quisque Petri pariter Paulique requiris./ Discipulos Oriens misit, quod sponte fatemur;/ sanguinis ob meritum Christumque per astra secuti/ aetherios petiere sinus regnaque piorum:/ Roma suos potius meruit defendere ciues./ Haec Damasus uestras referat noua sidera laudes'.

[58] R. Brändle, 'Petrus und Paulus als nova sidera', *Theologische Zeitschrift*, 48 (1992): pp. 207–17.

[59] D.E. Trout, 'Damasus and the Invention of Early Christian Rome', *Journal of Medieval and Early Modern Studies*, 33 (2003): pp. 517–36.

and martyr, city and saints, came to be forged.[60] The bishop's epigrams spell out a theology of *communitas*: the church is a community of saints – without being a community of *perfecti*. Damasus' martyrs are not models of perfection, but examples of human frailty and human heroism. Rejecting the rigorism of the schismatics, Damasus embraces the fallen. Reflecting the practical urgency of community building, martyr cults gave a new power base for the bishop. By putting his signature on the tomb of the martyrs, Damasus appropriated the martyrs of Rome for the Catholic church whose creed was prescribed, in 381, by Emperor Theodosius as a model of orthodoxy in the Roman empire. Damasus' sophisticated mixture of innovation and tradition cemented the relationship of bishop and martyrs and laid the ground for their successful co-operation in the future. Patrons of martyrs, the bishops organised the cultic commemoration of the heavenly sponsors of the church. Patrons of the church, the martyrs helped the bishop of Rome to weather imperial pressure, private ambition, heresy and schism.

---

[60] D.E. Trout, 'Saints, Identity and the City', in V. Burrus (ed.), *Late Ancient Christianity*, A People's History of Christianity (Minneapolis, 2005), pp. 165–87; and Sághy, 'Martyr Cult and Collective Identity', 17–35.

Chapter 3
Siricius and the Rise of the Papacy*

Christian Hornung

Introduction

The turn of the fourth to the fifth century is an important mark in the development of the papacy. The claim of the Roman bishops, as formulated in the extant Roman episcopal letters, tends more and more to that of an ecclesiastical primacy. In a short study, concerned with the 'popes' of the fourth and the fifth centuries, Jakob Speigl characterises the development in the following words:

> Ungefähr von der Mitte unseres Zeitraums (380) an stehen die römischen Bischöfe nicht mehr unter der Vorherrschaft der reichspolitischen Verhältnisse, sondern beginnen institutionell ihren Primat in West- und Ostkirche aufzubauen, wobei ein solcher Aufbau zunächst für die Westkirche schneller gelingt, die grundlegende Petrusdoktrin jedoch auch auf ein Ausgreifen des Primats nach dem Osten hinzielt.[1]

The episcopate of Siricius (384–98)[2] falls exactly into this time of ecclesiastical change. Damasus died on 12 December 384. As we are told in a short note by Prosper of Aquitaine, Siricius probably succeeded his deceased predecessor in

---

* An earlier version of this chapter was presented at the sixteenth International Conference on Patristic Studies, Oxford University, 8–12 August 2011.

[1] J. Speigl, 'Die Päpste in der Reichskirche des 4. und frühen 5. Jahrhunderts. Von Silvester I. bis Sixtus III.', in M. Greschat (ed.), *Das Papsttum*, vol.1: *Von den Anfängen bis zu den Päpsten in Avignon*, Gestalten der Kirchengeschichte, vol. 11 (Stuttgart, 1984), p. 43: 'From around the middle of our period (380) onwards, the Roman bishops are no longer under the predominance of the political conditions of the Roman empire, but are beginning in institutional terms to build up their primacy in the western and eastern churches. Initially, this is succeeding faster in the western church, but the fundamental Petrine doctrine also aims to extend the primacy to the East'. (my own translation).

[2] For the dating of Siricius' episcopate see Ch. Hornung, *Directa ad decessorem: Ein kirchenhistorisch-philologischer Kommentar zur ersten Dekretale des Siricius von Rom*, JbAC Erg.-Bd. Kleine Reihe, vol. 8 (Münster, 2011), pp. 19–22.

the episcopal see of Rome in the same month.³ A short imperial letter, directed to the urban prefect and preserved in the *Collectio Avellana*, recapitulates the incidents in a more differentiated way: hereafter Siricius was unanimously elected and Ursinus, the old rival in the episcopal election, was execrated.⁴ The Roman community remembered the violent conflicts in the aftermath of Damasus' election,⁵ a situation they wanted to avoid 20 years later. It seems then that this imperial letter was intended to give Siricius authority and protection against conflicts that might arise in the church after the election.⁶

We have only fragmentary information about the following 15 years of his episcopate. The extant correspondence shows communication with Illyricum Orientale. The topic of one letter, *Etiam dudum* (JK 259), concerns unauthorised episcopal ordinations, administered without the knowledge of the bishop of Thessaloniki.⁷ Siricius intervenes against this practice. Another letter sent to North Africa in 386 informs the provinces there of decisions made by a Roman synod. The letter *Cum in unum* (JK 258) is extant in the acts of the North African Synod of Thelepte of 417.⁸

The episcopate of Siricius occurred during the period in which the ecclesiastical influence of the bishop in the imperial residence of Milan exceeded the borders of northern Italy and was more and more perceptible in the whole

---

³   Prosper of Aquitaine, *Epit. chron.* 1182 (MGH.AA 9.461).

⁴   Valentinian II, *Ep. ad Pinianum* (*Collectio Avellana, Ep.* 4) (CSEL 35.47–8).

⁵   Ammianus Marcellinus 27.3.12: 'Damasus et Ursinus supra humanum modum ad rapiendam episcopi sedem ardentes scissis studiis asperrime conflictabant ad usque mortis vulnerumque discrimina adiumentis utriusque progressis ... '; *Collectio Avellana, Ep.* 1 (CSEL 35.1–4); A. Coşkun, 'Der Praefect Maximinus, der Jude Isaak und der Strafprozeß gegen den Bischof Damasus', *JbAC*, 46 (2003): pp. 17–44; and U. Reutter, *Damasus: Bischof von Rom (366–384): Leben und Werk*, Studien und Texte zu Antike und Christentum, vol. 55 (Tübingen, 2009), pp. 31–56.

⁶   See E. Wirbelauer, 'Die Nachfolgerbestimmung im römischen Bistum (3.–6. Jh.): Doppelwahlen und Absetzungen in ihrer herrschaftssoziologischen Bedeutung', *Klio*, 76 (1994): pp. 388–437, at p. 409.

⁷   Siricius, *Ep.* 4 (PL 13.1148–9) = *Collectio Thessalonicensis, Ep.* 3 (K. Silva-Tarouca, *Epistularum Romanorum pontificum ad vicarios per Illyricum aliosque episcopos. Collectio Thessalonicensis ad fidem codicis Vat. Lat. 5751*, Textus et documenta. Series theologica, vol. 23 [Rome, 1937], p. 19); the letter *Accepi litteras* (JK 259) was often classified as Siricius' second letter to Illyricum (PL 13.1176–8). Now it is ascribed to a synod chaired by Ambrose (F. Cavallera, 'La lettre sur l'évêque Bonose est-elle de saint Sirice ou de saint Ambroise?', *BLE*, 21 [1920]: pp. 141–7; and O. Faller and M. Zelzer [eds], *Sancti Ambrosi Opera*, part 10: *Epistulae et Acta*, t. 3: *Epistularum liber decimus, Epistulae extra collectionem, Gesta Concili Aquileiensis*, CSEL 82/3 [Vienna, 1996], pp. xxx–xxxi).

⁸   Siricius, *Ep.* 5 (CCL 149.59–63).

church. During their episcopates, Ambrose and Siricius took up correspondence with each other, a fact that has been interpreted in various ways. For example Joseph Langen concludes that they were on friendly terms.[9] However, this interpretation goes too far. In fact, Ambrose was acting independently in both ecclesiastical and political matters. He did not follow the Roman requirements,[10] with the consequence that his colleague Siricius was restricted in his influence.

Biographical details of Siricius are almost totally absent. His epitaph speaks of a career in the Roman clergy. During the episcopates of Liberius and Damasus he was first a lector, then a deacon, before finally being elected bishop.[11] Paulinus of Nola informs us about his arrogance[12] and Jerome scoffs at him. The latter had been defeated by Siricius in the election, which decided the succession of Damasus, and later on he criticised his successful competitor's simplicity (*simplicitas*).[13]

Notwithstanding the lack of information on Siricius' life and the exact organisation of his episcopate, scholars recognise his time in office as significant. Erich Caspar, in his still prominent history of the Roman bishops, describes him as the first pope,[14] and, in agreement with Caspar, Detlev Jasper writes in the introduction to his 2001 monograph dealing with the decretal as a literary genre:

> The obvious place to begin this discussion is with Pope Siricius' letters and decretals, because these decretals, which were issued mostly as *responsa*, reveal a new capacity of the popes to act as legislators. From the time of Siricius, popes claimed that their decretals were equal to conciliar decisions.[15]

---

[9] J. Langen, *Geschichte der römischen Kirche bis zum Pontifikate Leo's I. Quellenmäßig dargestellt* (Bonn, 1881), p. 648, n. 1.

[10] Hornung, *Directa*, pp. 23–4.

[11] Ps-Damasus, *Epigr*. 93.1–2 (M. Ihm [ed.], *Damasi epigrammata accedunt Pseudodamasiana aliaque ad Damasiana inlustranda idonea*, Anthologiae Latinae Supplementa, vol. 1 [Leipzig, 1895], p. 96): 'Liberium lector mox et levita secutus,/ post Damasum, clarus totos quos vixit in annos'.

[12] Paulinus of Nola, *Ep*. 5.14 (CSEL 29.33): ' ... urbici papae superba discretio ... '.

[13] Jerome, *Ep*. 127.9 (CSEL 56.152). See N. Adkin, 'Pope Siricius' "Simplicity" (Jerome, epist. 127, 9, 3)', *Vetera Christianorum*, 33 (1996): pp. 25–8.

[14] E. Caspar, *Geschichte des Papsttums von den Anfängen bis zur Höhe der Weltherrschaft*, vol. 1: *Römische Kirche und Imperium Romanum* (Tübingen, 1930), p. 261.

[15] D. Jasper, 'The Beginning of the Decretal Tradition: Papal Letters from the Origin of the Genre through the Pontificate of Stephen V', in D. Jasper and H. Fuhrmann (eds), *Papal Letters in the Early Middle Ages*, History of Medieval Canon Law (Washington, DC, 2001), pp. 1–133, at p. 4.

Caspar and Jasper agree in attributing a major importance to Siricius for the history of the popes. This importance they see revealed in the new form of Roman episcopal letters, the so-called decretals, which are known from the time of Siricius and clearly differ from the letters of his predecessors in form and style. As will be shown below, the decretals systematically adapt the style of the imperial chancery and transfer it to Roman ecclesiastical correspondence, assigning a hierarchy between writer and recipient. The first of these letters is *Directa* (JK 255),[16] dated 10 February 385.[17] It is a response, answering an enquiry, which had been sent to Damasus. The recipient of the Roman letter is Himerius, bishop of Tarragona in Spain. We only know of him due to the first decretal.

In the following sections of the chapter, I am going to investigate two aspects. Firstly, the *prooemium* has to be analysed in order to reconstruct the development of Roman primacy. As we have seen, Siricius is called the first pope. He points out his new concept of office in the *prooemium* of the letter to Himerius: What does Siricius refer to in formulating his new, already primatial concept of office? How does he legitimate it? Which methods can be observed only in the *prooemium* to give his position authority?

The episcopate of Siricius is seen as a turning point in the history of the papacy, because a new genre of Roman episcopal letters is developed at this time: the decretals. Siricius' successors also used them in order to come to a decision on different aspects of discipline and to give the Roman primacy validity. In a second part I want to show the change in the function of Roman episcopal letters. Although at first they are confined to answering single questions, they seem to transcend the single case and to claim more and more a general validity. One can ask how the Roman bishops used the different requests of colleagues, caused by different conflicts in the provinces, to establish a consistent discipline according to the Roman model, which gave the Roman bishops an increasing influence in other ecclesiastical areas. The first decretal of Siricius gives us important insights into this development which can also be observed in the episcopates of Innocent

---

[16] Siricius, *Ep.* 1 (PL 13.1131–47 = P. Coustant, *Epistolae Romanorum Pontificum et quae ad eos scriptae sunt a S. Clemente I usque ad Innocentum III*, t. 1 [Paris, 1721], cols 623–38) = JK 255.

[17] Authorship and date of the decretal *Ad Gallos episcopos* are disputed. The relationship between *Ad Gallos episcopos* and *Directa* has been discussed in Y.-M. Duval, *La décrétale* Ad Gallos episcopos: *son texte et son auteur. Texte critique, traduction française et commentaire*, Supplements to Viligiae Christianae, vol. 73 (Leiden and Boston, 2005); Reutter, *Damasus*, pp. 192–247; and Hornung, *Directa*, pp. 268–83. The latest research mentioned above gives more plausibility to the assumption that *Directa* is earlier than *Ad Gallos episcopos*, despite Duval.

I and Leo the Great: What does the first decretal reveal of its intended function? And which further indications of the new function of Roman episcopal letters can be found in the letters of his successors?

A New Concept of Office of the Roman Bishops

The response to the enquiry of Himerius of Tarragona may be one of Siricius' first actions in his episcopate. In his lost consultation, the Spanish colleague submitted a number of different questions related to the discipline of community and clergy, which today can only be reconstructed from the Roman answer.

The *prooemium*, which works on different levels of language and style, is especially important for Siricius' new concept of his office. Since it constitutes the foundation for the following argumentation, the text is presented in Latin (PL 13.1132–3) and an English translation.

> 1. Directa ad decessorem nostrum sanctae recordationis Damasum fraternitatis tuae relatio me iam in sede ipsius constitutum, quia sic Dominus ordinauit, inuenit. Quam cum in conuentu fratrum sollicitius legeremus tanta inuenimus, quae reprehensione et correctione sint digna, quanta optaremus laudanda cognoscere. Et quia necesse nos erat, in eius labores curasque succedere, cui per Dei gratiam successimus in honorem; facto, ut oportebat, primitus meae prouectionis indicio, ad singula, prout Dominus aspirare dignatus est, consultationi tuae responsum competens non negamus: quia officii nostri consideratione, non est nobis dissimulare, non est tacere libertas quibus maior cunctis Christianae religionis zelus incumbit. Portamus onera omnium qui grauantur: quin immo haec portat in nobis beatus apostolus Petrus, qui nos in omnibus, ut confidimus, administrationis suae protegit et tuetur haeredes.

> 2. The account which you, brother, directed to our predecessor of holy memory Damasus, found me now installed in his see because the Lord thus ordained. When we read that [account] more carefully in an assembly of brethren, we found to the degree we had hoped to recognize things which ought to be praised much which was worthy of reprimand and correction. And since it is necessary for us to succeed to the labors and responsibilities of him whom, through the grace of God, we succeeded in honor, having first given notice, as was necessary, of my promotion, we do not refuse, as the Lord deigns to inspire, a proper response to your inquiry in every point. For in view of our office there is no freedom for us, on whom a zeal for the Christian religion is incumbent greater than on all others, to

dissimulate or to be silent. We bear the burdens of all who are oppressed, or rather the blessed apostle Peter, who in all things protects and preserves us, the heirs, as we trust, of his administration, bears them in us.[18]

The passage begins with the information that Siricius has succeeded Damasus. Divine appointment legitimises his succession. From the second sentence onwards, Siricius briefly reports his motives for composing this letter: Himerius has written a consultative letter to Damasus, in which he has described threatening conditions in the Spanish church. Since he, Siricius, has succeeded Damasus and, as his heir (*haeres*), is responsible for the church as a whole, he responds in a detailed *responsum*. According to the text we can distinguish three parts of the *prooemium*: first, information about the succession, second, origin of the letter, and third, motivation.

A mere summary of the first chapter is not sufficient for conceiving his argumentation and his intention. For this reason, an analysis of the semantic field is necessary, which essentially draws our attention to analogies in Roman law. These are important for Siricius' concept of office. The Roman bishop uses it to describe his relations with the Spanish bishop and to give his succession the necessary legitimisation. This can be seen in three terms: *relatio*, *consultatio* and *responsum*. Siricius calls Himerius' epistle a *relatio*, somewhat later, and, in a terminological variation, a *consultatio*. On the other hand, he also calls his own letter a *responsum*. Thus, the Roman bishop chooses terms at the start of his letter that are familiar from imperial administration and which show a hierarchy between the emperor and his magistrates. *Relatio* or *consultatio* is the account of an inferior magistrate to a superior one, especially the emperor,[19] while *responsum* is a response of a lawyer, or later, of the emperor.[20] This terminology can also be found in the correspondence between Pliny the Younger and Trajan,[21]

---

[18] English translation of Siricius in R. Somerville and B.C. Brasington, *Prefaces to Canon Law Books in Latin Christianity: Selected Translations 500–1245* (New Haven and London, 1998), pp. 36–46.

[19] See O. Eger, 'Relatio', *Real-Encyclopädie*, vol. 1A/1 (Stuttgart, 1914), pp. 563–4; and L. Wenger, *Die Quellen des römischen Rechts*, Denkschriften der Gesamtakademie, vol. 2 (Vienna, 1953), p. 431.

[20] See Th. Mommsen, *Römisches Staatsrecht*, vol. 2/2 (Tübingen, 1952 [4th edn]), pp. 976–7; M. Bretone, *Geschichte des römischen Rechts: Von den Anfängen bis zu Justinian* (Munich, 1992), pp. 138–46; and T. Giaro, 'Responsa', *Der Neue Pauly*, vol. 10 (Stuttgart, 2001), pp. 931–2.

[21] Pliny the Younger, *Ep.* 10.96.9: 'Ideo dilata cognitione ad consulendum te decurri. Visa est enim mihi res digna consultatione, maxime propter periclitantium numerum'.

as well as in imperial constitutions of the fourth century.²² Using these terms, Siricius describes a subordination in the church, which is modelled after the relationship between the emperor and his magistrates, and places himself above his Spanish colleague.

However, in the first chapter the Roman law of succession has a greater importance than the terms discussed before. It is evident that the author borrowed both the idea and the terminology of its programme.²³ The verb *succedere*, an important term of the Roman law of succession, occurs twice: 'in eius labores curasque succedere' and 'successimus in honorem'. *Haeres* prominently stands at the end of the *prooemium*. Both expressions have a specific meaning in Roman law: *succedere* means the assumption of the universal rights of the deceased, the assumption of his property and his hereditary rights,²⁴ while *haeres* is the representative and the universal successor of the deceased.²⁵ When the heir is appointed in the will, there is no difference from the legal point of view between the deceased and the heir. The idea that the deceased lives on in his heir is related to this argumentation and is also present in Roman law.²⁶ Siricius seems to allude to it in his so-called *in*-phrases: ' ... quin immo haec portat in nobis beatus apostolus Petrus ... '.

---

²² See *CTh* 11.29.2 (Th. Mommsen and P. Krüger [eds], *Codex Theodosianus*, vol. 1: *Theodosiani Libri XVI cum constitutionibus Sirmondinis* [Hildesheim, 1990], p. 622); 11.29.4 (Mommsen and Krüger, *Codex Theodosianus*, p. 622); 1.2.11 (Mommsen and Krüger, *Codex Theodosianus*, p. 33): 'Rescripta ad consultationem emissa uel emittenda, in futurum his tantum negotiis opitulentur, quibus effusa docebuntur'; Ch. Lécrivain, 'Relatio', *Dictionnaire des antiquités grecques et romaines*, vol. 4/2 (Paris, 1911), p. 830; Ch. Lécrivain, 'Rescriptum', *Dictionnaire des antiquités grecques et romaines*, vol. 4/2 (Paris, 1911), pp. 844–6; and F. Wieacker, *Römische Rechtsgeschichte. Zweiter Abschnitt*, Handbuch der Altertumswissenschaft, vol. 10/3/1/2 (Munich, 2006), pp. 192–207.

²³ See W. Ullmann, 'Leo I and the Theme of Papal Primacy', *JThS*, n.s. 11 (1960): pp. 25–51; and W. Ullmann, *Gelasius I. (492–496): Das Papsttum an der Wende der Spätantike zum Mittelalter*, Päpste und Papsttum, vol. 18 (Stuttgart, 1981), pp. 23–31.

²⁴ Cf. Gaius in Justinian, *Dig.* 50.16.24 (Th. Mommsen and P. Krüger [eds], *Corpus Iuris Civilis*, vol. 1: *Institutiones, Digesta* [Hildesheim, 1993 (25th edn)], p. 901): 'Nihil est aliud hereditas quam successio in universum ius, quod defunctus habuit'.

²⁵ See J. Fellermayr, *Tradition und Sukzession im Lichte des römisch-antiken Erbdenkens. Untersuchungen zu den lateinischen Kirchenvätern bis zu Leo dem Großen* (Munich, 1979), pp. 391–7; and J. Fellermayr, 'Hereditas', *Reallexikon für Antike und Christentum*, vol. 14 (Stuttgart, 1988), pp. 626–48, at p. 627.

²⁶ A. Manigk, 'Hereditarium ius', *Real-Encyclopädie*, vol. 8/1 (Stuttgart, 1912), pp. 625–6.

From his use of *succedere* and *haeres* it can be deduced that the Roman law of succession forms the foundation of Siricius' new conception of office.[27] The other terms also familiar from Roman law (*relatio*, *consultatio* and *responsum*) only describe a hierarchy, but do not grant a sufficient legitimisation of the primacy. This is only achieved by referring to the law of succession. The same way the heir enters into the rights of the deceased, the Roman bishop succeeds those of Peter. According to this interpretation, he is the sole heir (*haeres*), the holder of his authority and of the promise of Matthew 16:18–19. The reference to Peter requires the tradition that the two finest of the apostles had suffered martyrdom in Rome,[28] but the authority of the Roman bishop, derived from this, results from the adaptation of the law of succession. The law of succession produces the medium which closes the temporal gap between Peter and his successors. Therefore it is understandable that in the following time the terms *haeres* and *succedere* are frequently used in the letters and homilies of Roman bishops.[29] The assumption of an inner identity between Peter and his successors, adumbrated in the *in*-phrases, gains its plausibility from the following idea that the deceased lives on in his heir.[30] For this reason, Siricius can claim that the apostle lives on in himself, a Roman bishop of the fourth century, and it legitimises at the same time the transfer of authority given in Matthew 16:18–19 to himself.

The Changed Function of Roman Episcopal Letters

The Roman law of succession and the characterisation of the ecclesiastical correspondence by the terms *relatio*, *consultatio* and *responsum* have been at the centre of interest in our interpretation of the *prooemium*. Using terms of the Roman law, Siricius tries to express his new papal conception of office at the beginning of his episcopate in his first letter. However, there are also noticeable analogies to Roman law in the remaining part of the decretal. In the following I shall point out parallels of structure between the decretal and imperial

---

[27] W. Selb, 'Erbrecht', *JbAC*, 14 (1971): pp. 170–84, at pp. 182–4.

[28] See O. Zwierlein, *Petrus in Rom: Die literarischen Zeugnisse: Mit einer kritischen Edition der Martyrien des Petrus und Paulus auf neuer handschriftlicher Grundlage*, Untersuchungen zur antiken Literatur und Geschichte, vol. 96 (Berlin and New York, 2010 [2nd edn]), especially pp. 332–3.

[29] Siricius, *Ep.* 5 (CCL 149.63); Innocent I, *Ep.* 1 (PL 20.465) = JK 285; Zosimus, *Ep.* 12.1 (PL 20.676) = JK 342; Sixtus III, *Ep.* 6.5 (PL 50.609) = JK 392; and Leo I, *Serm.* 3.4; and 5.4 (CCL 138.13, 24).

[30] K.-D. Schmidt, 'Papa Petrus ipse', *ZKG*, 54 (1936): pp. 267–75.

constitutions. By this means we can obtain knowledge of the modes by which the primacy was enforced.

In the first part of the decretal, Siricius follows the single points of the Spanish account exactly. This is made clear by phrases with which the Roman bishop refers to the consultation of Himerius: 'Prima itaque paginae tuae fronte signasti',[31] 'ut asseris'[32] or the impersonal construction 'adiectum est'.[33] The phrases serve as an introduction to the account of the ecclesiastical irregularities in which Siricius takes up information he has obtained from Himerius, probably in his lost consultation. Then, the ecclesiastical judgement follows in each chapter of the letter. The Roman bishop passes sentence on the irregularities, formulated in the first person plural (*decernimus*[34] and *censemus*[35]) or in the subjunctive.[36] A so-called 'Poenformel' can follow, by which the violation of law is made a punishable offence.

The first chapter of the decretal is a characteristic example of a regular structure. Siricius is trying to prohibit the rebaptism of heretics.

---

[31] Siricius, *Ep.* 1.I.2 (PL 13.1133).
[32] Ibid., 1.II.3 (PL 13.1134).
[33] Ibid., 1.III.4 (PL 13.1136).
[34] Ibid., 1.VIII.12 (PL 13.1142).
[35] Ibid., 1.V.6 (PL 13.1137).
[36] Ibid., 1.IX.13 (PL 13.1143); 1.X.14 (PL 13.1143); and 1.XV.19 (PL 13.1145): ' ... hac sibi conditione a nobis ueniam intelligat relaxatam ... '.

Prima itaque paginae tuae fronte signasti, baptizatos ab impiis Arianis plurimos ad fidem catholicam festinare, et quosdam de fratribus nostris eosdem denuo baptizare uelle:	On the first page of your letter, therefore, you indicated that multitudes who were baptised by the impious Arians were hastening to the Catholic faith, and that certain of our brothers wished to baptise these same people again.	Reference to Himerius' account
quod non licet, cum hoc fieri et apostolus uetet, et canones contradicant, et post cassatum Ariminense concilium, missa ad prouincias a uenerandae memoriae praedecessore meo Liberio generalia decreta prohibeant; quos nos cum Nouatianis aliisque haereticis, sicut est in synodo constitutum per inuocationem solam septiformis Spiritus, episcopalis manus impositione, Catholicorum conuentui sociamus, quod etiam totus Oriens Occidensque custodit:	This is not allowed, since both the apostle forbids and the canons oppose doing it; and after the Council of Rimini was annulled, the general decrees sent to the provinces by my predecessor of venerable memory Liberius prohibit it. We unite these people, and the Novatianists and other heretics, to the assembly of Catholics, just as it was constituted in the synod, solely through invocation of the sevenfold Spirit by imposition of the bishop's hand. Indeed all the East and the West preserves this practice,	Siricius' decision
a quo tramite uos quoque posthac minime conuenit deuiare, si non uultis a nostro collegio synodali sententia separari.	and it is also inappropriate henceforth for you to deviate from that path, if you do not wish to be separated from our company by synodal sentence.	Penalty, if decision is violated

Siricius' instruction against the rebaptism of heretics is a response to Himerius' account. The rule is formulated in a relative clause (*quod non licet*) and legitimated by reference to tradition (apostles, councils and the decisions of his predecessors). Siricius decides that baptised heretics should be initiated into the church by the imposition of hands and the invocation of the Holy Spirit. A penalty stands at the end of the chapter threatening everybody who violates this regulation with exclusion from the *collegium nostrum*.

The above-mentioned structure occurs very regularly in each chapter of the first part of the decretal (up to the eighth chapter). The structure is not the result of Siricius' literary competence, but of his orientation with regard to imperial constitutions. From these Siricius or the Roman episcopal chancery borrowed the structure of the letter, which can be illustrated as follows:[37]

Protocol	1. *Intitulatio*
	2. *Inscriptio*
Text	1. *Prooemium*
	2. *Narratio*
	3. *Dispositio*
	4. Publications mandate
	5. Penalty
Eschatocol	1. *Subscriptio*
	2. Date

As the structure reveals, *narratio*, *dispositio*, publications mandate and penalty are attached to the *prooemium* in the form of imperial constitutions.[38] The single parts are not obligatory, but can be regularly found in imperial laws. The parts in Siricius' decretal, as outlined above, correspond with them conspicuously. According to the structure, the 'Reference to Himerius' account' is the *narratio*, the part named 'Siricius' decision' can be seen as *dispositio* and the part labelled 'Penalty, if decision is violated' as penalty. There is no doubt that this is where Siricius borrowed the structure of his first decretal from.[39]

The uniformity of the structure shows that in the second part of the letter (from the eighth chapter onwards), concerned with the discipline of clergy, Siricius does not respond to single questions, but legislates independently. Only the instructions on the continence of the higher clergy and the interdiction of digamy are a result of the Spanish consultation, while the subsequent norms of an ecclesiastical *cursus honorum*, the recruitment of monks, and the

---

[37] See P.A. McShane, *La romanitas et le pape Léon le Great: L'apport culturel des institutions imperials à la formation des structures ecclésiastiques*, Recherches Théologie, vol. 24 (Tournai and Montreal, 1979), pp. 339–40; and Ch. Hornung, 'Die Sprache des römischen Rechts in Schreiben römischer Bischöfe des 4. und 5. Jahrhunderts', *JbAC*, 53 (2010): pp. 20–80, at pp. 43–52.

[38] See P. Classen, *Kaiserreskript und Königsurkunde: Diplomatische Studien zum Problem der Kontinuität zwischen Altertum und Mittelalter*, Byzantina keimena kai meletai, vol. 15 (Thessaloniki, 1977), pp. 60–80; P.E. Pieler, 'Die Rechtsliteratur', in L.J. Engels and H. Hofmann (eds), *Spätantike: Mit einem Panorama der byzantinischen Literatur*, Neues Handbuch der Literaturwissenschaft, vol. 4 (Wiesbaden, 1997), pp. 565–99; and S. Corcoran, *The Empire of the Tetrarchs: Imperial Pronouncements and Government AD 284–324* (Oxford, 1996).

[39] McShane, *Romanitas*, p. 339.

clerical prohibition of penance seem rather to be legislated by Siricius on his own authority.

The eighth chapter of the letter marks the turning point.[40] Having formulated the interdiction of clerical digamy, Siricius adds: ' ... quid ab uniuersis posthac ecclesiis sequendum sit, quid uitandum, generali pronuntiatione decernimus'.[41] With the term *generalis pronuntiatio* the Roman bishop again takes up Roman law: the phrase designates an official legal pronouncement.[42] Below, Siricius parallels his letter with precisely this process of the civil administration and decrees general instructions of canonical law, especially for the clergy. In so doing, it is quite obvious that Siricius here is referring to common experience rather than to specific abuses that have been reported to him. From a formal point of view, this can be illustrated by the changed structure of the norms. While the chapters in the first part of the decretal consist of a *narratio*, *dispositio* and (often) a penalty, the chapters in the second part are only short norms or, as we can now say, *dispositiones*.[43] The twelfth chapter, which is concerned with the institute of syneisacts, is only a main clause: 'Feminas uero non alias esse patimur in domibus clericorum, nisi eas tantum, quas propter solas necessitudinum causas habitare cum iisdem synodus Nicaena permisit'.[44]

The thirteenth chapter is more extensive than the twelfth. It allows Himerius to admit monks into the clergy and even asks him to do so, provided they have maintained a proper mode of life. Concerning its structure, it only consists of a *dispositio*, complemented by an implementation rule (*ita ut qui*):

> Monachos quoque quos tamen morum grauitas et uitae ac fidei institutio sancta commendat, clericorum officiis aggregari et optamus et uolumus; ita ut qui intra tricesimum aetatis annum sunt, in minoribus per gradus singulos, crescente tempore, promoueantur ordinibus: et sic ad diaconatus uel presbyterii insignia, maturae aetatis consecratione, perueniant. Nec saltu ad episcopatus culmen ascendant, nisi in his eadem, quae singulis dignitatibus superius praefiximus, tempora fuerint custodita.[45]

---

[40] Hornung, *Directa*, pp. 72–4 and 183.

[41] Siricius, *Ep.* 1.VIII.12 (PL 13.1142): ' ... what henceforth should be followed by all churches, what should be avoided, we decree by general pronouncement'.

[42] A. Berger, *Encyclopedic Dictionary of Roman Law* (Philadelphia, 1953), p. 657.

[43] Hornung, *Directa*, pp. 46–53.

[44] Siricius, *Ep.* 1.XII.16 (PL 13.1144): 'We certainly do not allow women in the houses of clerics, other than those alone whom the synod of Nicaea, for reasons only of necessity, permitted to live with them'.

[45] Ibid., 1.XIII.17 (PL 13.1144–5): 'We also desire and wish that monks who are commended by depth of character and a holy pattern of life and faith be added to the ranks

From a structural perspective it can also be followed that in the second part of the decretal Siricius transcends Himerius' consultation and gives instructions on his own authority. Regarding language and style, one can presumably attribute this part of the letter to a synod, which Siricius led at the beginning of the year 385.[46] This interpretation cannot be further elucidated here.[47]

The second part of the decretal consists solely of ecclesiastical instructions concerning the clergy. Siricius' intention is to confirm its *sanctitudo*. For this purpose, instructions on the career, the mode of life and the interdiction of penance are formulated. Attributes like *sanctus*[48] or *sacratus*[49] are frequently used in association with the clergy. The propagation of the norms was to be guaranteed by the order to publish the letter. At the end Himerius is instructed to send the decretal not only to the other Spanish bishops but also to those in provinces nearby, probably in Gaul.[50] This assignment indicates the general importance of the letter. Though Siricius at first answered the consultation of Himerius, the answer itself transcends the single case and is of general validity. The more comprehensive exposition of the canon law concerning clergy conforms to this intention.

In 404 Innocent I, one of Siricius' successors, sent a letter to Victricius of Rouen, answering several questions.[51] At the beginning of the letter he asks Victricius to publish the response and calls it a *liber regularum*.[52] This phrase is quite interesting concerning our topic: a Roman letter is supposed to serve as a book of ecclesiastical law for the future. Innocent, the author, claims that it is universal and transcends the single case. The claim is corroborated by the order to publish the letter. Again, the phrase *liber regularum* is familiar from Roman law:

---

of clerics in this way. Those under thirty years of age should be promoted in minor orders over time through the individual ranks and thus reach the honors of the diaconate and the priesthood with the dedication of maturity. They should not ascend in a jump to the height of the episcopate, but only after having served the same periods of time which we established above for the individual ranks'.

[46] See the phrase 'in conuentu fratrum' (Siricius, *Ep.* 1.1 [PL 13.1132]); and Hornung, *Directa*, p. 76.
[47] See Hornung, *Directa*, pp. 72–4.
[48] Siricus, *Ep.* 1.VII.10 (PL 13.1139).
[49] Ibid., 1.VII.8 (PL 13.1138).
[50] Ibid., 1.XV.20 (PL 13.1146).
[51] Innocent I, *Ep.* 2.1 (PL 20.469) = JK 286: ' ... Romanae ecclesiae normam atque auctoritatem magnopere postulasti ... '. See G.D. Dunn, 'Canonical Legislation on the Ordination of Bishops: Innocent I's Letter to Victricius of Rouen', in J. Leemans, P. van Nuffelen, S.W.J. Keough, and C. Nicolaye (eds), *Episcopal Elections in Late Antiquity*, AKG, vol. 119 (Berlin and Boston, 2011), pp. 145–66.
[52] Innocent I, *Ep.* 2.1 (PL 20.469).

libri regularum serve as 'Entscheidungsgrundlage im Rechtsvollzug römischer Provinzbeamter'.[53] They consist of basic rules and guidelines which were meant to support the course of justice. At the end of the letter Innocent uses the term *regula* once again: 'Haec itaque regula, frater charissime, si plena uigilantia fuerit ab omnibus Dei sacerdotibus obseruata, cessabit ambitio, dissensio conquiescet, haereses et schismata non emergent'.[54]

Retrospectively, Innocent confirms a development, which could be observed at the time of Siricius. Analysing the structure of the first decretal, it can be recognised that especially in the second part of the letter, in the part of the canon law concerning clergy, Siricius transcends the request of Himerius and establishes further norms. In this part of the letter he intends to decree a general canon law concerning clergy, which gives the clergy a clear profile and which can be transferred to future problems. The examples make clear that the function of the Roman episcopal letters change at the end of the fourth and the beginning of the fifth century. *Liber regularum*, the term of Innocent's letter, is an important indication for that. Roman episcopal letters gain a greater importance and can constitute, as far as we can judge from the words used, an early compendium of ecclesiastical law. If we follow the parallels to Roman law, the Roman episcopal letters sought to implement justice in the provinces, by way of offering legal principles.

Conclusion

About Siricius Erich Caspar wrote in his history of the Roman bishops that 'Man hat ihn wohl den "ersten Papst" genannt'.[55] This concisely summarises the importance of the episcopate of Siricius. The years between 384 and 398 mark an important turning point in the development of the papacy, not least because of the first decretal.

Here, right in the *prooemium* of his letter to Himerius, the ecclesiastical correspondence parallels with the imperial one by using the terms *consultatio*, *relatio* and *responsum*; in this way, the hierarchy extant between the emperor and his magistrates is transferred to the church, namely to the Roman bishop and

---

[53] H. Ohme, *Kanon ekklesiastikos: Die Bedeutung des altkirchlichen Kanonbegriffs*, AKG, Bd 67 (Berlin and New York, 1998), p. 58.

[54] Innocent I, *Ep.* 2.XIV.17 (PL 20.481): 'If henceforth the *regula* will be observed, insincere ambition will lose ground, dissent be reposed and heresy and schism will not arise'. (my own translation).

[55] Caspar, *Geschichte*, p. 261.

his colleagues. Siricius legitimates the new claim of primacy with the Roman law of succession (*succedere, haeres*). The law of succession alone permits him and his successors to apply the biblical passage of Matthew 16:18–19 to Roman bishops. Thus, as the deceased and his heir become one, Peter and the Roman bishop become one, so that Peter's successor obtains a still unknown authority and legitimation.[56]

Furthermore, the structure of the first decretal, its division into a first section referring to the consultation of Himerius and a second, in which Siricius legislates independently, shows the changed function of Roman episcopal letters. At first they are composed as responses, but then they become small compendia of early ecclesiastical law and develop into general norms. Innocent, one of the successors of Siricius, aptly introduces his letter to Victricius as a *liber regularum*, trying to present a sum of ecclesiastical discipline at the beginning of his episcopate.[57] Innocent's example indicates that the first decretal marks the beginning of a fundamental development. From Siricius onwards, Roman episcopal letters change their function. The casuistic consideration of the single case no longer takes centre stage, but rather, as in Roman law, the general rule of ecclesiastical discipline as a whole.[58]

In the context of this study, only the beginning of this development could be discussed. Later examples, such as letters from the episcopate of Leo the Great, confirm these observations,[59] but can only be mentioned here.[60] The results have to be put into the greater context of Roman episcopal correspondence as a whole. Certainly, not all the epistles of Peter's successors are responses or small compendia. Therefore, it is necessary and useful to distinguish between different

---

[56] See Ullmann, 'Leo', pp. 25–51, who assumes that Leo the Great is the first Roman bishop to claim the primacy with juridical terms.

[57] Ch. Pietri, *Roma Christiana. Recherches sur l'Église de Rome, son organisation, sa politique, son idéologie de Miltiade à Sixte III (311–440)*, BEFAR, vol. 2 (Rome, 1976), p. 983.

[58] This is also an interesting contrast with synodal law, which is restricted to individual causes. See A. Weckwerth, *Ablauf, Organisation und Selbstverständnis westlicher Synoden im Spiegel ihrer Akten*, JbAC Erg.-Bd. Kleine Reihe, vol. 5 (Münster, 2010), p. 230.

[59] See the following letters of Leo I, which also indicate that, in his answers, the Roman bishop transcends the single case and gives further general norms of ecclesiastical discipline: *Epp*. 4 (PL 54.610–14) = JK 402 (especially 4.3: 'Nec hoc quoque praetereundum esse duximus ... ' and 4.4: 'Illud etiam duximus praemonendum, ut ... '); 119.6 (PL 54.1045) = JK 495: 'Illud quoque dilectionem tuam conuenit praecauere, ut ... '; 120.5 (PL 54.1053) = JK 496: 'Vnde hoc quoque nos contra hostes ecclesiae prouidere condignum est, ut ... '; 120.6 (PL 54.1054): 'Quod superest, exhortamur ut ... '; 159 (PL 54.1135–40) = JK 536; and 167 (PL 54.1197–209) = JK 544.

[60] For detailed discussion see Hornung, 'Recht'.

forms (so-called 'disciplinary letters [Disziplinarbriefe]', 'pastoral letters [Lehrbriefe]', theological 'treatise letters [Traktatbriefe]', and, finally 'communal and accompanying letters [Gemeinschafts- und Begleitbriefe]'.[61] Here, too, a great diversity of form, style, and length is to be found. Even so, it is remarkable that from the time of the first decretal onwards the disciplinary letters turn into expanded letters and compendia. With regard to content and form, the first decretal seems to be an important document which gives insights into how the primacy was legitimised and enforced. Responding to questions of their colleagues, the Roman bishops legislate with respect to the whole church. They resolve conflicts in the provinces by regulating them in conformity with Roman discipline and obliging their colleagues to adherence. This is an important step on the path to Roman primacy.[62] However it must be admitted that the great number of arguments in the first decretal and the great number of letters in total directed by Siricius' successors to the various regions of the church are an unmistakable indication of the fact that the primacy was far from undisputed and would require a long time to take shape.

---

[61] See Hornung, 'Recht', pp. 32–43.
[62] Hornung, *Directa*, pp. 264–5.

Chapter 4
Pope Siricius and Himerius of Tarragona (385): Provincial Papal Intervention in the Fourth Century*

Alberto Ferreiro

In 385 Pope Siricius (384–99) sent a letter to Himerius of Tarragona in response to issues on which the bishop of Tarragona had sent to Rome seeking guidance. Himerius' letter had been sent to Pope Damasus, who did not respond due to his untimely death. Although we do not have the letter that Himerius wrote, the detailed response by Pope Siricius allows us to ascertain its content.[1] The pope considered the matter so pressing that he convened a synod in Rome rather than unilaterally responding. The letter has not gone unnoticed in contemporary scholarship for several reasons. One, since it is the first papal 'decretal', it has received considerable attention by scholars of the papacy.[2] Two, it is the earliest extant letter to Hispania from a bishop of Rome. Therefore for the history of papal relations with Hispania it is significant and a number of modern studies have considered its content.[3] This brief study will focus on specific questions

---

*   An earlier version of this chapter was presented at the sixteenth International Conference on Patristic Studies, Oxford University, 8–12 August 2011. I want to thank the Centro Fray Luis de León (Seattle-Salamanca) for the financial support that made my attendance possible.

[1]   Siricius, Ep. 1 (PL 13.1131–47 = P. Coustant, *Epistolae Romanorum Pontificum et quae ad eos scriptae sunt a S. Clemente I usque ad Innocentum III*, t. 1 [Paris, 1721], cols 623–38) = JK 255.

[2]   D. Jasper, 'The Beginning of the Decretal Tradition: Papal Letters from the Origin of the Genre through the Pontificate of Stephen V', in D. Jasper and H. Fuhrmann, *Papal Letters in the Early Middle Ages*, History of Medieval Canon Law (Washington, DC, 2001). An excellent discussion on what constitutes a decretal is at pp. 11–22.

[3]   For a prosopographical approach consult J. Vilella Masana, 'La *Epístola* 1 de Siricio: Estudio Prosopográfico de Himerio de Tarragona', *Aug*, 44 (2004): pp. 337–69; J. Vilella Masana, 'Las primacías eclesiásticas en *Hispania* durante el siglo IV', *Polis*, 10 (1998): pp. 269–85; and J. Vilella Masana, 'Los concilios eclesiásticos de la Tarraconensis durante el

regarding this papal letter. It also forms in part a comprehensive study that I am carrying out on the relationship of the bishops of Rome with the church in Hispania from Pope Siricius up to the Muslim invasion of 711.

The questions I consider here are: (1) Does the decretal represent a departure from previous papal letters that were pastoral in their approach to one expressing stern, authoritative and imposing language? (2) Did Pope Siricius condemn practices of the Priscillianists in Hispania and Gallia? (3) Was the pope's decretal intended for the universal church or only for bishops in Hispania and Gallia? (4) What contributions did the decretal make in the ongoing development of Petrine primacy?

Let us consider briefly a few observations regarding the background of the decretal.[4] We have enough information to reconstruct the pontificate of Pope Siricius, who succeeded Pope Damasus.[5] For example, Pope Siricius was also active in the North African church, to which he addressed decretals (*decretalia*).[6] In all cases – North Africa, Gallia and Hispania – he requested promulgation of his letters within each region.[7] The decretal to Hispania, therefore, directed at Himerius is not singular, it is one of several sent to provinces whose bishops sought papal guidance. Moreover, it was not the first intervention of a pontiff in Hispania. His predecessor Pope Damasus, for example, was involved in the emerging Priscillianist controversy, although his involvement was measured since the movement was not yet recognised unanimously as a heresy. Before Pope Damasus, however, active involvement in Hispania transpired in the pontificate of Pope Stephen I (254–57) after bishops Basilides and Martialis were removed by some bishops; the pope listened to an appeal from the deposed bishops and supported their restoration to their episcopal seats. Facing opposition from Rome the newly installed bishops of the churches of Mérida

---

siglo V', *Florentia Iliberritana*, 13 (2002): pp. 327–44. The most detailed study is the recent monograph by Ch. Hornung, *Directa ad decessorem: Ein kirchenhistorisch-philologischer Kommentar zur ersten Dekretale des Siricius von Rom*, Jahrbuch für Antike und Christentum Ergänzungsband Kleine Reihe, vol. 8 (Münster, 2011). See also Ch. Hornung, 'Die Sprache des römischen Rechts in Schreiben römischer Bischöfe des 4. und 5. Jahrhunderts', *JbAC*, 53 (2010): pp. 20–80.

[4] For the fourth-century background in Hispania see P. Ubric Rabaneda, *La Iglesia en la Hispania del siglo V* (Granada, 2004), pp. 111–32.

[5] J.N.D. Kelly, *The Oxford Dictionary of Popes*, (Oxford and New York, 1986), pp. 35–6.

[6] See Ibid., p. 35; and Jasper, 'The Beginning of the Decretal Tradition', pp. 9–10.

[7] Kelly, *The Oxford Dictionary of Popes*, p. 35.

and Astorga-León appealed to Carthage.[8] In view of this, Pope Siricius' decretal to Himerius was not a novel exercise of papal authority in Hispania, for, as Ricardo García Villoslada observed, 'Lo que si parece claro es que el recurso al centro del cristianismo occidental es cosa no infrequente en Hispana'.[9] What we witness with Pope Siricius is an ongoing recognition in the West of the apostolic authority of the bishop of Rome. The Roman pontiffs seized these opportunities to extend their authority in the churches of North Africa, Hispania and Gallia. In the early western Middle Ages papal authority and Petrine primacy would develop noticeably through Pope Siricius' successors, notably Innocent I and Leo the Great.

Concerning Himerius of Tarragona we know absolutely nothing of his personal biography other than he was bishop of Tarragona. We do not know, aside from this particular decretal, anything about his episcopal tenure before or after 385. Pope Siricius' decretal does reveal that Himerius of Tarragona held great prestige in Hispania since he was entrusted to promulgate the decretal in Hispania and Gallia. The pope, moreover, refers to the see of Tarragona as being beloved, ancient and glorious.[10] This privileged status that the see of Tarragona enjoyed was no doubt founded on the widespread belief that St Paul visited Hispania as expressed in his letter to the Romans (15:24 and 28), and the tradition is that the apostle did so in the region of Tarragona.[11]

---

[8] Cyprian, *Ep.* 67 (CCL 3C.446–62); and R. García Villoslada et al., *Historia de la Iglesia en España*, vol. 1: *La Iglesia de la España romana y visigoda (siglos I–VIII)*, Biblioteca de Autores Cristianos, Maior, vol. 16 (Madrid, 1979), pp. 125 and 148. See also A. Custodio Vega, *El Primado Romano y la Iglesia Española en los Siete Primeros Siglos* (El Escorial, 1942), pp. 31–8; G.D. Dunn, 'Cyprian of Carthage and the Episcopal Synod of Late 254', *REAug*, 48 (2002): pp. 229–47; and G.D. Dunn, *Cyprian and the Bishops of Rome: Questions of Papal Primacy in the Early Church*, ECS, vol. 11 (Strathfield, NSW, 2007), pp. 125–34.

[9] García Villoslada, *Historia de la Iglesia en España*, p. 125: 'What is quite clear is that recourse to the centre of western Christendom [Rome] was not infrequent in Hispania'. (my own translation). A full survey can be found in Custodio Vega, *El Primado Romano y la Iglesia Española*, where a series of articles by the author originally published in the journal *La Ciudad de Dios* are reproduced.

[10] Siricius, *Ep.* 1.XV.20 (PL 13.1146): ' ... utilius tamen, et pro antiquitate sacerdotii tui, dilectioni tuae esse admodum poterit gloriosum ... '. For an English translation see R. Somerville and B. Brasington, *Prefaces to Canon Law Books in Latin Christianity Selected Translations 500–1245* (New Haven and London, 1998).

[11] See the volume of essays, J.M. Gavaldà Ribot et al. (eds), *Pau, Fructuós i el cristianisme primitiu a Tarragona (segles I–VIII)*, Actes del Congres de Tarragona (19–21 de Juny de 2008), Biblioteca Tàrraco d'Arqueologia, vol. 6 (Tarragona, 2010), for in-depth research on this topic. The relevant essays are by A. Borrell Viader, 'Les tradicions sobre el viatge de sant Pau a Hispània en la Primera carta de Climent i en el Cànon de Muratori', pp. 157–66;

Since the content of the decretal has received more than adequate commentary from modern scholars a summary of its content here will suffice.[12] There are 20 sections in the decretal that I shall conflate by topic. Section 1 opens with cordial greetings to Himerius in which Pope Siricius states that the see of Rome exercises the ministry of Peter as its heir.[13] Section 2 addresses whether Arians need re-baptism if they return to the Catholic church. Section 3 continues with additional concerns regarding baptism. Section 4 treats briefly the persistence of paganism. Section 5 engages illicit marriages. Section 6 addresses penitents who fall back into sin. Sections 7 through 12 consider illicit sexual relations of women religious and monks. Sections 13 and 14 set forth the requirements necessary for promotion from reader step-by-step to bishop. Sections 15 through 19 legislate the discipline necessary to correct illicit sexual relations among clergy. Section 20 draws the decretal to conclusion with final directives to Himerius.

Now to our first question: whether the letter departs from a pastoral tone of previous letters to that of stern disciplinarian language. Jasper represents the view that Pope Siricius expressed himself sternly in contrast to the warm pastoral style of prior papal letters:

> As is generally found in early Christian letters, the oldest papal letters are characterised by a 'brotherly pastoral style'. The letters did not contain rules and commands. These early Christian writers preferred persuasion, instruction, and pastoral admonitions to affirm their common faith. The letters were basically substitutes for preaching and oral teaching. This style continued, without exception, until the time of Pope Damasus (366–384).[14]

Custodio Vega dissents, saying that Pope Siricius answered Himerius with 'a decretal filled with pastoral solicitude'.[15] What needs to be kept in mind is the distinction of style between letters that were meant to correct doctrinal error and impose discipline in contrast with personal letters not dealing with controversial

---

C. Godoy Fernández, 'Les tradicions del viatge de sant Pau a Hispània en la literature apòcrifa', pp. 167–80; and V. Mihoc, 'The Tradition on St. Paul's Journey to Spain in the Church Fathers', pp. 181–90.

[12] Consult the works cited in n. 3.

[13] Siricius, *Ep.* 1.1 (PL 13.1133): ' ... Quin imo haec portat in nobis beatus apostolus Petrus, qui nos in omnibus, ut confidimus, administrationis suae protegit et tuetur haeredes'.

[14] Jasper, 'The Beginning of the Decretal Tradition', p.18.

[15] Custodio Vega, *El Primado Romano*, p. 32: 'Le contestó con una Decretal llena de solicitud pastoral'.

issues. Although Pope Siricius' letter is disciplinary it does not exclude a warm pastoral expression, as I shall demonstrate.

While Pope Siricius' decretal contains what Jasper identifies as 'juristic, and often authoritative, language',[16] it is also warm in pastoral language. The pope, moreover, addressed serious moral lapses by the clergy. He was also attentive to offer conversion and penance in order to remain in full communion with the church. The language of imperial juridical force that some have highlighted was necessary to give added weight to his discipline. The decretal opens straightaway with a cordial greeting.[17] Furthermore, as the letter unfolds, Pope Siricius addresses Himerius with fraternal pastoral language: *fraternitatis tuae relatio*,[18] *dilectio tua*,[19] *charitate tua*,[20] *tua sanctitas*,[21] *frater charissime*,[22] *fraternitatis tuae*,[23] *dilectioni tuae*,[24] including the bishops in Hispania and Gallia, whom he calls *fratrum nostrorum*.[25] The overall tone is not merely that of a pontiff sternly issuing orders at Himerius and the clergy in Hispania and Gallia.

A topic that has elicited a lively scholarly discussion is whether the references to heresy were intended to include Priscillianists. The question is pertinent since the correspondence between Himerius and Pope Siricius transpired just as Priscillianism became increasingly a contentious issue. The decretal dates to 385, the same year Priscillian was executed in Trier, and just five years after the Synod of Zaragoza in 380, which some believe targeted Priscillianism.[26] No matter how one wishes to argue, the Synod of Zaragoza fails to mention even once by name Priscillian or his followers. This runs contrary to Sulpicius Severus who maintained that the synod did condemn Priscillian.[27] Priscillian's insistence to

---

[16] Jasper, 'The Beginning of the Decretal Tradition', p. 13.
[17] Siricius, *Ep.* 1.praef. (PL 13.1132): 'Siricius Himerio Tarraconensi episcopo [salutem]'.
[18] Ibid., 1.1 (PL 13.1132).
[19] Ibid., 1.V.6 (PL 13.1137).
[20] Ibid., 1.VII.8 (PL 13.1138).
[21] Ibid., 1.VII.11 (PL 13.1140).
[22] Ibid., 1. XV.20. (PL 13.1146).
[23] Ibid.
[24] Ibid.
[25] Ibid.
[26] See the collection of essays in G. Fatás Cabeza (ed.), *I Concilio Caesaraugustano MDC Aniversario* (Zaragoza, 1981).
[27] Sulpicius Severus, *Chron.* 2.47.2 (SC 441.336): 'Interim Instantius et Saluianus damnati iudicio sacerdotum Priscillianum etiam laicum, sed principem malorum omnium, una secum Caesaraugustana synodo notatum, ad confirmandas uires suas episcopum in Abilensi oppido constituunt, rati nimirum, si hominem acrem et callidum sacerdotali auctoritate armassent, tutiores fore sese'.

Pope Damasus that he was not condemned at the synod is vindicated by the acts of the synod.[28] Of significance, since Himerius of Tarragona did not attend the Synod of Zaragoza, scholars have proposed a variety of reasons for his absence.[29] Henry Chadwick weighed in on the absence of Himerius: 'Amazingly, Himerius can have said not a word overtly about Priscillianism, a silence which is deafening when one reflects on the situation in the late autumn of 384 when Himerius wrote to Rome'.[30] Perhaps Himerius did not attend the Synod of Zaragoza because the issues in dispute were of no immediate concern in Tarragona. I believe there is an additional reasonable explanation for his absence, which I shall propose below.[31]

Himerius asked whether the Arians who returned to the Catholic church required re-baptism. Pope Siricius forbade re-baptism, invoking the apostle Paul, the canons of synods, the annulment of the Synod of Rimini and the decree of his venerable predecessor Pope Liberius.[32] The pope did not pretend to be decreeing anything new. Pope Siricius, in other words, promulgated for Hispania and Gallia what was already universally practised in the East and West.[33] Albert Viciano i Vives aptly notes that papal legislation is rarely ever innovative; on the contrary, it is proposed in harmony with the consensus reached through

---

[28] Priscillian, *Tract.* 2 (M. Conti, *Priscillian of Avila: The Complete Works*, OECT [Oxford, 2010], p. 74, lines 110–13): 'In hac ergo ueritate fidei et in hac simplicitate uiuentibus nobis a Caesaraugustana synhodo Hydatius redit, nihil contra nos referens, quippe quos et ipse in eclesiis nostris secura etiam communicantes demiserat et quos nemo nec absentes quidem praesumpta accusatione damnauerat'.

[29] See T. Sardella, 'Papa Siricio e i movimenti ereticale nella Spagnadi Teodosio I', in R. Teja Casuso and C. Pérez González (eds), *La Hispania de Teodosio Congreso Internacional, Segovia 395–1995-Coca, Segovia*, Actas volumen 1 (Segovia, 1997), pp. 247–54, at p. 247; and J.M. Blázquez Martínez, 'Prisciliano, introductor del ascetismo en Hispania. Las Fuentes, Estudio de la investigación moderna', in Fatás Cabeza *I Concilio Caesaraugustano*, p. 93. Both authors believe Tarragona was yet untouched by the emerging sect.

[30] H. Chadwick, *Priscillian of Avila: The Occult and the Charismatic in the Early Church*. (Oxford, 1976), p. 29.

[31] Plausible is the comment in Chadwick, *Priscillian of Avila*, p. 29: 'Either the majority of the bishops were not yet meeting a serious problem in their dioceses or they saw little reason for becoming excited about Priscillian's activities. Probably only those directly confronted by active Priscillianist cells thought the agenda sufficiently urgent to require their voice at the council'.

[32] Siricius, *Ep.* 1.I.2 (PL 13.1133): ' ... quod non licet, cum hoc fieri et Apostolus uetet [Eph. 4:5], et canones contradicant, et post cassatum Ariminense concilium, missa ad prouincias a uenerandae memoriae praedecessore meo Liberio generalia decreta prohibeant ...'.

[33] Ibid., 1.I.2 (PL 13.1134): ' ... quod etiam totus Oriens Occidensque custodit ... '.

Scripture, Tradition, pontifical decrees and canons of synods. The decretal of Pope Siricius is a reaffirmation of the ongoing emerging ecclesial authority already well developed in the fourth century.[34] Furthermore, Pope Siricius decreed that the question regarding re-baptism also applied to Novatianists and other heretics.[35] Some scholars are convinced that the 'other heretics' is a couched reference to Priscillianism. To answer this question we have to consider the context and the status of the emerging sect in 385.

To ascertain if Pope Siricius had in mind the Priscillianists it is crucial to pinpoint when they were unanimously declared heretics. From 380 up to his execution in 385 there is no clear broad condemnation by the church. The opposition originated mainly from a few bishops in Hispania. Emperor Magnus Maximus' execution of Priscillian was not in concord with the church's desired course of action. On the contrary, his rash actions were condemned by Pope Siricius, Martin of Tours and Ambrose of Milan. Equally relevant in this period, Jerome in his *De uiris illustribus* (up to and including 393) was hesitant to declare Priscillianism a heresy; by 415, however, he was convinced they were the worst of heretics.[36] Even Pope Damasus, who had some doubt about the emerging sect, encouraged the bishops in Hispania to avoid any baseless judgements in view of the fact that no Priscillianists were present in Zaragoza to defend their views.[37] I propose as a benchmark date the year 400 when Priscillianism was authoritatively declared a heresy at a synod. Not much later Pope Leo the Great's detailed, point-by-point refutation of the heresy sealed it. With the force of papal and conciliar condemnation Priscillianism was irreversibly recognised a heresy.

From the Synod of Zaragoza (380), through the 390s, teachings later impugned exclusively upon the Priscillianists were initially associated with recognised heretics and anonymous groups and people. Priscillianism was a heresy in the making. Pope Siricius' comments about heresy, re-baptism and sexual indiscretions by clergy and religious need to be interpreted within this milieu; they should not to be associated exclusively with Priscillianists at this juncture.

---

[34] A. Viciano i Vives, 'La Decretal del Papa Sirici a Himeri de Tarragona', in Gavaldà Ribot, *Pau*, p. 662: 'La legislació pontifícia es presenta rarament com si fos innovadora. Al contrari, aquesta s'estima més de recolzar-se en la Tradició, les Escriptures, els decrets dels pontífex anteriors i la legislació dels concilis i sínodes'.

[35] Siricius, *Ep.* 1.I.2 (PL 13.1133): ' ... quos nos cum Nouatianis aliisque haereticis ... '.

[36] A. Ferreiro, 'Jerome's Polemic against Priscillian in the *Letter* to Ctesiphon (133, 4)', *REAug*, 39 (1993): pp. 309–32, at p. 310.

[37] A. Ferreiro, 'Petrine Primacy, Conciliar Authority, and Priscillian', in *I concili della cristianità occidentale secoli III–V*, XXX Incontro di studiosi dell'antichità cristiana, Roma, 3–5 maggio 2001, SEAug, vol. 78 (Rome, 2002), pp. 631–45, at p. 635.

There is another reason; the apparently endemic sexual indiscretions of clergy and religious to which Pope Siricius devoted so much attention could not have been directed exclusively at Priscillianists. The sources at every stage do not speak of large numbers of priests or bishops following Priscillian; some followed, but not in droves. The immoral clergy with whom Himerius and Pope Siricius were dealing were Catholic. In this extensive condemnation of libertine clergy they are identified as immoral, but never heretical. It is obvious that later some of them did become members of Priscillian's sect. In the absence of names we have no way of knowing who they were. In several studies I have cast serious doubts on the veracity of the sexual libertinism associated with the Priscillianists, in particular the charge of Nicolaitism.[38] The decretal did become relevant; it was read 15 years later at the first Synod of Toledo (400) with a letter of Ambrose to condemn the Priscillianists.[39] Since the letter was not reproduced at the synod, not even in part, it is not clear which directives of Pope Siricius they had in mind. We do get some idea at least in regard to baptism. In canon 18 of the first Synod of Toledo the Priscillianist form of baptism was rejected as being contrary to that of the see of Peter.[40] Certainly the rejection of re-baptism became useful when Priscillianists returned to the Catholic fold, although the synod did not specifically say so. The decree that clergy were not to live with other women, save their mothers, was not addressed at the first Synod of Toledo. At the first Synod of Braga (561) the lengthy rebuttal of Priscillianism by Pope Leo I was included in the acts and canon 15 did take up the issue of women living with clergy, although it was not as restrictive as the decree of Pope Siricius. It allowed more than just the mother as an acceptable living companion. Of significance for us, the canon states clearly that it was correcting an error of the Priscillianists.[41] Succinctly, from 400 onward Priscillian and his movement

---

[38] A. Ferreiro, 'Priscillian and Nicolaitism', *VChr*, 52 (1998): pp. 382–92; A. Ferreiro, 'Sexual Depravity, Doctrinal Error, and Character Assassination in the Fourth Century: Jerome against the Priscillianists', in E.A. Livingstone (ed.), *Studia Patristica*, vol.28, papers presented at the Eleventh International Conference on Patristic Studies held in Oxford 1991 (Leuven, 1993), pp. 29–38; and Ferreiro, 'Jerome's Polemic against Priscillian', pp. 309–32.

[39] *Exemplar* 74–8 (Chadwick, *Priscillian of Avila*, pp. 236–7): ' ... tamen litteris sanctae memoriae Ambrosii, quas post illud concilium ad nos miserat ... .(adde quae sanctae memoriae Siricius papa suasisset) ... '.

[40] First Synod of Toledo, can. 18 (*CCH* 4.344): 'Si quis in his erroribus Priscilliani sectam sequitur uel profitetur, ut aliud in salutare baptismi contra sedem sancti Petri faciat, anathema sit'.

[41] First Synod of Braga, can. 15 (J. Vives et al., *Concilios Visigóticos e Hispano-Romanos*, España Cristiana, Textos, vol. 1 [Barcelona-Madrid, 1963], p. 69): 'Si quis clericorum vel monachorum praeter matrem aut germanam vel thiam vel quae proxima sibi consanguinitate

will be universally condemned as a dangerous heresy, but much had transpired between 380 and 400.

Lastly, Isidore of Seville, in the seventh century, in his *De uiris illustribus*, dedicated chapter three to Pope Siricius, which is significant for the question of whether the bishop of Rome's decretal had the Priscillianists in its sight. Isidore highlighted exclusively the decretal to Himerius and the issue of re-baptism of heretics. Most telling is that he says not a word about Priscillianists nor for that matter even about the Arians, instead mentioning the Jovinianists and Auxentius as being the target of the discipline. Isidore had it correct by writing that Pope Siricius had in mind other heresies and omitting altogether Priscillian and his sect.[42]

We come now to our next subject: did Pope Siricius intend the decretal to be disseminated in the universal church or just in Hispania and Gallia? Jasper and Custodio Vega propose that Pope Siricius intended the decretal to have universal diffusion and enforcement: 'Not only is all of Spain supposed to be informed of the "statuta apostolicae sedis"; Siricius intended it for the whole Church'.[43] I maintain that initially the decretal was directed only at the church in Hispania and Gallia. Foremost, Pope Siricius nowhere said that his decrees were to be promulgated to the universal church, East and West. All of his directives to Himerius regarding its dissemination are confined to Hispania and (southern) Gallia.[44]

---

iunguntur alias aliquas quasi adobtivas faeminas secum retinent et cum ipsis cohabitant, sicut Priscilliani secta docuit, anathema sit'. It was previously promulgated at the Council of Nicaea, can. 3 (CCCOGD 1.21–2): "Ἀπηγόρευσε καθόλου ἡ μεγάλη σύνοδος μήτε ἐπίσκοπον μήτε πρεσβύτερον μήτε διάκονον μήτε ὅλως τῶν ἐν τῷ κλήρῳ τινὶ ἐξεῖναι συνείσακτον ἔχειν, πλὴν εἰ μὴ ἄρα μητέρα ἢ ἀδελφὴν ἢ θείαν ἢ ἃ μόνα πρόσωπα ὑποψίαν διαπέφευγεν'.

[42] Isidore, *De uir. illust.* 3 (C. Codoñer Merino [ed.], *El "De Viris Illustribus" de Isidoro de Sevilla, estudio y edición crítica*, Theses et Studia Philologica Salamanticensia, vol. 12 [Salamanca, 1964], pp. 135–6): 'Siricius clarissimus pontifex et Romanae sedis antistes, scripsit decretale opusculum directum ad Eumerium Tarraconnensem episcopum: In quo inter alias ecclesiasticas disciplinas constituit haereticorum baptisma nequaquam ab ecclesia rescindenda. Reperimus et aliam eius epistolam ad diuersos episcopos missam, in qua condemnat Iovinianum haereticum atque Auxentium ceterosque eorum sequaces. Praefuit Romae annos quattuordecim obiitque sub Theodosio et Valentiniano imperatoribus'. See Codoñer Merino's discussion of this entry at pp. 70–71.

[43] Jasper, 'The Beginning of the Decretal Tradition', p. 21; and Custodio Vega, *El Primado Romano*, p. 38: 'Siricio, en una palabra, decide, establece, ordena y decreta como un supremo jerarca espiritual, a quien incumbe el cuídado y la potestad omnímoda sobre todas las Iglesias'.

[44] The church in northern Gallia in the fourth century did not have as highly developed a relationship with Rome as that in the south. This situation was still largely prevalent in the

There are instances in the decretal where Pope Siricius mentioned the universal church. A significant one regards the re-baptism of Arians. He told Himerius that rejection of re-baptism of heretics was already upheld in the East and West.[45] Pope Siricius was informing Himerius what was already agreed upon in the universal church; therefore, teaching nothing new. Himerius' task was to make it known and enforced in Hispania and Gallia where apparently the teaching needed to be promulgated and implemented. He also warned Himerius and the clergy not to deviate from this established norm, lest they find themselves not in communion (with the universal church) by synodal sentence.[46] In another directive he invoked the universal and provincial church; he warned 'all priests' (Hispania-Gallia) who did not want to be separated from the church of Rome, upon which Christ built his church, to embrace his teaching.[47]

The intended provincial diffusion of the decretal is found in a number of other places. The pope chastised the 'bishops of your regions' of sexual indiscretions.[48] Moreover, his censure and directive that it was to be upheld 'by all churches' is to be understood within Hispania and Gallia.[49] In section 19 he ordered the bishops 'of all provinces' – in Hispania and Gallia – to be diligent in enforcing his recommendations.[50] In the concluding section 20 of the decretal Pope Siricius clearly entrusted Himerius to have it promulgated not just to the Tarragonans, but to all of the Carthaginians, Baeticians, Lusitanians, Galicians and those in the neighbouring provinces [Gallia].[51] These are the 'provinces' and 'regions' that the pope had in mind. Jasper proposes, contrary to this view, as evidence for the intended dissemination of the decretal in the entire

---

sixth century of Gregory of Tours and Caesarius of Arles. See A. Ferreiro, '"Petrine Primacy" and Gregory of Tours', *Francia*, 33 (2006): pp. 1–16.

[45] Siricius, *Ep.* 1.I.2 (PL 13.1134): ' ... quod etiam totus Oriens Occidensque custodit ...'.

[46] Ibid.: ' ... a quo tramite uos quoque posthac minime conuenit deuiare, si non uultis a nostro collegio synodali sententia separari'. The Council of Nicaea did not order the rebaptism of Arians, as it did the Paulianists. In Hispania Arians were being rebaptised. Pope Siricius sought to put a stop to this practice.

[47] Ibid., 1.II.3 (PL 13.1135–6): ' ... nunc praefatam regulam omnes teneant sacerdotes, qui nolunt ab apostolicae petrae, super quam Christus uniuersalem contruxit ecclesiam, soliditate diuelli'.

[48] Ibid., 1.VIII.12 (PL 13.1142): 'Quae omnia ita a uestrarum regionum despiciuntur episcopis ... '.

[49] Ibid.: ' ... quid ab uniuersis posthac ecclesiis sequendum sit, quid uitandum, generali pronuntiatione decernimus'.

[50] Ibid., 1.XV.19 (PL 13.1145): ' ... scituri posthac omnium prouinciarum ... '.

[51] Ibid., 1.XV.20 (PL 13.1146): ' ... et non solum eorum qui in tua sunt dioecesi constituti: sed etiam ad uniuersos Carthaginenses ac Baeticos, Lusitanos atque Gallicios, uel eos, qui uicinis tibi collimitant hinc inde prouinciis ... '.

church the concluding remarks just after this: '... ea quae ad te speciali nomine generaliter scripta sunt per unanimitatis tuae sollicitudinem in universorum fratrum nostrorum notitiam perferantur ...', the focus being on *uniuersorum*.[52] The context demands that *uniuersorum* was a provincial reference to Hispania and Gallia only and not beyond. Administratively Himerius was hardly in a position to carry out the distribution of the decretal to the universal church. Since the teaching, according to Pope Siricius, was already known in East and West there would be no need to promulgate it elsewhere. Similar to the canons of the earlier Synod of Elvira, Pope Siricius' decretal was intended primarily to resolve regional problems first and foremost.[53]

Another subject that needs attention is Pope Siricius' contribution to the development of Petrine primacy. Jasper weighs in on this topic by observing that in this first decretal 'the identification of the Roman bishop with Peter is complete' and Kelly adds that Pope Siricius 'was as fully aware as Damasus I of Rome's primatial status and his own role as successor of St. Peter'.[54] Minnerath, in his seminal study on the Petrine primacy in the first millennium, demonstrated how earlier Roman pontiffs such as Pope Calixtus (217–22) already had developed the link between the see of Rome and Matthew 16:18–19, where Jesus designates Peter as the 'rock' of the church.[55] Another significant event is that by 354 the feast of the 'birth of Peter's chair' was added to the western liturgical calendar for 22 February.[56] It appears that Pope Siricius' decretal of 385 was written at a time when the Petrine primacy was fundamentally well established. Therefore, his appeal to Petrine authority is not a unique contribution. The theological

---

[52] Jasper, 'The Beginning of the Decretal Tradition', p. 21. See Siricius, *Ep.* 1.XV.19 (PL 13.1146): '... si ea, quae ad te speciali nomine generaliter scripta sunt, per unanimitatis tuae sollicitudinem, in uniuersorum fratrum nostrorum notitiam perferantur ...'.

[53] M. Maccarrone, '"Sedes Apostolica – Vicarius Petri": La perpetuità del primato di Pietro nella sede e nel vescovo di Roma (Secoli III–VIII)', in M. Maccarrone (ed.), *Il primato del vescovo di Roma nel primo millennio. Ricerche e testimonianze*, Atti del Symposium Storico-Teologico, Roma, 9–13 Ottobre 1989. Pontificio Comitato di Scienze Storiche, Atti e Documenti, vol. 4. (Vatican City, 1991), pp. 275–362, at p. 292.

[54] Jasper, 'The Beginning of the Decretal Tradition', p. 9; and Kelly, *The Oxford Dictionary of Popes*, p. 35.

[55] R. Minnerath, 'La tradition doctrinale de la primauté Pétrinienne au premier millénaire', in *Il primato del successore di Pietro*, Atti del Simposio teologico, Roma, 2–4 Dicembre 1996, Atti e Documenti, vol. 7 (Vatican City, 1998), pp. 117–46, at p. 121: 'Calliste [217–222] en appelait à Mt 16, 19 pour légitimer son pouvoir de pardonner les péchés. Il s'agirait du premier usage connu du *Mt* 16 par un successeur de Pierre'.

[56] Ibid., p. 128: 'Le chronographe romain de 354 atteste au 22 février la fête du *Natale Petri de cathedra*, commémorant le jour où le Christ a conféré à Pierre sa *cathedra* par les paroles de Mt 16, 18'.

fullness of the Petrine primacy arrived soon after with his successors. Jasper reminds us that 'Pope Innocent I (402–17) made Siricius' well-known phrase that the apostolate and the episcopacy originated in Peter (JK 258) famous in his decretal to Victricius of Rouen ... '.[57] The Petrine ecclesiology reached its apogee in this early phase in the pontificate of Pope Leo the Great (440–61).[58]

Now let us consider the Petrine content of the decretal. As we saw earlier, the pontiff cautioned all clergy in Hispania and Gallia not to risk becoming separated from the apostolic rock upon which Christ built the universal church.[59] He commended Himerius for consulting the apostolic see.[60] In a stern moment, the pope declared that those who refused to heed his discipline should be expelled by the authority of the apostolic see.[61] In the closing section of the decretal Pope Siricius moderated his temperament by warmly telling Himerius that the issues he sent to the Roman church for review, as if to the 'head of the body', have been adequately answered.[62]

The main innovation of the decretal is noted by Kelly who says it is ' ... couched in the authoritative style of imperial edicts and, like them, carrying the force of law'.[63] Minnerath identified yet another: 'Qui inaugure la pratique des "décrétales" comme nouvelles sources du droit canonique en Occident, fait volontiers sienne la *sollicitudo omnium ecclesiarum* de 2 Co 11, 28. Ses décrétales emploient le langage du droit. L'Église romaine est la tête du corps de l'Église entière'.[64] Pope Siricius, by equating the authority of the see of Rome with that of conciliar canons, marks a significant contribution. He warned Himerius and all

---

[57] Jasper, 'The Beginning of the Decretal Tradition', pp. 14–15.

[58] The comment by Viciano i Vives, 'La Decretal del Papa Sirici', p. 662, is relevant here: 'En el curs del segle V, el poder legislatiu dels papes s'aferma amb força i es justifica per l'autoritat romana, basada en la successió de sant Pere ... culmina amb el Papa Lleó el Gran (440–461)'. Relevant for the primacies in Hispania, see Vilella Masana 'Las primacías eclesiásticas en *Hispania*', pp. 269–85; and Vilella Masana, 'Los concilios eclesiásticos de la Tarraconensis', pp. 327–44.

[59] See n. 47 above.

[60] Siricius, *Ep.* 1.V.6 (PL 13.1137): 'De his uero non incongrue dilectio tua apostolicam sedem credidit consulendam ... '.

[61] Ibid., 1.VII.11 (PL 13.1140): ' ... quo indigne usi sunt, apostolicae sedis auctoritate deiectos ... '.

[62] Ibid., 1.XV.20 (PL 13.1146): ' ... ad Romanam ecclesiam, utpote ad caput tui corporis ... '.

[63] Kelly, *The Oxford Dictionary of Popes*, p. 35.

[64] R. Minnerath, 'La tradition doctrinale de la primauté Pétrinienne', p. 128.

priests that they could not ignore the apostolic see and canons.⁶⁵ In the ensuing centuries in Hispania papal authority was cited in several important synods – Toledo I (400), Braga I (561) and Toledo III (589) – to bolster the authority of the canons that were decreed by the bishops.⁶⁶ It was utilised with all of its juridical-papal authority in subsequent centuries to enforce its directives when needed in the Latin West. Several centuries later *Liber pontificalis* anachronistically spoke of the decretal as originally intended for universal application: 'He issued a decree about the whole church and against every heresy, and he broadcast it through the whole world, to be kept in the archive of every church for rebutting every heresy'.⁶⁷

The decretal of Pope Siricius marked an important advancement of Petrine ecclesiology and the authority of the Roman see in the Latin West. The decretal is to be contextualised as part of an already emerging pattern of intervention of the popes in Hispania and Gallia, mainly the result of provincial bishops seeking apostolic guidance from Peter's successor in Rome and rarely ever Rome imposing its will without initial solicitation. Pope Siricius' decretal not only represents novelty and continuity in the exercise of papal authority in the fourth century, it will also become one of the most cited decretals in the Middle Ages by popes, councils and canon lawyers. It is only then that the decretal experienced broad diffusion mainly in the Latin West.

---

⁶⁵ Siricius, *Ep.* 1.XV.20 (PL 13.1146): ' ... statuta sedis apostolicae uel canonum uenerabilia definita, nulli sacerdotum Domini ignorare sit liberum ... '. For further discussion of decretals and councils see Jasper, 'The Beginning of the Decretal Tradition', pp. 16–18.

⁶⁶ See Ferreiro, 'Petrine Primacy, Conciliar Authority, and Priscillian', pp. 631–45; and Jasper, 'The Beginning of the Decretal Tradition', p. 17.

⁶⁷ *Lib. pont.* 40.1 (L. Duchesne and C. Vogel [eds], *Le* Liber pontificalis*: Texte, introduction et commentaire*, BEFAR [Paris, 1955 (2nd edn)], vol. 1, p. 216): 'Hic constitutum fecit de omnem ecclesiam uel contra omnes hereses et exparsit per uniuersum mundum ut in omnem ecclesiae archibo teneantur ob oppugnationem contra omnes hereses'. (English translation in R. Davis, *The Book of Pontiffs [Liber Pontificalis]: The Ancient Biographies of the First Ninety Roman Bishops to AD 715*, TTH, vol. 6 [Liverpool, 2000 (2nd edn)]). It also highlights his opposition to the Manichaean heresy and the necessary protocols for readmitting heretics into the church, a directive as we saw mainly intended for Arians, Novatianists and unnamed heretics. It also records (40.3) that, 'He decreed that a heretic should be reconciled by the laying on of hands in the presence of the whole church'.

PART II
The Fifth Century

Chapter 5

Innocent I and the First Synod of Toledo*

Geoffrey D. Dunn

Sometime in the first years of the fifth century, Hilary and Elpidius, a Spanish bishop and presbyter, journeyed to Rome. They informed its bishop, Innocent I, that some of the 20 canons to address perceived irregularities in the lives of Spanish clergy and lay people, as well as the solution to the Priscillianist crisis, adopted by 19 bishops, including Hilary,[1] at the first Synod of Toledo (ancient Toletum in the province of Carthaginensis) in September 400 were being rejected. The synod had agreed to accept repentant Priscillianist bishops back into communion as bishops, but some Spanish colleagues in Baetica or Carthaginensis disagreed with such leniency and broke off communion.[2] As a consequence of the visit of the two Spanish clerics Innocent wrote his letter *Seape me* to the 19 bishops who had been in Toledo.[3]

The synod has been studied, particularly concerning Priscillianism.[4] Less studied has been the involvement of Innocent I, bishop from 402 to 417, in the

---

* An earlier version of this chapter was presented at the sixteenth International Conference on Patristic Studies, Oxford University, 8–12 August 2011. Funding for my research was provided by the Australian Research Council and for my participation by Australian Catholic University.

[1] First Synod of Toledo (*CCH* 4.326).

[2] Innocent I, *Ep.* 3.1–3.I.2 (PL 20.486–87).

[3] Ibid., 3 (PL 20.485–93 = P. Coustant, *Epistolae Romanorum Pontificum et quae ad eos scriptae sunt a S. Clemente I usque ad Innocentum* III, t. 1 [Paris, 1721], cols 763–71) = JK 292.

[4] See H. Chadwick, *Priscillian of Avila: The Occult and the Charismatic in the Early Church* (Oxford, 1976), pp. 170–88; R. Van Dam, *Leadership and Community in Late Antique Gaul*, TCH, vol. 7 (Berkeley and Los Angeles, 1985), pp. 108–10; J. Orlandis and D. Ramos-Lissón, *Historia de los Concilios de le España Romana y Visigoda* (Pamplona, S.A., 1986), pp. 80–100; V. Burrus, *The Making of a Heretic: Gender, Authority, and the Priscillianist Controversy*, TCH, vol. 24 (Berkeley and Los Angeles, 1995), pp. 104–14; J. Vilella Masana, 'Priscilianismo Galaico y política antipriscilianista durante el siglo V', *AntTard*, 5 (1997): pp. 177–85; A. Ferreiro, 'Priscillian and Nicolaitism', *VChr*, 52 (1998): pp. 382–92; D. Ramos-Lissón, 'El tratamiento de la mujer en los cánones del Concilio I de Toledo (a. 400)', in *I concili della cristianità occidentale secoli III–V*, XXX Incontro di studiosi dell'antichità cristiana, Roma, 3–5 maggio 2001, SEAug, vol. 78 (Rome, 2002), pp. 607–18;

affairs of the Spanish churches at this time.[5] Erich Caspar mentioned this letter only once, not in his chapter on Innocent I, but as a footnote to the relationship between Siricius of Rome and Ambrose of Milan, where he described Innocent's letter as an 'Antwort' to the synod.[6] In more recent years Josep Vilella Masana, J. Orlandis and Alberto Ferreiro have turned their attention to the relationship between Rome and the Spanish churches.[7] With regard to Innocent, Ferreiro states that 'the pontiff ordered the excommunication of anyone who did not submit to the said council or to his apostolic authority'.[8]

Here I wish to examine Innocent's letter both in terms of context and content. It is one of rich but largely untapped significance for our knowledge of Spanish Christianity in late antiquity. The Priscillianist crisis did have a lengthy impact and Innocent's letter is early evidence for the ways in which it was handled.[9] It is the only surviving letter from Innocent to Spain. It is virtually the last piece of

---

A. Weckwerth, 'Aufbau und Struktur der *Constitutio* des ersten Konzils von Toledo (400)', in *I concili della cristianità occidentale secoli III–V*, XXX Incontro di studiosi dell'antichità cristiana, Roma, 3–5 maggio 2001, SEAug, vol. 78 (Rome, 2002), pp. 619–30; and S.J.G. Sánchez, *Priscillien, un chrétien non conformiste. Doctrine et pratique du Priscillianisme du IVe au VIe siècle*, Théologie historique, vol. 120 (Paris, 2009).

[5] Ch. Pietri, *Roma Christiana. Recherches sur l'Église de Rome, son organisation, sa politique, son idéologie de Miltiade à Sixte III (311–440)*, BEFAR, vol. 224 (Rome, 1976), pp. 1062–7, offers the most detailed analysis. E.G. Weltin, *The Ancient Popes*, The Popes through History, vol. 2 (Westminster, MD, 1964), does not mention this letter. Chadwick, *Priscillian of Avila*, pp. 186–7; M.R. Green, 'Pope Innocent I: The Church of Rome in the Early Fifth Century', (DPhil diss., Oxford 1973), pp. 118–20; and M. Kulikowski, *Late Roman Spain and its Cities* (Baltimore, 2004), p. 43, mention the letter only briefly.

[6] E. Caspar, *Geschichte des Papsttums von den Anfängen bis zur Höhe der Weltherrschaft*, Bd 1: *Römische Kirche und Imperium Romanum* (Tübingen, 1930), p. 281, n. 1.

[7] J. Vilella Masana, 'La correspondencia entre los obispos Hispanos y el Papado durante el siglo V', in *Cristianesimo e specificità regionali nel Mediterraneo Latino (sec. IV–VI)*, XXII Incontro di studiosi dell'antichità cristiana, Roma, 6–8 maggio 1993, SEAug, vol. 46 (Rome, 1994), pp. 457–81; J. Orlandis, 'El Primado Romano en la España Visigoda', in M. Maccarrone (ed.), *Il primato del vescovo di Roma nel primo millennio. Richerche e testimonianze*, Atti del Symposium storico-teologico, Roma, 9–13 Ottobre 1989, Atti e Documenti, vol. 4 (Vatican City, 1991), pp. 453–72; and A. Ferreiro, 'Petrine Primacy, Conciliar Authority, and Priscillian', in *I concili della cristianità occidentale secoli III–V*, XXX Incontro di studiosi dell'antichità cristiana, Roma, 3–5 maggio 2001, SEAug, vol. 78 (Rome, 2002), pp. 631–45.

[8] Ferreiro, 'Petrine Primacy', p. 640.

[9] For a completely different kind of impact see K. Bowes, '"... Nec sedere in uillam". Villa-Churches, Rural Piety, and the Priscillianist Controversy', in T.S. Burns and J.W. Eadie (eds), *Urban Centers and Rural Contexts in Late Antiquity* (East Lansing, MI, 2001), pp. 323–48.

literary evidence we have for Roman Spain before the arrival of the Visigoths.[10] It has much to contribute to our knowledge of the expanding primacy of the Roman bishop in late antiquity. My interest is not so much in the developments in Spain in the aftermath of Priscillian's execution in 385 as it is with the perceptions held by the Spanish and by Innocent himself about the authority of the Roman church in Spain. I argue that nowhere did Innocent assert a full-blown apostolic authority or any notion of Petrine primacy over Spain. An examination of Innocent's letter in the context of the earlier involvement of other Italian bishops, such as Damasus, Ambrose and Siricius, will reveal also that the Spanish turned to Rome because it, along with places like Milan, could offer support, influence and, uniquely, judicial oversight. The first two items were what Hilary and Elpidius were seeking. We may begin by considering that historical context.

Historical Context of the Relationship between Rome and Spain

We need not go back as far as the third century to examine the relationship between Rome and Spain; yet, if we did, we would find in the time of Cyprian that the Spanish bishops turned not only to Stephen I, bishop of Rome, but to Cyprian, bishop of Carthage, as well.[11] They were not seeking someone to make a decision for them but for someone to share his expert opinion and experience so they could reach their own decision. Both bishops offered their thoughts, though they were contradictory. Rome would continue to be a church to which Spanish bishops would turn for advice and support, but it was not the only one.

Sulpicius Severus believed that Priscillian, by then bishop of Ávila (ancient Abila in the province of Lusitania), together with the two Spanish bishops who ordained him, Instantius and Salvian, after the 380 Synod of Zaragoza (ancient Caesaraugusta in the province of Tarraconensis) in which they had been condemned,[12] travelled to Rome to clear themselves of charges before Damasus,

---

[10] On the transition from Roman to Visigothic Spain see R. Collins, *Early Medieval Spain: Unity in Diversity, 400–1000*, New Studies in Medieval History (New York, 1995 [2nd edn]); and R. Collins, *Visigothic Spain 409–711*, A History of Spain (Oxford, 2004).

[11] See Cyprian, *Ep.* 67 (CCL 3C.446–62); G.D. Dunn, 'Cyprian of Carthage and the Episcopal Synod of Late 254', *REAug*, 48 (2002): pp. 229–47; and G.D. Dunn, *Cyprian and the Bishops of Rome: Questions of Papal Primacy in the Early Church*, ECS, vol. 11 (Strathfield, NSW, 2007), pp. 125–34.

[12] Chadwick, *Priscillian of Avila*, pp. 33–4, noted that Priscillian's episcopal ordination was never challenged on the grounds that only two bishops ordained him or that the

Roman bishop between 366 and 384.[13] Sulpicius offered no comment about whether or not Damasus had the authority to do so, but presumably he believed that Damasus did.

In his own version produced for Damasus,[14] Priscillian not only asserted that no one had been condemned at Zaragoza,[15] but that it was because Damasus had written to the Spanish bishops before their meeting and ordered them (*praeceperas*) not to condemn anyone absent that no such condemnation had occurred.[16] It is certainly true, as Ferreiro observes, that Priscillian made statements about Damasus' authority and Petrine authority.[17] At the beginning of his letter Priscillian called Damasus 'the chief of us all'[18] and begged him to order (*facias*) Hydatius of Mérida (ancient Emerita Augusta), the metropolitan of Lusitania and bishop in the civil diocesan capital for Spain,[19] Priscillian's chief opponent, to appear before a synod in Rome itself, or at least to give letters to his Spanish colleagues to call a synod to investigate both antagonists.[20] Yet, even though Ferreiro describes Priscillian's attitude as 'one of heartfelt conviction',[21] it could be argued equally that there was a calculated element of flattery here designed to win over Damasus to exercise his *auctoritas* rather than any supposed *potestas* he had in Spain.

---

metropolitan, Hydatius of Mérida, was not involved, as required by the Council of Nicaea. A. Ferreiro, in his chapter in this volume, doubts that Priscillian was condemned in 380.

[13] Sulpicius Severus, *Chron.* 2.48.1 (SC 441.336): ' ... ut apud Damasum, urbis ea tempestate episcopum, obiecta purgarent'.

[14] While J. Matthews, *Western Aristocracies and Imperial Court A.D. 364–425* (Oxfords, 1998 [2nd edn]), pp. 163–4; and Chadwick, *Priscillian of Avila*, pp. 27–8, think that the synod must have issued some condemnation, Burrus, *The Making of a Heretic*, pp. 55–6; and Ferreiro, 'Petrine Primacy', pp. 635–6, support Priscillian's version.

[15] Priscillian, *Tract.* 2 (M. Conti, *Priscillian of Avila: The Complete Works*, OECT [Oxford, 2010], pp.70, lines 27–30, and 78, lines 180–84).

[16] Priscillian, *Tract.* 2 (Conti, *Priscillian of Avila*, p. 70, lines 32–5).

[17] Ferreiro, 'Petrine Primacy', pp. 637–40.

[18] Priscillian, *Tract.* 2 (Conti, *Priscillian of Avila*, p. 68, line 7): ' ... senior omnium nostrum ... '. See M. Maccarrone, '"Sedes Apostolica – Vacarius Petri". La perpetuità del primato di Pietro nella sede e nel vescovo di Roma (Secoli III–VIII)', in M. Maccarrone (ed.), *Il primato del vescovo di Roma nel primo millennio. Richerche e testimonianze*, Atti del Symposium storico-teologico, Roma, 9–13 Ottobre 1989, Atti e Documenti, vol. 4 (Vatican City, 1991), pp. 275–362, at pp. 284–5.

[19] Kulikowski, *Late Roman Spain and its Cities*, p. 71.

[20] Priscillian, *Tract.* 2 (Conti, *Priscillian of Avila*, p. 78, lines 183–5 and 187–8).

[21] Ferreiro, 'Petrine Primacy', p. 637.

When Damasus refused to see them, Priscillian's group moved to Milan and sought in vain for support from Ambrose.[22] It makes little practical difference if the attempted visit to Ambrose was before rather than after the attempted visit to Damasus.[23] The fact that Priscillian's group wanted to see Ambrose indicates that, even if Damasus gave them nothing, to have received some support from Ambrose would have been helpful.[24]

I would like to offer a tentative solution as to why Damasus refused to see Priscillian and what kind of authority Damasus had in this matter. What we need to consider is the 378 Synod of Rome and the corresponding imperial reply (*Ordinariorum*).[25] These documents reveal an envisaged process for dealing with trials of bishops in the West. First-instance trials were to be before a metropolitan bishop in synod (and the synodal letter was primarily concerned with Italian bishops, for whom the bishop of Rome was metropolitan), except for western metropolitans outside Italy (*in longinquioribus partibus*) who were to be tried at first instance either in Rome or before Rome's delegate. Appeals against the first-instance sentences of remote provincial synods (at second-instance trials) could be to Rome or to 15 neighbouring bishops (presumably from another province).[26] Gratian's reply indicated that this process was to be available also in

---

[22] Sulpicius Severus, *Chron.* 2.47.2 (SC 441.338). Priscillian, *Tract.* 2 (Conti, *Priscillian of Avila*, p. 76, lines 151–4), suggests that this document was written after Damasus had refused to see them. For differing explanations for Damasus' refusal see Chadwick, *Priscillian of Avila*, pp. 39–40; Burrus, *The Making of a Heretic*, pp. 90–92; and Ferreiro, 'Petrine Primacy', p. 637.

[23] While Chadwick, *Priscillian of Avila*, p. 40 and N.B. McLynn, *Ambrose of Milan: Church and Court in a Christian Capital*, TCH, vol. 22 (Berkeley and Los Angeles, 1994), p. 151, accept Sulpicius Severus' order of events, E.-Ch. Babut, *Priscillien et le priscillianisme* (Paris, 1909), p. 153 and Burrus, *The Making of a Heretic*, pp. 84–5, on the basis of what Priscillian, *Tract.* 2 (Conti, *Priscillian of Avila*, p. 76, lines 154–6), said about not receiving an answer from the quaestor, reverse it.

[24] According to Sulpicius Severus, *Chron.* 2.48.2 (SC 441.338), even without Ambrose they were able to elicit imperial help from Macedonius, the *magister officiorum*. On Priscillian's ultimate failure with appealing to civil authority see A.R. Birley, 'Magnus Maximus and the Persecution of Heresy', *BJRL*, 66 (1982–3): pp. 13–43; R.W. Mathisen, *Ecclesiastical Factionalism and Religious Controversy in Fifth-Century Gaul* (Washington, DC, 1989), pp. 12–13; and E. Fournier, 'Exiled Bishops in the Christian Empire: Victims of Imperial Violence?', in H. Drake (ed.), *Violence in Late Antiquity: Perceptions and Practices* (Aldershot, 2006), pp. 157–66, at pp. 159–60.

[25] Ambrose, *Ep. extra collect.* 7 (CSEL 82/3.191–7); and Gratian, *De rebap.* (*Collectio Avellana, Ep.* 13) (CSEL 35.54–8).

[26] Ambrose, *Ep. extra collect.* 7.9 (CSEL 82/3.195–6). The process does not specify what second-instance options were available to bishops who were tried at first instance before the Roman bishop. It could be argued that the synod was not clear about the option

the praetorian prefecture of Gaul, of which Spain was one civil diocese.[27] Even though by 405 the provisions of Gratian's rescript no longer featured in imperial law, there is no reason to doubt that, in the first few years after it was issued, Rome would have been keen to utilise it.[28]

On this basis, since Priscillian was not a bishop at the time of Zaragoza and since no one was deposed by that synod there was no reason or basis for Damasus to be involved. Any trials of Priscillian, Instantius and Salvian ought to have been conducted in a provincial synod in Lusitania, headed by Hydatius of Mérida.[29] Perhaps the visiting group was trying to convince Damasus that their metropolitan would be biased against them and that Rome should hear the matter. If that were the case then Damasus obviously declined to become involved. Charges against Hydatius could be heard in Rome and so Priscillian's entreaty that Damasus order Hydatius to appear there could also be an appeal to the provisions of the 378 synod. Perhaps Damasus' refusal to see the Spanish bishops was also because a charge against a metropolitan needed to come from a provincial synod, not individual bishops or, more probably, could not come from individual bishops who were themselves the subject of accusation, which Hydatius had instigated by then.[30] Priscillian himself suggests this was Hydatius' tactic when he writes: 'ne iudices haberet, si omnes diuersis obstrectantionibus infamasset ... '. If so, it was successful, since Damasus appears to have dismissed their counter charge against Hydatius as nothing more than an attempt to avoid facing the charges hanging over them.

What emerges here from all this, I would contend, is not a legislative or executive primacy of the Roman bishop over Spain, but a growing judicial

---

of a second-instance trial. How are we to understand 'Certe si uel metropolitani uel cuiusce alterius sacerdotis suspecta gratia uel iniquitas fuerit, uel ad Romanum episcopum uel ad concilium certe quindecim episcoporum finitimorum ei liceat prouocare'.? Is the appeal to Rome or the 15 other bishops permitted to take place after a first-instance verdict, as I have suggested above, or is the accusation of bias made before a first-instance trail commences, such that the Roman bishop or the 15 neighbouring bishops hear the matter at first instance, and that there is no second-instance provision in this letter at all? See Pietri, *Roma Christiana*, pp. 741–8; McLynn, *Ambrose of Milan*, pp. 90–91; J.H.W.G. Liebeschuetz and C. Hill, *Ambrose of Milan: Political Letters and Speeches*, TTH, vol. 43 (Liverpool, 2005), pp. 244–8; and G.D. Dunn, 'The Development of Rome as Metropolitan of Suburbicarian Italy: Innocent I's *Letter to the Bruttians*', *Aug*, 51 (2011): pp. 161–90, at pp. 171–5.

[27] Gratian, *De rebap.* (*Collectio Avellana, Ep.* 13.10–12) (CSEL 35.57–8).

[28] *Const. Sirmon.* 2 (Th. Mommsen and P. Krüger [eds], *Codex Theodosianus*, vol. 1: *Theodosiani Libri XVI cum constitutionibus Sirmondinis* [Hildesheim, 1990], pp. 908–9).

[29] I accept Chadwick, *Priscillian of Avila*, p. 20, that the other two bishops were Lusitanian.

[30] Priscillian, *Tract.* 2 (Conti, *Priscillian of Avila*, p. 76, lines 146–9).

one recognised by Priscillian (here demonstrated by Damasus' refusal to short circuit the process), if such a modern threefold distinction legitimately can be applied to the situation in late antiquity, which I think can be even though no one at the time thought in such categories. Rome was at the apex of an evolving ecclesiastical court system in the West, which first emerged in the canons from the Synod of Sofia (ancient Serdica) in 343.[31] This must be seen as distinct from the idea that Rome could direct operations (in an executive or legislative sense) in the churches of Spain.

Interestingly, Hydatius did not appeal to Rome (or Milan) when charges were levelled against him for moral turpitude and for organising the harsh treatment given to Instantius and Salvian when they attempted to visit Mérida, but appealed to civil power in the person of Gratian in Milan, where he obtained a rescript ordering the heretics[32] to leave their churches, a provision provided for in *Ordinariorum*.[33] It would not be wrong to conclude that Hydatius found imperial authority more satisfying than any Roman ecclesiastical authority, and that even Rome's increasing judicial authority could be bypassed.

Around this time another Spanish bishop, Himerius of Tarragona (ancient Tarraco, capital of the province of Tarraconensis) wrote to Damasus with disciplinary questions, to which Siricius responded in 385 with his letter *Directa*, now most often regarded as the first papal decretal.[34] While some argue that Siricius' letter was a definitive and binding ruling,[35] and therefore an example of legislative or executive primacy, this is not the only way to interpret it. This is

---

[31] See H. Hess, *The Early Development of Canon Law and the Council of Serdica*, OECS (Oxford, 2002).

[32] On Hydatius labelling his opponents as Manichean see S.N.C. Lieu, *Manichaeism in the Later Roman Empire and Medieval China*, WUNT, vol. 63 (Tübingen, 1992 [2nd edn]), p. 149.

[33] Priscillian, *Tract.* 2 (Conti, *Priscillian of Avila*, p. 76, 141–5); Sulpicius Severus, *Chron.* 2.47.2 (SC 441.336). In lines 145–7 Priscillian states that Ambrose knew of Hydatius' message to Gratian, but I do not know if we must accept Chadwick, *Priscillian of Avila*, p. 35; and Burrus, *The Making of a Heretic*, p. 54, that Hydatius had appealed for Ambrose's support in getting Gratian to issue a rescript against Priscillian and his supporters. Even if we accept that interpretation, all that this means is that it was Ambrose's connectedness not his authority over other bishops that interested Hydatius. McLynn, *Ambrose of Milan*, pp. 149–50, makes no claim other than Ambrose's knowledge of proceedings.

[34] Siricius, *Ep.* 1 (PL 13.1132–47 = Coustant, *Epistolae Romanorum Pontificum*, cols 623–38) = JK 255. See Chapters 3 and 4 in this volume for recent discussion on this letter.

[35] See Pietri, *Roma Christiana*, pp. 1045–56; and V. Escribano, 'Heresy and Orthodoxy in Fourth-Century Hispania: Arian and Priscillianism', in K. Bowes and M. Kulikowski (eds), *Hispania in Late Antiquity: Current Perspectives*, The Medieval and Early Modern Iberian World, vol. 24 (Leiden and Boston, 2005), pp. 121–49.

how Siricius saw his own position, but Himerius seems to have been asking for advice about how the Roman bishop would proceed or for information about how Rome handled similar situations, at least as far as I read the letter, so that he could make his own decision, rather than asking Rome to make the decision for him. So my point about limiting Rome's authority in remote western provinces to one of judicial oversight remains.

Synod of Toledo and Rome

Although Priscillian's efforts in appealing to civil authority resulted in his execution in 385, in a move which shocked Ambrose, Siricius, Martin of Tours (ancient Ciuitas Turonum) and Sulpicius Severus, and cost Hydatius his see[36] (where he was replaced by Patruinus), his extreme asceticism attracted numerous followers including some bishops, particularly in Gallaecia.[37] Efforts in both Spain and Gaul to entice Priscillianists back to the mainstream church resulted in the Synod of Toledo, under the presidency of Patruinus, the new bishop of Mérida and metropolitan of Lusitania.

Although they had been guided by non-extant letters from Ambrose and Siricius about the conditions under which repentant Priscillianists could be received back into communion, when the bishops met in Toledo in 400 they

---

[36] See Ambrose, *Ep.* 68.3 (CSEL 82/2.169–70); Magnus Maximus, *Ep. ad Siric.* (*Collectio Avellana* 40) (CSEL 35.90–91); and Sulpicius Severus, *Chron.* 2.50.1–2 (SC 441.340–2); 2.51.3 (SC 441.344). Prosper of Aquitaine, *Epit. chron.* 1193 (MGH.AA 9.462), reports that Hydatius and Ithacius of Faro (ancient Ossonuba in Lusitania) were excommunicated and exiled.

[37] With regard to these followers, Van Dam, *Leadership and Community*, p. 109, n. 100, is disinclined to accept Symphosius' see as being Astorga and him being the same individual who was at Zaragoza in 380, instead following Hydatius of Chaves (ancient Aquae Flaviae), *Chron.* 31 (SC 218.112). S. Muhlberger, *The Fifth-Century Chroniclers: Prosper, Hydatius, and the Gallic Chronicler of 452*, ARCA Classical and Medieval Texts, Papers and Monographs, vol. 27 (Leeds, 1990), p. 206, notes that Hydatius misdates Toledo from 400 to 399. On Priscillian Hydatius of Chaves probably used Sulpicius Severus, *Chron.* 2.48 (CSEL 1.101) at *Chron.* 13 (SC 218.52). However, *Exemplar* 70–73 (Chadwick, *Priscillian of Avila*, p. 236) is clear in linking the Symphosius at Zaragoza with the one at Toledo. On Paternus see *Exemplar* 96–100 (Chadwick, *Priscillian of Avila*, p. 237), on Vegetinus see *Exemplar* 120–122 (Chadwick, *Priscillian of Avila*, p. 238), on Isonius see *Exemplar* 101–3 (Chadwick, *Priscillian of Avila*, p. 237), on Herenias see *Exemplar* 108–11 (Chadwick, *Priscillian of Avila*, pp. 237–8), on Donatus, Acurius and Emilius, who together with Herenias were non-repentant see *Exemplar* 114–15 (Chadwick, *Priscillian of Avila*, p. 238), and on Anterius see *Exemplar* 141 (Chadwick, *Priscillian of Avila*, p. 238).

were prepared to readmit to communion and their former positions the now repentant Priscilliants, provided that, in some cases, approval for this decision was ratified by the Roman bishop (the unnamed and unknown Anastasius I, referred to as *papa*) and Simplician of Milan, Ambrose's successor.[38] It mystifies me how Pietri can reach the conclusion that the consultation of *both* Milan and Rome reveals Spanish acknowledgement of Roman primacy![39]

What is interesting is what this reveals about the Spanish attitude towards Rome. We must not conclude that the Spanish bishops were required to obtain the ratification of their synod by the Roman bishop in virtue of his universal primacy of jurisdiction. Just as in 404 when, in the letter preserved in Palladius, John Chrysostom wrote to Innocent, Venerius of Milan and Chromatius of Aquileia,[40] the fact that more than one bishop is addressed indicates that they were seeking support from several influential bishops whose opinions were hoped to hold enough sway as to overturn the opinion of one's opponents. Allowing excommunicated clergy to regain their positions upon reconciliation was contrary to ecclesiastical practice, about which Siricius had reminded Himerius of Tarragona,[41] although it was not without exception.[42] Indeed,

---

[38] *Exemplar* 130–32 (Chadwick, *Priscillian of Avila*, p. 238): ' ... expectantes pari exemplo quid papa qui nunc est, quid sanctus Simplicianus episcopus Mediolanensis reliquique ecclesiarum rescribant sacerdotes'. A few lines later, 142–3 (Chadwick, *Priscillian of Avila*, pp. 238–9), a further restriction is placed upon the capacity of Dictinius and Anterius to ordain until word has been heard back from Rome and Milan.

[39] Pietri, *Roma Christiana*, p. 1066: 'Lorsque les évêques réunis à Tolède en septembre 400 envisageaient de consulter Rome et Milan sur la réconciliation des priscillianistes repentis, ils reconnaissaient surtout le primat de la communion romaine'.

[40] John Chrysostom, *Ep ad Innoc.* 1 = Palladius, *Dial.* 2 (SC 342.94). See G.D. Dunn, 'Roman Primacy in the Correspondence between Innocent I and John Chrysostom', in *Giovanii Crisostomo. Oriente e Occidente tra IV e V secolo*, XXXIII Incontro di studiosi dell'antichità cristiana, Roma, 6–8 maggio 2004, SEAug, vol. 93 (Rome, 2005), pp. 687–98.

[41] Cyprian, *Ep.* 55.11.3 (CCL 3B.269); Synod of Elvira, can. 51 (*CCH* 4.258); and Siricius, *Ep.* 1.XIV.18 (PL 13.1143). In addition laymen could not be ordained after reconciliation. On the Synod of Elvira see J. García Sánchez, 'El derecho romano en el concilio de Elvira (s. IV)', in *I concili della cristianità occidentale secoli III–V*, XXX Incontro di studiosi dell'antichità cristiana, Roma, 3–5 maggio 2001, SEAug, vol. 78 (Rome, 2002), pp. 589–606.

[42] First Council of Nicaea, can. 8 (CCCOGD 1.24). The validity of Novatianist ordination might have been recognised see P. L'Huillier, *The Church of the Ancient Councils: The Disciplinary Work of the First Four Ecumenical Councils* (Crestwood, NY, 1996), pp. 59–60. Augustine, *De bapt.* 1.1.2 (NBA 15/1.268–70), argued that whether or not such a schismatic cleric ought to be allowed to resume ministry when reconciled from schism depended upon the needs of the church. See *Ep.* 185.10.44 (NBA 23.66), where Augustine was prepared to accept this for repentant Donatist clergy; and Innocent I, *Ep.* 17.V.9 (PL

one of the canons produced by the 19 bishops at Toledo stated that penitents were not to be admitted to the clergy.[43] Therefore it is little wonder the Spanish bishops wanted the support of several major figures like the bishops of Rome and Milan for their radical plans.[44]

My reading of the context is that the Spanish churches looked to Rome (and Milan) in order to gain a heavyweight supporter (or supporters) and were prepared to flatter Rome's apostolic sensitivities to help win it over, but that the Spanish did not have a sense of Rome being the ultimate decision-maker in the church, except in some limited instances of legal appeal. Perhaps one could even go further and agree with Ralph Mathisen's recent suggestion that by not mentioning Anastasius by name the Spanish bishops were more attracted to the current influence of the church of Milan more than that of Rome.[45] Now we are in a position to consider what Innocent's letter itself contributes to our understanding of the relationship between Rome and the Spanish churches in late antiquity.

Innocent's Letter

The conclusion of both Chadwick and Burrus is that the death of Anastasius might have slowed Rome's response to the synod, which was then forthcoming in Innocent's letter.[46] Indeed, as we noted earlier, Caspar referred to Innocent's

---

20.531). See G.D. Dunn, 'Innocent I and the Illyrian Churches on the Question of Heretical Ordination', *JAEMA*, 4 (2008): pp. 65–81, at p. 71. Siricius, *Ep*. 1.VII.11 and 1.XV.19 (PL 13.1140 and 1143), himself had provided exceptions: sexually incontinent clergy ignorant of the requirement to live celibately or anyone who had performed penance prior to ordination could continue in office but never be advanced (while those who claimed that they had a right not to live celibately were to be removed from office).

[43] First Synod of Toledo, can. 2 (*CCH* 4.328–9): 'Item placuit ut de paenitente non admittatur ad clerum, nis tantum, si necessitas aut usus exegerit, inter ostiarios deputetur uel inter lectores, ita ut euangelia et apostolum non legat. Si qui autem ante ordinati sunt subdiacones, inter subdiacones habeantur, ita ut manum non imponant aut sacra non contingant. Ex paenitente uero dicimus de eo qui posst baptismum aut pro homicidio aut pro diuersis criminibus grauissimisque peccatis publiccam paenitentiam gerens sub cilicio, diuino fuerit reconiliatus altario'. Of course, the canon is not entirely relevant in that it is talking about admission to the clergy rather than the readmission of higher clergy.

[44] Burrus, *The Making of a Heretic*, p. 109.

[45] R.W. Mathisen, 'The Council of Turin (398/399) and the Reorganization of Gaul ca. 395/406', *Journal of Late Antiquity* 6 (2014): p. 294.

[46] Chadwick, *Priscillian of Avila*, p. 185, and Burrus, *The Making of a Heretic*, p. 212, n. 30.

letter as an 'Antwort', a view also held by Pietri, who noted that '[l]a sentence romaine ne s'occupe guère de la procédure prévue en 400 par le synode espagnol'.[47] However, if Mathisen is correct, perhaps the Spanish were slow to inform Rome about their synod. The whole thrust of Innocent's letter, in any event, is not to endorse the synod but to react to post-synodal events.

When they went to Rome, Hilary and Elpidius were not bringing news about the synod but about local reaction to the synod, updating Rome on what had happened since the synod had concluded. Of course, their update was for a very specific purpose. What Innocent did in response was not to criticise the Spanish for failing to follow Roman directives, but to exhort them ('exhortándoles' as Orlandis notes) to repair internal ruptures.[48] The letter therefore is not what Pietri described as an example of 'la législation pontificale'.[49] Innocent felt such a care (*cura*) for the problems besetting the Spanish churches, which he described as schism, that a correction (*emendatio*) or medicine was needed to rectify things. The problem was the lack of unity that flowed from a breakdown of discipline, the disregard for the canons of the fathers, and the seizure of churches.[50] Who was responsible for providing that remedy is not specified, although Innocent no doubt understood that the intervention of the apostolic see, which is how he describes his church, would make a contribution. Innocent offered strong guidance, which I am sure he believed would be followed, rather than directives to be obeyed. The difference may be subtle but is at the heart of how we understand the Roman bishop's standing in the late antique churches of the West.

Interestingly, Innocent did not discuss this matter with a provincial synod of Italian bishops but with the presbyters of Rome.[51] This is a singular reference to such a role for the Roman presbyters in Innocent's correspondence and it is not entirely clear how we are to interpret its significance. Was the topic not important enough to take to an episcopal synod or was it so pressing that it could not wait until the next scheduled meeting of regional bishops in Italy? We are left without an answer.

The Spanish bishops who broke off communion after Toledo insisted upon traditional discipline, as found in Siricius' letter to Himerius: those clergy who had been Priscillianists, like Symphosius and Dictinius, could be reconciled with the church, but only as lay men. In this they stood in the tradition of such

---

[47] Pietri, *Roma Christiana*, p. 1065.
[48] Orlandis, 'El primado Romano', p. 456.
[49] Pietri, *Roma Christiana*, p. 1065.
[50] Innocent I, *Ep.* 3.1 (PL 20.486).
[51] Ibid.

Spanish bishops as Gregory of Granada (ancient Elvira in Baetica), who followed Lucifer of Cagliari (ancient Caralis in Sardinia), staunch opponents of Arianism in the fourth century who refused to have anything to do with repentant Arian bishops.[52] That Innocent mentions Lucifer, who had died a little after 370, and links him with the current hardliners, suggests that he was trying to shame them by making this link and that therefore Lucifer's policy had come to be regarded by all in Spain as unacceptable. On the other hand, if the current hardliners idolised Gregory to any extent, it is understandable that Innocent failed to mention him by name.

We do not know how the bishops at Toledo justified their lenient policy, but we do know how Innocent supported it. Innocent painted the hard-line bishops as opponents of peace, and the bishops at Toledo as promoters of unity.[53] He turned to the Scriptures. Peter himself, as well as Thomas and King David, had sinned, and not only had been reconciled, but had continued to serve the Lord.[54] Such willingness to reconcile and deviate from harsh norms would be a regular feature of Innocent's episcopate. In *Epistula* 16 we find him confirming the Illyrian practice of readmitting repentant schismatic clergy to ministry, provided they had been ordained validly before joining schism, although in *Epistula* 17 he rejected their practice of 'reordaining' schismatic clergy ordained in schism, arguing that they could be received into the church but only as lay men.[55] Since the latter ordinations were invalid they were parallel to the situation in canon 2 from Toledo: repentant lay men (and this is how Innocent considered invalidly ordained schismatic clergy) could be reconciled with the church but could not be ordained.[56] So there are exceptions to Innocent's willingness to make exceptions! Furthermore, as another example of his openness to reconciliation, he was willing to accept the church of Antioch, which he had excommunicated because

---

[52] Ibid., 3.2 (PL 20.486–7). Cf., Pietri, *Roma Christiana*, p. 1066, who says that Innocent mentioned not only the followers of Lucifer but Novatian as well, but I do not find any such latter reference in this letter.

[53] Innocent I, *Ep.* 3.I.2 (PL 20.486–7).

[54] Ibid., 3.I.3 (PL 20.488).

[55] Ibid., 16 (PL 20.519–21) = JK 299; and 17 (PL 20.526–37) = JK 303. See G.D. Dunn, 'The Letter of Innocent I to Marcian of Niš', in D. Bojpvić (ed.), *Saint Emperor Constantine and Christianity*, International Conference Commemmorating the 1700th Anniversary of the Edict of Milan, 31 May–2 June 2013, 2 vols (Niš, 2013), 1.319–38; and Dunn, 'Innocent I and the Illyrian Churches', p. 70.

[56] Innocent I, *Ep.* 3.I.4 (PL 20.488–9).

of its involvement in the exile of John Chrysostom, back into communion with Rome when a move was made by Alexander, its new bishop.⁵⁷

Dissension over the clerical status of repentant Priscillianist bishops was not the only topic of complaint brought by Hilary and Elpidius to Rome. The bishops at Toledo agreed that the Nicene canons on ordination were to be observed and that anyone aware of the canons who disregarded them was to be excommunicated unless he made amends.⁵⁸ Norton considers that the problem was bishops like Rufinus and Minicius ordaining outside their province.⁵⁹ Burrus thinks this refers to canon 4 of Nicaea about the necessity of having three bishops from the province ordain a new bishop, provided that the other bishops of the province consented and that the metropolitan confirmed their action.⁶⁰ It is her contention that not only were Priscillianist bishops like Symphosius and Dictinius guilty of disobeying this canon but that non-Priscillianist bishops like Rufinus and Minicius were doing likewise.⁶¹ Chadwick and Pietri think that the bishops at Toledo had canon 6 of Nicaea more in mind.⁶² This canon requires the consent of the metropolitan prior to the ordination of a new bishop.⁶³ Here I wish to endorse Chadwick and Pietri. In Innocent's letter it is clear that Hilary complained that Rufinus had been ordaining bishops without the prior consent of the metropolitan. It would seem that Rufinus apologised to the bishops at Toledo for having engaged in this practice.⁶⁴ This would suggest that Rufinus knew of the canons of Nicaea and escaped condemnation by promising to stop the practice. It is clear from the fact that Hilary complained about him to Innocent that Rufinus had not ceased. Not only was this a violation of the policy of discipline, it was done in secret and contrary to the will of the people.⁶⁵

---

⁵⁷ Ibid., 19 (PL 20.540–2) = JK 305. See G.D. Dunn, 'The Roman Response to the Ecclesiastical Crises in the Antiochene Church in the Late-Fourth and Early-Fifth Centuries', in D. Sim and P. Allen (eds), *Ancient Jewish and Christian Texts as Crisis Management Literature: Thematic Studies from the Centre for Early Christian Studies*, Library of New Testament Studies, vol. 445 (London, 2012), pp. 112–28.

⁵⁸ First Synod of Toledo (*CCH* 4.327–8).

⁵⁹ P. Norton, *Episcopal Elections 250–600: Hierarchy and Popular Will in Late Antiquity*, OCM (Oxford, 2007), p. 154.

⁶⁰ First Council of Nicaea, can. 4 (CCCOGD 1.21–2).

⁶¹ Burrus, *The Making of a Heretic*, p. 110. On p. 214, n. 46, she suggests that canon 8 might also have been in the minds of the bishops at Toledo.

⁶² Chadwick, *Priscillian of Avila*, p. 173; and Pietri, *Roma Christiana*, p. 1066.

⁶³ First Council of Nicaea, can. 6 (CCCOGD 1.23).

⁶⁴ Innocent I, *Ep.* 3.II.5 (PL 20.489): ' ... et dudum in concilio Toletano erroris sui ueniam postulasse ... '.

⁶⁵ Ibid., 3.II.5 (PL 20.489): ' ... contra populi uoluntatem et disciplinae rationem, episcopum lucis abditis ordinasse ... '.

The question of the rights of metropolitans in the ordinations of bishops is one to which Innocent would turn his attention on another occasion in 404 when he wrote to Victricius of Rouen.[66] It was also a topic treated earlier by Damasus in his letter to the Gallic churches (*Dominus inter*), if he was the author, and Siricius in his letter after an Italian synod in 386 (*Cum in unum*), which ended up preserved in an African synod from 418.[67]

Minicius had ordained a bishop for Girona (the ancient Gerunda) in Tarraconensis. Hilary could bring the complaint of the Tarragonan bishops to Innocent. This would suggest that Hilary himself was not from Tarraconensis (and therefore it is extremely likely that Hilary and Rufinus were both from the same province). Innocent did not decide these cases. His directive was that the Spanish bishops themselves ought to hear these matters by applying the Nicene canons[68] and that those bishops who had been ordained illegally by Rufinus and Minicius be removed.[69] Innocent had no doubt as to the guilt of Rufinus and Minicius but he left it to the Spanish bishops to investigate fully and pronounce sentence. This contrasts with Siricius, who stated to the Spanish bishops through Himerius that the apostolic see would give judgement on issues that would arise regarding irregular ordinations after any Spanish ignorance on the practice had been dispelled.[70]

Innocent also was informed of Bishop John who had sent legates (*legati*) in his place to Toledo. They had agreed to the synod's positions on the reception of Priscilliant bishops back into communion as bishops, but their action was then reversed by their bishop. Innocent instructed the Spanish bishops to investigate this matter also and to excommunicate those who perpetuated the schism.[71]

---

[66] Ibid., 2.I.3 (PL 20.471). See G.D. Dunn, 'Canonical Legislation on the Ordination of Bishops: Innocent I's Letter to Victricius of Rouen', in J. Leemans et al. (eds), *Episcopal Elections in Late Antiquity*, AKG, Bd 119 (Berlin, 2011), pp. 145–66.

[67] [Damasus], *Ep. ad Gallos epis.* 18 (Y.-M. Duval, *La décrétale* Ad Gallos Episcopos: *son texte et son auteur. Texte critique, traduction française et commentaire*, Supplements to Vigiliae Christianae, vol. 73 [Leiden and Boston, 2005], p. 46); and Siricius, *Ep.* 5.1 (CCL 149.60–1) = JK 258.

[68] Innocent I, *Ep.* 3.II.5 (PL 20.489): 'Dehinc Tarraconensium episcoporum est causa tractanda, qui pari modo Minicium in Gerundensi ecclesia episcopum ordinasse conquesti sunt; et iuxta Nicaenos canones ferenda est de tali usurpatione sententia'.

[69] Ibid., 3.II.5 (PL 20.489–90): 'Illorum etiam episcoporum, qui a Rufino uel a Minicio contra regulas ordinati sunt, habeatur plena discussio: ut quia perperam facti sunt, intelligant id, quod uitioso initio adepti sunt, se diutius obtinere non posse'.

[70] Siricius, *Ep.* 1.XV.19 (PL 13.1143).

[71] Innocent I, *Ep.* 3.III.6 (PL 20.490): 'Et prorsus super omnibus, quorum in dubium uenit de cessatione communio, plena inquisitio uestigetur ...'.

Once again Innocent is clear about the outcome and is quite happy to tell the Spanish bishops what they ought to do, but leaves it to them to do it. He did not order them but he certainly did not expect there to be any disagreement with his proposals.

The next item concerns the lack of qualifications for episcopal office of some men who held that position. Who had complained about this? Two bishops are mentioned as having been ordained bishops even though they ought not to have been: Rufinus and Gregory. The mention of Rufinus again would suggest that this is another complaint against him by Hilary himself. In that case it would seem likely that it was Hilary who was complaining also about Gregory. We read of a Gregory a little further on in the letter and the understanding of Chadwick was that they are one and the same individual, viz., Gregory of Mérida, the metropolitan of Lusitania, who had succeeded Patruinus (and, before him, Hydatius) in the short time since the Synod of Toledo over which Patruinus had presided. This could suggest that Hilary was a suffragan bishop somewhere in Lusitania, complaining about the man who recently had become his metropolitan. This would make Hilary a true defender of Toledo against both a hard-line anti-Priscillianism and a laxist approach to the synod's canons. Alternatively, perhaps someone else had complained about Rufinus and Gregory for, in the next section, Hilary seems to have presented a complaint on behalf of Gregory against others who were infringing his rights. It seems unlikely that Hilary would both complain about Gregory on the one hand and then act on his behalf on the other. As with the extreme anti-Priscillianists, perhaps Hilary was informing Innocent not of his own complaint in this instance but of that of others against what bishops like Hilary thought was a fair compromise.

The trouble with bishops like Rufinus and Gregory was their backgrounds. Both it seems, after initiation, had continued in forensic practice before becoming bishops.[72] In his letter to Exsuperius of Toulouse in 405 Innocent would touch upon this matter indirectly. There he would note that none of his predecessors had dealt with the matter of accepting as Christians those who had been involved in the Roman justice system, particularly as judges and executioners.[73] The parallel is not exact since the subject matter is initiation rather than ordination and the level of involvement in the judicial system might have been different in both cases. In Innocent's opinion such a background ought to make one ineligible for ordination, as would other things like military service, membership of the *curiales*, and providing public entertainment in theatres and

---

[72] Ibid., 3.IV.7 (PL 20.491).
[73] Ibid., 6.III.7–8 (PL 20.499).

amphitheatres.⁷⁴ The reason for this was that one would be expected to act in such official or civic capacities in ways contrary to the Gospel. Military service (including – or sometimes particularly – civil service, which by this time was organised as a form of military service) was clearly forbidden to Christians at the Council of Nicaea and was repeated in Damasus' letter *Dominus inter*, Siricius' letter *Cum in unum* and would be found repeated in Innocent's letter to Victricius of Rouen.⁷⁵ Indeed, the bishops at Toledo had decreed that those who served in the military or civil service could only be ordained as clerics below the rank of deacon.⁷⁶ Repeated imperial attempts to keep *curiales* in civic rather than religious service made recruitment of men from this level of society increasingly unattractive for the church, even though Innocent would plead for some former *curiales* to be exempt from imperial recall.⁷⁷

However, in the case of the Spanish churches, to insist upon all these eligibility criteria would have seen the removal of many bishops, who must otherwise have been quite acceptable. Knowing that to ask the Spanish bishops to investigate this matter would create riots in Spain, Innocent counselled that the past not be looked into and the rigour of ecclesiastical law be imposed only from that time forward, with penalties for the one so promoted and those who would promote him.⁷⁸ He repeated much of what he said a little later in the letter.⁷⁹

In response to Gregory of Mérida's complaint against those infringing his rights, presumably against his rights as metropolitan in the ordination of bishops for his province, although this is not specified, Innocent states simply that it needs to be heard (*audiatur*).⁸⁰

---

74 Ibid., 3.IV.7 (PL 20. 491).
75 See Dunn, 'Canonical Legislation', pp. 159–62.
76 First Synod of Toledo, can. 8 (*CCH* 4.331–2): 'Si quis post baptismum militauerit et chlamydem sumpserit aut cingulum, etiamsi grauia non admiserit, si ad clerum admissus fuerit, diaconii non accipiat dignitatem'.
77 Innocent I, *Ep.* 2.XII.14 (PL 20.478). On the situation of the *curiales* as bishops see A. Di Berardino, 'The Poor must be Supported by the Wealth of the Church (*Codex Theodosianus* 16.2.6)', in G.D. Dunn, D. Luckensmeyer, and L. Cross (eds), *Prayer and Spirituality in the Early Church*, vol. 5: *Poverty and Riches* (Strathfield, NSW, 2009), pp. 249–68.
78 Innocent I, *Ep.* 3.IV.7 (PL 20.491): 'Sed ne deinceps similia committantur, dilectionis uestrae maturitas prouidere debebit, ut tantae usurpationi saltem nunc finis necessarius imponatur: eo uidelicet constituto, ut si qui post haec aduersus formas canonum uel ad ecclesiasticum ordinem, uel ad ipsum sacerdotium uenire tentauerint, una cum creatoribus suis ipso, in quo inuenti fuerint, ordine et honore priuentur'.
79 Ibid., 3.VI.9 (PL 20.492).
80 Ibid., 3.V.8 (PL 20.491).

The letter finishes touching upon other qualifications for the ordination of clerics including the *cursus* of clerical office and the marriage of clergy, which have already been set out previously. This is a clear reference to Siricius' letter to Himerius.[81] Only on the topic of marriage does Innocent go into detail: clergy are to have married virgins and they are to have been married only once, regardless of whether the first marriage was before or after baptism. This was a topic Innocent would revisit in his letter to Exsuperius of Toulouse and in one of his letters to the Illyrian bishops.[82]

Given Hilary's whole thrust in visiting Rome, I think we can conclude that he was not there to complain about Siricius' attitude towards clerical marriage, but about the fact that the new provisions were still being ignored. What Siricius had urged upon Himerius seems to have been taken up by Spanish synods, for at Toledo there is reference to previous provisions issued by the Lusitanian bishops.[83] At Toledo itself canons had been issued putting into effect regulations about clerical marriage: a lector who marries a widow can only be promoted to sub-deacon, and a sub-deacon who marries a second time is to be demoted and if a third time is to do penance and be reduced to the lay state.[84]

In particular, since Innocent's reply focused on the topic of whether or not a marriage entered into prior to baptism should count as a first marriage, it would seem that Hilary had alerted Innocent to the situation of those like Carterius, the Spanish bishop who had remarried after his first wife, whom he had married while unbaptised, had died. We know about this because Oceanus, Fabiola's husband, wrote to Jerome seeking his comment. Jerome was of the opinion that baptism washed away everything from one's former life, including marriage.[85] To counter the passage in 1 Timothy 3:2 about clergy being the husband of one wife, he argued that what the author had banned was simultaneous polygamy not sequential polygamy.[86] We read a summary of Jerome's position in the first book of his *Apologia contra Rufinum*.[87]

---

[81] Siricius, *Ep.* 1.IX.13 – 1.X.14 (PL 13.1142–3) on the *cursus* and 1.VIII.2 (PL 13.1141–2) on the marriage of clergy. See G.D. Dunn, 'The Clerical *cursus honorum* in Late Antique Rome', *Scrinium*, 9 (2013): pp. 132–45.
[82] Innocent I, *Epp.* 2.IV.7 – 2.VI.9 (PL 20.473–5); and 17.I.2–6 (PL 20.527–30).
[83] First Synod of Toledo, can. 1 (*CCH* 4.328).
[84] Ibid., cans 3 and 4 (*CCH* 4.329–30).
[85] Jerome, *Ep.* 69.2 (CSEL 54.680). See D.G. Hunter, 'The Raven Replies: Ambrose's *Letter to the Church at Vercelli* (*Ep.ex.coll.* 14) and the Criticisms of Jerome', in A. Cain and J. Lössl (eds), *Jerome of Stridon: His Life, Writings and Legacy* (Farnham, 2009), pp. 175–89, at pp. 182–6.
[86] Jerome, *Ep.* 69.5 (CSEL 54.686).
[87] Jerome, *Apol.* 1.32 (CCL 79.33).

Other than point out his interpretation of the Scriptures, strongly in opposition to what Jerome advocated, Innocent did not issue any directives or suggestions.

Conclusion

It is clear from the letter of Gratian in 378 that he considered that all of the churches in the West looked to Rome to some extent and that in the matter of the deposition of bishops Rome was the point of legal appeal for those who believed they could not or did not receive a fair hearing at first instance. This does equate to a certain degree of primacy held by the Roman bishop over his western colleagues, at least at the judicial appeal level (but not at the legislative or executive level). However, even when Priscillian went to Rome to see Damasus (although he failed to see him because there was no basis for Damasus to hear his appeal, I would contend, and it suited Damasus not to get involved) he attempted to see Ambrose in Milan as well. This suggests that Rome was not the only church to which others turned for advice (and that it was advice and not a decision that was being sought). When Siricius wrote to Himerius of Tarragona in 385 his language reveals that he thought (or at least wanted the Spanish bishops to think) that he had the authority to dictate to them how to administer their churches, something far broader.

There is a whole different tone about Innocent's letter in response to the visit of Hilary and Elpidius to Rome. Nowhere in it does he assert himself as the successor of Peter or make claims about what Petrine authority meant. The most he claimed about Rome was that it was 'the bosom of faith' and an apostolic see.[88] He wrote giving the Spanish churches his opinion about how they should respond to ongoing problems of disunity caused by their lenient policy of readmitting repentant Priscillians back into communion and into clerical office. He reminded them also of the legislation enacted at Nicaea, which ought to be observed in Spain as elsewhere, but left it up to the Spanish bishops themselves to apply. Although he was offering an opinion it was not one that he expected could be disregarded.

The question of Innocent's authority over the Spanish churches rests ultimately, I would think, on the degree to which he could ensure compliance with what he wrote. A Roman bishop could issue what could appear to be binding directives to other churches (but Innocent certainly did not engage in

---

[88] Innocent I, *Ep.* 3.1 (PL 20.486): ' ... in ipso sinu fidei ... '.

language to imply that he had), but without a sufficient mechanism to enforce it, such directives were little better than personal opinions. This is certainly true the further from Rome the correspondence travelled. Early in the fifth century Rome still had to rely upon persuasion, influence and accumulated prestige if it had any hope of getting remote churches to implement and imitate what Rome wanted. As we conclude it must be noted that we have no information at all about how the Spanish reacted to Innocent's letter, although, since he was supportive of their efforts, they would have welcomed it as helpful support from the most important church in the West.

Chapter 6

Reconsidering a Relationship: Pope Leo of Rome and Prosper of Aquitaine[*]

Michele Renee Salzman

The relationship between Pope Leo I (440–61) and Prosper of Aquitaine has been problematic for centuries. Following on from Gennadius' late fifth-century rumour about Prosper's involvement with Leo's letters against Eutyches, Prosper has been cast as Leo's secretary, adviser or ghostwriter for all or some of Leo's works.[1] Scholars have assumed that Leo, as bishop of Rome, was either too busy or too theologically unsophisticated to be able to craft his own letters, sermons and treatises. Yet, even among scholars who see Prosper as Leo's theological ghostwriter, there is no agreement on when the two men met, if they did. Some scholars propose an initial meeting in 431 when Leo was archdeacon and Prosper went with Hilary from Marseille to Rome to inform Celestine I, then bishop of Rome, about Pelagianism in Gaul.[2] Others suggest the two men met in 440,

---

[*] An earlier version of this chapter was presented at the sixteenth International Conference on Patristic Studies, Oxford University, 8–12 August 2011, at a panel on Prosper of Aquitaine organised by Alexander Hwang. I want to thank Rita Lizzi Testa for her helpful reading of this chapter and Colin Whiting for his assistance. I appreciate greatly the funding from University of California, which made possible my research and travel to present the ideas in this chapter.

[1] The disputed relationship goes back to seventeenth-century scholarship, and is well summarised by F. Di Capua, 'Leone Magno e Prospero di Aquitania', in A. Quacquarelli (ed.), *Scritti minori*, vol. 2 (Rome, 1959), pp. 184–90. For an excellent discussion of the issues see B. Green, *The Soteriology of Leo the Great*, OTM (Oxford, 2008), pp. 195–201; and B. Neil, *Leo the Great*, The Early Church Fathers (London and New York, 2009), pp. 15–16. For specific articles on their relationship see nn. 3, 4 and 7 below. For Gennadius' rumour see Gennadius, *De uir. illust.* 85 (E.C. Richardson [ed.], *Hieronymus. Liber de uiris inlustribus, Gennadius. Liber de uiris inlustribus*, TU, vol. 14/1 [Leipzig, 1896], p. 90) and my discussion below.

[2] For Prosper's mission to Rome see Celestine I, *Ep.* 21 (PL 50.528–37 = P. Coustant, *Epistolae Romanorum Pontificum et quae ad eos scriptae sunt a S. Clemente I usque ad Innocentum III*, t. 1 [Paris, 1721], cols 1185–95) = JK 381. For their initial meeting see the suggestion of J. Gadioz, 'Prosper d'Aquitaine et le Tome à Flavien', *RSR*, 23 (1949): pp. 270–301.

when Leo was in Gaul on a diplomatic mission before his episcopal election.[3] In any case, it is widely stated that Prosper was in Rome either by 435 or, at the latest, by 440 so that he could serve Leo, now pope.[4] Their presumed relationship lies behind scholarly assessment of many of their works; so, for example, Muhlberger presumes their bond to explain in part why Prosper's *Chronicon* makes Leo into the paradigm of a saint and the key figure in his account of events.[5]

The problem with this neat biography of the pope and his lay theologian or stenographer or adviser is that there is little in the way of evidence to support it. There are three ancient texts that have been used to argue for this relationship, the fifth-century Gallic writer, Gennadius, and two ninth-century writers, Ado of Vienne and the Byzantine encyclopedist, Photius.[6] The allusions in these texts have led generations of scholars to hunt for internal evidence, namely similarities in the writings of Leo and Prosper, which would show Prosper's influence on Leo.[7] But scholars have failed to resolve this relationship on the internal evidence. As Bernard Green observes, echoes of Prosper's language or ideas in Leo's extant works show only that Leo had read Prosper's writings

---

[3] For Leo in Gaul see Prosper of Aquitaine, *Epit. chron.* 1341 (MGH.AA 9.478), who mentions his diplomatic mission to restore relations between Aetius and Albinus. For Prosper and Leo meeting ca. 440 in Gaul see A.Y. Hwang, *An Intrepid Lover of Perfect Grace: The Life and Thought of Prosper of Aquitaine* (Washington, DC, 2009), pp. 189–91, with discussion of earlier scholars who take this view.

[4] See M. Cappuyns, 'Le premier représentant de l'augustinisme médiéval, Prosper d'Aquitaine', *RTAM*, 1 (1929): pp. 309–37, who dates Prosper's move to Rome to ca. 435 as the result of Cassian's death and the resulting theological quiet in Gaul, an atmosphere disputed by Hwang, *An Intrepid Lover*, pp. 183–6.

[5] S. Muhlberger, *The Fifth-Century Chroniclers: Prosper, Hydatius, and the Gallic Chronicler of 452*, ARCA Classical and Medieval Texts, Papers and Monographs, vol. 27 (Leeds, 1990), pp. 52–3, acknowledges that we do not know much about Prosper's time in Rome, but presumes it to explain his theological development. On Leo as Prosper depicted him see pp. 110–13 and 127–35.

[6] For these writers see my discussion and nn. 20, 33 and 34 below.

[7] Gadioz, 'Prosper d'Aquitaine et le Tome à Flavien', pp. 270–301; N.W. James, 'Leo the Great and Prosper of Aquitaine: A Fifth-Century Pope and his Adviser', *JThS*, n.s. 44 (1993): pp. 554–84; and N.W. James, 'Prosper of Aquitaine Revisited: Gallic Correspondent or Resident Papal Adviser', in M. Vizent (ed.), *Studia Patristica*, vol. 69, papers presented at the Sixteenth International Conference on Patristic Studies, Oxford 2011 (Leuven, 2013), pp. 267–76. James, 'Leo the Great', pp. 557–8, observed Leo varied terms such as *natura* and *substantia* depending on the audience, hence the earlier arguments of Gadioz and others that terms such as 'nature' (*natura*) in Leo's *Tomus* were the result of Prosper's hand are not possible to sustain. Nonetheless, James did not acknowledge that this shows the weakness of ascribing authorship on the basis of verbal echoes that he adduced in the 2011 Oxford paper. For more discussion and bibliography see also Green, *The Soteriology of Leo*, pp. 195–201.

and been influenced by them; conversely, echoes of Leo's *Sermones* or theology in Prosper's writing – notably citations from Leo's *Sermones* in Prosper's *De uocatione omnium gentium* – show that Prosper had access to Leo's *Epistulae* and *Sermones*.[8] Suffice it to say that originality was not valued as highly antiquity as it is today, and so verbal echoes are to be expected and appreciated. Moreover, such similarities do not at all remove the other problem raised by Green, who observed that there are 'marked differences in style between the two writers'.[9]

Rather than undertaking another inconclusive study of alleged similarities in the works of Leo and Prosper, I shall instead reconsider the ancient testimony for the scholarly view that Prosper was Leo's secretary or ghostwriter. As I shall show in the first part of this chapter, these texts have been seriously misread. In truth, they provide no good evidence to secure the notion that Prosper was in Rome in this capacity, or even in Rome at all after 431. Scholars who continue to support this view of the pope and his adviser are working on modern assumptions about the extent and influence of the bishop and the church's organisation in Rome in the middle of the fifth century. Indeed, viewing Prosper as Leo's secretary suggests that Leo was essentially an administrator, dependent on specialists for advice on theological issues in a large, efficient papal bureaucracy. Instead, I suggest, Leo's administration was more *ad hoc* and less organised than that. Moreover, Leo was himself deeply engaged with pastoral care and theological considerations. He was influenced by other theologians, including Prosper, but there is little in either the style or content of Leo's works to prove that he was not engaged in the composition of his works.

In part two of this chapter, I shall consider some implications of removing Prosper from direct involvement in Roman papal circles and placing him, instead, in Gallic aristocratic ones. First, we can see that Prosper's theology developed independently. Assuming that Prosper was the author of the *De prouidentia Dei*,

---

[8] Green, *The Soteriology of Leo*, pp. 195–201. Surprisingly, Neil, *Leo the Great*, p. 96, accepts Green's criticism of the view of Prosper as Leo's secretary, but she nonetheless accepts the suggestion of A. Chavasse (ed.), *Sancti Leonis magni Romani Pontificis Tracttus Septem et Nonaginta*, CCL, vol. 138 (Turnhout, 1973), p. cliii, that ' ... likely ... Prosper prepared the materials that were used in the compilation of [Leo's] *Tome* and that he may have been involved in editing the text'. However, Chavasse's citations do little more than show that Prosper had access to Leo's published sermons. Green's conclusion – that the theology in Leo's *Tomus* is entirely his, and Prosper's works show the influence of Leo's theology and not the reverse – remains valid. Moreover, the work generally attributed to Prosper, *De uocat.*, dated after 440, advances an ideal of universal salvation beyond the empire that is generally explained as showing Leo's influence on Prosper. See Green, *The Soteriology of Leo*, pp. 195–201.

[9] Green, *The Soteriology of Leo*, p. 201.

as has been proposed by Marcovich and Hwang, his was an independent, Gallic aristocrat's view of the papacy.[10] Second, viewing Prosper as an independent aristocrat also helps to explain the attribution to him of the *Epistula ad Demetriadem*; like Demetrias, Prosper was an independent, ascetically oriented, aristocratic supporter of Leo. And third, reconsidering the relationship between Prosper and Leo supports the view of the pope as a man eager to build ties to Roman aristocrats, be they in Rome or, like Prosper, in Gaul. Indeed, Leo was happy to have Gallic elite supporters for, as has been shown for early fifth-century Gaul, churches and clerics selectively accepted Rome's opinions, only agreeing to them when they so desired.[11] Reconsidering the relationship between Leo and Prosper as one of bishop and Gallic aristocrat, and seeing Leo as engaged with making ties with Gallic supporters in the West fits in with more recent studies of the fifth-century bishops of Rome that see them as rather more limited leaders of a less than fully unified western Christendom.[12]

Reconsidering the Evidence

Was Prosper Leo's Notary or Secretary?

It is often stated that Prosper was a well-educated member of the Gallo-Roman aristocracy in the late fourth century because of the attribution to him of a series of works, most specifically *De prouidentia Dei*, which tells of his being, at some time before ca. 415, caught up in barbarian invasions and then released; the circumstances of his release in this biographical poem are not clearly indicated, but soon after, ca. 416, he is alleged to have written these verses in Marseille.[13] In these years, Prosper's pro-Augustinian position made him an ally of another layman in the city, Hilary, and placed him in opposition to Pelagius' ideas. Hilary and Prosper consequently joined together and went to Rome between 428 and 431 to appeal to the pope to act against Pelagianism in Marseille.[14]

---

[10] Hwang, *An Intrepid Lover*, p. 37, following the arguments of M. Marcovich (ed.), *Prosper of Aquitaine: De providentia Dei. Text, Translation and Commentary*, Supplements to *Vigiliae Christianae*, vol. 10 (Leiden and New York, 1989), pp. ix–xii.

[11] R.W. Mathisen, *Ecclesiastical Factionalism and Religious Controversy in Fifth-Century Gaul* (Washington, D.C., 1989), pp. 44–68.

[12] For more on this view see K. Sessa, *The Formation of Papal Authority in Late Antique Italy: Roman Bishops and the Domestic Sphere* (Cambridge, 2012), pp. 25–30.

[13] Hwang, *An Intrepid Lover*, p. 37.

[14] If the embassy had wanted the pope to take a public stand, they failed, though they did get the pope to praise Augustine. Indeed, no pope confronted this issue in Gaul openly

Disappointingly, Celestine I, the pope, did not act against the Pelagians in Gaul, but he did issue an encomium of Augustine.[15]

As a result of this trip to Rome, some scholars suggest that Prosper gained access to documents and made connections with members of the papal establishment in Rome, including the then archdeacon Leo who, however, was in the opposing camp at this moment; Leo had asked Prosper's enemy, Cassian, to write *De incarnatione Domini contra Nestorium*.[16] At some point soon after this trip, Prosper wrote a work that attacked Cassian and Pelagianism; he authored *De gratia Dei et libero arbitrio contra Collatorem* attacking Cassian and likely also wrote the two-dozen lines attacking his Gallic opponents, *Epitaphium Nestorianae et Pelagianae haereseon*. Though we have no other evidence, these works suggest a Gallic audience and hence the idea that Prosper had returned to Gaul at this date; the Gallic material in the first version of *Chronicon* ascribed to Prosper also suggests access to Gallic information, and hence a return to Gaul at least for the version of *Chronicon* that ended in 433.[17]

After this point, many scholars assert that Prosper moved to Rome. The arguments rest on circumstantial evidence, namely because the first edition of Prosper's *Chronicon* shows a break after 433 and an allegedly increased focus on papal matters.[18] Other scholars claim that Prosper was still in Gaul until ca. 440 when he met the then archdeacon Leo; Leo had come to Gaul on a diplomatic mission to try to patch up relations between Albinus, the praetorian prefect of Gaul, and Aetius, the general.[19] These scholars assert that when Leo returned to

---

until Hormisdas in 520. See Celestine I, *Ep.* 21 (PL 50.528–37).

[15] Green, *The Soteriology of Leo*, p. 108; and Celestine I, *Ep.* 21.1–2 (PL 50.528–30).

[16] John Cassian, *De incarn. Dom.* pref. (CSEL 17.253); and see Green, *The Soteriology of Leo*, pp. 32–4. For supposed access to papal documents see A. Elberti, *Prospero d'Aquitania: teologo e discepolo* (Rome, 1999), pp. 248–50; M. Cappuyns, 'L'auteur du *De vocatione omnium gentium*', *RB*, 39 (1927): pp. 198–226, at p. 226; the discussion by R.A. Markus, 'Chronicle and Theology: Prosper of Aquitaine', in C. Holdsworth and T.P. Wiseman (eds), *The Inheritance of Historiography 350–900* (Exeter, 1986), pp. 31–43, at p. 35; and Di Capua, 'Leone Magno', pp. 177–83 and 184–90.

[17] Prosper, *Con. Collat.* (PL 51.215–76), attacks Cassian, especially in *Conl.* 13 (CSEL 13.362–96). For this work of Prosper's and for dating his *Epit. Nest. et Pelag.* see Hwang, *An Intrepid Lover*, pp. 14–16 and 156–72. For Prosper's *Epit. chron.* see Muhlberger, *The Fifth Century Chroniclers*, p. 85, n. 77.

[18] For discussion of the significance of the break in Prosper's *Epit. chron.* see Markus, 'Chronicle and Theology', pp. 31–43; and Muhlberger, *Fifth-Century Chroniclers*, pp. 113–27.

[19] Prosper of Aquitaine, *Epit. chron.* 1341–2 (MGH.AA 9.478), mentions his diplomatic mission to restore relations between Aetius and Albinus. B. Studer, *La riflessione teologica nella Chiesa imperiale (secoli IV e V)*, Sussidi Patristici, vol. 4 (Rome, 1989), p. 27,

Rome to become pope in 440, Prosper returned with him, having joined his staff as a papal adviser.

The only explicit evidence for Prosper's presence in Rome after 440 is the late fifth-century work of Gennadius, which continued Jerome's *De uiris illustribus* down to his day. Gennadius ended his entry on Prosper as follows: 'Epistulae quoque papae Leonis aduersus Eutychen de uera Christi incarnatione ad diuersos datae ab isto dictatae creduntur'.[20] One translation prints: 'Epistles of Pope Leo against Eutyches, *On the true incarnation of Christ*, sent to various persons, are also thought to have been dictated by him [i.e. Prosper]'.[21] Some scholars have taken this to mean that Prosper composed Leo's letters against Eutyches, namely Leo's *Epistulae* 1, 2 and 18, while others have seen this as including the idea that Prosper wrote also Leo's *Tomus*, i.e., *Epistula* 28 to Flavian.[22]

But scholars have not remarked that this statement contradicts what Gennadius said about Leo in a previous section: 'Leo, urbis Romae episcopus, scripsit ad Flauianum, Constantinoplitanae ecclesiae episcopum, *Aduersus Eutychen* presbyterum ... epistolam'.[23] Gennadius does not reference Prosper's input in any way here.

Part of the problem in interpreting Gennadius' passage at *De uiris illustribus* 85 is understanding what Gennadius meant by *dictatae*. *Dicto*, in classical and late-Roman usage, can signify simply saying something out loud; from this it came to be used for writing down what is said aloud, i.e., dictation in the modern sense, and hence composing. From this *dicto* can also mean to set out or publish.[24] Though Gennadius' remark is generally taken to mean dictation, and hence that Prosper authored the work, it is possible that Gennadius is publishing a rumour that Prosper published copies of Leo's letters. When Gennadius wants to indicate composition, he regularly uses the verbs *scribere* or *componere*. Gennadius uses *dictare* one other time in the *De uiris illustribus* to discuss the works of a certain

---

suggests that Leo was sent to Gaul by Empress Galla Placidia but gives no specific reason for this notion. For Prosper's alleged return to Rome in 440 see especially Hwang, *An Intrepid Lover*, pp. 189–91; and Elberti, *Prospero d'Aquitania*, pp. 248–50.

[20] Gennadius, *De uir. illust.* 85 (TU 14/1.90).

[21] E.C. Richardson, 'Jerome and Gennadius: Lives of Illustrious Men', in P. Schaff and H. Wace (eds), *Nicene and Post-Nicene Fathers*, second series, vol. 3: *Theodoret, Jerome, Gennadius, Rufinus: Historical Writings, etc.* (Edinburgh, 1892), pp. 349–402, at p. 399.

[22] See James, 'Leo the Great', p. 565; and P. Barclift, 'Shifting Tones of Pope Leo the Great's Christological Vocabulary', *CH*, 66 (1993): pp. 221–39.

[23] Gennadius *De uir. illust.* 71 (TU 14/1.85): 'Leo, bishop of Rome, wrote a letter *to Flavianus*, bishop of the church at Constantinople, against Eutyches the presbyter ... '. (For English translation see n. 21).

[24] *Thesaurus Linguae Latinae*, sv. *Dicto*.

Theodoulus, a priest: 'In quo ostendit ... nec diuersa credi debere aut non uno spiritu et uno auctore dictata ... '.²⁵ Here Gennadius makes clear that the one composing is also the author by adding the noun *auctor* in the ablative. ²⁶

But even if Gennadius intended to say that Prosper had dictated Leo's letter, it is worth emphasising that, as Gennadius acknowledges (*De uiris illustribus* 85), he is reporting only a rumour (*dicuntur*), and one that disparages both Prosper and Leo. Gennadius, it should be remembered, did not approve of Prosper's theology and was very pro-Cassian.²⁷ This helps explain why Gennadius' entries for Leo and Prosper show a certain degree of disdain; Gennadius ignores most of Leo's activities, focusing only on *Tomus ad Flauianum*.

Moreover, Gennadius is not as well informed about Prosper as is generally assumed by scholars who see him as closer in time and place to Prosper and hence more knowing of what he reports. As Muhlberger observed, Gennadius mistakenly ascribed an Easter cycle to Prosper based on Gennadius' mistaken reading of Victorius of Aquitaine; Victorius partly used the consular list provided by Prosper's *Chronicon* to draw up an Easter cycle, but he did not say that Prosper made one, though that is what Gennadius assumed.²⁸ Hence, arguments that Prosper helped Leo with the dating of the Easter controversy based on this passage of Gennadius are similarly flawed.²⁹

As I have shown Gennadius' evidence is unreliable in its information about Prosper composing or editing Leo's *Epistulae*. One key to Gennadius' testimony, is his dislike of Prosper's theology, which views were also shared by Leo. This theological affinity is what is remembered, too, in ninth-century accounts of their relationship. The ninth-century *Codex Thuaneus* attributes Leo's *Sermo* 5

---

²⁵ Gennadius, *De uir. illust.* 92 (TU 14/1.93-4): 'In this work he shows ... that they [the laws of Moses and of Christ] should not be considered different, but as dictated by one spirit and one author ... '.

²⁶ For *scribere* see, for instance, Gennadius, *De uir. illust.* 101 (TU 14/1.97): 'Ego Gennadius, Massiliae presbyter, scripsi "Aduersum omnes hereses" libros octo ... et epistulam "De fide mea" misam ad beatum Gelasium, episcopum urbis Romae'. Confusion over Gennadius' sentence about Prosper is noticeable, too, in the manuscripts. The eleventh-century *Codex Bambergensis* in Nuremberg tries to clarify by revising the verbs: 'epistulae ... ab isto dictae conduntur'. The eleventh-century *Codex Bernensis* in Bern is similarly aiming for clarification: 'ab ipso dictante'.

²⁷ Gennadius *De uir. illust.* 62 (TU 14/1.82). Gennadius was not insistent on absolute adherence to the church for, as Colin Whiting observed in private correspondence, his entry on Faustinus (*De uir. illust.* 16 [TU 14/1.67]) mentions that Faustinus may have been a Luciferian, hence a schismatic, without any condemnation or criticism.

²⁸ Muhlberger, *The Fifth Century Chroniclers*, p. 52, n. 12.

²⁹ James, 'Leo the Great', p. 568.

to Prosper, a view that gets almost no support from scholars. Chavasse's work on the manuscripts of Leo's *Sermones* as well as the internal evidence shows that the author of this fifth-anniversary sermon was also the author of Leo's *Sermones* 1–4.[30] And all five sermons of Leo are consistent with his other sermons.[31] Moreover, as Green observed, how Prosper could have imitated Leo's style before he had yet written anything makes little sense.[32]

The ninth century also saw the ascription of the office of 'secretary' to Prosper in *Martyrologium* of Ado of Vienne. This is a work of notorious fictions, so it can do no more than support the ninth-century view that these two men shared theology.[33] But it is striking that a close look at the ninth-century text used to argue for Prosper's presence in Rome as Leo's secretary does not say that exactly. In *Bibliotheca* Photius says:

ἀλλὰ Πρόσπερός τις ἄνθρωπος ὡς ἀληθῶς τοῦ θεοῦ, λιβέλλους κατ' αὐτῶν ἐπιδεδωκὼς ἀφανεῖς αὐτοὺς ἀπειργάσατο, ἔτι Λέοντος τοῦ προειρημένου τὸν Ῥωμαϊκὸν θρόνον ἰθύνοντος.[34]

This adds nothing to the question of Prosper's position in the church or his location; the passage as a whole is interested in writings against heretics in the

---

[30] Chavasse, *Sancti Leonis magni*, pp. cl–clii.
[31] Green, *The Soteriology of Leo*, p. 194, spoke only about the affinities to Leo's *Serm.* 1–4, but there is nothing in *Sermo* 5 that distinguishes it in style or vocabulary from *Serm.* 1–4 or from the remaining sermons in Chavasse's edition; based on the manuscripts, *Sermo* 5 is likely the result of editing, which Chavasse, *Sancti Leonis magni*, pp. cl–clii, dates to the end of 445. See too Neil, *Leo the Great*, pp. 13–14. The first five sermons are all devoted to commemorating Leo's taking office, and that gives them a unity and coherence, but does not distinguish them from his remaining sermons.
[32] Green, *The Soteriology of Leo*, p. 201.
[33] G. Renaud and J. Dubois (eds), *Le martyrologe d'Adon: ses duex familles, ses trios recensions. texte et commentaire* (Paris, 1984), discuss the fictionalised information that Ado included.
[34] Photius, *Bibliotheca* 54 (R. Henry [ed.], *Bibliothèque* [Paris, 1959], p. 44): 'But Prosper, a certain man who was really a man of God published against those [heretics] *libelli* (pamphlets/petitions) which cut them down, at the time that Leo then was holding the Roman episcopal see ... ' (my own translation). Mathisen, *Ecclesiastical Factionalism*, p. 138, n. 100, asserts that it is probably the heresy of Eutychianism. But others have suggested Pelagianism; see, for one, P.A. McShane, *La romanitas et le pape Léon le Great: L'apport culturel des institutions imperials à la formation des structures ecclésiastiques*, Recherches Théologie, vol. 24 (Tournai and Montreal, 1979), p. 370.

age of Leo, but these are not set in Rome. Hence the notion that Prosper was in Rome is baseless.[35]

So, to summarise, there is no good ancient testimony for Prosper as Leo's secretary, ghostwriter, or notary. Prosper's aristocratic status and high level of education as manifested by works and poems that scholars now attribute to him add to the evidence against his being an ecclesiastical notary for the pope.[36] By the fifth century, papal notaries were generally free men who possessed special skills of stenography, but not a single aristocrat is so noted.[37] Ecclesiastical notaries either worked in the church archives (*scrinia*) or were directly attached to the person of the bishops.[38] Some also served on diplomatic missions, carrying letters or accompanying episcopal legations. Indeed, we know of two of Leo's notaries who were so employed, and a third is known from correspondence, for they are so named in our documents.[39] Prosper is never so named, nor does anyone say that he was. Nothing indicates that he had the stenographic skills that some scholars have claimed; moreover, his education shows that he was likely from a well-educated, aristocratic background, not the typical, relatively humble background of most notaries.[40]

Prosper's expertise was as a theologian, not a secretary. Yet, Leo never commissioned him to write a tract, as he had Cassian. If he were Leo's private ghostwriter there is no evidence of this in any of Prosper's prefaces or works, as there was, for example, when Cassian indicates he wrote something on the

---

[35] This is a correction of Green, *The Soteriology of Leo*, p. 194, whose analysis of the connection between Prosper and Leo is otherwise persuasive.

[36] For more recent assessments of his works see Hwang, *An Intrepid Lover, passim*.

[37] H.C. Teitler, *Notarii and Exceptores: An Inquiry into the Role and Significance of Shorthand Writers in the Imperial and Ecclesiastical Bureaucracy of the Roman Empire (from the Early Principate to c. 450 A.D.)* (Amsterdam, 1985), pp. 86–94.

[38] These are attested as organised since 412 according to C. Sotinel, 'Le personnel épiscopal. Enquête sur la puissance de l'évêque dans la cité', in É. Rebillard and C. Sotinel (eds), *L'Évêque dans la cité du IV*ᵉ *au V*ᵉ *siècle. Image et autorité*, CEFR, vol. 248 (Rome, 1998), pp. 105–26.

[39] In 449 Dionysius was ordered by Leo to carry a message to Constantinople; see Leo I, *Ep.* 59 (E. Schwartz [ed.], *ACO*, t. 2: *Concilium Vniversale Chalcedonense*, vol. 4: *Leonis papae I epistularum collectiones* [Berlin, 1932], pp. 34–7) = JK 447. Again in 449, Dulcitius was a papal delegate to the Council at Ephesus; see Leo I, *Ep.* 28.6 (E. Schwartz [ed.], *ACO*, t. 2: *Concilium Vniversale Chalcedonense*, vol. 2: *Versiones particulares*, pars 1: *Collectio Novariensis de re Eutychis* [Berlin, 1932], pp. 24–33) = JK 423. A notation in another hand was added to another of Leo's letters by the *notarius* Tiburtius (likely = Turibus); see Leo I, *Ep.* 28.6 (PL 54.781, note c): 'Tiburtius notarius iussu domni mei venerabilis pape Leonis edidi'. For more on this last *notarius* see Teitler, *Notarii and Exceptores*, pp. 173–4.

[40] For scholars who see Prosper as Leo's stenographer see notes 3, 4 and 7 especially.

incarnation at Leo's request, or when Jerome wrote at Damasus' request.[41] Indeed, when Jerome fulfilled certain tasks at Damasus' behest, he indicates this in his prefaces, and he did so not as Damasus' notary but as a presbyter, a position that Prosper did not hold; consequently, using the relationship between Jerome and Damasus as evidence for Prosper as Leo's notary is not compelling.[42]

Was Prosper in Rome after 440 in Leo's Papal Administration?

The most frequently referenced argument for Prosper's presence in Rome after 440 and his being part of Leo's papal administration is Prosper's *Chronicon*, which, it is alleged, shows a break after 433 with a new focus on and awareness of events at Rome. Many scholars have pointed to this shift as the moment of Prosper's move to Rome.[43] But this is hard to accept in the light of Robert Markus's study of *Chronicon*. Markus counted the sheer number of items devoted to Rome and Gaul and concluded: 'His [Prosper's] *Chronicle* certainly records an increasing interest in Roman affairs from the mid-430s and especially great admiration for Leo. It does not necessarily show any less knowledge of Gaul, so it cannot be presented as evidence for his move'.[44]

Markus stopped short of making the more radical suggestion that Prosper wrote the remainder of his *Chronicon* in Gaul, but I see no reason not to make it. Prosper could have used his Roman contacts for information for the later versions of *Chronicon*, assuming that he wrote them.[45] The dossier of information that filled the 451 edition described the sudden rise of the Eutychian heresy and its defeat by Leo, things that could have been known through Leo's letters (which circulated) and through ecclesiastical circles. There is no information in *Chronicon* that necessitated Prosper being in Rome. Even the last reference in *Chronicon* in 455 that notes Leo's letters to Emperor Marcian to protest the Alexandrian computations for the date of Easter do not, *pace* Markus, require that Prosper be in Rome. Prosper simply mentions these letters exist (*extant*) and that Leo agreed to compromise for the peace of the church, facts that he

---

[41] Sotinel, 'Le personnel épiscopal', pp. 105–26; and Green, *The Soteriology of Leo*, pp. 194–5.

[42] For Jerome and Damasus see A. Cain, *The Letters of Jerome: Asceticism, Biblical Exegesis, and the Construction of Christian Identity in Late Antiquity*, OECS (Oxford, 2009).

[43] See notes 1, 3 and 4 above.

[44] Markus, 'Chronicle and Theology', p. 33, does note that Prosper has detailed knowledge – and ascribes motives to Pope Celestine in *Epit. chron.* for 431 that he might have gained after his trip to Rome in 431.

[45] *Epit. chron.* was updated at various times, according to Muhlberger, *Fifth Century Chroniclers*, pp. 445, 451 and 455.

could have learned from these letters and from the obvious dating of Easter in that year as was known to anyone living in the West.[46] The controversy between the Roman and Alexandrian dates was an old one and required no direct contact with Leo to surmise reasons for compromise. Indeed, the second version of *Chronicon* ended in 444 with a mention of the date of Easter.[47] Ending the 455 edition with a mention of Easter echoes this earlier version and is not necessarily a sign of a personal tie to Leo.

Nonetheless, Prosper's admiration for Leo and his support for the primacy of the Roman see are noteworthy elements in the version of *Chronicon* that ends in 455.[48] Prosper shows Leo's success in battling spiritual errors because Leo 'relied on the help of God, who one should know is never missing from the labors of the pious'.[49] Prosper sees Leo as a specially sacred holder of his office. Nonetheless, it is the office that Prosper wants to praise, for, little noticed in this discussion is the fact that Prosper takes a positive view of all the fifth-century bishops of Rome; so, for example, Prosper omits anything negative about Leo's predecessor, Celestine, at the expense of leading Gallic ecclesiastics.[50] Prosper's support for the Roman see is consistent in this version of *Chronicon*, but we need not then believe that he was attached to it.

---

[46] Leo I, *Epp.* 121 (K. Silva-Tarouca [ed.], *S. Leonis Magni: Epistulae contra Eutyches haeresim*, pars 2: *Epistulae post Chalcedonense concilium missae (aa. 452–458)*, Texta et documenta. Series theologica, vol. 20 [Rome, 1935], pp. 126–8) = JK 497; 137 (E. Schwartz [ed.], *ACO*, 2/4.89–90) = JK 511; and 142 (Silva Tarouca, *S. Leoni Magni*, pp. 147–8) = JK 517, were sent to Emperor Marcian, but Prosper's *Epit. chron.* does not indicate that he knew the precise nature of their contents other than knowing that they were about the Easter controversy.

[47] Prosper of Aquitaine, *Epit. chron.* 1352 (MGH.AA 9.479): 'Hoc anno pascha domini VIIII kal. Maias celebratum est, nec erratum est, quia in die XI kal. Mai. dies passionis fuit. Ob cuius reuerentiam natalis urbis sine circensibus transiit'.

[48] Muhlberger, *Fifth Century Chroniclers*, p. 130. Prosper consistently refers to Leo after his accession as a 'sanctus' or 'beatissimus papa'.

[49] Ibid., p. 121; and Prosper of Aquitaine, *Epit. chron.* 1367 (MGH.AA 9.482). Prosper contrasted Leo's success with Aetius' failure; Aetius had relied only on his own judgement, and so his fate demonstrates the problem with Pelagianism, as Muhlberger, *Fifth-Century Chroniclers*, p. 122, observed. This reliance on God explains Leo's successful meeting with Attila: Prosper of Aquitaine, *Epit. chron.* 1367 (MGH.AA 9.482): 'Suscepit hoc negotium cum uiro consulari Auieno et uiro praefectorio Trygetio beatissimus papa Leo auxilio dei fretus, quem sciret numquam piorum laboribus defuisse'.

[50] What is unusual, as Muhlberger, *Fifth-Century Chroniclers*, p. 133, observes, is Prosper's veneration of Leo when he was still alive. This goes alongside Prosper's positive focus on the see of Rome as an institution.

We have no extant letters from Leo to Prosper or *vice versa* that could tell us where either man lived. But if Leo wrote to Prosper, it would not likely have survived; Leo's extant letters have to do with matters of discipline and ecclesiastical jurisdiction, and have thus been preserved in canon law collections.[51] Since Prosper was not a cleric, any letters to him would not have been preserved in these collections.[52] Finally, the verbal and theological influences of Prosper on Leo and *vice versa*, indicate that documents circulated freely, but provide no evidence for Prosper being in Rome when Leo was pope.

Seeing Bishop Leo and the Gallic Aristocrat Prosper in a New Light

If Prosper were not in Rome after 435, his access to information about Leo came primarily through Leo's writings – Leo's *Epistulae* and *Sermones*. But if Prosper remained in Gaul, then the notion that Prosper developed his theology after periods of reading and reflection becomes far more likely. Indeed, Hwang has argued recently that we need to appreciate Prosper as a theologian and scholar whose understanding of the church and its doctrines evolved over his lifetime.[53] Prosper came to his positions on grace, the incarnation of Christ and universal salvation through his own reading and thinking. He drew on Augustine and Leo, but came to advance his own theological position, a fact perhaps easier to accept if we do not see him as an attaché at the Roman see.

Revising Prosper's biography also raises the question of the audience for his writing. So, for example, Prosper's notion of universal salvation extending beyond the borders of the empire in a work that is generally attributed to him, *De uocatione omnium gentium*, is an idea that he might have found in Leo (*Sermo* 82.1 [CCL 138A.508-9]). But Prosper sees God's universal salvific will as an expression of God's grace, whereas Leo used this idea in support of the renewal of the papal see in Rome.[54] This divergence is one sign of Prosper's independent analysis, but it also would be appropriate for a Gallic audience.

Certainly, many of Prosper's works advance support for the bishop of Rome over and above local Gallic ecclesiastics. If we compare Prosper's *Chronicon* with

---

[51] Neil, *Leo the Great*, p. 14.

[52] One sixth-century chronicle does say Prosper was a cleric, though there is no basis for this other than his theological writings. See the *exordium* of *Paschale Campanum* pref.5 (MGH.AA 9.745). This chronicle is dated between 464 and 599.

[53] Hwang, *An Intrepid Lover*, pp. 1–10, 94, and 207–8, on Prosper's re-evaluation of the conflict inspired by Augustine's doctrine of predestination in Gaul.

[54] Ibid., p. 216.

the roughly contemporary anonymous *Chronica Gallica ad annum 452*, we find in the latter a text in which the bishop of Rome hardly matters. Rather, it is the Gallic ecclesiastic elite who are central to the narrative; so, for example, the Gallic chronicler praises the bishop of Marseille for investigating scandals but omits the role of Pope Zosimus in resolving conflict over the primacy of the province of Narbonensis Secunda.[55] Prosper's *Chronicon*, however, advances a strikingly different agenda, highlighting Leo's successes in theological debates within the empire and minimising the role of the Gallic church.[56] This in itself has suggested to some scholars that Prosper was in Rome. Yet the reasoning here is faulty.

Certainly, the fifth-century papacy was eager to support the loyalty of elite provincials, such as Prosper, especially as popes tried to assert their authority outside Rome. Indeed, popes had only limited means to move western bishops; so, for example, although Leo's *Epistulae* 1 and 2 (JK 398 and 399) to the bishops of Aquileia and Altinum in Italy had instructed them to call a provincial synod to address Pelagianism, they never did this.[57] Leo was eager to assert papal primacy and to develop the church bureaucracy, as I have argued elsewhere, but his resources were limited.[58] Philippe Blaudeau observes that aside from the presence of Julian of Cos in the years 451–57, Leo had no network of trustworthy correspondents or agents with adequate connections even to the important imperial court in Constantinople.[59] Rome had to rely only on delegations, which were irregular and were therefore paid less attention. Both the size and organisation of the church bureaucracy under Leo were far less developed than was previously thought; we know the names of three of Leo's notaries, a sign of the bishop's resources, but we do not have certain numbers for the mid-fifth-century church bureaucracy in Rome.[60] No doubt Leo's church organisation was larger than the 140 clergy mentioned for the third-century

---

[55] Muhlberger, *Fifth-Century Chroniclers*, pp. 163–5.

[56] Prosper of Aquitaine, *Epit. chron.* 1247 (MGH.AA 9.466), is the next to last reference to the Gallic church, dated to 412.

[57] Neil, *Leo the Great*, p. 132, notes for *Ep.* 2: 'Leo is careful to respect the local provincial hierarchy of bishops and metropolitans, instructing Bishop Septimus to cooperate with his metropolitan bishop in Venice, to whom he had sent similar letters'.

[58] M.R. Salzman, 'Leo in Rome: The Evolution of Episcopal Authority in the Fifth Century', in G. Bonamente and R. Lizzi Testa (eds), *Istituzioni, carismi ed esercizio del potere (IV-VI secolo d.C.)* (Bari, 2010), pp. 343–56.

[59] P. Blaudeau, 'Between Petrine Ideology and Realpolitik: The See of Constantinople in Roman Geo-ecclesiology (449–536)', in G. Kelly and L. Grig (eds), *Two Romes: Rome and Constantinople in Late Antiquity* (Oxford, 2012), pp. 364–86.

[60] Sotinel, 'Le personnel épiscopal', pp. 105–26; and Sessa, *The Formation of Papal Authority*, pp. 25–30.

church by Eusebius, but it was far less disciplined and efficient than its medieval counterpart.[61]

Political upheavals placed further restrictions on Leo's resources, and made him all the more eager to rely on imperial or aristocratic assistance when possible. Not surprisingly, then, Leo would have been pleased to have a strong supporter like Prosper in Gaul. Moreover, Prosper's works, with their poetry as well as theological focus, were aimed not only at the clergy, but at lay people and elites.[62] It is Prosper's reputation as an independent theologian, an aristocrat and likely an ascetic, yet a supporter of the pope and church of Rome, that may lend further support to the attribution to him of *Epistula ad Demetriadem*. In 1965 Krabbe made a forceful case for Prosper as the author of this work based on its similarities in prose rhythm and scriptural citations to *De uocatione omnium gentium*.[63] Other scholars have pointed to these two works as sharing theological positions.[64] I want to point to another aspect of the letter in support of Prosper's authorship.

Demetrias, daughter of the wealthy Anicii Probi, allegedly wrote to Prosper for spiritual direction. She is so praised as follows:

---

[61] Eusebius, *Hist. eccl.* 6.43.11 (SC 41.156). See n. 60 above for more discussion of the relative lack of organisation of the fifth-century church bureaucracy.

[62] See, for example, J. Delmulle, 'Le *Liber epigrammatum* de Prosper d'Aquitaine, un petit catéchisme augustinien', in M.-F. Gineste-Guipponi and C. Urlacher-Becht (eds), *La renaissance de l'épigramme dans la latinité tardive*. Actes du colloque de Mulhouse, 6–7 October 2011, Collections de l'Université de Strasbourg, Études d'archéologie et d'histoire ancienne (Paris, 2013), 193–209, and the work of M. Cutino.

[63] K.C. Krabbe, *Epistula ad Demetriadem De Vera Humilitate: A Critical Text and Translation with Introduction and Commentary*, Catholic University of America Patristic Studies, vol. 97(Washington, DC, 1965), pp. 77–92, included a lengthy statistical overview of Prosper's prose rhythm and that of *De uocat.* and came to the conclusion that the same person wrote both works. Moreover, on pp. 59–61, Krabbe documented that approximately one-third of the scriptural citations in *Ep. ad Dem.* are found in *De uocat*. B. Neil, 'On True Humility: An Anonymous Letter on Poverty and the Female Ascetic', in W. Mayer, P. Allen and L. Cross (eds), *Prayer and Spirituality in the Early Church*, vol. 4: *The Spiritual Life* (Strathfield, NSW, 2006), pp. 233–46, at pp. 234–5, is more inclined to leave the authorship undecided.

[64] Hwang, *An Intrepid Lover*, pp. 20 and 29, lists it as disputed but authentic. Not all scholars accept this letter's authenticity. See, for one, A. Kurdock, '*Demetrias ancilla dei*: Anicia Demetrias and the Problem of the Missing Patron', in K. Cooper and J. Hillner (eds), *Religion, Dynasty, and Patronage in Early Christian Rome, 300–900* (Cambridge, 2007), pp. 190–224, who mistakenly argued that it was only its inclusion with *De uocat.* in the manuscripts that had suggested Prosper as author.

> Cum splendidissimae sanctimoniae tuae sublime propositum super humilitatis fundamenta consistere pie et sapienter intelligis, in hoc usque, o sacra uirgo Demetrias, dignationem tuae dignitatis inclinas, ut prouectiones tuas etiam meo stilo exigas adiuuari ... tam maturo et erudite animo ... [65]

Demetrias' alleged request is surely a sign of her stature and independence, as Jacobs argued, in contrast to what had happened earlier in her life when, after taking the veil as a teenager (ca. 413–14), Demetrias' mother had written soon after (413/414–417) to the most eminent Christian leaders of the age – Pelagius, Augustine and Jerome – for advice for her daughter's ascetic lifestyle.[66] The mature Demetrias' independence is reinforced by what we know about her. She established in her house (*domus Pincianae*) an ascetic retreat for women.[67] Some scholars date this effort to the period after her return to Rome ca. 414, though others would see it in Africa.[68] Regardless of location, Demetrias' initiative remains, and we see it again at some later date, as Kim Bowes has shown, when she established a church to St Stephen on her estate on Via Latina with features, namely a crypt and altar above, that suggest that the relics to the protomartyr were located here on this private estate.[69] An inscription from the site, as well

---

[65] [Prosper], *Ep. ad Demet.* 1 (Krabbe, *Epistula ad Demetriadem*, p. 138): 'Since in your piety and wisdom you realise that the lofty ideal of your radiant holiness rests upon the foundation of humility, despite your dignity, O holy virgin Demetrias, you even condescended to the point of urging me to write something to assist your progress ... to a soul so mature and well-instructed ... '. (English translation by Krabbe).

[66] A. Jacobs, 'Writing Demetrias: Ascetic Logic in Ancient Christianity', *CH*, 69 (2000): pp. 719–48. Pelagius had written a letter to Demetrias (PL 30.15–45) in 414, and that had apparently spurred Augustine to write letters to her grandmother and mother (*Epp.* 130 [NBA 22.72–108]; 150 [NBA 22.498]; and 188 [NBA 23.176–92]); Jerome followed with *Ep.* 130 (CSEL 56.175–201) to her. As G.D. Dunn, 'The Elements of Ascetical Widowhood: Augustine's *De bono viduitatis* and *Epistula* 130', in W. Mayer, P. Allen and L. Cross (eds), *Prayer and Spirituality in the Early Church*, vol. 4: *The Spiritual Life* (Strathfield, NSW, 2006), pp. 247–56, points out, Augustine was not writing with advice for Demetrias, but, to counter any influence from Pelagius, about how her mother and grandmother should live their widowhood. See also G.D. Dunn, 'The Christian Networks of the Aniciae: The Example of the Letter of Innocent I to Anicia Juliana', *REAug*, 55 (2009), pp. 53–72.

[67] Jerome, *Ep.* 130.6 (CSEL 56.181).

[68] Pelagius, *Ep. ad Demet.* 23 (PL 30.37). Krabbe, *Epistula ad Demetriadem*, p. 4, accepts *in urbe* as the manuscript reading and as a reference to Demetrias' house in Rome. However, there are problems with the manuscript, and alternative readings would locate this ascetic establishment in Africa. See Dunn, 'The Christian Networks of the Aniciae', p. 59.

[69] K. Bowes, *Private Worship, Public Values, and Religious Change in Late Antiquity* (Cambridge, 2007), pp. 94–6.

as *Liber pontificalis*, claimed that Leo had helped in executing this church at Demetrias' wish;[70] he might have had no choice but to accept her putting the relics of the protomartyr in her private church, but the bishop could not have been pleased by this independent assertion of ownership of relics. No wonder, as Bowes notes, soon after this the bishop of Rome built a bigger basilica to Stephen in an attempt to reclaim control of his cult and to diminish the impact of Demetrias' church.[71] Indeed, this letter might have encouraged Demetrias to build her church, for Prosper, assuming his authorship, follows Leo's notion of redemptive almsgiving and advises charity along with humility as a means of spiritual advancement.[72]

It would thus appear as quite plausible if the independent-minded, mature Demetrias, with her aristocratic notions of Christianity and asceticism, wrote to Prosper at some point after 440, the usual dating of this letter.[73] By these decades, Prosper was a known, prominent lay theologian. Like Demetrias, he was not a member of the clergy. Like Demetrias, he too, was probably an aristocrat. These attributes would have appealed to Demetrias. If Prosper were in Gaul, the choice of letter as a genre makes sense, though it is certainly true that letters could also be sent to people when in the same city.[74]

Conclusion

As I have argued, there is no good ancient evidence to see Prosper as Leo's notary or his personal secretary/theological adviser. Yet, based on weak evidence, scholars have hunted for verbal or theological similarities in order to support the notion that Prosper authored some of Leo's writings. That Leo consulted Prosper's works, as those of others, is plausible, but so is it plausible that Prosper consulted Leo's writings. In truth, we cannot say with any certainty that Prosper

---

[70] For the inscription from the site, see E. Diehl, *ILCV*, 1765 = H. Dessau, *ILS*, 8988. Reference to the church is in *Lib. pont.* 47.1 (L. Duchesne and C. Vogel [eds], *Le* Liber pontificalis*: Texte, introduction et commentaire*, BEFAR [Paris, 1955 (2nd edn)], vol. 1, p. 238. Eng. trans. in R. Davis, *The Book of Pontiffs* (Liber Pontificalis): *The Ancient Biographies of the First Ninety Roman Bishops to AD 715*, TTH, vol. 6 (Liverpool, 2000 [2nd edn]).

[71] Bowes, *Private Worship*, pp. 94–6.

[72] [Prosper], *Ep. ad Demet.* 5 (Krabbe, *Epistula ad Demetriadem*, p. 158). The letter writer cites 1 Tim. 5:8 for the need to take care of your household before giving charity.

[73] We cannot date the letter with certainty, but most scholars place it between 440 and 460, based on its ties to *De uocat*. See Hwang, *An Intrepid Lover*, pp. 201–21.

[74] Most of Jerome's letters to Marcella, for instance, were written when they were both in Rome, according to Cain, *The Letters of Jerome*, p. 68.

authored any of Leo's writings, or even was in Rome at the time of Leo's papacy, that is from 440 to 461.

The historiography of the relationship between Prosper and Leo is, however, most interesting for what it says about modern notions of the papal bureaucracy. Instead of a fully organised, efficiently run papal organisation with influential intellectuals like Prosper at its head, ghost-writing papal documents, I have proposed that Leo was a bishop deeply engaged with pastoral care and theological speculation. Moreover, the bishop of Rome, Leo, was eager to gain assistance from lay officials and aristocrats, both at home and abroad. Christian aristocrats like Prosper and Demetrias were key patrons and supporters of the bishop in his quest to assert a unified western Christendom in the face of numerous competing Christian sects and confessional groups.

Chapter 7
Narrating Papal Authority (440–530): The Adaptation of *Liber Pontificalis* to the Apostolic See's Developing Claims[*]

Philippe Blaudeau

There is scarcely need to exaggerate the importance of *Liber pontificalis*, or *Liber episcopalis in quo continentur acta beatorum pontificum urbis Romae (The Pontifical Book in which are gathered the activities of the blessed pontiffs of the City of Rome)*. The series of biographical notices that makes up *Liber pontificalis* was carried on from one continuator to the next until, in 1479, Bartolomeo Sacchi da Platina replaced it with a model better suited to the dawn of the modern age.[1] In this sense, *Liber pontificalis* is a written monument, even if not properly speaking a literary one, able both to stimulate its own perpetuation for almost a millennium and to provoke a famous imitation by Agnellus of Ravenna (around 839), otherwise extremely hostile to Roman initiatives regarding his church.[2] Its capacity to do this, a form of continual rebirth, is perplexing and calls for a consideration of the work's original characteristics in order to discern its dynamic force. Such an investigation, initiated long ago and pursued with the characteristic rigour and insight of two of the greatest scholars, Mommsen[3] and Duchesne,[4] at the end of the nineteenth century, has been recently renewed,

---

[*] This chapter was translated into English by Mathew Dal Santo. It is dedicated to Françoise Prévot, emeritus professor of Roman and Ancient Christian History at University of East-Paris (France).

[1] Cf. W. Berschin, *Biographie und Epochenstil im lateinischen Mittelalter*, vol. 1: *Von der Passio Perpetuae zu den Dialogi Gregors des Großen*, Quellen und Untersuchungen zur lateinischen Philologie des Mittelalters, vol. 8 (Stuttgart, 1986), p. 270.

[2] *Liber pontificalis ecclesiae Ravennatis*. The most recent edition is D. Mauskopf-Deliyannis, CCM, vol. 199 (Turnhout, 2006).

[3] Th. Mommsen (ed.), *Liber pontificalis*, MGH.GPR, vol. 1 (Berlin, 1898).

[4] L. Duchesne and C. Vogel (eds), *Le Liber pontificalis: Texte, introduction et commentaire*, BEFAR, 3 vols (Paris, 1955–7 [2nd edn]). The notes and commentary proposed in recent translations in modern languages (Davies and Auburn) have not been considered as decisive for the purposes of this chapter.

above all by H. Geertman.[5] It has allowed us to appreciate just how Roman the biographical genre was from which *Liber pontificalis* stemmed. Its subject was none other than the head of the institution that stepped into the shoes of imperial power, concentrating in the *urbs* the display of its religious power and establishing, with the *urbs* at its centre, an efficient network of command and representation. In this way, each pontifical biography is fashioned according to identifiable categories with distinct rubrics, to which we shall come back later. It is enough to note for the moment that our series of lives belongs to a long tradition which, notwithstanding significant transformations, reaches back to Suetonius.[6]

Yet the deep-rootedness of *Liber pontificalis* in a peculiarly Roman tradition is not accidental but deliberate: its authors intended to make use of a form of historiography that deliberately challenged alternative influences coming from the East. For, at Rome,[7] no text is to be found that illustrates, in detail, the role played by the see of St Peter in salvation history by collating the most important documents and inserting them in an orderly, chronological narrative. Hardly atoned for by the brief chronicle (complete up to 455) by Prosper of Aquitaine, this absence is surprising. Doubtless, it is connected to the limited impact of Eusebius of Caesarea's works, despite Rufinus's continuation, with Jerome's failure to compose his own church history also perhaps adding to what otherwise appears to be a remarkable lacuna.[8] Equally, it probably also reflects a

---

[5] See H. Geertman (ed.), *Atti del colloquio internazionale 'Il Liber Pontificalis e la storia materiale' (Rome, 21–22 février 2002)*, Mededelingen van het Nederlands Instituut te Rome, Antiquity, vols 60–61 (Rome, 2003). Two of the contributions by Geertman himself are especially important here: 'Documenti, redattori e la formazione del testo del Liber Pontificalis', pp. 267–84 (reprinted in H. Geertman [ed.], *Hic fecit basilicam: Studi sul Liber Pontificalis e gli edifici ecclesiastici di Roma da Silvestro a Silverio* [Leuven, 2004], pp. 149–67); and 'Le biografie del Liber Pontificalis dal 311 al 535. Testo e commentario', pp. 285–355 (reprinted in Geertman, *Hic fecit basilicam*, pp. 169–235). Some more precision is to be found in the contribution of H. Geertman, 'La genesi del *Liber Pontificalis* romano. Un processo di organizzazione della memoria', in F. Bougard and M. Sot (eds), *Liber, Gesta, histoire. Écrire l'histoire des évêques et des papes, de l'Antiquité au XXIᵉ siècle* (Turnhout, 2009), pp. 37–107.

[6] See Berschin, *Biographie*, pp. 275–6 and R. McKitterick, 'Roman Texts and Roman History in the Early Middle Ages', in C. Bolgia, R. McKitterick and J. Osborne (eds), *Rome across Time and Space: Cultural Transmission and the Exchange of Ideas, c. 500–1400* (Cambridge, 2011), pp. 28–33.

[7] Cf. N. Ertl, 'Diktatoren frühmittelalterlichen Papstbriefe', *Archiv für Urkundenforschung*, 15 (1938): pp. 57–60.

[8] For his intention see *Vita Malchi* 10 (PL 23.60); and Y.-M. Duval, 'Jérôme et l'histoire de l'Église du IVᵉ siècle', in B. Pouderon and Y.-M. Duval (eds), *L'historiographie*

setting characterised by lower polemical intensity than in the East, where the rise of Constantinople led to a certain intensification of expressions of identity that were all the more impassioned for being aware of the imperative of persuading imperial power.

But the main reason is surely to be found elsewhere, stemming in all likelihood from an entrenched Petrine ideology, one so clearly organised by Leo that with him we may properly speak of 'Petrinology'. For the conception of this ideology, however gladly affirmed later, presupposed a highly peculiar understanding of time or, more precisely, duration. Interpreted as applying impartially to his heir, however personally unworthy the latter might have been, Christ's promise bestowed on Peter's successor the *principatus*, the *plenitudo potestatis* in a church by definition immune to Augustine's law regarding the evolution of earthly institutions. As a result, it was never deemed necessary, with a few notable exceptions,[9] to make historical the instrument for affirming papal authority. On the contrary, this was far better guaranteed by the unchanging Divine Voice and much better established in fact by recourse to the law.

In the eyes of Leo and Gelasius, therefore, the papacy's mission received no more than confirmation from history's facts and events, necessary but nevertheless secondary. Under these conditions, the best display of Rome's faithfulness to its vocation lay not so much in demonstrating the correctness or even the farsightedness of its actions as in recalling the faultlessness of its theological and juridical positions. While it was occasionally necessary to compose a brief outline of the historical facts, as for example in *Gesta de nomine Acacii*,[10] until the end of the fifth century it was viewed as counter-productive and to some extent inadvisable to expose, by way of a more ample narrative, the teachings of the apostolic see to the risks of contingency and variability inherent in the writing of history.

It took an important quarrel to modify this conception without doing away with it entirely, giving birth thereby to a text that was original and yet typically Roman and whose roots lay in existing papal lists and catalogues. Dating from

---

de l'Église des premiers siècles, Théologie historique, vol. 114 (Paris, 2001), pp. 381–408, at 398-9.

[9] Cf. Prosper of Aquitaine, *Epit. Chron.* 1367 (MGH.AA 9.482): 'nam tota legatione dignanter accepta ita summi sacerdotis praesentia rex [Attila] gauisus est et bello abstinere praecipit et ultra Danuuium pace discederet ... '; and 1369 (MGH.AA 9.482): 'Synodus Calchedonensis peracta Eutyche Dioscoroque damnatis ... confirmata uniuersaliter fide, quae de incarnatione uerbi secundum euangelicam et apostolicam doctrinam per sanctum papam Leonem praedicabatur'.

[10] *Gesta de nomine Acacii* (*Collectio Avellana*, Ep. 99) (CSEL 35.440–53).

the beginning of the sixth century, the first compilation of *Liber pontificalis* betrayed the necessity of recording the memory of a recent period of conflict – the Laurentian schism – by locating it within the framework of the apostolic succession. Thus, what we may call the *Urtext* was almost certainly motivated by a polemical goal: indeed, it exists in lively competition (without being able to do more than merely guess at an order of priority) with another version, a fragment of which is conserved in the manuscript *Veronensis* XXII (20). According to Duchesne's observations, the latter, clearly Laurentian in prejudice, cannot have been as lengthy as the rival version, despite containing a complete catalogue of popes. Further, that part of it that is preserved (no more than a few concluding lines from the *uita* of Anastasius II and a very hostile account of Symmachus and his episcopacy) suggests that a certain development took place in respect of those papal *uitae* most exposed to continuing adverse claims (from Simplicius? or only from Gelasius?) in the context of schism (with the East or within the Roman church), with the whole inhering within a broader apologetic and polemic purpose.[11] According to Wirbelauer, the text favourable to Laurentius's party was composed in order to apply pressure (in a conciliatory spirit towards the East) to one of Hormisdas's legations, with that of 515 being doubtless the best candidate.[12] In contrast to this short text, *Liber pontificalis*, otherwise composed in much less sophisticated language, is introduced by a fictional exchange of letters in which Jerome beseeches Damasus for a history lesson.[13] If we accept that this alleged correspondence formed part of the original text, its purpose seems to have been to signify that its authority derived from the

---

[11] Duchesne and Vogel, *Le* Liber pontificalis, pp. xxx–xxxii and xlvii–xlviii.

[12] E. Wirbelauer, *Zwei Päpste in Rom: der Konflikt zwischen Laurentius und Symmachus (498–514): Studien und Texte*, Quellen und Forschungen zur antiken Welt, vol. 16 (Munich, 1993), pp. 143–5.

[13] Duchesne and Vogel, *Le* Liber pontificalis, p. 117: 'Vt actus gestorum a beati Petri apostoli principatum usque ad uestra tempora, quae gesta sunt in sedem tuam, nobis per ordinem enararre digneris ... ' On what was surely the original relation between *Lib. pont.* and Damasus' figure, see K. Blair-Dixon, 'Memory and Authority in Sixth-Century Rome: The *Liber Pontificalis* and the *Collectio Avellana*', in K. Cooper and J. Hillner (eds), *Religion, Dynasty, and Patronage in Early Christian Rome, 300–900* (Cambridge, 2007), p. 60. In this paper, however, Blair-Dixon is unaware of Geertman's hypothesis (2002) and proposes an analysis of how the *Collectio Avellana* emerged that we do not share. See my own communication 'A propos des sections 3 et 4a de l'Avellana (n°51–78): comment documenter le rejet de Chalcédoine manifesté en Orient?', in A. Evers (ed.), *Emperors, Bishops, Senators: The Significance of the Collectio Avellana (367–553 AD)*, Rome, 1–2 April 2011 (Loyola Universiy of Chicago John Felice Rome Center, Royal Netherlands Institute of Rome, Istituto Patristico Augustinianum) (forthcoming).

apostolic see itself rather than from a merely personal initiative, even that of a father of the church.

A succession of *uitae* then unfolds which, starting with St Peter, each offers a narrative whose internal organisation deliberately prioritises the following elements:

1. Prosopographical and chronological information relative to each pope;
2. Developments in ecclesiastical administration, liturgy and doctrine at Rome;
3. The narration of episodes preferably concerning external relations;
4. Material preoccupations and papal munificence; and
5. Figures regarding ordinations.

These, the main supports of the narrative framework of each *uita*, are readily found in the extant versions.[14] For all that, the content of the first *Liber pontificalis* is not easy to reconstitute with regard to its witnesses. As mentioned, the models that aim to reconstitute it are today themselves under revision. For Geertman's recent hypotheses have shaken a certain number of propositions taken for granted since Mommsen and Duchesne. Rather than seeing the Felician (F) and Cononian (K) abridgements as the versions closest to the first edition, the Dutch scholar considers them to be summaries from a later stage of publication, the result of a re-writing of *Liber pontificalis* aimed at a broader correction of grammar and style. If this is so, then the most complete version preserved (P) would be the relic of the oldest redaction.[15] But Geertman goes further, on the one hand comparing the text of the abridgements with that of the long version for the pontificates of Hormisdas and John I,[16] while on the other minutely examining the letter of the notices from Miltiades to John II.[17] He believes that this first phase (P1) is the work of several redactors charged with three rubrics (corresponding to numbers 1, 5 and 2 – whose contents are limited in this case to the administration and the liturgy, as indicated above). To this same period of re-writing belong some nearly contemporaneous additions that relate to rubric 4.[18] Geertman then suggests that fuller accounts were rapidly introduced into the *editio prior*. These are most often dedicated either to double

---

[14] Geertman, 'Documenti, redattori', p. 267.
[15] Ibid., pp. 268–71.
[16] This is the specific aim of Geertman, 'Documenti, redattori'.
[17] See Geertman, 'Le biografie'.
[18] Geertman, 'Genesi', pp. 39–40.

ordinations (in the case of Liberius, Boniface I, Symmachus and Boniface II) or to theological disputes and schismatic movements.[19]

Moreover, Geertman postulates that those who compiled and introduced into *Liber pontificalis* the more detailed historical notices began their redaction following the pontificate of Hormisdas, partly in order to highlight the latter pope's merit as a peace-maker in the aftermath of the quarrels occasioned by the Acacian schism, an insertion partly revealed by the use of the formula *sub huius episcopatum* (or *huius temporibus*),[20] typical of such additions. In this respect, those responsible for this amplification (called Phase 2 – P2 – and realised by a different bureau in the papal chancery) not only described Rome's often fraught relations with the court at Ravenna and Constantinople, but also took care to list the donations made to the bishop of Rome by the representatives of temporal power.[21] This suggestion is particularly compelling because it allows us to form a vision of the whole that corresponds to the insights uncovered by the research we propose to reproduce here: that is, the date of the original composition of the *Urtext* must be located at the beginning of the sixth century. Duchesne placed the latter's origins under the reign of Hormisdas, assuming that several years were necessary to ensure the adoption of the historical fictions peddled by the false partisans of Symmachus. According to Duchesne, the work must have been continued as far as the notice regarding Felix IV (III) (526–30),[22] the end point of our thesis here, by two authors distinguished only with difficulty from each other. Following Geertman's persuasive revision of the more complex models, however, the second phase of composition must have been completed around 535, extending *Liber pontificalis* from the *uita* of St Peter to that of John II.[23]

To summarise, the initial version (P1) of *Liber pontificalis* does not derive from a propaganda initiative by Pope Hormisdas, despite appearing remarkably faithful to his underlying preoccupations, including the method chosen to win over the clergy. In the framework of the conflict of memory that continued to mark the Roman church, therefore, this text declared itself in favour of Symmachus at a time when renewed contact with Constantinople had revived the contemporary

---

[19] Geertman, 'Documenti, redattori', pp. 268–70.

[20] Geertman, 'Le biografie', p. 349, n. 197. See also Geertman, 'Documenti, redattori', p. 289, n. 3.

[21] Geertman, 'Genesi', p. 42.

[22] The first edition, from which two abbreviated forms would have been the nearest according to Duchesne and Vogel, *Le* Liber pontificalis, p. lxvii. On pp. xxxix–xli and xlviii Duchesne also thinks that it would have been prolongated to Silverius' pontificate (badly treated in the first part of the existing notice) by someone faithful to the former legate, Dioscorus, notably interested in the double elections.

[23] Geertman, 'La genesi', p. 42. Geertman concedes that the second phase is linked with the strong conflict between the supporters of Dioscorus and Boniface II (p. 43).

repercussions of the crisis. All the same, the text is not entirely dependent on the line the false Symmachans defended, remaining instead silent on their favourite argument: namely, the impossibility of judging a pope (doubtless because it would allow an intolerable doubt to persist regarding Symmachus's blameworthiness). This edition targeted a public primarily composed of Roman clerics,[24] including the lower orders, which obviously does not rule out the possibility that lay circles were also concerned. It set itself the task of re-establishing the support of the ministers of the holy see for their head, identifying their majority approval as the legitimising criterion of the pope's accession.[25] This promotion of the union between pope and Roman clergy in mutual respect for their obviously unequal functions[26] led shortly thereafter to the exaltation of a second theme much debated at the end of Theodoric's reign: the expression of unflinching support for the popes' eastern policies so long as they were conducted coherently, that is to say in conformity with Leo's actions. For the embellishments applied to the narrative underline an idea too easily overlooked at first sight: the least sign of a papal backflip in eastern matters was not only serious, but a leading cause of internal division. What is more, by bringing a somewhat weightier geo-ecclesial affair to the relevant rubric (3), our embellishers recast the original lesson of the *uitae*: the initiatives taken by the popes to put an end to what were obviously eastern-born controversies have now become determinative. They confirmed the appropriateness of the apostolic see's claim to primacy, lending weight to its centrality and testifying to its acknowledgement, even when the latter was delayed.

Let us examine each of these elements:

(1) The claim of primacy underwent, it is known, a significant extension during Leo's pontificate. When doctrinal conflict erupted, Leo took it upon

---

[24] This would be recognised, according to P. Carmassi, 'La prima redazione del *Liber Pontificalis* nel quadro delle fonti contemporanee. Osservazioni in margine alla *vita* di Simmaco', in *Atti del colloquio internazionale 'Il* Liber Pontificalis *e la storia materiale' (Rome, 21–22 février 2002)*, Mededelingen van het Nederlands Instituut te Rome, Antiquity, vols 60–61 (Rome, 2003), pp. 235–66, at p. 254, under the *curiositas temporum sacerdotalis* formula used as the main reason for giving satisfaction to Jerome by the alleged Damasus.

[25] Neither the place of consecration nor the identity of the ordaining prelate is decisive. Even the *sententia plurimorum* once alleged by Symmachus has shown its own limits (Wirbelauer, *Zwei Päpste*, pp. 14–15).

[26] This gives the opportunity for a further part (Boniface II to Silverius) of the tale. Maybe this one was written under the influence of the party still partisan to Dioscorus, the legate, because the official practice of papal designation by the living pope (as in the case of Boniface II or the former, as suggested, Felix IV [III] is strongly denounced). See Carmassi, 'Prima redazione', p. 252 and Duchesne and Vogel, *Le* Liber pontificalis, p. 281.

himself to preach the 'correct' apostolic doctrine direct to the eastern churches, declining merely to limit himself to guaranteeing the position adopted by one of the parties involved (usually Alexandria).[27] This conviction finds a revealing echo in *Liber pontificalis*, where Leo appears responsible not only for uncovering and denouncing the Eutychian heresy, but also, as pope, for unmasking and condemning the Nestorian heresy.[28] The works of Cyril of Alexandria, like Celestine's involvement in the matter, are thus conveniently erased. Moreover, Leo's christological teaching becomes an integral part of the timeless deposit of the faith,[29] reflected in *Liber pontificalis* through the generic insistence on its place in the papal archives.[30] This conviction was accompanied by the equal certainty that later difficulties in no way affected the accuracy of Leo's refutation.[31] On the contrary, the popularised papal version broadcast at length in the letters and treatises of a Felix or a Gelasius – otherwise famous for his writings –[32] encourages the belief that the rupture in relations between Rome and Constantinople was exclusively the result of the doings of Peter Mongus and then Acacius.[33] Reduced to such a portrayal of the characters involved in notices which, so far as the pontificates of Simplicius and Gelasius are concerned, are often only rough sketches, this simplification – which makes surprisingly little

---

[27] See E. Schwartz, *Der Prozeß des Eutyches,* Sitzungsberichte der Bayerischen Akademie der Wissenschaften, Philosophisch-historische Abteilung, vol. 5 (Munich, 1929), p. 91.

[28] Duchesne and Vogel, *Le* Liber pontificalis, p. 238. See P. Blaudeau, 'Rome contre Alexandrie? L'interprétation pontificale de l'enjeu monophysite (de l'émergence de la controverse eutychienne au schisme acacien 448–484)', *Adamantius*, 12 (2006): pp. 140–216, at 169–72.

[29] The belief was taken willingly from the pope's expressions after 461. See Blaudeau, 'Rome contre Alexandrie?', pp. 197–9.

[30] Duchesne and Vogel, *Le* Liber Pontificalis, p. 238: 'Iterum multas epistulas fidei misit beatissimus Leo archiepiscopus quae hodie reconditae archiuo tenentur'. On the notion of the late antique Roman archive see the remarks of Blair-Dixon, 'Memory', pp. 74–6.

[31] *Lib. pont.* surprisingly also asserts the importance of Hilary's legacy (Duchesne and Vogel, *Le* Liber pontificalis, p. 242 : 'Hic fecit decretalem et per uniuersas Orientem exparsit et epistulas de fide catholica, confirmans III synodos Niceni, Epheseni et Calcedonense uel tomum sancti episcopi Leonis; et damnauit Eutychem et Nestorium uel omnes sequaces eorum et uel omnes hereses; et confirmans dominationem et principatum sanctae sedis catholicae et apostolicae ... '), probably in order to assign to him a strenuous action against Eutychian beliefs – and to give him a significant place in the list dramatically cut off by Anastasius II.

[32] Duchesne and Vogel, *Le* Liber pontificalis, pp. 255 and 257, n. 14.

[33] See ibid., p. 252 and 255; and P. Blaudeau, 'Motifs et structures de divisions ecclésiales. Le schisme acacien', *AHC*, 39 (2007): pp. 65–98.

of Timothy Aelurus, despite his vilification in the corresponding papal letters[34] – places the blame on Pope Anastasius II's perfidy. His attempt to find a negotiated settlement with the church of Constantinople, where Acacius' memory was still venerated, is portrayed as a betrayal,[35] whereas the Laurentian fragment credits the pope with it as a success.[36] For *Liber pontificalis'* embellishers, the divine punishment that struck the pope down – a *mors haeretici* that recalled the *mors persecutorum*[37] – was retribution for Anastasius' betrayal while its inevitable result was the quarrelling that arose upon his death.

Although the account of Symmachus's pontificate completely ignores eastern issues, this was perhaps less a reflection of any lack of information – since the period's events were by then well-known[38] – than of intent.[39] The silence only lent weight to the notion that the exercise of Rome's primacy had been interrupted in the East. What mattered was to draw attention to the causes that lay behind this unfortunate situation and to establish responsibility for it: thus, the Laurentian schism was presented as entirely the fault of the Roman factions (in the Senate as in the church),[40] as if only on such grounds could papal authority be impaired. However, the schism had been indirectly brought about

---

[34] Blaudeau, 'Rome contre Alexandrie?', pp. 184–9. On the report on the Acacian schism preserved in *Lib. pont.* see also Blair-Dixon, 'Memory', p. 67.

[35] Duchesne and Vogel, *Le* Liber pontificalis, p. 258.

[36] Ibid., p. 44: ' ... imperatorem Anastasium directa per Cresconium et Germanum episcopos, quae tanta scripturarum caelestium auctoritate suffulta est, ut qui hanc intenta mente sub diuino timore perlegerit, inaniter hactenus inter ecclesias Orientis et Italiae tam schisma nefarium perdurare cognoscit ... '

[37] This identification is permitted by two communications given to the pope of the condemnation inflicted on Emperor Anastasius, who would be so strongly associated with ancient pagan emperors so vehemently denounced by Lactantius. Duchesne and Vogel, *Le* Liber pontificalis, p. 270. This supposed imperial death during a storm on the night of 9 July 518 is widespread among the sources (see Duchesne and Vogel, *Le* Liber Pontificalis, p. 273, n.13; and C. Capizzi, *L'imperatore Anastasio I [491–518]. Studio sulla sua vita, la sua opera e la sua personalità*, Orientalia Christiana Analecta, vol. 184 [Rome, 1969], pp. 261–73). The most ancient text to say so is probably Theodorus Lector's (written in 518–19) if we agree with Hansen (*Chron.*, a. 518 = F 77, G.Ch. Hansen [ed.], *Theodoros Anagnostes. Kirchengeschichte*, GCS n.F., vol. 3 [Berlin, 1995,2nd edn], p. 151) that Victor of Tonnona witnessed it. Here one finds that the *basileus* was struck by lightning in the bedroom where he hid.

[38] See Duchesne and Vogel, *Le* Liber pontificalis, pp. xxxv–xxxvi; and Geertman, 'Documenti, redattori', p. 271.

[39] On the rapport between Symmachus and the eastern empire see P. Blaudeau, *Le Siège de Rome et l'Orient (448–536)*, CEFR, vol. 460 (Rome, 2012), pp. 166–9.

[40] Duchesne and Vogel, *Le* Liber pontificalis, pp. 260–1. See Wirbelauer, *Zwei Päpste*, pp. 10 and 64 especially.

by the situation in the East, itself provoked by the scheming of a 'Eutychian' and the inconstancy of an archbishop of Constantinople.

To believe *Liber pontificalis*, therefore, Hormisdas was responsible for seizing the initiative with the empire, 'displaying the humanity of the apostolic see,'[41] in contrast to those whom the text hardly bothers to distinguish other than by the unflattering title, 'the Greeks'.[42] This somewhat misleading representation implicitly suggested that, the Roman clergy having regained its unity, the empire's leading see was now free to demonstrate its concern for external affairs. Emperor Anastasius, doubtless seeing through such benevolence, forestalled any agreement and rejected the pope's *libellus* (also known as the Formulary of Hormisdas).[43] But after Anastasius' death, also attributed to the *nutus diuinitatis*,[44] this formulary, accompanied as it was by a justification of Acacius's culpability by the papal legate, Dioscorus,[45] became the condition for a return to the *pax ecclesiae*. Indeed, the ending of the schism required the written acceptance – an obligation specifically imposed to underline its irrevocability – of a *libellus*[46] whose much-vaunted preservation in the Roman archives guaranteed both its content and its conformity with the changeless *praedicatio* found in Leo's letters.[47] For its part, Dioscorus's supplementary gloss merely strengthened the representation thus broadcast by portraying the conflict as one of personalities. It thereby reaffirmed the immovability of Rome's position even as it signalled a

---

[41] Duchesne and Vogel, *Le* Liber pontificalis, p. 269.

[42] On the generic significance of this term on the Roman side see P. Blaudeau, '*Vice mea* : Remarques sur les représentations pontificales auprès de l'empereur d'Orient dans la seconde moitié du Ve siècle (452–496)', *MEFRA*, 113 (2001): pp. 1059–1123, at pp. 1104–5; and P. Blaudeau, 'Symbolique médicale et dénonciation de l'hérésie: le cas monophysite dans les sources pontificales de la seconde moitié du Ve siècle', in V. Boudon and B. Pouderon (eds), *Les Pères de l'Église face à la science médicale de leur temps*. Actes du 3e colloque d'études patristiques (Paris, 9–11 septembre 2004) organisé par l'Institut Catholique de Paris et l'Université de Tours avec la participation de l'UMR –CNRS 8062 'Médecine grecque', Théologie historique, vol. 117 (Paris, 2005), pp. 497–524, at pp. 515–17.

[43] Duchesne and Vogel, *Le* Liber pontificalis, p. 269.

[44] Ibid., p. 270.

[45] The P text, in its three classes (Duchesne and Vogel, *Le* Liber pontificalis, p. 270), is lacunary concerning Dioscorus' explanation, when compared with the Felician abbreviated form (Duchesne and Vogel, *Le* Liber pontificalis, pp. 102–3). On the reasons for such a situation see Duchesne and Vogel, *Le* Liber pontificalis, pp. 273–4, n. 19 ; and especially Geertman, 'Le biografie', p. 348, n. 195, who distinguishes himself from them forcefully.

[46] Duchesne and Vogel, *Le* Liber pontificalis, p. 270.

[47] Ibid., p. 102. See also Geertman, 'Le biografie', p. 348, n. 195. On the value of such an arrangement in the Roman performative communication see Blaudeau 'Rome contre Alexandrie?', pp. 157–9.

clear division of responsibilities. To the historical efficiency thereby lent to this action – no resistance being recorded other than the fleeting objections of John of Constantinople and his clergy[48] – corresponds that of Pope John I, doubtless narrated by a continuator.[49] Obliged by Theodoric to go to Constantinople, John, according to *Liber pontificalis*, gained the emperor's complete agreement to his requests.[50] To be sure, the text does not neglect to underline that the embassy owed its success just as much to the senators who accompanied the pope, but this only strengthens the overall message: by their presence the senators demonstrated Rome's unanimity behind a pope who had been manhandled by a heretic king (an Arian, as the Felician abridgement clarifies at this point).[51] Revered by Emperor Justin, Pope John I thus exalted a primacy whose logical outcome was to make St Peter's successor spiritual father to the emperor.

(2) The portrayal of the Acacian schism and its consequences, to which each of the *uitae* returns, leads naturally to the question of steady relations with Constantinople properly speaking, a subject that undergoes much development in *Liber pontificalis*. Faced with what it identifies as a major issue, whatever its risk of turning to Rome's disfavour, the redactor of the additions seemingly wished to underline the apostolic see's power of attraction. With the expression, *uenit de Graecia(s) relatio*, repeated no fewer than three times,[52] the author stressed how far the pope, assisted by his synod, found himself called upon to judge the issue; he did not arrogate to himself the investigation's initiative. Once the papal throne had been solicited in this manner, it was then its vocation to become the *ecclesia executrix*,[53] which rather clumsily translated the theory of the leading see's rights developed by Gelasius.[54] In addition to inserting a juridical reference of this kind

---

[48] Duchesne and Vogel, *Le* Liber pontificalis, p. 102.

[49] One cannot explain the radical change of treatment concerning King Theodoric in another way. See infra.

[50] Duchesne and Vogel, *Le* Liber pontificalis, p. 275: 'Qui vero papa Iohannes vel senatores viri religiosi omnia meruerunt'. On the different considerations of this result in various sources see P. Goubert, 'Autour du voyage à Byzance du pape S. Jean I', *OCP*, 24 (1958): pp. 339–52, at pp. 350–51.

[51] See Duchesne and Vogel, *Le* Liber pontificalis, p. 104.

[52] Simplicius (Duchesne and Vogel, *Le* Liber pontificalis, p. 249); Felix III [II] (Duchesne and Vogel, *Le* Liber pontificalis, p. 252 – with the variant *uenit relatio ab imperatorem Zenonem* [sic!]); and Gelasius (Duchesne and Vogel, *Le* Liber Pontificalis, p. 255).

[53] Duchesne and Vogel, *Le* Liber pontificalis, p. 249.

[54] See Gelasius' third letter to the Dardanians (*Collectio Avellana, Ep.* 95 [CSEL 35.372, 374 and 384). The formula used in *Lib. pont.* may come from Simplicius' letter, as some of Gelasius' allusions would suggest (*Collectio Avellana, Ep.* 95 [CSEL 35.379, 383, 386 and 397). See Blaudeau, '*Vice mea*', pp. 1087–93.

into the biographical narrative, the account also conveys another, somewhat offbeat assertion, suggesting a particular intensification of envoys from the East up to the end of the fifth century. Historically, however, it was rather Acacius' silence that characterised the lead-up to the schism.[55] Preferring contradiction to silence, *Liber pontificalis* thus manages to publish a curious annotation washing Simplicius clean of all suspicion of dissimulation.[56] The image thereby projected was one in which the Roman see remained constantly at the centre of events. That John Talaïa found refuge at Rome (an event mistakenly placed under Gelasius' pontificate) further accentuated this impression.[57] As a result, Rome emerges as that place where all relevant information converges, where the victims come to plead their case, a place of judgement and condemnation,[58] but also where the means for repentance were to be found.[59] Indeed, it is from Rome that flows, under Hormisdas, the desire to re-establish union, depriving Emperor Justin's 518 initiative of all originality in advance.

(3) To this polarised construction of space was added, insofar as the account echoed recent events, an intensification of the honours shown by the emperor or his representatives to the pope. From this perspective, the welcome that the papal legates received at Constantinople in 519 – unlike similar missions in 483, 515 or 517 – 'repeated' the manner of John I's advent, so much so that the emperor himself, rather than his nephew, was presented as meeting the apostolic see's envoys.[60] Indeed, the novelty of John I's journey to Constantinople made it a model for other narratives (one taken up again in part in the notice dedicated to Pope Agapetus), by presenting an ideal image of the relationship obtaining between a

---

[55] Blaudeau, 'Rome contre Alexandrie?', pp. 153–5.

[56] This is to the astonishment of Duchesne and Vogel, *Le* Liber pontificalis, p. 251, n. 6.

[57] Duchesne and Vogel, *Le* Liber pontificalis, p. 255. On the coming of Talaïa in 483 and its consequences see P. Blaudeau, *Alexandrie et Constantinople (451–491). De l'histoire à la géo-ecclésiologie*, BEFAR, vol. 327 (Rome, 2006), pp. 199–215 and 478–80.

[58] Duchesne and Vogel, *Le* Liber pontificalis, pp. 252 and 254. The condemnation of Acacius and Mongus in perpetuity would be a result, according to the tale, of Gelasius' and his synod's judgement. This is not true. See P. Blaudeau, 'Condamnation et absolution synodales. Le cas du légat pontifical Misène de Cumes (483, 495)', in *I concili della cristianità occidentale secoli III-V*, XXX Incontro di studiosi dell'antichità cristiana, Roma 3–5 maggio 2001, SEAug, vol. 78 (Rome, 2002), pp. 513–21. It shows how important Gelasius' decisions remained, even though they were imperfectly recorded.

[59] To such an extent, a similar *libellus*, so to speak, would have been prepared already while Felix III [II] was pope (Duchesne and Vogel, *Le* Liber pontificalis, p. 252). But, at that time, conditions for the restoration of the Roman communion were not so strictly and dryly expressed. See Blaudeau, 'Symbolique médicale', pp. 511–17.

[60] Duchesne and Vogel, *Le* Liber pontificalis, p. 270. See recently B. Croke, 'Justinian under Justin: Reconfiguring a Reign', *ByzZ*, 100 (2007): pp. 13–56, at p. 29.

pope and an emperor about to become a direct protagonist in Italy's affairs. Yet the glorious reception shown the 'vicar of Blessed Peter' was meaningful only to the extent that the emperor was, unquestionably, catholic.[61] Only then could he perform the three gestures that were supposed to display his acceptance of the apostolic see's leading role in the church: the emperor bowed down (*humiliauit*) before the pope, venerated (*adorauit*) him and had himself crowned by him.[62] Research has shown that such a representation far exceeded both events as then observed and the meaning attributed to them at Byzantium.[63] Unapologetically maximalist in conception, *Liber pontificalis*' account functioned as a narrative rendition of the relationship between priesthood and empire that, however elaborated by Felix and Gelasius, had lacked even the slightest opportunity for dramatisation during the reigns of either Zeno (now consigned to oblivion)[64] or Anastasius. Thus, the powerful expressiveness with which the events of 526 were described reflected the intense satisfaction aroused by the apparent, if illusory, agreement which the emperor had finally given to papal theories regarding Rome's role. Such expressiveness also anticipated the pope's personal triumph when, shortly thereafter, he was called not only to a confessor's glory but to a martyr's, on account of the maltreatment to which he was subjected, on his return to Italy, by an aged Theodoric, himself soon to be punished with death, *nutu dei*.[65]

To complete this demonstration, a final observation can be added. On the basis of the list of donations signalled at the start, a catalogue of famous gifts from

---

[61] Duchesne and Vogel, *Le* Liber pontificalis, p. 275. This expression (*cum gloria et laudem*) had already been used in order to describe the *aduentus* of Roman legates in 519 (Duchesne and Vogel, *Le* Liber pontificalis, p. 270).

[62] Ibid., p. 275.

[63] W. Enßlin, 'Papst Johannes I. als Gesandter Theoderichs des Grossen bei Kaiser Justinus I', *ByzZ*, 44 (1951): pp. 127–34, at pp. 129–32. Enßlin's analysis is not overturned by Vitiello, who shows the parallelism between imperial, or royal, ritual at St Peter's grave in Rome and the form of veneration at the moment of the papal *aduentus* in Constantinople (M. Vitiello, '*Cui Iustinus Imperator venienti ita occurit ac si beato Petro*. Das Ritual beim ersten Papst-Kaiser Treffen in Konstantinopel : eine römische Auslegung ?', *ByzZ*, 98 [2005]: pp. 81–96, at pp. 90–92) and admits that the papal welcome by Justin, only known to us thanks to *Lib. pont.* and *Excerpta Valesianus*, has been written in accordance with western representation, in order to confirm the acceptance of *primatus Petri*.

[64] Zeno is mentioned only once in *Lib. pont.*, sending a relatio, which is not correctly situated nor interpreted. On the facts see Blaudeau, *Alexandrie et Constantinople*, p. 202.

[65] Duchesne and Vogel, *Le* Liber pontificalis, 276.

the East,[66] adding to those from Clovis or Theodoric on the death of Hormisdas,[67] had been drawn up already. But the redactors of the second phase inserted a new list that inventoried the gifts (patens, chalices, cups) sent to Rome by Justin, the only donor this time mentioned.[68] In other words, the discourse regarding the devotion displayed to the apostolic see went even as far as the reception of the sacred vessels distributed among Rome's churches, the historicised inventory of gifts attesting that henceforth no ruler could ignore or oppose the papacy with impunity – not even the emperor of the East.

While *Liber pontificalis* hardly deals with doctrine, the progressive compilation of the *uitae* none the less displays, behind its mediocre style, a sharp awareness of the transformations underway during the decades separating Leo's pontificate from that of John II. Through the regular adaptation of its rubrics, the narrative reflects the apostolic see's consolidation as an institution without, however, entirely concealing its growing pains or the obstacles it encountered. In particular, *Liber pontificalis* underlined the papal claim to exercise in the East a primacy founded on the principle of condemning any resurgence of miaphysitism after 451, in conformity with the creed of Chalcedon. For this reason, it gave special weight to the Acacian schism, which challenged the prevailing order as Rome saw it without being able to prevent its ultimate acceptance, a success all the more striking for being delayed. In these circumstances, it can be readily understood how Hormisdas's pontificate, emblematised in the restoration of links with Constantinople in 519, assumed considerable significance. Indeed, the noticeable amplification of the narrative soon begun gained added intensity through the frank expression of a certain philo-Byzantinism. Thus, the narrative offered an enlarged readership an *aide-mémoire* designed to articulate and give clear lessons for the relationship between Rome and Constantinople, a relationship as yet untroubled by the Justinianic reconquest. At the price of certain changes of course (as with the presentation of Theodoric), *Liber pontificalis* effectively affirmed that the glory of the apostolic see, like the quarrels that might occasionally beset it, only acquired true meaning if set in the perspective of Rome's activities in respect of the East. Indeed, at the very time or thereabouts that *Liber pontificalis* was composed, with Agapitus (535–6) at Constantinople, papal authority appeared to enjoy an unprecedented degree of imperial favour.

---

[66] At the risk of attributing to Emperor Justin gifts offered by others, especially Archbishop Epiphanius see Duchesne and Vogel, *Le* Liber pontificalis, p. 274, n. 24; and Geertman, 'Le biografie', p. 349, n. 197.

[67] Duchesne and Vogel, *Le* Liber pontificalis, p. 271. It seems probable that these gifts were given by the pope before his journey to Constantinople.

[68] Ibid., p. 276.

Chapter 8

Are All Universalist Politics Local? Pope Gelasius I's International Ambition as a Tonic for Local Humiliation*

George Demacopoulos

If one were to read Pope Gelasius I's *Epistula* 12 to Emperor Anastasius in a vacuum, one might draw the conclusion that Gelasius was a powerful pope, able to speak with considerable authority. Indeed, the letter is one of the oldest and boldest papal criticisms of a Roman emperor. It famously differentiates between the earthly authority, administered by the emperor, and the priestly authority, administered by the bishop of Rome. It also famously subordinates the earthly authority to the priestly on the premise that even emperors need the sacraments (and therefore the clergy) for their salvation.[1] But the letter does far more than offer a theoretical conceptualisation of a church/state binary; it censures the emperor's past actions, condemns his theological advisors for heresy and insists that the correct interpretation of any theological question can only emerge from the see of Rome because of its special association with St Peter, the prince of the apostles.[2] If this were the only surviving document from Gelasius' tenure, or if we were to read this text through the prism of what the papacy would become, then yes, rightly might we read *Ad Anastasium* as though Gelasius were

---

* An earlier version of this chapter was presented at the sixteenth International Conference on Patristic Studies, Oxford University, 8–12 August 2011. The author would like to thank his fellow panellists and the many others present for their constructive criticisms and collaboration. This essay is drawn from a much larger study of Gelasius' use of the Petrine *topos* that appears in G. Demacopoulos, *The Invention of Peter: Apostolic Discourse and Papal Authority in Late Antiquity* (Philadelphia, PA, 2013).

[1] Gelasius, *Ep.*12.2 (A. Thiel [ed.], *Epistolae Romanorum pontificum genuinae et quae ad eos scriptae sunt a s. Hilaro usque ad Pelagium II*, vol. 1 [Braunsberg, 1867], p. 351) = JK 632.

[2] In short, one can read *Ad Anast.* as a late-ancient testimony to an international papal consciousness that could and did insert itself into the political arena with force and conviction.

a powerful and assertive pontiff, boldly censuring imperial folly and righting heretical wrongs around the world.

This, in fact, was the way that the papal biographers of the early Middle Ages understood Gelasius.[3] It is also the presentation of Gelasius and the fifth-century papacy that we find in many modern collections of medieval sources in translation, which frequently include a few paragraphs of *Ad Anastasium* as evidence of papal strength at the transition from late antiquity to the early Middle Ages.[4] Unfortunately, this was also the view that all too many twentieth-century historians perpetuated in their grand narratives of the so-called 'rise of the papacy'.[5]

But if we read *Ad Anastasium* without the blinders of what the papacy would later become, if we view it through the lens of what was actually going on in the city of Rome at the time, and if we dispel ourselves of the myth that the late-ancient bishops of Rome automatically commanded the respect of the citizens and clergy of Rome itself, then we gain a very different perspective from *Ad Anastasium*. It is the thesis of this essay that however much Gelasius may have insisted that his opinions should be respected by the emperor and the ecclesiastical leaders in the East, the real threats to his position were local. And, as a consequence of that reality, I believe that there is a great deal to learn by viewing his international claims through the prism of local conflict. Thus, this paper proposes that Gelasius' assertions of international ecclesiastical authority do not document ecclesiological or political realities as they were but instead testify to a discourse of papal ambition born from frustration by a bishop who, at the moment of writing, enjoyed little tangible authority either at home or abroad.

Trouble in Rome

To help us ascertain Gelasius' standing in the city of Rome, we shall focus our attention upon two incidents that reveal the pontiff's domestic troubles but have never been adequately connected to his international efforts. The first concerns

---

[3] Note, for example, the treatment of Gelasius I in *Lib. pont.* 51 (L. Duchesne and C. Vogel [eds], *Le* Liber pontificalis: *Texte, introduction et commentaire*, BEFAR, vol. 1 [Paris, 1955 (2nd edn)], pp. 255–7).

[4] See, for example, J.H. Robinson, *Readings in European History* (Boston, MA, 1905), pp. 72–3, whose thoughts have been reprinted frequently both in books and online.

[5] Note, especially, E. Caspar, *Geschichte des Papsttums*, Bd 2: *Das Papsttum unter byzantinischer Herrschaft* (Tübingen, 1933); and W. Ullmann, *Growth of the Papal Government in the Middle Ages: A Study in the Ideological Relation of Clerical to Lay Power* (London, 1970 [3rd edn]), especially pp. 14–28.

his condemnation of the *Lupercalia* festival and reveals the extent to which Gelasius could be easily humiliated by the local aristocracy. The second concerns the 'retrial' of an excommunicated Italian bishop, Misenus, and exposes the extent to which internal divisions within the Roman clergy belie the narrative of a Christian community united by a powerful and respected pontiff.

What is known of the altercation between Gelasius and the senatorial patrons of the *Lupercalia* festival derives entirely from a single Gelasian text, which Thiel lists as *Tractatus* 6 but the *Collectio Avellana* transmits as an epistle.[6] The treatise rebukes and threatens to excommunicate an unnamed magistrate (identified by the *Avellana* editors as the senator Andromachus).[7] It also delivers a series of loosely aimed critiques at other elite patrons, including a tongue-in-cheek accusation that they were failing to perform the pagan ritual properly.[8] But taken in its totality, the treatise may best be characterised as an extended charge of hypocrisy designed to undermine the credibility of lay Christians who were all too willing to criticise the clergy.[9] How could they, Gelasius reasoned, who were guilty of drunken buffoonery and demonic superstition, have been in a position to judge the ministers of the Church?

A careful reading of the first paragraph, in fact, sets the entire treatise in context. A local priest has been found guilty of an adulterous relationship, bringing public scrutiny to the church.[10] What is more, Gelasius has come under personal criticism for not acting swiftly enough to punish the derelict priest.[11]

---

[6] Gelasius I, *Tract.* 6 (Thiel, *Epistolae Romanorum pontificum*, pp. 598–607) = Gelasius I, *Adu. Androm.* (*Collectio Avellana, Ep.* 100) (CSEL 35.453-64) = JK 672. A translation of the title of the epistle in the *Collectio Avellana* is 'Against Andromachus and the other Romans who hold that the Lupercalia should be celebrated according to the ancient custom'. It is worth noting that the paragraph designations differ between the two editions, which can lead to inconsistencies in the secondary literature. I have followed Thiel's paragraph divisions.

[7] The identification of Andromachus as the ringleader of the *Lupercalia* celebration goes back to the eleventh-century manuscript that serves as the basis for the *Collectio Avellana*. N. McLynn, 'Crying Wolf: The Pope and the Lupercalia', *JRS*, 98 (2008): pp. 161–75, at p. 163, identifies Andromachus with a prominent member of Odoacer's administration, who served as both *magister officiorum* and *consiliarius* in 489.

[8] This Gelasian charge has led to a number of divergent interpretations. Most likely, it was meant sarcastically, to the effect of 'if you think that this festival is really important, then why don't you perform it according to the traditional form?' In antiquity, the aristocrats themselves ran the semi-nude race, whereas, by Gelasius' time, the patrons paid actors to perform the race for them. See McLynn, 'Crying Wolf', pp. 162–3.

[9] The charge of hypocrisy is followed by an appeal for Christian mercy and forgiveness.

[10] Gelasius I, *Tract.* 6.1 (Thiel, *Epistolae Romanorum pontificum*, p. 598).

[11] Ibid.

Several paragraphs later we learn that an added element in that particular year's festivities would be a theatrical mocking, through lewd songs, of the guilty priest.[12] Clearly, Gelasius is embarrassed by the fact that the clergy (including, by extension, himself) were going to be to the target of drunken buffoonery. Andromachus has been unresponsive to Gelasius' attempts to suppress the mocking of the clergy – he has even posted a public announcement of the festival – and so Gelasius responds with the maximum force that he can – a threat of excommunication.[13] But given that Andromachus is not actually named in the treatise and given that Andromachus would likely have had access to a private oratory, the threat of excommunication contained in the document would have amounted, in practical terms, to little more than bluster. In the end, Gelasius can do nothing to stop the event, nor can he really do anything to diminish Andromachus' standing in the city. Gelasius' concluding declarations that the festival must come to an end should not be misconstrued as evidence of the cessation of the festival.[14] There is nothing in the text, in fact, to suggest that the *Lupercalia* came to an end. Instead, Gelasius' concluding exhortation should be read as a kind of political or religious slogan for reform – a desire for moral change that was more idealistic than realistic and that was more likely intended to reinforce the ideology of those who already shared his viewpoint than it was designed to persuade those who did not.

But why is it that Gelasius, the bishop of Rome and heir of Peter, proves so powerless to shut down the *Lupercalia* and why would his declaration of excommunication have meant so little? The answers to both of these questions are to be found, in part, in recent scholarship on the private oratories of aristocratic Roman Christians from this period. Kristina Sessa and Kimberly Bowes independently have demonstrated that the continuation of the pre-Nicene domestication of Christian liturgical practice (such as daily prayer and domestic communion)[15] would have served as a formidable barrier to papal

---

[12] Ibid., 6.8 (Thiel, *Epistolae Romanorum pontificum*, pp. 603–4).

[13] Ibid., 6.10–12 (Thiel, *Epistolae Romanorum pontificum*, pp. 605–6), implies that he and Andromachus have had a previous conversation about the festival. Here, Gelasius presents Andromachus' arguments in defence of the festival only to counter them one by one. The threat of excommunication appears in paragraph 4.

[14] Several scholars have fallen victim to Gelasius' rhetoric by assuming that Gelasius' call for an end to the event led to the cessation of the festival.

[15] K. Bowes, *Private Worship, Public Values, and Religious Change in Late Antiquity* (Cambridge, 2008), p.76, argues that weekday public liturgies were not practised in Rome until the sixth century. Although Christians would attend public masses at meeting houses and the new basilicas on Sunday and feast days, the majority of communion acts necessarily took place within the home.

assertions of religious hegemony in the city.[16] One of the unique characteristics of the development of Christianity in the city of Rome was that the private households of the senatorial elite would have remained a space decidedly free of episcopal oversight (whether political, economic or ethical). This was due, in large part, to the carefully guarded and ancient legal protections granted to all aspects (including the religious) of the private domain, the *domus*, through the principle of the *paterfamilias*. As Sessa notes, the Roman *domus* 'was not a blank slate onto which the bishop simply etched his power to build his church'.[17] Rather, the householder remained an active agent in the process by which Roman bishops did, eventually, gain access into the home. But that process was a long and uneven one, far from complete during Gelasius' tenure. In short, the evidence that Sessa, Bowes and others have provided for household worship in Rome dramatically contradicts the traditional scholarly narratives for this period as being one of the so-called 'rise of the papacy', which has been thought to have come at the expense of the lay householders' religious and domestic autonomy.[18]

On this point, it is interesting to take notice of the very first line of Gelasius' *Tractatus* 6, which begins with the assertion that 'Some folks are sitting in their houses and are unaware of what they are saying or of what they approve of, trying to judge others because they don't know how to judge themselves.'[19] In short, Gelasius is suggesting that Andromachus and his fellow aristocrats are not adhering to the ethical parameters of the Christian life. Not only are they judging those to whom they should show mercy, but they are doing so from a vantage point that marks them as somehow *para-ecclesial* – outside of the church. Gelasius, thus, implies that the authentic church is that of basilica churches within the episcopal administrative system. The domesticated churches of the senatorial elite fly in the face of that system. They are both a threat to and competition for the episcopal structure. It is not surprising, therefore, that we find in Gelasius' correspondence the most concerted attempt of any pontiff in

---

[16] See K. Sessa, 'Christianity and the *Cubiculum*: Spiritual Politics and Domestic Space in Late Antique Rome', *JECS*, 15 (2007): pp. 171–204, especially pp. 196–204; and K. Sessa, 'Domestic Conversions: Household and Bishops in the Late Antique "Papal Legends"', in K. Cooper and J. Hillner (eds), *Religion, Dynasty, and Patronage in Early Christian Rome 300–900* (Cambridge, 2007), pp. 79–114. For a more thorough discussion see K. Sessa, *The Formation of Papal Authority in Late Antique Italy: Roman Bishops and the Domestic Sphere* (Cambridge, 2012). See also Bowes, *Private Worship*, especially pp. 61–103.

[17] Sessa, 'Domestic Conversions', p. 84.

[18] Ibid., pp. 82–5.

[19] Gelasius I, *Tract*. 6.1 (Thiel, *Epistolae Romanorum pontificum*, p. 598): 'Sedent quidam in domibus suis nescientes, neque quae loquantur, neque de quibus affirment, de aliis iudicare nitentes, quum se ipsi non iudicent …'.

the late-ancient period to regulate the construction and consecration of new churches.[20] In one letter, he goes so far as to insist that the building of any new church or oratory in all of Suburbicarian Italy must first gain papal approval.[21] Similarly we may view his unprecedented efforts to scrutinise clerical ordinations as an attempt to regulate the clergy who might ultimately serve in one of these domestic churches.[22] For now, we can simply conclude that *Tractatus* 6 on the *Lupercalia* reveals Gelasius' frustration with a fractured ecclesiological system for which he has no immediate recourse other than rhetorical performance.

Turning from Gelasius' troubles with the Roman lay elites to his altercations with the Roman clergy, we can focus our attention on a text that Thiel lists as *Epistula* 30. The document is not an actual letter and is probably best described as a redacted and partisan transcript from a legal proceeding in which an Italian bishop, Misenus, is restored to his previous dignity after having endured a long period of excommunication.[23] Misenus, in fact, had been the bishop of Cumae during the tenure of Pope Felix III (II) (Gelasius' predecessor) and had served as a papal ambassador to Constantinople in 384 at the height of the altercation with Acacius.[24] Misenus had made the career-ending mistake of validating Acacius' orthodoxy by receiving the eucharist from him.[25] Felix had been embarrassed

---

[20] Concerning the construction and consecration of new churches see ibid., *Epp.* 14.4 (Thiel, *Epistolae Romanorum pontificum*, p. 364) = JK 636; 25 (Thiel, *Epistolae Romanorum pontificum*, pp. 391–2) = JK 643; 35 (Thiel, *Epistolae Romanorum pontificum*, p. 449) = JK 680; and 41 (Thiel, *Epistolae Romanorum pontificum*, p. 454) = JK 995 (assigned to Pelagius I).

[21] Ibid., *Ep.*25 (Thiel, *Epistolae Romanorum pontificum*, pp. 391–2).

[22] Examples of Gelasius' attempts to oversee ordinations throughout Italy include ibid., *Epp.* 14 (Thiel, *Epistolae Romanorum pontificum*, pp. 360–79); 15 (Thiel, *Epistolae Romanorum pontificum*, pp. 379–80) = JK 675; 20 (Thiel, *Epistolae Romanorum pontificum*, pp. 386–8) = JK 651; 21 (Thiel, *Epistolae Romanorum pontificum*, p. 388) = JK 653; 22 (Thiel, *Epistolae Romanorum pontificum*, p. 389) = JK 658; 23 (Thiel, *Epistolae Romanorum pontificum*, pp. 389–90) = JK 727; 29 (Thiel, *Epistolae Romanorum pontificum*, pp. 436–7) = JK 715; 34 (Thiel, *Epistolae Romanorum pontificum*, pp. 448–9) = JK 679; and 41 (Thiel, *Epistolae Romanorum pontificum*, p. 454).

[23] The text ends with the following attribution: 'Sixtus notarius sanctae Romanae ecclesiae iussu domini mei beatissimi papae Gelasii ex scrinio editi die tertio Idus Martii, Flauio Viatore uiro clarissimo consule'. ('I, Sixtus, the notary of the Roman church by the order of my lord most blessed Gelasius, gave this from my desk on the third day before the Ides of March [495]'.).

[24] *Lib. pont.* 51.2–3 (Duchesne and Vogel, *Le* Liber pontificalis, p. 255).

[25] According to *Lib. pont.* 50.3 (Duchesne and Vogel, *Le* Liber pontificalis, p. 252), the two envoys had succumbed to bribes (which is a common motif in *Lib. pont.*, used to explain behaviour with which the editors find error). Interestingly, there is no mention of bribery in *Ep.* 30 (Thiel, *Epistolae Romanorum pontificum*, pp. 437–47), which, instead, describes Misenus' acknowledgement of having previously held heretical views.

and his hard-line diplomatic stance towards the eastern patriarch had been compromised. Not surprisingly, Felix's response was swift. Misenus was recalled from Constantinople and condemned by a Roman synod upon his return.[26]

As the chief architect of Felix's eastern strategy, Gelasius must have concurred with (if not orchestrated) the punitive action against Misenus in 484. Thus, the rehabilitation of Misenus in 495 is a rather surprising development. Although only a few scholars have taken notice of *Epistula* 30, it has led to radically divergent interpretations. J.N.D. Kelly, for example, saw Misenus' rehabilitation as evidence of an increasingly powerful clerical element within the city, which had grown tired of the schism with the East. In Kelly's view, Misenus' rehabilitation amounts to a clerical repudiation of Gelasius' eastern policy.[27] In contrast, Jeffrey Richards views Misensus' restoration as a sign of increasing papal strength.[28] Saying nothing of the motives for why Gelasius would seek to restore Misenus, Richards emphasises what he considers to be a surprisingly small minority of priests who boycotted the synod – 18 of the 76 Roman priests did not attend.[29] But Richards's analysis leaves us with more questions than answers. Why, for example, should we view an 80 per cent majority opinion as an example of strength when even Richards concedes that a 100 per cent agreement in such matters was typical at this time?[30] Moreover, how can we reconcile Gelasius' hard-line approach towards the East in all other matters if we are supposed to believe that the rehabilitation of Misenus was orchestrated by Gelasius – a change of course that is not only inconsistent with Gelasius' continuing eastern policy but that was somehow refused by a group of Roman priests that we are supposed to believe to have been more rigid than Gelasius himself? But even if Richards were correct, and I think he is not, and the decision to rehabilitate Misenus was the pope's, Gelasius was clearly unable to gain full clerical support for the endeavour, which alone evinces a limit to the pontiff's ability to control clerical opinion in Rome.

And it is precisely because of this weakness that the unprecedented affirmations of Gelasius' sovereignty contained within *Epistula* 30 are so

---

[26] *Lib. pont.* 50.4 (Duchesne and Vogel, *Le Liber pontificalis*, p. 255).

[27] J.N.D. Kelly, *The Oxford Dictionary of Popes* (Oxford, 1986), p. 48.

[28] J. Richards, *The Popes and the Papacy in the Early Middle Ages, 476–752* (London, 1979), p. 66.

[29] Ibid. P.A.B. Llewelyn, 'The Roman Clergy during the Laurentian Schism (498–506): A Preliminary Analysis', *Ancient Society*, 8 (1977): pp. 245–75, at p. 253, eyeing a rather different scenario, attributes some of the missing priests to a clerical shortage brought on by episcopal ordinations. Llewelyn's thesis, though not inconceivable, is mostly born of silence.

[30] Richards, *The Popes and the Papacy*, p. 66.

arresting.[31] Following Misenus' confession of guilt and affirmation of faith (paragraphs 1–5), the document informs us that Gelasius asked the assembled bishops to offer their own opinions on the matter. Here, the text boasts:

> All of the bishops raised themselves up, calling and saying: 'Christ hear us, give Gelasius a long life!' This was said twenty times. 'Since God gave you authority, rule!' This was affirmed twelve times. 'Do what [our] Lord Peter does!' This was said ten times. 'We ask you to be lenient!' This was said nine times.[32]

This characterisation of Gelasius in full control of a sycophantic synod, of course, echoes similar portraits of a Roman emperor whose authority was publicly proclaimed by both Senate and people. No doubt, this is not the first time that a discourse of papal authority had mirrored imperial models nor the first time that a Roman bishop had been cheered in imperial fashion, but the hyperbole is all the more noteworthy given the apparent divisions among the Roman clergy, which this partisan account seems to have been designed to conceal.

The document concludes by transcribing a second episode of euphoric affirmation. Many of the previous assertions are repeated, but in this case, there are two significant additions: 'We acknowledge you as the vicar of Christ!' and 'We see you to be the apostle Peter!'[33] *Epistula* 30 is, in fact, the oldest extant text affirming the papal title 'Vicar of Christ'. The second addition, linking Gelasius directly to Peter, is perhaps less grandiose but no less rhetorically significant. Indeed, it is precisely because Gelasius is 'Peter' that he is able to 'loose' the sin of Misenus (cf. Matthew 16:19: 'what sins you bind are bound and whatever sins you loose are loosed').[34]

---

[31] For an alternative reading of *Ep*.30 as indicating 'authentic' and unbiased courtroom events, see J. Taylor, 'The Early Papacy at Work: Gelasius I (492–496)', *JRH*, 4 (1975): pp. 317–32, especially pp. 322–3.

[32] Gelasius I, *Ep*.30.6 (Thiel, *Epistolae Romanorum pontificum*, p. 440): 'Leuauerunt se omnes episcopi et presbyteri rogantes et dicentes: "exaudi Christe: Gelasio uita!" dictum uicies. "Quod uobis Deus dedit in potestate, praestate!" dictum duodecies. "Hoc fac quod facit domnus Petrus!" dictum decies. "Ut indulgeas, rogamus!" dictum nouies'.

[33] Ibid., *Ep*.30.15 (Thiel, *Epistolae Romanorum pontificum*, p. 447): '"Vicarium Christi te uidemus!" dictum undecies. "Apostolum Petrum te uidemus!" dictum sexies'.

[34] An interesting element of the text is the protracted (and rather strained) justification that the author must give for overturning a previous synodal decision. See ibid., *Ep*.30.11–14 (Thiel, *Epistolae Romanorum pontificum*, pp. 444–7). Is this, perhaps, one of the reasons that some of the local clergy objected to Misenus' rehabilitation (i.e., that Gelasius did not have the right to overturn a previous synod)?

While no objective interpreter would assume that *Epistula* 30 accurately reflects everything that took place during the synod nor would anyone presume that the very public proclamations of Gelasius' popularity represents the universal view of the city's priests, the surviving evidence presents a real interpretive challenge for assessing Gelasius' functional authority among the Roman clergy. On the one hand, no Roman bishop has ever enjoyed universal support and it may well be that Gelasius' efforts to defend the Roman clergy in the *Lupercalia* episode made him more popular among that constituency than some other popes. On the other hand, it is also possible that the letter's exaggerated proclamations of Gelasius' authority, especially the introduction of new and more exalted titles such as 'Vicar of Christ', were inserted into the only surviving record of the trial for the explicit purpose of concealing what might otherwise have been understood to have been a humiliating experience for the pontiff. Indeed, it is significant that the entire document seems fixated on asserting Gelasius' authority vis-à-vis the rest of the church (whether the assembled bishops who acknowledge his authority, the eastern heretics who do not, or some silent third party that seems to have questioned the pope's right to overturn a previous synod).[35] The text does not at all seem to be concerned with the actual matter at hand – the redemption of a penitent cleric. My feeling is that Gelasius was forced into this rehabilitation against his will by a significant faction of local clergy and bishops (with those who would have supported him in continuing to refuse reconciliation to Misenus not turning up), but that the document in which the evidence is found has tried to cover up this humiliating retreat by Gelasius.

Ad Anastasium

As we turn our attention to *Ad Anastasium*, there are two contextual factors to keep in mind. First, let us remember that papal letters to Constantinople, especially those to the emperor, would likely have been posted around the city of Rome for others to see. Correspondence was a public act, anything that Gelasius might have wished to confer privately would have been handled directly by his envoys, not by letters. Second, let us remember that the political situation in Italy at this time was such that the emperor was emperor of Italy in name only – Italy was ruled by the Ostrogoths in Ravenna. The emperor had no real ability – or interest for that matter – to control the church or political structures within

---

[35] Ibid.

the city of Rome. In other words, papal demands of the eastern emperor – just like imperial demands upon the papacy – were largely for show. This, of course, does not mean that anyone in Rome or Constantinople was particularly excited about the fact that the churches were in schism; it simply means that neither the emperor nor the pope had significant leverage against the other at this time.

Ad Anastasium is a long and extremely sophisticated letter, ripe for political, theological and/or cultural analysis. As a consequence, we shall limit our examination of this letter to a few particular statements that are especially relevant to our understanding of Gelasius' situation within the city of Rome. The first is his claim to be 'Roman born'. The second is his referring to the emperor as his 'son'. The third is the claim that only the bishop of Rome, the heir of St Peter, has the authority to resolve theological questions. While it may be that each of these elements had its own purpose in Gelasius' diplomatic strategy for the East, they are equally illuminating of his domestic concerns.

We shall begin with Gelasius' claim to be 'Roman born'. In the first paragraph of the letter, following an awkward and specious justification for having failed to announce his election to the emperor, Gelasius declares: 'most glorious son, I, being born a Roman, love, care for, and hold you as the ruler of the Romans'.[36] Gelasius' claim of Roman birth is a fascinating assertion. In fact, he was not a Roman, he was born in North Africa.[37] Ostensibly, Gelasius' statement of Roman-ness is an affirmation of his patriotism and is followed by his pledge of loyalty to the emperor.[38] But the same claim serves as a rhetorical mask for one of Gelasius' most significant political liabilities at home. Indeed, Gelasius was one of the only post-Constantinian popes to have been neither Roman born nor a member of the provincial aristocracy. Thus, it is quite possible that the framing of this particular sentence had more to do with Gelasius' desire to speak to the members of the Roman Senate (who likely would have viewed him as a low-born 'outsider') as it does his desire to defend his patriotism to the emperor. As such, we can interpret to the claim to be 'Roman born' as a marker of Gelasius' own insecurity that his financial and provincial background put him at a distinct

---

[36] Ibid., *Ep.*12.1 (Thiel, *Epistolae Romanorum pontificum*, p. 350): ' ... gloriose fili, et sicut Romanus natus Romanum princepem amo, colo, suspicio ... '.

[37] As noted, Llewellyn, 'The Roman Clergy during the Laurentian Schism', pp. 254–8, has argued that Gelasius' well-known trouble with the senatorial families in Rome was related to the fact that he was not a Roman.

[38] F. Dvornik, 'Pope Gelasius and Emperor Anastasius I', *ByzZ*, 44 (1951): pp. 111–16, at p. 112, interprets the passage in a straight-forward fashion, arguing that Gelasius was not 'yet' willing to break with contemporary understandings of the supreme leadership of the emperor.

disadvantage with the Roman senators with whom he was vying for authority and influence in the capital.

Second, the very same sentence refers to the emperor as 'son', which we can view as a careful rhetorical subordination of the emperor to the pope.[39] Although it was a commonplace of late-ancient and medieval episcopal correspondence to address a secular correspondent from a paternal vantage point, Gelasius was actually one of the first popes to employ the father/son paradigm in his imperial correspondence.[40] By framing the emperor as 'son', Gelasius is able to present himself as a nurturing spiritual father who is concerned for the religious well-being of a spiritual disciple. But, at the same time, using the father/son paradigm enabled Gelasius to subordinate the emperor in the process – there would have been no mistaking the diminution of 'sons' to 'fathers' in the Roman world. However irritated the distant emperor might have become from Gelasius' use of this calculated ploy, the naming of the emperor as 'son' would likely have drawn the attention of local aristocrats who could not, themselves, have justifiably subordinated the emperor in the same way. In other words, by invoking the biblical and episcopal language of the paternal shepherd, Gelasius was able to present himself as presiding from a position of paternal authority vis-à-vis the emperor in a way that no senator or secular aristocrat could ever hope to possess. However ineffective Gelasius might have been in exerting any real authority over the secular rulers of Rome, the naming of emperor as 'son' provided him with a rhetorical position of strength that no Roman senator could match.

Because this is not the proper forum to rehearse all of the ways in which *Ad Anastasium* asserts papal ecclesiastical authority via the Petrine privilege,[41] we can simply summarise Gelasius' claims in this letter in the form of the following syllogism: (1) orthodoxy is enshrined in the teaching of St Peter; (2) the apostolic see, more than any other see, remains faithful to Peter's teaching; therefore (3) the apostolic see is the guardian of orthodoxy. One of the important ways that *Ad Anastasium* marks an important escalation of Gelasius' development of the Petrine theme is the extent to which it uses 'St Peter' as a grammatical substitute for the apostolic see. The apostolic see, through its *pontifex* (i.e., Gelasius), acts on behalf of St Peter, in solidarity with St Peter, because it is St Peter. In short, the emperor cannot himself evaluate the orthodoxy of Acacius, nor should he

---

[39] Gelasius I, *Ep.* 12.1–2 (Thiel, *Epistolae Romanorum pontificum*, pp. 349–52).

[40] Technically, Pope Felix III (II) was the first pope to employ this convention, but it has long been presumed that Gelasius, who served as Felix's secretary, was responsible for much of Felix's diplomatic and rhetorical decisions.

[41] For a more extensive analysis of Gelasius' use of Petrine authority, see Demacopoulos, *The Invention of Peter*, ch. 3.

rely on his eastern advisors to do so. St Peter alone can interpret christological orthodoxy and, of course, Gelasius is St Peter.

One of the fascinating elements of *Ad Anastasium* is that, despite all of the bluster about his Petrine authority, there are a number of internal markers (particularly in paragraph 9) that reveal that Gelasius is fully aware that he and his office command little respect within the eastern church.[42] One of the ways that we may, thus, comprehend the disconnect between the assertions of Petrine authority and the recognition that such assertions meant little in the East, is that the promotion of Petrine authority in *Ad Anastasium* was not designed to persuade the eastern church, or even the emperor, of Gelasius' importance so much as it was offered for the benefit of Gelasius' domestic audience. Perhaps, in fact, we should view the production of *Ad Anastasium* as an effort to address domestic issues rather than international ones. In other words, because there is little reason to think that Gelasius actually believed that his letter would heal the Acacian schism or that it would effect imperial subordination to the papacy, we should view *Ad Anastasium* from the perspective of what Gelasius might have hoped to achieve at home. Indeed, from this standpoint the design and argumentation of the letter appear to be more logical.

To the extent that *Ad Anastasium* allowed Gelasius to assert for his domestic audience that all foreign bishops took their theological cues from the heir of St Peter and to the extent that he could instruct his spiritual 'son', the emperor, to be mindful of the fact that his salvation was dependent upon his adherence to Gelasius' dogmatic instruction, the pontiff could fabricate a level of international respect that no other domestic authority, whether lay or ecclesiastical, could possibly equal. However many challenges Gelasius faced in his daily interactions with the other actors of Rome, be they the powerful ruling families of the Senate or the entrenched and often insubordinate clergy in the city and surrounding area, Gelasius possessed the ability to claim through the Petrine privilege a degree of international primacy and respect that no other inhabitant of Rome could match. While it is likely that some of Gelasius' domestic contemporaries knew that the claim of international primacy was more rhetorical than actualisable,[43]

---

[42] For example, Gelasius I, *Ep.* 12.9 (Thiel, *Epistolae Romanorum pontificum*, pp. 356–7), acknowledges that eastern clerics have been critical of him to the emperor. This is an astonishing admission by Gelasius that the eastern bishops believe that it is within their purview to evaluate the orthodoxy of the Roman bishop. And that acknowledgement is a rather dramatic internal contradiction to the very claims of papal sovereignty asserted throughout the letter.

[43] The Roman senator Faustus, who was charged by Theodoric to embark upon a political mission to the emperor's court in Constantinople, got an eye-witness account of

with time, treatises like *Ad Anastasium* would serve to ground a Gelasian and papal legacy in which the late-ancient bishops of Rome wielded their authority all over the empire, even bringing the emperor himself to learn that his salvation depended upon Peter's heir. That the biographers of the Middle Ages and even our own time have come to believe such a fiction is a testament, I believe, to the force of Gelasius' rhetorical sophistication.

Gelasius' lack of standing in the eastern church. It is noteworthy that the strongest assertions of Petrine privilege to be found anywhere within the Gelasian corpus exist in a letter that Gelasius sent to Faustus (*Ep.* 10 [Thiel, *Epistolae Romanorum pontificum*, pp. 341–8] = JK622) as he was returning from Constantinople to Rome. It is quite possible, in fact, that Gelasius' strong assertions of privilege in the letter to Faustus represent something of a preemptive public relations strike, which was designed to diminish the damage that Faustus' return might cause. See Demacopoulos, *The Invention of Peter*.

Chapter 9
Crisis in the Letters of Gelasius I (492–96): A New Model of Crisis Management?*

Bronwen Neil

Introduction

Fifth-century Rome was a city under siege from many directions. Its crises included threats to its religious, civil and political security, as well as an ongoing identity crisis with the permanent move of the imperial residency to Ravenna in the 450s.[1] The letters written by bishops of Rome between 410 and 500 offer a limited picture of the types of crisis that impinged specifically on the city of Rome in the fifth centuries, and the strategies bishops adopted for dealing with them. Within this corpus of some 300 letters, those of Gelasius stand out as offering a markedly different approach. As deacon and then bishop of Rome, Gelasius (492–96) had to deal with the ongoing Acacian schism with Constantinople, as well as fallout from the recent transition of Italy to Gothic rule.[2] By comparing

---

*   An earlier version of this chapter was presented at the sixteenth International Conference on Patristic Studies, Oxford University, 8–12 August 2011. I thank Australian Catholic University for giving me financial support to attend the conference.

[1]   A. Gillett, 'Rome, Ravenna, and the Last Western Emperors', *PBSR*, 69 (2001): pp. 131–67, points out that the imperial residency alternated between Rome and Ravenna until ca. 457.

[2]   Recent research on Gelasius is relatively sparse. Past researchers have concentrated on the whole on his attitude to papal primacy: W. Ullmann, *Gelasius I. (492–496): Das Papsttum an der Wende der Spätantike zum Mittelalter*, Päpste und Papsttum, vol. 18 (Stuttgart, 1981); and A.K. Ziegler, 'Pope Gelasius and His Teaching on the Relation of Church and State', *CHR*, 27 (1942): pp. 412–47 (with older bibliography). An important exception is J. Taylor, 'The Early Papacy at Work: Gelasius I (492–496)', *JRH*, 8 (1975): pp. 317–32, and more recently, N. McLynn, 'Crying Wolf: The Pope and the Lupercalia', *JRS*, 98 (2008): pp. 161–75. George Demacopoulos offers a radical reappraisal of Gelasius' claims for leadership of the universal church, in G. Demacopoulos, *The Invention of Peter: Apostolic Discourse and Papal Authority in Late Antiquity* (Philadelphia, PA, 2013); see also Demacopoulos's Chapter 8 in this volume. For reviews of current research see F.W. Bautz,

his letters with other sources – histories, inscriptions, *uitae* and *Liber pontificalis* among them – we can establish who or what failed to register in the episcopal record. Gelasius' approach to his role emerges most clearly in his management of various crises. The categories of crisis that may be identified as relevant to the pontificate of Gelasius are:

1. crises in structures of dependency;[3]
2. population displacement, including exiles, prisoners of war, refugees and asylum seekers;
3. violent conflict, within the church and without; and
4. failure of the justice system, both secular and ecclesiastical (*audientia episcopalis*).[4]

Using the letters of the fifth-century bishop of Hippo, Augustine, and Pope Gelasius, I explore the thesis that Gelasius' management of crisis was based on an African model of episcopacy.

African Origins?

The early sixth-century redactor of *Liber pontificalis* asserts that Gelasius was 'African' (*natione Afer*).[5] This statement has not been accepted without question in modern scholarship, with some pointing to Gelasius' profession of loyalty in his famous letter to Emperor Anastasius: 'as one Roman born, I love the Roman emperor'.[6] Thiel points out that Gelasius may have been referring to

---

'Gelasius I', in *Biographisch-Bibliographisches Kirchenlexikon*, vol. 2 (Hamm, 1990), pp. 197–99; and R. Bratož, 'Gelasio', *Enciclopedia dei Papi*, vol. 1 (Rome, 2000), pp. 458–62.

[3] The phrase 'structures of dependency' neatly encapsulates both the causes and consequences of a highly stratified social structure, although people in late antiquity remained oblivious to continuing generational poverty and the structural reasons for that phenomenon.

[4] Another category of crisis, natural disasters, is not mentioned at all in the Gelasian corpus. Two other categories – religious controversies, especially the Acacian schism and Pelagianism, and crime and corruption within the church – have been omitted here for lack of space. These are dealt with in B. Neil and P. Allen (intro. and trans.), *The Letters of Gelasius I (492–496): Pastor and Micromanager of the Church of Rome*, Adnotationes, vol. 1 (Turnhout, 2014).

[5] *Lib. pont.* 51.1 (L. Duchesne and C. Vogel [eds], *Le Liber pontificalis; Texte, introduction et commentaire*, BEFAR, vol. 1 [Paris, 1955 (2nd edn)], p. 255).

[6] Gelasius I, *Ep.* 12.1 (A. Thiel [ed.], *Epistulae Romanorum pontificum genuinae et quae ad eos scriptae sunt a s. Hilaro usque ad Pelagium II*, vol. 1 [Braunsberg, 1867]), p. 350 = JK 632: '... sicut Romanus natus Romanum principem amo ...'.

Roman citizenship rather than Roman birth.[7] It is possible that Gelasius had African parentage but was raised in Rome. I agree with Thiel that there is no reason to question the testimony of *Liber pontificalis,* in which case this pope shared his origins with Victor (ca. 195) and Miltiades (310–14). Naturally I make no claims for the colour of their skin.[8] Gelasius served as deacon under his predecessor Felix III (II), writing at least one letter in his name.[9]

It is well known that the North African church was divided into some 600 sees, each with its own bishop, and these had developed a collegial system of operation in the third century, with annual synods to settle disciplinary and doctrinal issues, under the presidency of the bishop of Carthage.[10] The synods

---

[7] Thiel, *Epistulae Romanorum pontificum,* pp. 285 and 350, n. 5. Three late manuscripts read *Romae natus*: two from the pseudo-Isidorian Collection: 1. Vatican, BAV, lat. 630 (*saec.* XI); 2. Vatican, BAV, lat. 1340 (*saec.* XII); and another from the *Collectio Dionysio-Hadriana*: 3. *Remensis S. Remigii,* then *Jesuit. Parisinus* 569; now Berlin, SBPK, Phill. 1741 (*saec.* VIII or IX): see *sigla* in Thiel, *Epistulae Romanorum pontificum,* pp. xxxvii–xxxviii.

[8] Cf. M. Browne, 'The Three African Popes', *The Western Journal of Black Studies,* 22 (1998): pp. 57–70, who argues that all three African-born popes were black, as were Tertullian, Cyprian and Augustine. This is not a point I should like to labour. On p. 65 he claims: 'Despite the centuries that separated Victor, Miltiades, and Gelasius from one another, one looks for a sign of their common African heritage – a common outlook, perhaps, a mutual motivation for their behavior. One looks, too, for some contribution that they made to Western Christianity, something especially African. However it is impossible to do this. Works on the early Chruch (*sic*) in Africa are almost non-existent'. She concludes on the next page: 'It is difficult to see Victor, Miltiades, and Gelasius very clearly or to understand them very well'. I hope to challenge Browne's grim prognosis, at least in the case of the last bishop.

[9] E.g. Felix III (II), *Ep.* 14 (Thiel, *Epistulae Romanorum pontificum,* pp. 266–9) = JK 613, to Flavitas of Constantinople (488–89). See discussion in Thiel, *Epistulae Romanorum pontificum,* pp. 17 and 285; and Bratož, 'Gelasio', pp. 458–60.

[10] On late-antique Africa and the African church in general in this period see A. Leone, 'Christianity and Paganism, IV: North Africa', in A. Casiday and F.W. Norris (eds), *Constantine to c. 600,* Cambridge History of Christianity, vol. 2 (Cambridge, 2006), pp. 231–47; A. Leone, *Changing Townscapes in North Africa from Late Antiquity to the Arab Conquest,* Munera, vol. 28 (Bari, 2007); C. Lepelley, *Les Cités de l'Afrique romaine au bas-empire,* 2 vols, EAA, vols 80–81 (Paris, 1979–81); C. Lepelley, 'La crise de l'Afrique romaine au début du Ve siècle, d'après les Lettres nouvellement découvertes de saint Augustin', *Comptes rendus des séances de l'Académie des Inscriptions et Belles Lettres,* 125 (1981): pp. 445–63; C. Lepelley, 'La Cité africaine tardive, de l'apogée du IVe siècle à l'effondrement du VIIe siècle', in J.-U. Krause and C. Witschel (eds), *Die Stadt in der Spätantike – Niedergang oder Wandel?* Akten des internationalen Kolloquiums in München am 30. und 31. Mai 2003, Historia Einzelschriften, Bd 190 (Stuttgart, 2006), pp. 13–32; P. Allen and E. Morgan, 'Augustine on Poverty', in P. Allen, B. Neil, and W. Mayer, *Preaching Poverty in the Later Roman Empire: Perceptions and Realities,* Arbeiten zur Kirchen- und Theologiegeschichte, Bd 28 (Leipzig, 2009), pp. 119–70, at pp. 120–22; F. Decret and M. Fantar, *L'Afrique du Nord dans l'antiquité*

seem to have ceased for nearly a century after Cyprian's death in 257, up until the mid-fourth century. Either Augustine or Aurelius decided to hold a series of synods to rejuvenate the African church, starting in Carthage in 393.[11] Jane Merdinger has convincingly argued that African bishops, starting with Augustine, became increasingly dependent on bishops of Rome for upholding church discipline in the course of the fifth century.[12] Thus, the transition from North Africa to Rome might not have been as radical for an ambitious young cleric as first appears. We will see that Gelasius relied on synods to implement his decisions, and used the office of *defensor ecclesiae* to manage crises in the structures of dependency in Italy and beyond, as did the bishops of Carthage and Hippo.

It is important to distinguish between crisis management and acts of evergetism that bishops of Rome were required to perform at least from the time of Sixtus III and Leo I, in the middle decades of the fifth century. These included: redeeming of captives, maintaining and repairing church buildings for public use, provision of handouts to citizens such as the *annona*, especially in times of famine, and undertaking diplomatic missions.[13] Many of the crises listed above demanded these civic responses, and Gelasius was no different from Leo before him or Symmachus after him in undertaking such works as a public benefactor for the city. Our attention here is on a more intimate involvement with individuals of various social and religious backgrounds. Of course, we can only know about such cases if letters to such people survive. So before we begin I need to acknowledge that only those letters that had some bearing on canon law were redacted from the letter collections of popes of the fourth and fifth centuries. Archival practices might have excluded just such cases as those that

---

: *histoire et civilisation, des origines au Ve siècle* (Paris, 1998 [2nd edn]); S. Raven, *Rome in Africa* (London and New York, 1993 [3rd edn]); and M. Marin and C. Moreschini (eds), *Africa cristiana. Storia, religione, letteratura*, Letteratura Cristiana Antica (Brescia, 2002).

[11] Augustine, *Ep.* 22.2 (NBA 21A.108) to Aurelius, bishop of Carthage. See J.E. Merdinger, *Rome and the African Church in the Time of Augustine* (Yale, 1997), pp. 64–6. On the early African synods see G.D. Dunn, *Cyprian and the Bishops of Rome: Questions of Papal Primacy in the Early Church*, ECS, vol. 11 (Strathfield, NSW, 2007).

[12] Merdinger, *Rome and the African Church*, p. 205: '[Yet] the cherished independence of the North African church was gradually giving way, as the Divjak letters prove, to increasing reliance on the Apostolic see'. On the 'Divjak' letters of Augustine, see 'Crisis 4' below.

[13] The reasons for this shift are examined by B. Neil, 'Imperial Benefactions to the Fifth-Century Roman Church', in G. Nathan and L. Garland (eds), Basileia. *Essays on Imperium and Culture in Honour of E.M. and M.J. Jeffreys*, Byzantina Australiensia, vol. 17 (Brisbane, 2011), pp. 55–66.

survive in the Gelasian corpus.[14] If so, we have to ask whether it was the rationale of the collector that had changed or the actual *modus operandi* of the bishops of Rome.

Gelasius' Epistolary Corpus

The first similarity that strikes us between Gelasius and Augustine is the prolific output of these letter-writing bishops. Augustine published some 350 letters in his 34 years as bishop of Hippo. Gelasius too was one of the most prolific bishops of late antiquity, publishing 102 extant letters during his relatively short pontificate of less than five years.[15] Of earlier bishops of Rome, only Leo the Great outranks him, with 143 letters from a 21-year pontificate. The majority of Gelasius' letters (34 in all) concern matters of clerical discipline and church management. A change in the function of papal letters is first signalled in the letters of his predecessor Felix III (II), the first demonstrably aristocratic pope.[16] Felix wrote to Emperor Zeno commending the papal legate, Terrentianus, in the context of the Acacian controversy. This is the first surviving letter on behalf of any individual other than clergy involved in religious controversies or disciplinary enquiries.[17] However, we note that the beneficiary was a nobleman, like Felix (*uir clarissimus*). Here we see one nobleman commending another to the emperor in terms that are familiar from patron–client correspondence. Whether Gelasius was also of aristocratic origins is an open question: certainly

---

[14] I examine these methodological concerns in B. Neil, 'Papal Letter Collections', in E. Watts, C. Sogno and B. Storin (eds), *A Critical Introduction and Reference Guide to Letter Collections in Late Antiquity* (Berkeley and Los Angeles, forthcoming). For a sixth-century example see B. Neil '*De profundis*: The Letters and Archives of Pelagius I of Rome (556–561)', in B. Neil and P. Allen (eds), *Collecting Early Christian Letters: From the Apostle Paul to Late Antiquity* (Cambridge, forthcoming).

[15] Forty letters survive in full (Thiel, *Epistulae Romanorum pontificum*, pp. 85–483) and 49 in fragments (Thiel, *Epistulae Romanorum pontificum*, pp. 483–509), some of them as brief as two or three lines, and I have excluded from the count *Ep.* 11 to Gelasius from the bishops of Dardania. In addition there are 22 extra letters edited by S. Loewenfeld, *Epistolae pontificum Romanorum ineditae* (Leipzig, 1895), pp. 1–12. These are asterisked wherever they are cited below. Other occasional letters have been preserved elsewhere, such as *Ep.* 4 (P. Ewald [ed.], 'Die Papstbriefe der Brittischen Sammlung, 2', *Neues Archiv*, 5 (1880): pp. 503–96, at p. 510, n. 2) of the British Collection.

[16] J. Richards, *The Popes and the Papacy in the Early Middle Ages, 476–752* (London, 1979), p. 235; and J. Moorhead, 'On Becoming Pope in Late Antiquity', *JRH*, 30 (2006): pp. 279–93, on Felix as the probable great-great-grandfather of Pope Gregory I.

[17] Felix III (II), *Ep.* 5 (Thiel, *Epistulae Romanorum pontificum*, p. 242) = JK 618, from 483.

the fact that he was chosen to succeed Felix, having served as his archdeacon, seems to me to suggest that it was likely.

Crisis 1: Crises in the Structures of Dependency

The strongest evidence for a new model of crisis management is found in Gelasius' responses to the crises of structures of dependency which occurred in the fifth century. The term 'structures of dependency' was coined by Nicholas Brooks to cover social and economic relations between rich and poor in a period when traditional patronage structures were readjusting to a new set of social and economic circumstances.[18] The dispatch of the last Roman emperor in 476, followed by the rule of Odoacer and the transition of Italy to Ostrogothic rule in 493–94, created a new set of patron–client obligations and threw old established social networks into disarray. Those who were most vulnerable – widows, orphans and the sick – found themselves in need of new protectors. Augustine was the earliest adopter of the eastern system of poor-rolls (*census matriculorum*), brought to the West by Cassian, in which the needy were enrolled for charity from a particular church or diaconate.[19] Leo I was the first bishop of Rome to institutionalise the poor-roll with a team of seven deacons to administer it.[20] Some security was offered to the poor outside Rome with the introduction of the *quadraticum*, a fourfold division of episcopal revenue that was first signalled in the letters of Felix III (II)'s predecessor, Simplicius.[21] Five letters illustrate this innovation.[22] A quarter of the church's income he

---

[18] The term was used by N. Purcell, 'The Populace of Rome in Late Antiquity: Problems of Classification and Historical Description', in W.V. Harris (ed.), *The Transformations of Urbs Roma in Late Antiquity*, Journal of Roman Archaeology Supplementary Series, vol. 33 (Portsmouth, RI, 1999), pp. 135–61, at pp. 152–6.

[19] Augustine, *Ep.* 20* (NBA 23A.160–88). See M. Rouche, 'La Matricule des pauvres. Evolution d'une institution de charité du Bas Empire jusqu'à la fin du Haut Moyen Âge', in M. Mollat (ed.), *Etudes sur l'Histoire de la pauvreté (Moyen âge – XVIe siècle)*, vol. 1 (Paris, 1974), pp. 83–110, at p. 96. See also R.D. Finn, *Almsgiving in the Later Roman Empire. Christian Promotion and Practice (313–450)*, OCM (Oxford, 2006), p. 75.

[20] See B. Neil, 'Leo I on Poverty', in P. Allen, B. Neil and W. Mayer, *Preaching Poverty in the Later Roman Empire: Perceptions and Realities*, Arbeiten zur Kirchen- und Theologiegeschichte, Bd 28 (Leipzig, 2009), pp. 171–208, at p. 198.

[21] Simplicius, *Ep.* 1.2 (Thiel, *Epistulae Romanorum pontificum*, pp. 176–7) = JK 570, from 475.

[22] Gelasius II, *Epp.* 14.27 (Thiel, *Epistulae Romanorum pontificum*, p. 378) = JK 636; 17 (Thiel, *Epistulae Romanorum pontificum*, pp. 381–2) = JK 637; *frag.* 20 (Thiel, *Epistulae Romanorum pontificum*, pp. 494–5) = JK 710; *frag.* 23 (Thiel, *Epistulae Romanorum*

reserved for the bishops (*cathedraticum*), a quarter for the poor, a quarter for church buildings and the rest for the clergy. In *fragment* 20 Gelasius warns Bishop Sabinus that the *cathedraticum* should not be more than is prescribed by ancient custom; Gelasius advises Sabinus to keep the custom that is prescribed for all churches about collections made on the day of dedication of offerings.[23] A letter to brother bishops in Sicily instructs them to distribute stipends to widows, orphans, paupers and clerics.[24] Bishops may claim the remainder for themselves, so that they can offer largesse to travellers (*peregrini*) and captives. Only bishops had the power to direct the resources of the church. In *fragment* 23 the patrimony of the church of Volaterra was entrusted to Archdeacon Justin and *defensor* Faustus. Gelasius gave detailed instructions for its repair and restoration of its property, including slaves. Annual rents should be given to the bishop, and legal and other expenses paid: the rest was to be divided into four (for the bishop, the clergy, fabric of the church and the poor). Anything left over could be invested.[25] We note here Gelasius' use of the title 'your pontiff' (*pontificem uestrum*) for his addressee – not a title he reserved for himself. If any bishops owned properties of the church and someone made a claim against them, he again invoked the imperial law that permitted no appeals more than 30 years after the event.[26]

As in Augustine's letter, the clerical class emerges as a key recipient of papal aid, but the association of this group with elite background or particular wealth is problematic. The same applies to the class of religious men and women (monks and nuns), who might or might not have had personal wealth. The author of *Liber pontificalis*, who compiled Gelasius' entry with others in the early sixth century, claims that he delivered the city from famine,[27] which is quite likely but not witnessed in his correspondence. The anonymous author adds that Gelasius 'was a lover of the clergy and the poor, and increased the clergy'.[28]

---

pontificum, pp. 496–7) = JK 741; and *frag.* 28 (Thiel, *Epistulae Romanorum pontificum*, pp. 499–500) = JK 738.

[23] Ibid., *frag.* 20 (Thiel, *Epistulae Romanorum pontificum*, p. 495).

[24] Ibid., *Ep.* 17 (Thiel, *Epistulae Romanorum pontificum*, pp. 381–2), dated 15 May 494.

[25] Ibid., *frag.* 23 (Thiel, *Epistulae Romanorum pontificum*, p. 497). See Taylor, 'The Early Papacy at Work', p. 331.

[26] Gelasius I, *Ep.* 17.2 (Thiel, *Epistulae Romanorum pontificum*, p. 382).

[27] *Lib. pont.* 51.2 (Duchesne and Vogel, *Le Liber pontificalis*, p. 255): 'Hic liberauit a periculo famis ciuitatem Romanam'.

[28] Ibid.: 'Hic fuit amator <cleri et> pauperum et clerum ampliauit'.

Defensores *of the Poor*

Augustine's concern to defend the interests of the poor is evident in many of his letters, especially the recently discovered Divjak corpus.[29] However, as Lepelley observes, he was largely powerless to help them in the face of oppression by even those imperial officials who were meant to defend their interests.[30] The office of *defensor plebis* or *defensor ciuitatis* was founded by Valentinian I in 368 so that the poor of each city would have an advocate against oppression.[31] Augustine laments the lack of suitable candidates for the office ' ... who might protect them somehow from the wickedness of more powerful personages who trample them down, and also guard the laws passed on their behalf against those who scorn them ... '.[32] Its ecclesiastical counterpart was the *defensor ecclesiae*, instituted first in Rome (367–68) and later in North Africa (after an appeal by the African bishops in 407) to act on behalf of the poor and clergy in legal cases.[33] The first instance of the office of *defensor ecclesiae* in papal letters appears in Innocent's

---

[29] Allen and Morgan, 'Augustine on Poverty', pp. 119–70; see also P.R.L. Brown, *Poverty and Leadership in the Later Roman Empire*, The Menahem Stern Jerusalem Lectures (Hanover, NH and London, 2002); and Finn, *Almsgiving*, *passim*.

[30] C. Lepelley, 'Facing Wealth and Poverty: Defining Augustine's Social Doctrine', The Saint Augustine Lecture, 2006, *AugSt*, 38 (2007): pp. 1–17, at p. 17; D. Grodzynski, 'Pauvres et indigents, vils et plebeians (Une étude terminologique sur le vocabulaire des petites gens dans le Code Théodosien)', *Studia et documenta historiae et iuris*, 53 (1987): pp. 140–218, at p. 199. On p. 214, he reports that there was little difference between the pre-Christian Roman imperial period and the Christian empire of the fourth and fifth centuries in their regard for the poor as expressed in imperial legislation: the rigid social hierarchy of social-juridical categories that were property-dependent and reversible pertained just as much to the early Christian centuries as before.

[31] *CTh* 1.29.1–8 (Th. Mommsen and P. Krüger [eds], *Codex Theodosianus*, vol. 1: *Theodosiani Libri XVI cum constitutionibus Sirmondinis* [Hildesheim, 1990], pp. 64–6). On the fifth-century development of this office see R.M. Frakes, *Contra potentium iniurias: The Defensor Civitatis and Late Roman Justice*, Münchener Beiträge zur Papyrusforschung und antiken Rechtsgeschichte, vol. 90 (Munich, 2001), pp. 165–93.

[32] Augustine, *Ep.* 22*.2 (NBA 23A.192–4): ' ... quia scilicet defensores desunt qui eos ab improbitate personarum potentiorum, a quibus conteruntur, utcumque tueantur et leges pro eis latas aduersus eos, a quibus contemnuntur'. (my own translation). See F. Jacques, 'Le défenseur de cité d'après la Lettre 22* de saint Augustin', *REAug*, 32 (1986): pp. 56–73. Cf. Augustine, *Ep.* 20*.6 (NBA 23A.164–6), where a *defensor ecclesiae* is named as part of the company of Antony of Fussala.

[33] Valentinian I, *Ep. ad Praext.* (*Collectio Avellana*, Ep. 6) (CSEL 35.49); *Reg. eccl. Cathag. excerpta* 87 (CCL 149.215). See C. Humfress, 'A New Legal Cosmos: Late Roman Lawyers and the Early Medieval Church', in P. Lineham and J.L. Nelson (eds), *The Medieval World* (London and New York, 2001), pp. 557–75.

letter to Lawrence (of Siena?).³⁴ Innocent reports that he had successfully used *defensores ecclesiae* to remove heretical Photinians from Rome. The first reference in *Liber pontificalis* is during the pontificate of Felix III (II), who sent an unnamed *defensor* as legate to Constantinople in the course of the Acacian schism.³⁵ In *fragment* 6 to Bishop Sabinus, Gelasius recommends the appointment of a fourth *defensor* for the people of Frumenta, at their request.³⁶ Bishops Rufinus and Justus are ordered to initiate a trial in the presence of Lawrence, *defensor* of the Roman church, to investigate the calumnies brought against the deacon, Agnellus of Verulana.³⁷

Slaves

The Gelasian epistolary corpus reveals an expanded focus on individuals of various social backgrounds who requested aid from the bishop. Like Augustine, Gelasius was greatly concerned with the breakdown of structures of dependency between slaves and their masters. As head of the Roman church, he was also the owner of many church slaves. Slaves and their children were not allowed to inherit property, and slaves of the church did not get special treatment, as the case of the contractor (*conductor*), Ampliatus, shows. Ampliatus, a slave of the church, had left property in Dalmatia to his children. In *fragment* 28 to Honorius, bishop of Salona, Gelasius insists that the 'stolen' property which Ampliatus left to his children is to be reclaimed by the church, while maintaining that care for the poor is the pontiff's responsibility. Gelasius ordered Bishop Honorius to void the will: the *status quo* had to be maintained.

One of the major threats to the traditional structures of dependency involved the liberation of slaves for service in the clergy. *Epistulae* 20 to 24 concern the ordination of slaves and soldier-settlers (*originarii*). Most of the slave-owners in these disputes were women (Placidia, Maxima and Theodora). From 494 to 495, following the precedent set by Pope Leo I,³⁸ Gelasius ruled against the

---

³⁴ Innocent I, *Ep.* 41 (PL 20.607–8) = JK 318. See the discussion of G.D. Dunn, 'Innocent I's Letter to Lawrence: Photinians, Bonosians, and the *Defensores ecclesiae*', *JThS*, n.s., 33 (2012): pp. 136–55. Cf. C. Humfress, *Orthodoxy and the Courts in Late Antiquity* (Oxford, 2007), pp. 262–3, on the *defensor ecclesiae*.

³⁵ *Lib. pont.* 50.2 (Duchesne and Vogel, *Le* Liber pontificalis, p. 255).

³⁶ Gelasius I, *frag.* 6 (Thiel, *Epistulae Romanorum pontificum*, p. 486) = JK 678, to Bishop Sabinus.

³⁷ Ibid., *frag.* 15 (Thiel, *Epistulae Romanorum pontificum*, pp. 491–2) = JK 655, to Bishops Rufinus and Justus.

³⁸ Leo I, *Ep.* 4.2 (H. Wurm [ed.], 'Decretales selectae ex antiquissimis Romanorum Pontificum epistulis decretalibus', *Apollinaris*, 12 [1939]: pp. 40–93, at pp. 87–9) = JK 402.

ordination of such persons in contravention of Valentinian's *Nouella* 36.6. The agents of a nobleman, Amandianus, had complained that some of his bondsmen had been ordained – some as clerics, some as deacons – without their master's permission. The letter to Bishops Martyrius and Justus starts in a reproving tone:

> Et antiquis regulis et nouella synodali explanatione comprehensum est, personas obnoxias coelestis militiae cingulo non praecingi. Sed nescio, utrum ignorantia an uoluntate rapiamini, ut ex hac culpa nullus pene episcoporum uideatur extorris.[39]

The 30-year law (*tricennalis lex*) applied in this instance, which stipulated that crimes could only be prosecuted for up to 30 years after their occurrence.[40] In *Epistula* 16 he repeated the proscription against ordaining 'any illiterate or servile person', in a form letter to be sent out to all new bishops.[41]

A similar decree pertains to the ordination of two slaves of the noblewoman Placidia, who were ordained when their mistress was absent. One was to be given back but his brother could remain because his ordination to the priesthood precluded his being returned to his mistress.[42] Likewise, two *originarii* of the noblewoman Maxima were rejected from holy offices.[43] Gelasius advised Bishop Felix to deal with the slave-owner Claudius (*uir spectabilis*) concerning certain servile persons who had been ordained clerics.[44] The priest Genitor was

---

[39] Gelasius I, *Ep.* 20 (Thiel, *Epistulae Romanorum pontificum*, p. 386) = JK 651: 'It is explained in both ancient canons and in a *novella*, with the support of a synod, that servile persons should not be girt with the girdle of the heavenly army. I do not know whether you are seized by ignorance or will so that it seems that none of the bishops is banished from this crime'. (my own translation). Martyrius and Justus are probably bishops of Acherontinus and Terracina (Thiel, *Epistulae Romanorum Pontificum*, p. 386, n. 1).

[40] *CTh* 4.14 (Mommsen and Krüger, *Codex Theodosianus*, pp. 194–6); Council of Chalcedon, can. 17 (CCCOGD 1.145); Valentinian III, *Nou.* 27 (Th. Mommsen and P.M. Meyer [eds], *Codex Theodosianus*, vol. 2: *Leges Novellae ad Theododianum pertinentes* [Hildesheim, 1990], pp. 122–6). The last is cited by Gelasius I, *Ep.* 17.2 (Thiel, *Epistulae Romanorum pontificum*, p. 382).

[41] Gelasius I, *Ep.* 16.1 (Thiel, *Epistulae Romanorum pontificum*, pp. 380–1) = JK 647: ' ... ne ... illiteratum uel obnoxium ... ad sacros ordines permittat accedere'. (' ... lest he allow any illiterate or servile person to attain holy orders'.).

[42] Ibid., *Ep.* 21 (Thiel, *Epistulae Romanorum pontificum*, p. 386) = JK 653, to Herculentius, Stephan and Justus: ' ... quia propter sacerdotium non jam potest retolli ... '.

[43] Ibid., *Ep.* 22 (Thiel, *Epistulae Romanorum pontificum*, p. 386) = JK 658, to Bishops Rufinus and April.

[44] Ibid., *Ep.* 4* (Loewenfeld, *Epistolae pontificum Romanorum ineditae*, pp. 2–3) = JK 644, to Bishop Felix, from end of 494 to beginning of 495.

instructed to return Septimus, one of two slaves ordained without his mistress' knowledge, to his owner.⁴⁵

This firmness even applied to Christian slaves of Jews. A slave with the unfortunate name of Judas who did not want to serve a Jewish master who had recently had him circumcised, had fled to a church in Venefrana, claiming that he had been a Christian since infancy. Gelasius advises three bishops to investigate the case, to verify that Judas had not attempted by lying to impugn the rights of his legitimate master.⁴⁶ By the time of Gregory the Great (590–604) no Christians could be forced to serve Jewish masters if it imperilled their salvation.⁴⁷ Like other bishops of Rome and North Africa, Gelasius was not concerned to challenge the *status quo*. We have demonstrated this elsewhere in the cases of Leo I and Augustine of Hippo.⁴⁸

The interests of the ruling class did not always triumph, however, for either Gelasius or Augustine, and this is a change from preceding bishops of Rome, especially Leo. This is evident in the case of Sylvester and Faustinian, clerics of the church of Grumentium. The two former slaves complained with tears that their liberty, granted by their master, was threatened by his heir Theodora, who had oppressed them with violence. She sought to remove their clerical rank and reclaim them as her slaves, even though their manumitter was still alive. Gelasius promised to look into their case,⁴⁹ and recommended to a Gothic count (*zaja*) that he do the same.⁵⁰ We can see here that Gelasius is attempting to use

---

⁴⁵ Ibid., *Ep.* 10* (Loewenfeld, *Epistolae pontificum Romanorum ineditae*, p. 6) = JK 653, to Bishops Herculentius and Stephan, from end of 494 to August 495.

⁴⁶ Ibid., *frag.* 43 (Thiel, *Epistulae Romanorum pontificum*, p. 507) to Bishops Siracusius, Constantius and Laurence: 'Quapropter diligenter uestra inter utrumque sollicitudo rerum fideliter examinet ueritatem, quatenus nec religio temerata uideatur, nec seruus hac obiectione mentitus competentis iura dominii declinare contendat'.

⁴⁷ Gregory I, *Ep.* 2.45 (CCL 140.137). See the discussion of A. Serfass, 'Slavery and Pope Gregory the Great', *JECS*, 14 (2006): pp. 77–103, esp. p. 99.

⁴⁸ See Allen and Morgan, 'Augustine on Poverty', pp. 147–50; Neil, 'Leo I on Poverty', pp. 198 and 203; and B. Neil, 'Conclusions', in P. Allen, B. Neil and W. Mayer, *Preaching Poverty in the Later Roman Empire: Perceptions and Realities*, Arbeiten zur Kirchen- und Theologiegeschichte, Bd 28 (Leipzig, 2009), pp. 209–31, at pp. 227–8.

⁴⁹ Gelasius I, *Ep.* 23 (Thiel, *Epistulae Romanorum pontificum*, p. 390) = JK 727, to Bishops Crispinus and Sabinus.

⁵⁰ Ibid., *Ep.* 24 (Thiel, *Epistulae Romanorum pontificum*, p. 391) = JK 728, from 494 to 495. Taylor, 'The Early Papacy at Work', p. 328, suggests that *zaja* or *zeia* was the Gothic equivalent of *comes*. The *zaja* is mentioned also in *Ep.* 14 (Ewald, 'Die Papstbriefe der Brittischen Sammlung, 2', pp. 513–14) = JK 650, in the context of correcting another kind of abuse.

traditional patronage networks to enforce church discipline. These structures were no longer adequate, however.

Interventions on Behalf of the Needy

Gelasius penned several other letters of recommendation to bishops and the aristocracy on behalf of those with no protectors. He ordered two bishops to help Maximus and Januarius, clerics who had no relatives, and had been robbed of their property by their guardian, the deacon Olympius.[51] Gelasius recommended the widow Antonina to the care of Bishops John, Bassus and Alexander.[52] He petitioned Januarius, a nobleman, to help and defend the poor. Not only the nobility but also royalty were enlisted to aid the poor. In a letter to the mother of the Gothic king Theodoric, he asked the queen to help the poor 'for the sake of [her] salvation and the increase of [her] prosperity'.[53] It seems that Gelasius' letters to her son the king, delivered by the *defensor* of the church, had gone unanswered. Gelasius also wrote letters of recommendation for Jewish converts, as in the case of the nobleman Telesinus.[54]

Crisis 2: Managing Population Displacement

With the Vandal invasion of North Africa from 429, the persecution of Nicene Christians as well as Manichees and Donatists meant that bishops of Rome had to deal with a torrent of displaced persons. The impact of this was only glimpsed by Augustine before his death in 430. The influx of refugees from North Africa to Rome was a cause of grave concern to Leo the Great in the 440s after the taking of Carthage in 439, due to the burdens it imposed on the already stretched resources of the city. Rome suffered a mass exodus of its richer citizens with the sieges of Alaric and Geiseric in 410 and 455 respectively, and the narrowly averted invasion by Attila in 452. With its native population

---

[51] Gelasius I, *frag.* 32 (Thiel, *Epistulae Romanorum pontificum*, p. 500) = JK 726, to Anastasius; and *frag.* 33 (Thiel, *Epistulae Romanorum pontificum*, p. 501) = JK 734, to Fortunatus.

[52] Ibid., *frag.* 1 (Theil, *Epistulae Romanorum pontificum*, pp. 483–4) = JK 671, to Bishop John.

[53] Ibid., *frag.* 36 (Thiel, *Epistulae Romanorum pontificum* p. 502) = JK 683, to Hereleuva: '… ut pro uestrae salutis et prosperitatis augmentis egentium causas iuuare dignemini'.

[54] Ibid., *frag.* 45 (Thiel, *Epistulae Romanorum pontificum*, p. 508) = JK 654, to Bishop Quinigesius.

reduced to half its earlier levels of around one million, Rome's food supplies had shrunk accordingly.

In the early 490s, however, the influx was renewed by the civil war between Odoacer and Theodoric, and it fell to the bishop of Rome to feed, clothe and house them. It seems that some unscrupulous Romans had benefited from the chaos. Gelasius lamented the increase of immigrant mouths to feed in a letter to a Roman noblewoman,[55] and asked Firmina to arrange that those estates of the Roman church (*praedia*) that had been stolen, whether by barbarians or by Romans, be returned for the feeding of the poor. Adopting the rhetoric of civic evergetism, he maintained that her almsgiving would be in her spiritual interest: 'Think how much good work you will acquire, if the estates, which individuals donated for the good of their souls to the blessed apostle Peter, are given back by your aid and released to God'.[56] The only instance of Gelasius' direct correspondence with a refugee is his reprimand to a North African bishop, Succonius, ca. the end of 493 (*Epistula* 9). Bishop Succonius, having fled the Arian persecution of Nicene Christians in North Africa, had fallen in with the supporters of Acacius in Constantinople. Gelasius admonished him for his cowardice: 'Surely you are not he who scorns the threats of kings and despises the feral laws of raging barbarians ... ?'.[57] This kind of plain speech suggests a familiarity between the letter-writer and his addressee which might also be read as evidence that Gelasius had a particular interest in the North African situation.

The redemption of captives was a key responsibility of bishops in this period, especially those of Gaul and North Africa. From their letters one would never guess that Roman bishops were involved in this problem in the fifth century. However, we know for instance that thousands of Romans were taken captive by

---

[55] Ibid., *frag.* 35 (Thiel, *Epistulae Romanorum pontificum*, p. 502) = JK 685: 'Cuius tanta de prouinciis diuersis, quae bellorum clade uastatae sunt, Romam multitudo confluxit, ut uix ei Deo teste sufficere ualeamus'. ('For such a multitude has converged on Rome from diverse provinces, that we are hardly able to manage it, with God as our witness.').

[56] Ibid.: 'Conspicitis ergo, quantum boni operis acquiratis, si beato Petro apostolo praedia, quae pro sua quisque anima contulit, uestro post Deum praesidio liberata reddantur'.

[57] Ibid., *Ep.* 9.2 (Thiel, *Epistulae Romanorum pontificum*, p. 340) = JK 628: 'Nonne ille es qui spretis regum minis et saeuientium barbarorum feralia iura despiciens ... ?' Cf. *Ep.* 9.4 (Thiel, *Epistulae Romanorum pontificum*, pp. 340–41): 'Nunc uere de patria conuersatione discessum est, nunc uerum sentitur exilium ... ' ('Now have you truly abandoned the ways of your homeland, now you feel your true exile ... '); and *Ep.* 9.3 (Thiel, *Epistulae Romanorum pontificum*, p. 340): 'Itane non senseras, quod duobus cornibus praeludendo uno eodemque tempore non minus in Oriente quam in Africa Iesum soluere niteretur Antichristus?' ('Did you not realise that, by playing on two horns at the same time, the Antichrist was attempting to destroy Jesus no less in the East than in Africa?').

Geiseric in the 450s. There is no evidence of Gelasius funding redemptions, but his successor Symmachus (496–514) certainly did, though this is not mentioned in his letters.[58] Gelasius did however offer letters of recommendation to clergy whose job it was to find and redeem captives in other parts. In *Epistula* 13 (25 January 494), Gelasius recommended to Rusticus of Limoges another bishop, Epiphanius of Lyons, who was about to arrive in Limoges to find and redeem captives of his own people.[59] Ennodius, in his *Vita Epiphanii*, confirms that Epiphanius did indeed arrive in Lyons by crossing the river Rhodanus.[60]

Like Augustine, Gelasius had to deal with several crises concerning those who sought refuge or asylum in churches, a practice that had gained acceptance during the siege of Rome in 410, as Augustine recounted in *De ciuitate Dei*.[61] Augustine seems to have exercised his own judgement about who was worthy of sanctuary: in *Epistulae* 1* and 250, he reprimanded a young bishop for anathematising Augustine's friend Callinicus, and his whole family, when Callinicus violated the sanctuary of a younger bishop's church to retrieve some unworthy persons.[62] Churches initially offered asylum only when the claimant had a legitimate grievance, but the legal right of sanctuary was not always respected even in these cases. *Fragments* 39 and 40 stipulate that those who are said to have violated the asylum of churches should not be deemed worthy of entering them, i.e. they should be anathematised.

Like his predecessors, Gelasius recognised that the limitations of sanctuary excluded slaves – however, a slave could only be given back to his master when an

---

[58] On Symmachus' collaboration with Caesarius of Arles to raise funds from the Roman Senate for the ransoming of Gallic and Italian prisoners, as reported in *Vita Caesarii*, see W.E. Klingshirn, 'Charity and Power: Caesarius of Arles and the Ransoming of Captives in Sub-Roman Gaul', *JRS*, 75 (1985): pp. 183–203, at pp. 198–9. On the ransoming of prisoners in Liguria and Milan by Symmachus see also *Lib. pont.* 53.11 (Duchesne and Vogel, *Le* Liber pontificalis, p. 263); cf. his dictum at the Roman synod of 502 in *Acta synodi Romani anno 502* (MGH.AA 12.449, lines 16–18).

[59] Gelasius I, *Ep.* 13 (Thiel, *Epistulae Romanorum pontificum*, p. 359) = JK 634. Gelasius also seeks information about the Acacian schism, on which see below.

[60] Ennodius of Pavia, *Vita Epiphanii*, 151 (MGH.AA 7.103).

[61] Augustine, *De ciu. Dei*, 1.1 (NBA 5/1.18–20). The first recorded case of Christian exile in a church is Martin of Tours, in Sulpicius Severus, *V. sancti Martini* (SC 133.254).

[62] See A. Ducloux, *Ad ecclesiam confugere. Naissance du droit d'asile dans les églises (IVe – milieu du Ve s.)*, De l'archéologie à l'histoire (Paris, 1994); and G. Folliet, 'Le dossier de l'affaire Classicianus (Epist. 1* and 250)', in C. Lepelley (ed.), *Les lettres de saint Augustin découvertes par Johannes Divjak. Communications présentées au colloque des 20 et 21 Septembre 1982*, EAA, vol. 98 (Paris, 1983), pp. 129–46.

oath had been sworn that the slave would not be punished.[63] This stricture was imposed by *Codex Theodosianus* in 432, and ratified by Emperor Leo in 466.[64] Both orthodox and Arian churches served as sanctuaries: in the case of Felix, who had sought asylum in the church of the 'barbarians' (that is, the Goths), Gelasius ruled that if Felix was found innocent of the crimes alleged against him he could go free, but when the *uir spectabilis* Heorthasius gave evidence against him, Gelasius ordered Felix to be taken off into custody.[65]

Crisis 3: Violence, Within the Church and Without

Violence against persons of the clergy seems to have been a relatively frequent occurrence at the end of the fifth century. *Epistulae* 36 to 39 concern the murder of a bishop in Calabria. First, Gelasius instructed Bishop John to deprive Archdeacon Asellus of office, because since the death of his bishop he had been canvassing for election without consulting the holy see (*Epistula* 36). He condemned the church of Scyllaceum in Calabria for the double killing of its bishops (*Epistula* 37). It would not be allowed its own priest; Bishops Majoricus and John should visit it for eucharist. He forbade absolutely the sacrilegious division of the holy eucharist attempted by those who only took the bread but not the cup. *Epistula* 38 to Phillip and Cassiodorus records that the priest Coelestinus had been convicted of killing his father and bishop, and was deprived of office. A letter to Bishops Majoricus, Serenus and John brought down judgement on the Dionysians, who brought ruin to the church of Vibo, a town in the territory of the Bruttii.[66] They were to be kept away from the

---

[63] Gelasius I, *frag.* 41 (Thiel, *Epistulae Romanorum pontificum*, pp. 505–6) = JK 711, to Bishop Boniface. Cf. *frag.* 43 (Thiel, *Epistulae Romanorum pontificum*, pp. 506–7) = JK 742, on the fate of a slave of a Jewish master who sought refuge in a church of Venefrana, discussed above. See also K. Sessa, *The Formation of Papal Authority in Late Antiquity: Roman Bishops and the Domestic Sphere* (Cambridge, 2012), pp. 158–61.

[64] *CTh* 9.45.5 (Mommsen and Krüger, *Codex Theodosianus*, p. 526), from 432. See discussion of Ducloux, *Ad ecclesiam confugere,* pp. 243–50, and texts, pp. 288–91.

[65] Gelasius I, *frag.* 42 (Thiel, *Epistulae Romanorum pontificum*, p. 506) = JK 732. This could be the same Felix as in *frag.* 13 (Thiel, *Epistulae Romanorum pontificum*, p. 490) = JK 743, namely, Felix of Nola, who accused Bishop Serenus of violence.

[66] Ibid., *Ep.* 39 (Thiel, *Epistulae Romanorum pontificum*, p. 453) = JK 733. The identity of the 'Dionysians' is unknown – from their appearance in this context, one may speculate that they were the party who opposed the taking of the bread without the cup at eucharist. The Manichees also refrained from drinking wine at eucharist.

eucharist, and the bishops were ordered not to neglect anything that could be done against them through secular laws.

More violence against bishops is addressed in *fragment* 14. Bishops Justus and Stephan were told to look into the claim of Proficius, bishop of Salpina, that Brumarius, a *uir spectabilis*, physically attacked the servant of the church with no reason, and then, to increase his violence, spread serious slanders against the bishop. If Brumarius confessed, they should look into it; if not, the bishops should invoke the judgement of the province. This appears to mean that they should invoke the powers of secular law.

A letter to Justus of Lerins and Probus (bishop of an unnamed city in Apulia) responds to the complaint of a priest, Mark, that he was beaten in his church on Easter day. The bishops should defend him from injuries by enemies, and the bishop of Luceria should make sure lest condemnation be brought on his monastery on the Lucerian estate.[67] Violence, even accidental, against persons of the clergy could result in them being made unfit for office. Self-inflicted injury is the subject of *fragment* 9 to Bishop Palladius, concerning a priest, Stephan, who had brought a petition to Gelasius. Stephan wounded his nether regions when jumping a fence trying to escape a barbarian attack. Thus, he was now not 'whole' and could not be a priest according to the canons, so he had been deposed. Gelasius generously ruled that since the accident happened several years after his ordination, he should be restored to office.[68]

The invocation of secular power for the protection of bishops occurs in a group of three final letters. *Fragment* 11 describes how his fellow bishop, Serenus of Nola, was attacked by such contumelies that he was forced to come to the court of King Theodoric.[69] It transpired from *fragment* 13 that two clerics of Nola, Felix and Peter, had inflicted serious injuries and losses on Bishop Serenus after he had redeemed barbarian captives by proper authority.[70] Addressing Theodoric, Gelasius insisted that, just as Theodoric had ordained that the laws of Roman emperors (*principes Romani*) should be observed, he would wish surely them to be kept all the more when the matter concerned the reverence due to

---

[67] Ibid., *Ep.* 3* (Lowenfeld, *Epistolae pontificum Romanorum*, p. 2) = JK 631, from the end of 493 to January 494.

[68] Ibid., *frag.* 9 (Thiel, *Epistulae Romanorum pontificum*, p. 488) = JK 706.

[69] Ibid., *frag.* 11 (Thiel, *Epistulae Romanorum pontificum*, p. 489) = JK 723, to Bishops Gerontius and John.

[70] Ibid., *frag.* 13 (Thiel, *Epistulae Romanorum pontificum*, p. 490) = JK 743, to Bishops Quinigesius and Constantinus: ' ... et auctoritate promerita contra ciuilitatem redemptis sibi barbaris suprascriptum episcopum suum grauibus injuriis et dispendiis affecerunt'.

the apostle Peter (*fragment* 12).[71] His petition seems to have been successful: Theodoric sent the rebel clerics Felix and Peter of Nola back to Gelasius for trial (*fragment* 13).

Gelasius upheld a relatively enlightened attitude to violence against women in ruling that rape was committed against a girl who was abducted before her marriage, as 'that law of previous princes declared'.[72] This was in line with previous fifth-century papal rulings, for example by Innocent and Leo.[73]

Crisis 4: Failure of the Legal System

Concern with social abuses resulting from the failure of the legal system is most obvious in the 29 newly discovered 'Divjak' letters of Augustine. The bishop of Hippo wrote several impassioned letters about indentured child labour and the slave trade.[74] Between the years 415 and 420, Augustine defended the release of victims of the Numidian slave-traders who operated off the coast of North Africa. Members of his congregation in his absence had bought about 120 captives as their ship was passing through the port of Hippo, and released

---

[71] Ibid., *frag.* 12 (Thiel, *Epistulae Romanorum pontificum*, pp. 489–90) = JK 722: 'Certum est, magnificentiam uestram leges Romanorum principum, quas in negotiis hominum custodiendas esse praecepit, multo magis circa reuerentiam beati Petri apostoli pro suae felicitatis augmento uelle seruari'. See the discussion of this incident in P. Amory, *People and Identity in Ostrogothic Italy, 489–554*, Cambridge Studies in Medieval Life and Thought, 4th series (Cambridge, 1997), pp. 82–4.

[72] Gelasius I, *frag.* 47 (Thiel, *Epistulae Romanorum pontificum*, p. 508), to an unknown recipient: 'Lex illa praeteritorum principum ibi raptum dixit esse commissum, ubi puella, de cujus ante nuptiis nihil actum fuerit, uideatur abducta'.

[73] Innocent rejected the Roman law on the dissolution of marriage after abduction of one of the spouses and their enslavement, in *Ep.* 36 (PL 20.602–3) = JK 313. See G.D. Dunn, 'The Validity of Marriage in Cases of Captivity: The Letter of Innocent I to Probus', *ETL*, 83 (2007): pp. 107–21. On Leo's *Ep.* 159 (PL 54.1138–40) of 21 March 458 to Nicetas of Aquileia, which upheld Innocent's ruling on the validity of first marriages, see B. Neil (trans.), *Leo the Great*, The Early Church Fathers (London and New York, 2009), pp. 139–40; and K. Sessa, 'Ursa's Return: Captivity, Remarriage, and the Domestic Authority of Roman Bishops in Fifth-Century Italy', *JECS*, 19 (2011): pp. 401–32, at 423–9.

[74] See J. Rougé, 'Escroquerie et brigandage en Afrique romaine au temps de saint Augustin (Epist. 8* and 10*)', in C. Lepelley (ed.), *Les Lettres de saint Augustin découvertes par Johannes Divjak. Communications présentées au colloque des 20 et 21 Septembre 1982*, EEA, vol. 98 (Paris, 1983), pp. 177–88.

them.[75] Free-born women and children were among those stolen by the 'people traffickers' (*mangones*); some were children sold into slavery by their parents.

Gelasius encouraged bishops to look after the law suits of widows and orphans with zeal.[76] The intercession of priests in court cases (*negotiis*) in Gelasius' name was not denied to those who requested it.[77] Gelasius took only limited action against social abuses resulting from failure of the legal system, but it should be noted that no popes before him took any action at all except Leo, who condemned usury by clerics and lay persons.[78] In 419 the Synod of Carthage had made the same prohibition for clergy and laity alike.[79] Two of Gelasius' interventions against social abuses concerned women. An honourable woman accused a deacon who had 'sought [her] out for indecent crimes' (*fragment* 16). The deacon was convicted on various charges, including magic. *Epistula* 40 addresses the tearful petition of Olibula, a religious woman, who was being deprived of her share of her parents' estate by her sisters and their husbands. The local *audientia episcopalis* had clearly failed this woman. Gelasius instructed Bishop John of Spoleto to see to it that Olibula can serve God with a quiet mind, having received the portion of their wealth she is owed.

The majority of abuses concern similar cases of property theft, often by members of the clergy.[80] *Epistula* 16* to Mercurius deals with law suits about rents (*pensiones*), that cannot be transferred before judgement is carried against some person.[81] Gelasius rules that property under legal proceedings should not

---

[75] Augustine, *Ep.* 10*.2–3 (NBA 23A.80–82). Of the 120 released by members of his congregation only 26 had been sold by their parents. See Augustine, *Ep.* 10*.7 (NBA 23A.84–6). The text is discussed by Finn, *Almsgiving*, p. 23.

[76] Gelasius I, *frag.* 31 (Thiel, *Epistulae Romanorum pontificum*, p. 500) = JK 707, to Bishops Gerontius and Peter.

[77] Ibid., *frag.* 30 (Thiel, *Epistulae Romanorum pontificum*, p. 500) = JK 730, to Bishops Leontius and Peter.

[78] Leo I, *Ep.* 4.3 (Wurm, 'Decretales selectae', p. 91).

[79] *Canones in causa Apiarii*, can. 5 (CCL 149.102/134), although Augustine, *Serm.* 77A.4 (NBA 30/1.550–552); 86.3.3 (NBA 30/2.10); 113.2.2 (NBA 30/2.414–16); and 239.5 (NBA 32/2.626); and Augustine, *En. in Ps.* 36.3.6 (NBA 25.818–20); and 54.14 (NBA 26.100–102), acknowledged that, while forbidden by the church, it was permitted for lay persons under secular law. Usury had been forbidden to clerics as long ago as the 345 Synod of Carthage, can. 13 (CCL 149.9). On Augustine and usury see Allen and Morgan, 'Augustine on Poverty', p. 135 and n. 118.

[80] Sessa, *The Formation of Papal Authority*, pp. 190–91, deals with Gelasius' handling of this problem briefly, setting it in the wider context of stewardship of the church's assets by the bishop of Rome. See also pp. 94 and 108.

[81] Gelasius, I *Ep.* 16* (Loewenfeld, *Epistolae pontificum Romanorum ineditae*, p. 9) = JK 691.

be transferred to any person until the case is concluded.[82] No one should be allowed to exact rents from any property until it is settled. Some people were clearly losing patience with the legal system and taking matters into their own hands. *Epistula 6** concerns law suits between members of the clergy:[83] Gelasius appointed as judges three bishops – Victor, Serenus and Melior – to settle a dispute between an archdeacon and his deacon.

Conclusion

On the basis of this epistolary evidence we discern a major shift occurring at the end of the fifth century in the production, function and preservation of papal letters. The many similarities between the Gelasian corpus and Augustine of Hippo's use of letters to make personal interventions on behalf of the needy seem to me to reveal in Gelasius an approach to episcopal government that is distinct from that of previous bishops of Rome, and which perhaps might be 'African' in its origins. Far more frequently than any Roman bishop before him Gelasius involved himself in crises of the kinds I have discussed. In his personal dealings with Gallic prisoners of war and asylum seekers, victims of famine, and victims of crisis, Gelasius was breaking new ground for a bishop of Rome. This is not to say that he was a revolutionary challenger of the *status quo*. He respected traditional ties of obligation as his letters on the status of slaves demonstrate. However, his many letters of personal recommendation, even on behalf of a Jew on one occasion, demonstrate the new approach. His involvement in the financial management of church property is also quite novel. His attempts to impose a fourfold division of church income on churches in Italy and Sicily, and his appeals to imperial law, show that his interventions were more than *ad hoc* or *ad hominem*. On the other hand he insisted that the secular powers uphold imperial laws to protect the clergy.

The new focus on financial management and personal recommendations for those in need is evident in the early sixth century in the corpus of Symmachus (498–514). Similar moves are made by Pelagius I (556–61), who sought to help the needy of Rome and Portus Romanus using the produce and revenues

---

[82] Ibid., *frag.* 46 (Thiel, *Epistulae Romanorum pontificum*, p. 508) = JK 712, to Bishop Quinigesius.

[83] Ibid., *Ep. 6** (Loewenfeld, *Epistolae pontificum Romanorum ineditae*, pp. 3–4) = JK 646, from end of 494 to beginning of 495.

of papal estates.[84] The pontificate and crisis-management style of Gregory the Great marks the end of the period of transition to a new style of papal leadership inspired by Gelasius, which possibly might be African in origin.[85]

---

[84] Pelagius I, *Epp.* 4 and 9 (P.M. Gassó and C.M. Batlle [eds], *Pelagii I Papae epistulae quae supersunt [556 – 561]*, Scripta et Documenta, vol. 8 [Montserrat, 1956], pp. 11–13, 28–30) = JK 943 and 947, to Bishop Sapaudus. See Richards, *The Popes*, p. 53.

[85] The continuities between the three popes are examined by B. Neil, 'The Papacy in the Age of Gregory the Great', in B. Neil and M. Dal Santo (eds), *Companion to Gregory the Great*, Brill's Companions to the Christian Tradition, vol. 47 (Leiden, 2013), pp. 3–27.

PART III
The Sixth Century

Chapter 10

Ipsis diebus Bonifatius, zelo et dolo ductus: The Root Causes of the Double Papal Election of 22 September 530[*]

Dominic Moreau

The sixth century was a period of significant political, social and economic changes for Italy. As the main territory of an Ostrogothic kingdom allied to the eastern Roman empire since the early 500s, the peninsula eventually became the centre of a war between the two 'states' from 535 to 553/4. After this date, Constantinople believed it had sustainably recovered the historic centre of its empire, but the Lombards broke this illusion in 568. Never again were the Byzantines going to control the entirety of Italy.

With all this turmoil, the sixth century was also the period of late antiquity that saw the largest number of controversial elections for the headship of the Roman church: the double elections of Symmachus and Lawrence (498/501–506/7), and of Boniface II and Dioscorus (530), the probable appointment of Felix IV (III) by Theodoric (526), of Silverius by Theodahad (536) and of Vigilius and Pelagius I by Justinian I (537 and 556). The best documented of these cases is certainly that of 530, when Felix IV (III) (526–30), on his deathbed, appointed Boniface II as his successor, which was not supported by the majority of the Roman clergy who instead nominated Dioscorus.

Before the last quarter of the nineteenth century, Felix's initiative, contrary to the ecclesiastical canons, had been forgotten. This episode came to light again through the discovery of a small dossier related to this case by Guerrino Amelli – known as Ambrogio Maria Amelli after his entry to the Abbey of Monte Cassino – in the *Codex Novariensis XXX (66)* (tenth century).[1] Yet, the

---

[*] This chapter derives from some results of the postdoctoral research programme on the *Collectio (Ecclesiae) Thessalonicensis* I carried out under the supervision of Eckhard Wirbelauer at Université de Strasbourg (UMR 7044 – ARCHIMÈDE), with financial support of the Fonds de recherche du Québec 'Société et Culture'.

[1] See A.M.(G.) Amelli, *Nuovi contributi alla teologia positiva. San Leone Magno e il primato del romano pontefice in Oriente* (Monte Cassino, 1908); A.M.(G.) Amelli,

exact reasons that drove Felix to make such a decision, as well as those that led him to choose Boniface as his successor, have remained unknown. This is also the case for the exact sequence of the schism. Biographies of Boniface II thus usually focus on the details of his appointment as well as on his failed attempt to appoint his own successor in the person of Vigilius, this last episode having been well recounted by *Liber pontificalis*.[2]

Nevertheless, the episcopacies of Felix and Boniface were not limited to endeavours by the highest ecclesiastical authorities in Rome to establish, under pressure from or with the support of the Ostrogothic court, a new system of appointment for Roman bishops. The papal history of the 520s and 530s was actually extremely rich in many other ways, for example in the production of canonical collections. However, the willingness of Roman pontiffs to interfere directly in the election of their successors fully fits in the context of major changes to the established political order. In reality, we cannot understand one question without examining the others.

By looking at all the sources at our disposal from a fresh perspective, this chapter will focus on the atmosphere surrounding the events of 22 September 530, with the aim of reinserting the simultaneous appointments of Boniface and Dioscorus within the politico-religious ambience of the time in order to suggest why Felix chose Boniface and why Dioscorus emerged in opposition to that appointment. To fulfil adequately these objectives, the work is divided into three parts: after a quick overview of the background of the two popes, it will question the importance of the context following the Laurentian-Symmachian schism and the impact of John I's death on the double papal election of 530. The chapter will conclude with a proposed explanation of the

---

Spicilegium Casinense complectens analecta sacra et profana e codd. Casinensibus aliarumque bibliothecarum collecta atque edita, t. 1 (Monte Cassino, 1888–93), pp. 179–81. On the Felix–Boniface dossier see also L. Duchesne, 'La succession du pape Félix IV', *Mélanges d'archéologie et d'histoire*, 3 (1883): pp. 239–66; P. Ewald, 'Acten zum Schisma des Jahres 530', *NA*, 10 (1885): pp. 412–3; Th. Mommsen, 'Actenstücke zur Kirchengeschichte aus dem Cod. Cap. Novar. 30', *NA*, 11 (1886): pp. 367–8; Th. Mommsen, *Gesammelte Schriften*, Bd 6: *Historische Schriften. Dritter Band* (Berlin, 1910), pp. 605–9; L. Duchesne, *L'Église au VIe siècle* (Paris, 1925), pp. 143–6; A. von Harnack, 'Der erste deutsche Papst (Bonifatius II., 530/32) und die beiden letzten Dekreten des römischen Senats', *Sitzungsberichte der Preussischen Akademie der Wissenschaften. Philosophisch-historische Klasse* (1924): pp. 24–42; L. Duchesne and C. Vogel (eds), *Le* Liber pontificalis: *Texte, introduction et commentaire*, t. 1, BEFAR (Paris, 1955 [2nd edn]), pp. 282–3, n. 4–10 and 14; E. Wirbelauer, 'Die Nachfolgerbestimmung im römischen Bistum (3.–6. Jh.). Doppelwahlen und Absetzungen in ihrer herrschafts-soziologischen Bedeutung', *Klio*, 76 (1994): pp. 388–437 at pp. 417–21.

[2] *Lib. pont.* 57.3–4 (MGH.GPR 1.139 and H. Geertman, *Hic fecit basilicam: Studi sul* Liber pontificalis *e gli edifici ecclesiastici di Roma da Silvestro a Silverio* [Leuven, 2004], p. 234).

root causes of the event, which was one of the first steps to what Ernst Stein considers 'la plus grandiose des guerres justiniennes'.[3]

Background of Boniface and Dioscorus

The major difficulty in the analysis of what took place on 22 September 530 is due to the fact that we know few details about the past of the two figures elevated to the pontificate. It is important, however, to place what we do know within the context of the political events of the time. We indeed know almost nothing of Boniface II's life before that date, only that he made his career in the Roman church and that he was archdeacon when Felix IV (III) chose him as his successor.[4] Also, *Liber pontificalis* presents him as a native of Rome, but the name of his father in the same book, Sigibuldus, suggests a Germanic origin, which leaves open the idea that he might have had some sympathy for the kingdom of the Ostrogoths and that he could even have belonged to this 'nation'.[5]

Apart from almost certain Alexandrian origin, the personal history of the Roman deacon Dioscorus is not much better known than that of his rival. Unlike with Boniface, we are however more aware of his involvement in church affairs. As a close associate of Popes Symmachus and Hormisdas, he played a key role in the resolution of the Acacian schism (484–519). For some time, he was even seen by Emperor Justin I (518–27) – and his nephew Justinian! – as a potential candidate for bishop of Antioch.[6] It is impossible to prove it, but Dioscorus

---

[3] E. Stein, *Histoire du Bas-Empire*, t. 2: *De la disparition de l'Empire d'Occident à la mort de Justinien (476–565)*, J.-R. Palanque (ed.) (Paris, Brussels and Amsterdam, 1949), p. 339.

[4] Felix IV (III), *Praeceptum* (E. Schwartz [ed.], *ACO*, t. 4: *Concilium universale Constantinopolitanum sub Iustiniano habitum*, vol. 2: *Johannis Maxentii libelli – Collectio codicis Novariensis XXX – Collectio codicis Parisini 1682 – Procli Tomus ad Armenios – Johannis papae II Epistula ad viros illustres* [Strasbourg, 1914], p. 97) = P. Jaffé, *Regesta pontificum Romanorum ab condita ecclesia ad annum post Christum natum MCXCVIII*, vol. 2: *Ab a. MCXLIII ad a. MCXCVIII*, rev. W. Wattenbach (Leipzig, 1888 [2nd edn]), supplementum regestorum 879a; and *ICUR* n.s. 2.4153.

[5] *Lib. pont.* 57.1 (MGH.GPR 1.139 and Geertman, *Hic fecit basilicam*, p. 234); von Harnack, 'Der erste deutsche Papst', pp. 24–5; P. Amory, *People and Identity in Ostrogothic Italy, 489–554*, Cambridge Studies in Medieval Life and Thought, 4th series (Cambridge, 1997), p. 415 (Sigibuldus); and *PCBE* 2.2066 (Sigibuld).

[6] *Frag. Laurentianum Lib. pont.* 52.fol. 2 (MGH.GPR 1.x); *Lib. pont.* 54.5 and [7] (MGH.GPR 1.128–9 and Geertman, *Hic fecit basilicam*, pp. 227–9) = *Epit. Feliciana Lib. pont.* 54.§ 6 (MGH.GPR 1.259–60); Ennodius of Pavia, *Epp.* 6.33; 7.28.4; and 9.16.1 (MGH. AA 7.229, 259 and 304); John Maxentius, *Libellus fidei, superscriptio* 2 (CCL 85A.5); John Maxentius, *Responsio adu. ep. [124] Horm.* 1.1 (7).81; 4 (20).276 and (21).283; 8 (26).350; and 9 (35).487, 492 and 495 (CCL 85A.125, 132, 134 and 138–9); Hormisdas, *Epp.* 50

might also have been the anonymous cleric whom the Ostrogothic king, Theoderic the Great (471/93–526), had blocked previously from obtaining the apostolic see, by placing Felix IV (III) on it *ex iusso*, in order to avoid the return of a certain *pristina contentio*.[7] This expression from a letter of Ostrogothic king Athalaric (526–34) – actually from his mother Amalasuintha († 535) and Cassiodorus († ca. 580) – has always been interpreted as referring to the Laurentian-Symmachian schism (498/501–506/7), in which the Alexandrian participated actively against Lawrence's party.[8]

Dioscorus was a supporter of the religious – and political? – union between Rome and Constantinople, but a union in the full Chalcedonian orthodoxy and not in the ambiguity of the *Henotikon*. Based on this position, it is often suggested that he could have arrived in Rome at the same time as John Talaïa

---

(*Collectio Avellana, Ep.* 149) (CSEL 35.594–8) = JK 806; 52.7 (*Collectio Avellana, Ep.* 150.7) (CSEL 35.599) = JK 808; 72–4 (*Collectio Avellana, Ep.* 219–21) (CSEL 35.680–2) =JK 815–6 and 818; 87 (*Collectio Avellana, Ep.* 170) (CSEL 35.627) = JK 827; 97 (*Collectio Avellana, Ep.* 226) (CSEL 35.690–2) = JK 838; 104–6 (*Collectio Avellana, Ep.* 173, 175 and 171) (CSEL 35.629–32 and 627–8) = JK 841–3; 107.2–3 (*Collectio Avellana, Ep.* 172.2–3) (CSEL 35.628–9) = JK 844; and 123 (*Collectio Avellana, Ep.* 229) (CSEL 35.694) = JK 849; John II the Cappadocian, *Ep. ad Horm.* (*Redditis mihi*) 1 and 7 (*Collectio Avellana, Ep.* 159.1 and 7) (CSEL 35.607 and 610); Dioscorus, *Suggestiones ad Horm.* (*Ineffabilis Dei*) (*Collectio Avellana, Ep.* 167) (CSEL 35.618–21); (*Verum est*) (*Collectio Avellana, Ep.* 216) (CSEL 35.675–6); (*Erat optabile*) (*Collectio Avellana, Ep.* 222) (CSEL 35.682–3); (*Per Eulogium*) (*Collectio Avellana, Ep.* 224) (CSEL 35.685–7); Justin I, *Ep. ad Horm.* (*Quanto flagramus*) 2 (*Collectio Avellana, Ep.* 181.2) (CSEL 35.636); *Ep. ad Horm.* (*Summa quidem*) (*Collectio Avellana, Ep.* 192) (CSEL 35.649–50); Germanus of Capua et al., *Suggestiones ad Horm.* (*Reuerenda uestri*) (*Collectio Avellana, Ep.* 185) (CSEL 35.641–2); (*In ciuitate*) (*Collectio Avellana, Ep.* 213) (CSEL 35.671–3); (*Cum Dei*) (*Collectio Avellana, Ep.* 217) (CSEL 35.677–9); (*Filius uester*) (*Collectio Avellana, Ep.* 218) (CSEL 35.679–80); (*Non miramur*) (*Collectio Avellana, Ep.* 223) (CSEL 35.683–4); (*Magna est*) (*Collectio Avellana, Ep.* 225) (CSEL 35.688–90); Epiphanius of Constantinople, *Relatio ad Horm.* (*Deus, qui*) 7 (*Collectio Avellana, Ep.* 195.7) (CSEL 35.654). On the Acacian schism see E. Schwartz, *Publizistische Sammlungen zum acacianischen Schisma*, Abhandlungen der Bayerischen Akademie der Wissenschaften. Philosophisch-historische Abteilung. Neue Folge, vol. 10 (Munich, 1934); and P. Blaudeau, 'Motifs et structures de divisions ecclésiales. Le Schisme acacien (484–519)', *AHC*, 39 (2007): pp. 65–98.

[7] Cassiodorus, *Variae* 8.15 (MGH.AA 12.246); *Epit. Cononiana Lib. pont.* 56.§ 2 (MGH.GPR 1.263). See also P. Blaudeau, *Le Siège de Rome et l'Orient (448–536). Étude géo-ecclésiologique*, CEFR, vol. 460 (Rome, 2012), p. 149, n. 82. It is interesting to note that the non-abbreviated text of *Lib. pont.*, that has reached us, specifies that Felix was ordained *cum quietem*. See *Lib. pont.* 56.2 (MGH.GPR 1.138).

[8] On the Laurentian-Symmachian schism see mainly E. Wirbelauer, *Zwei Päpste in Rom. Der Konflikt zwischen Laurentius und Symmachus (498–514). Studien und Texte*, Quellen und Forschungen zur antiken Welt, vol. 16 (Munich, 1993).

(Chalcedonian bishop of Alexandria in 481–2) or immediately after.[9] Anyway, written sources suggest that it was the Catholic-Orthodox sympathies of the Alexandrian deacon that might have encouraged him to support Symmachus against Lawrence, since the latter was an agent of the ex-consul Rufius Postumius Festus in arguing to Emperor Zeno (474–91) that Anastasius II (496–8) would accept the *Henotikon*.

There is no intention here to assert that Dioscorus was fully in favour of the religious current defended at that time by the eastern imperial court or to reduce the Laurentian-Symmachian schism to a simple opposition between supporters and opponents of Constantinople. Nonetheless, it must be acknowledged that the division of the churches of the two *partes* held a significant (and underestimated!) importance in the Laurentian-Symmachian conflict.[10] On the one hand, the abbreviator of Theodorus Lector says that Festus was one of the most loyal protectors of Lawrence after his return from an embassy to Constantinople on behalf of Theodoric, during which it had promised the Byzantine authorities that they would get the Roman pontiff, Anastasius II to sign the *Henotikon*.[11] On the other hand, the 'philo-Symmachian' edition of *Liber pontificalis* states that Anastasius drew the wrath of several Roman clerics by taking the initiative to enter into communion with a Thessalonian deacon named Photinus, who was a follower of Acacius of Constantinople (471–89), in order to rehabilitate the Constantinopolitan bishop.[12] Symmachus was one of these opponents of his predecessor in the apostolic see.[13]

---

[9] See for example *PCBE* 2.571 (Dioscoros).

[10] See Wirbelauer, *Zwei Päpste*, pp. 44–50.

[11] *Epit. hist. eccl. Theodori Anagnostae (uel Lectoris) et Johannis Diacrinomeni* 441 (GCS n.F. 3.129–30); J. Moorhead, 'The Laurentian Schism: East and West in the Roman Church', *CH*, 47 (1978): pp. 125–36, at pp. 128–9; J. Moorhead, *Theoderic in Italy* (Oxford, 1992), pp. 57–9; and Wirbelauer, *Zwei Päpste*, p. 57.

[12] *Lib. pont.* 52.2 (MGH.GPR 1.119 and Geertman, *Hic fecit basilicam*, p. 222) = *Epit. Feliciana Lib. pont.* 52.§ 2 (MGH.GPR 1.256); E. Caspar, *Geschichte des Papsttums von den Anfängen bis zu Höhe der Weltherrschaft*, Bd 2: *Das Papsttum unter byzantinischer Herrschaft* (Tübingen, 1933), pp. 84–7 and 758 (Zu S. 82); H. Chadwick, *Boethius. The Consolations of Music, Logic, Theology, and Philosophy* (Oxford, 1981), pp. 30–1 and 38; Moorhead, *Theoderic*, pp. 56–8; and T.F.X. Noble, 'Theodoric and the Papacy', in CISAM, *Teoderico il Grande e I Goti d'Italia. Atti del XIII Congresso internazionale di studi sull'Alto Medioevo* (Milan, 2–6 November 1992), Atti dei Congressi, vol. 13 (Spoleto, 1993), pp. 395–423, at p. 404.

[13] The disapproval of Anastasius II's policy can be seen in Symmachus, *Epp.* 2–3 (MGH.Epp. 3.33–5) = JK 753–4; and Wirbelauer, *Zwei Päpste*, pp. 17 and 133–4, n. 94.

This would suggest a reasonable ground for rivalry between Boniface and Dioscorus based on opposing stances they had taken in the Laurentian-Symmachian schism a generation previously, if we could suggest a reason why Boniface was opposed to Symmachus or attracted to Lawrence. However, nothing is evident and we must look elsewhere to explain their differences.

The Legacy of the Laurentian-Symmachian Schism from 507 to 530

Theoretically, the Laurentian-Symmachian schism was completely resolved by 507, as well as the Acacian schism by 519. Assuming a progressive deterioration of the relations between Ravenna and Constantinople in the 520s, some scholars explain the intrusion of the Ostrogothic monarchy in the papal elections of 526 and 530 as some kind of 'nationalistic reaction' – both times against Dioscorus given his role in the resolution of the Acacian schism – in order to prevent the unification of the western and eastern churches in the Chalcedonian orthodoxy. That widely received view is based nevertheless on an argument from silence. In fact, it seems preferable not to see Felix IV (III) or Boniface II as representing a pro-Gothic/anti-Byzantine party especially because we have no evidence of their attitude towards the *Henotikon* prior to their elections.

It is true that the ecclesiastical agreement between the Romans of the two *partes* was never a priority for the kings of the Ostrogoths and that the division had rather benefited them. Whatever the case, nothing allows us to assert, however, that the persons who occupied the Ostrogothic throne before 535 took concrete steps to prevent the normalisation of East–West relations in religious matters, inasmuch as Theodoric and Athalaric – in reality, his mother, Amalasuintha – had almost always sought to accommodate and to retain a good relationship with Constantinople (as we shall see, the year 525–6 was an exception). Tolerance within the socio-political order established by the first Ostrogothic ruler of Italy, as well as in the external affairs of the kingdom, appears, in fact, to have been for the Amals a better guarantee of peace and prosperity, than would have been a position too settled in favour of or against the religious policy of the emperor.[14]

---

[14] See for example G.B. Picotti, 'Osservazioni su alcuni punti della politica religiosa di Teoderico', in CISAM, *I Goti in Occidente. Problemi* (Spoleto, 29 March – 5 April 1955), Settimane di studio del CISAM, vol. 3 (Spoleto, 1956), pp. 173–226; T.S. Brown, 'Everyday Life in Ravenna under Theoderic: An Example of his "Tolerance" and "Prosperity"?', in CISAM, *Teoderico il Grande e i Goti d'Italia. Atti del XIII Congresso internazionale di studi sull'Alto Medioevo* (Milan, 2–6 November 1992), Atti dei Congressi, vol. 13 (Spoleto, 1993), pp. 77–99; Noble, 'Theodoric', pp. 395–423; and B. Saitta, *La* civiltas *di Teoderico*.

This might explain why Theoderic first appears to have been more responsive to the protests of the 'Laurentians' – some of whose key members advocated a dialogue, even a compromise, with the Monophysite/Miaphysite East – rather than to those of the 'Symmachians', although ultimately he had no real bias in favour of one candidate or the other.[15] In reality the Amals would have preferred not to talk about religious matters, especially after the *pristina contentio*. The fact that the emperor was Orthodox or Monophysite did not matter for the Goths. As is suggested by Thomas Noble, it is surely not by chance that Theoderic's recognition of Symmachus' 'victory', obtained, it must be pointed out, with the help of Dioscorus, dates back to the year 507 (or 508?).[16] More or less at the time of the promulgation of the royal *praeceptum*, which put an end to the conflict between the two pretenders to the apostolic see, Emperor Anastasius I

Rigore amministrativo, "tolleranza" religiosa e recupero dell'antico nell'Italia ostrogota, Studia historica, vol. 128 (Rome, 1993), pp. 63–99. One cannot exclude that Theoderic's main adviser, Cassiodorus, was one of the architects of the tolerance policy. See for example T. Canella, 'Gli *Actus Silvestri*: l'invenzione di un'identità statale cristiana', *Annali di storia dell'esegesi*, 21 (2004): pp. 289–302; and T. Canella, *Gli* Actus Silvestri. *Genesi di una leggenda su Costantino imperatore*, Uomini e mondi medievali. Collana del Centro italiano di studi sul Basso Medioevo – Accademia Tudertina, vol. 7 (Spoleto 2006), pp. 135–77.

[15] If there is a constant in the diverging *uitae Symmachi* of the different versions of *Lib. pont.*, it is that Symmachus is always the accused one – sometimes wrongly, sometimes rightly – before Theoderic. Moreover, *Frag. Laurentianum* suggests that it was the king himself who allowed Lawrence to return to Rome in 502. As *Epit. Feliciana* would be the closest text to the first 'philo-Symmachian' edition of *Lib. pont.* – according to the *communis opinio*, even if it is not certain – one wonders if we should not retain the adjectives *hereticus* applied to Theoderic and *eutychianus* to Emperor Anastasius I, in the biography of Symmachus, as elements of the original vocabulary, unless these are additions made after the death of Pope John I in an Ostrogothic gaol. See *Frag. Laurentianum Lib. pont.* 52 (MGH. GPR 1.ix–x); *Lib. pont.* 53.2–5 (MGH.GPR 1.120–2 and Geertman, *Hic fecit basilicam*, pp. 223–4) = *Epit. Feliciana Lib. pont.* 53.§ 1–5 (MGH.GPR 1.256–7) = *Epit. Cononiana Lib. pont.* 53.§ 1–4 (MGH.GPR 1.256–8); A. Goltz, *Barbar – König – Tyrann. Das Bild Theoderichs des Großen in der Überlieferung des 5. bis 9. Jahrhunderts*, Millennium-Studien. Studien zu Kultur und Geschichte des ersten Jahrtausends n. Chr., Bd 12 (Berlin and New York, 2008), pp. 334–41. See also Moorhead, *Theoderic*, pp. 138–9 and 242, n. 138; Noble, 'Theodoric', pp. 410–2; and L. Capo, *Il* Liber pontificalis, *i Longobardi e la nascita del dominio territoriale della Chiesa romana*, Istituzioni e società, vol. 12 (Spoleto, 2009), p. 42.

[16] *Praeceptum Theoderici Magni contra sacerdotes substantiae ecclesiarum alienatores* (MGH.AA 12.392); Noble, 'Theodoric', p. 411–2. On the date of 507 see Schwartz, *Publizistische Sammlungen*, p. 169; R.S. Bagnall et al., *Consuls of the Later Roman Empire*, Philological Monographs of the American Philological Association, vol. 36 (Atlanta, 1987), p. 548; and Wirbelauer, *Zwei Päpste*, pp. 39–40. Nevertheless, the end of Lawrence's pontificate might have been officialised by the Roman clergy as early as 506. See Wirbelauer, *Zwei Päpste*, pp. 37–9.

(491–518), Zeno's successor, would officially recognise Lawrence as legitimate pontiff.[17] The Goths did not want the Romans to engage in negotiations, especially not secret ones, and did not want the Byzantines to take positions in Italian affairs, hence the problem when Anastasius I recognised Lawrence. The mistrust between the two 'states' would now follow an exponential curve. About 513 or 514, Priscian of Caesarea, a friend of Boethius, was able to announce a project of Byzantine re-conquest of the West in his famous eulogy to the Constantinopolitan ruler.[18]

The imperial succession of 518, which marked the coming to power of the Justinianic dynasty, and the conclusion of the schism of Acacius in favour of the Chalcedonian party, whose main leaders sought no compromise with other religious traditions, would make things worse between the two political entities. The breaking point with Theodoric was reached shortly before the last months of 525, following the proclamation by Emperor Justin I of measures against the Arians, in particular the confiscation of worship places belonging to them and/or some (forced?) conversions to the Catholic-Orthodox faith.[19] It is in this strained context of 525, heralding future hostilities, that Boethius and his father-in-law, Quintus Aurelius Memmius Symmachus Junior were executed, perhaps also (Faustus or Flavius?) Albinus Junior († after 522), accused of high treason for conspiring with Constantinople or defending conspirators. The first two were very likely members of the 'Laurentians', while the other appears to

---

[17] Symmachus, *Ep.* 10 (Schwartz, *Publizistische Sammlungen*, pp. 151–7; see also p. 169, n. 100). This testimony is not decisive, but it is interesting to note that pseudo-Zacharias of Mytilene, *Hist. eccl.* 7.12, fol. 131 r° b (CSCO 83/Scriptores Syri 38.56) clearly suggests that Symmachus' intransigence in matters of Diophysism was the key reason for his misunderstanding with Anastasius I.

[18] Priscian of Caesarea, *Carmen in laudem Anastasii imperatoris* 265 (A. Chauvot [ed.], *Procope de Gaza, Priscien de Césarée. Panégyriques de l'empereur Anastase Ier*, Antiquitas. Reihe 1: Abhandlungen zur alten Geschichte, Bd 35 [Bonn, 1986], pp. 66, 81, 98–107 and 190–92); Chadwick, *Boethius*, p. 43; and Noble, 'Theodoric', pp. 411–2.

[19] *Excerpta Valesiana* 2.15.88 (I. König [ed.], *Aus der Zeit Theoderichs des Großen. Einleitung, Text, Übersetzung und Kommentar einer anonymen Quelle*, Texte zur Forschung, Bd 69 [Darmstadt, 1997], pp. 92–3); and *Lib. pont.* 55.1 (MGH.GPR 1.133 and Geertman, *Hic fecit basilicam*, p. 231) = *Epit. Feliciana Lib. pont.* 55.§ 2–3 (MGH.GPR 1.260) = *Epit. Cononiana Lib. pont.* 55.§ 2 (MGH.GPR 1.260). On Justin's anti-Arian measures see also Theophanes, *Chron.* A.M. 6016 (C. de Boor [ed.] *Theophanis Chronographia*, vol. 1 [Leipzig, 1883], p. 169) and G. Greatrex, 'Justin I and the Arians', in M.F. Wiles and E.J. Yarnold (eds), *Studia Patristica*, vol. 34, paper presented at the Thirteenth International Conference on Patristic Studies held in Oxford 1999 (Leuven, 2001), pp. 72–81.

have been part of the 'Symmachians', but it was no longer the time for a *pristina contentio* between Roman aristocrats.[20]

To negotiate a repeal of the anti-Arian laws, Theodoric tried to play the diplomatic card, by sending an embassy to Constantinople at the end of 525 or beginning of 526.[21] It is not known choice of legates was deliberate or if he had a specific goal, but at least three of the delegates were former notorious supporters of Lawrence: Flavius Inoportunus, Flavius Theodorus and the Roman bishop (Caelius?) John I (523–6).[22] Could it have been possible that the Ostrogothic

---

[20] On the allegiances and the divisions within the Roman aristocracy, sometimes within the same family, during the Laurentian-Symmachian schism see Chadwick, *Boethius*, pp. 6–16, 29–46, and 287, n. 27; J. Moorhead, 'The Decii under Theoderic', *Historia*, 33 (1983): pp. 107–15; Moorhead, *Theoderic*, pp. 129–33, 166–72 and 238–40; Wirbelauer, *Zwei Päpste*, pp. 57–65; and T. Sardella, *Società, Chiesa e Stato nell'età di Teoderico. Papa Simmaco e lo scisma laurenziano*, Armarium. Biblioteca di storia e cultura religiosa, vol. 7 (Soveria Mannelli, 1996), pp. 53–7. See also Ch. Pietri, *Christiana respublica. Éléments d'une enquête sur le christianisme antique*, CEFR, vol. 234 (Rome, 1997), pp. 1007–57, although several elements of this need to be revised with regard to the subsequent bibliography, especially as regards the supposed abstention of Cassiodorus' family members in the conflict between 'Laurentians' and 'Symmachians'. It is surprising that some still defend today the idea of Boethius' total neutrality – and that of other great historical figures – during Roman affairs of 498/501–506/7, by simply brushing aside works which tend to prove the opposite. See A. Galonnier, *Boèce. Opuscula sacra*, vol. 1: Capita dogmatica *(Traités II, III, IV)*, Philosophes médiévaux, vol. 47 (Louvain-la-Neuve, Louvain and Paris, 2007), pp. 114–9; and n. 37 below.

[21] See M. Rosi, 'L'ambasceria di papa Giovanni I a Constantinopoli secondo alcuni principali scrittori', *Archivio della R. Società romana di storia patria*, 21 (1898): pp. 567–84; Caspar, *Geschichte*, pp. 183–92 and 766–7 (Zu S. 183ff); Stein, *Histoire*, pp. 258–61; W. Enßlin, 'Papst Johannes I. als Gesandter Theoderichs des Grossen bei Kaiser Justinos I.', *ByzZ*, 44 (1951): pp. 127–34; P. Goubert, 'Autour du voyage à Byzance du pape saint Jean I. (523–526)', *OCP*, 24 (1958): pp. 339–52; Moorhead, *Theoderic*, pp. 235–42; J. Wojda, *Communion et foi. Les trois premiers voyages des papes de Rome à Constantinople (484–555). Étude historique et théologique* (Siedlce, 2006), pp. 121–62 (even if it is useful for the narrative and bibliography, this book must be used with great caution, because the demonstration and the conclusions are highly ideological); and Goltz, *Barbar*, pp. 400–425, 451–75 and 510–13.

[22] Flavius Inoportunus and Flavius Theodorus were two brothers of the Albinus Junior who was accused of high treason in the 520s. Being among the most loyal supporters of Lawrence, the first two continued to use the circus factions to cause riots in Rome during the two to three years following the end of the Laurentian-Symmachian schism, a situation probably not to the liking of Theodoric. See Cassiodorus, *Variae* 1.27 (MGH.AA 12.29). Even though the king raised Inoportunus to the rank of *patricius* in 509/12 – perhaps not without a second thought – and although there is no trace of any involvement of the two 'Laurentians' in civil troubles after 510, it is not impossible that they never really reconciled with the Ostrogothic monarchy. See Cassiodorus, *Variae* 3.6 (MGH.AA 12.82–3). The impeachment and eventual execution of their brother, despite diverging positions during

ruler thought they were going to search, as in the past, for a compromise with the Orient? Perhaps he wanted to test their loyalty, in this period of tensions and reprisals. In any case, the legation obtained from the emperor almost everything the king had asked, with the sole exception of the return to Arianism of (forced?) converts to Chalcedonian orthodoxy. Besides this failure, Theodoric was made aware of the triumphal reception and of the gifts made to John by Justin, as well as, perhaps, of other – secret – negotiations between ambassadors and imperial authorities. All the legates who returned were therefore put in jail under suspicion of conspiracy with Justin. Already weakened, the Roman pontiff did not survive this ultimate ordeal.

John I's 'Martyrdom': The Straw that Broke the Camel's Back

John I's death strongly and durably marked minds. Henceforth, the Ostrogothic monarchy would no longer let papal elections escape its vigilance. It is in this context that the Ostrogoths appointed Felix IV (III) and, most likely, Boniface II, in order to counter the aspirations of a party which, at least in 530, was represented by a character who had been at the forefront of the negotiations during the schisms of the beginning of the sixth century, a Roman from the East whose unfailing loyalty to the Chalcedonian faith gave no room for doubt: the deacon Dioscorus. Did the Ostrogoths decide to control the papal election for religious/theological reasons?

One might think, as the sources tell us, that certain anti-Arian measures constituted the breaking point between Justin I and Theodoric and that it was the reaction of the latter to John I on his return from Constantinople that completed the break between the Ostrogothic monarchy and the Roman aristocrats.[23] To illustrate Roman perception of Theodoric in 526, the second

---

the conflict between Symmachus and Lawrence, possibly prompted them to take advantage of their stay in the imperial capital to conspire against the Ostrogothic ruler. On the use by the parties of the circus during the Laurentian-Symmachian schism and thereafter see E. Condurachi, 'Factions et jeux du cirque à Rome au début du VIe siècle', *Revue historique du Sud-Est européen*, 18 (1941): pp. 95–102; Moorhead, 'The Decii', pp. 107–15; Wirbelauer, *Zwei Päpste*, pp. 51–65; Sardella, *Società*, pp. 43–58; and Pietri, *Christiana respublica*, pp. 771–87.

[23] Procopius, *B.Goth.* 1.1.39, fails to mention the death of John I and presents the death sentence over Boethius and Quintus Aurelius Memmius Symmachus Junior as first and last an error of Theodoric. Maybe Justinian did not want to attract too much attention to the (secret?) negotiations with Pope John. See Procopius, (*B.Goth.* 1.3.15 and 17 (O. Veh [ed.], *Prokopius von Caesarea*, vol. 2: *Gotenkriege* [Munich, 1970], pp. 14–5).

Anonymus Valesianus states that he reigned henceforth no longer as *rex*, but as *tyrannus* and that it is in consequence of the last measures taken against the Catholics-Orthodox that he died of violent diarrhoea.[24] This text confirms that reconciliation would no longer be possible between the elite of the two 'nations'.

Nevertheless one does not want to push this hostility too far, since it was not until nearly a decade later that the eastern empire initiated the re-conquest of Italy, even if some actions of the Ostrogoths could have triggered a state of war before then,[25] and no religious reason was used as pretext for its outbreak. In 535, Byzantium was in 'eternal peace' with Persia and the integration of the former Vandal Africa was well underway, whereas nothing was going right between the king of the Ostrogoths, Theodahad (534–6), and his Roman subjects.[26] The barbarian ruler offered to Constantinople an excellent *casus belli* by murdering his cousin Amalasuintha, daughter and heiress of Theodoric. With this assassination, Theodahad indeed broke the almost personal link which united the Amals' rule to the empire. The marriage of Theodahad's successor, Wittigis (536–40, † ca. 542), with the daughter of Amalasuintha, Matasuentha († ca. 550), did not change anything.[27]

Moreover, the Catholic-Orthodox religioos policy of Amalasuintha does not seem at all to have been a cause for her assassination. During the 12 years between the death of Pope John I and Cassiodorus' departure for the eastern capital (ca. 538), the latter never ceased to defend the utopian civil and religious union of the *Gothi* and *Romani* and there is every reason to think that it was the official position of all the Ostrogothic rulers of this period, even Theodoric in 526 and

---

[24] *Excerpta Valesiana* 2.16.94 (König, *Aus der Zeit*, pp. 94–5). Regarding the origin and the objectives of the second Anonymus Valesianus, see G. Zecchini, *Ricerche di storiografia latina tardoantica*, vol. 2: *Dall'*Historia Augusta *a Paolo Diacono*, Centro ricerche e documentazione sull'Antichità classica. Monografie, vol. 34 (Rome, 2008), pp. 201–8; and Goltz, *Barbar*, pp. 476–526.

[25] For example, the Ostrogoths drove out the Gepids from Sirmium at the beginning of the 530s and they pursued them as far as Gratiana (currently Dobra in Serbia), in the province of Moesia Prima, in the diocese of Dacia, so right inside the empire's political borders. See Procopius, *B.Goth.* 1.3.15 and 17 (Veh, *Gotenkriege*, pp. 24–7); and Stein, *Histoire*, pp. 307–8 and 336.

[26] On the general situation on the eve of the Gothic War see for example Stein, *Histoire*, pp. 294–6, 318–22 and 338–41, as well as pertinent pages in A. Cameron, B. Ward-Perkins and M. Whitby (eds), *The Cambridge Ancient History*, vol. 14: *Late Antiquity: Empire and Successors, A.D. 425–600* (Cambridge, 2000 [2nd edn]).

[27] *PLRE* 3.851–2 (Matasuentha) and 1382–6 (Vitigis); Amory, *People*, p. 452 (Matasuentha) and 460–61 (Witigis); and S. Cosentino, *Prosopografia dell' Italia bizantina (493–804)*, 2 vols (Bologna, 1996–2000), 2.351 (Matasuntha).

Theodahad in 535.[28] Of course, just the opposite happened, as one witnesses a real strengthening of the respective identities of Ostrogothic and Roman populations, especially around the affirmation of the Arian faith of the one and the Catholic-Orthodox faith of the other.[29] There is however no sign that this explicit desire for differentiation had a real impact on the general policy of the Ostrogothic court. The social consequence of John I's death on the inhabitants of Italy was, in fact, the inevitable result of a process initiated well before 526 and their Amal kings always had to manage it. This, the extremely tense situation at the end of the Laurentian-Symmachian schism, when the Ostrogothic and the Byzantine leaders were no longer in agreement about the preferred candidate for the Roman pontificate, did not result in any bellicose action. It was just a minor disagreement in itself, but it was in fact the tip of an iceberg.

Without challenging the profoundly theological nature of the various religious crises which separated the West and the East under Emperor Anastasius I and without calling into question the sincerity of his faith, it must be recognised that his particularly zealous involvement in these conflicts was only the symptom of an incurable syndrome, dating back to the last quarter of the fifth century, namely the effective inability of the Roman emperor in Constantinople to assert concretely his rights over the *pars Occidentis*. This problem, coupled with the proliferation of episcopal rivalries arising from the affirmation of the see of Constantinople, led, ultimately, to major geopolitical and geo-ecclesiological transformations in the administrative field, as well as in that of the imperial ideology of power.[30] The most enduring dispute between

---

[28] On the project defended by Cassiodorus see in particular, C. Kakridi, *Cassiodors Variae. Literatur und Politik im ostgotischen Italien*, Beiträge zur Altertumskunde, Bd 223 (Munich and Leipzig, 2005), pp. 292–347; S. Teillet, *Des Goths à la nation gothique. Les origines de l'idée de nation en Occident du Ve au VIIe siècle*, Histoire, vol. 108 (Paris, 2011 [2nd edn]), pp. 281–303.

[29] Concerning the development of the ethno-cultural identities in Ostrogothic Italy see Amory, *People*; Teillet, *Des Goths*, pp. 271–334; and P. Heather, 'Merely an Ideology ? – Gothic Identity in Ostrogothic Italy', in S.J. Barnish and F. Marazzi (eds), *The Ostrogoths from the Migration Period to the Sixth Century. An Ethnographic Perspective* (San Marino, 8–12 September 2000), Studies in Historical Archaeoethnology, vol. 7 (Woodbridge and San Marino, 2007), pp. 31–79.

[30] The geopolitics of the 'ante-Justinian' protobyzantine empire has not, so far, really been the subject of a complete synthesis. Regarding the geo-ecclesiology see P. Blaudeau, *Alexandrie et Constantinople (451–491). De l'histoire à la géo-ecclésiologie*, BEFAR vol. 327 (Rome, 2006); and Blaudeau, *Le Siège*. See also P. Blaudeau, 'Rome contre Alexandrie ? L'interprétation pontificale de l'enjeu monophysite (de l'émergence de la controverse eutychienne au Schisme acacien 448–484)', *Adamantius* 12 (2006): pp. 140–216; Blaudeau, *Motifs*; and P. Blaudeau, 'Between Petrine Ideology and Realpolitik: The See of

the two *partes* in matters of administrative geography, both civil and religious, was without a doubt about control over Illyricum. The envenoming of this old quarrel, dating back more than a century and in which the Goths were involved more than once, would constitute the background of the major event of the pontificate of Boniface II, namely the Roman synod of 531. As the acts of this synod are a most concrete source for the relationship between Roman East and Ostrogothic West during the pontificate of Boniface II, the analysis of these acts can be very instructive.

The goal of this synod was to examine the appeal of Stephen, bishop of Larissa (in Thessalia), following his dismissal by the patriarch of Constantinople, Epiphanius, who had acted on the request or with the support of the imperial power. The central issue of the case was the attachment of Eastern Illyricum to the jurisdictional sphere of the church of Rome rather than to that of Constantinople, while the region was politically part of the empire. The end of the acts of the synod is missing, but we know that Boniface II had seriously annoyed Constantinople on this occasion, certainly by defending the privileges of his episcopal see.[31] Yet, he never presented himself as an advocate of the Ostrogothic monarchy during this case and the sources never accuse him of being one. It was a dispute between Romans and Romans. Furthermore, nothing indicates that Dioscorus' position with regard to Constantinople's initiative of 531 would have been different if he were the judge. What we know about him makes one even think that he could have been more zealous in his defence of the apostolic see's privileges than Boniface. If both popes do not appear to differ in their attitude towards Ostrogothic and Roman regimes, what can be the root causes of their elections? Nothing is sure – because we do not know much about the two figures – but the answer may be of a religious nature: not in the opposition between some anti-Arian/pro-Byzantine and pro-tolerance/pro-Ostrogothic movements, but in the relations of Catholic-Orthodox westerners to imperial propositions of the moment in matters of theology.

Constantinople in Roman Geo-Ecclesiology (449–536)', in L. Grig and G. Kelly (eds), *Two Romes: Rome and Constantinople in Late Antiquity*, Oxford Studies in Late Antiquity (New York, 2012), pp. 364–84.

[31] Agapitus I, *Ep. ad Iustinianum* (*Licet de*) 10–14 (*Collectio Avellana*, *Ep.* 88.10–14) (CSEL 35.337–8) = JK 894; and Blaudeau, *Le Siège*, pp. 104, 151 and 279.

The Double Election: Possible Religious Causes Hushed up in the Sources

Considering the strongly deleterious atmosphere in the Ostrogothic kingdom in the time after the Laurentian-Symmachian schism, especially the atmosphere established after John I's death, there was probably a difference in Boniface's and Dioscorus' positions towards this regime and the eastern Roman empire. Yet, as no source refers to it, it does not seem to be the central issue of the double election of 530.

One often reads that Boniface and Dioscorus represented respectively the pro-Gothic and pro-Byzantine parties, i.e. the maintenance of the relative independence of the Ostrogothic kingdom versus a total political union with the Roman empire. Louis Duchesne came to such a conclusion by highlighting the Germanic origin of the first and the convinced Chalcedonianism of the second, this in the light of those who appointed Boniface (his predecessor, himself named by the king) and those who elected Dioscorus (the majority of the Roman clergy).[32] This reconstruction is not flawless. The issues of the papal election of 530 are more complex, depending upon events that occurred well before, without the exact links being totally clear.[33]

To the pro-Ostrogoths versus pro-Byzantines hypothesis, we can immediately oppose one simple question: how could Amalasuintha, a good friend of Constantinople, have let her 14-year-old son sponsor the appointment of a pope to antagonise the Roman East? An affirmative answer is extremely difficult to sustain, as nothing indicates that the queen and her minister, Cassiodorus, had completely lost control of the state in 530. According to Jordanes, the testament of Theodoric commanded his heirs to honour their king, to love the Senate and Roman people and always to ensure the peace and favour of the emperor, and these recommendations would have been observed as long as Athalaric reigned.[34] The picture perhaps seems too beautiful, especially in light of the end of the second Anonymus Valesianus, but it does not go totally against Procopius of Caesarea's account, which clearly

---

[32] Duchesne, 'La succession', p. 244; and Blaudeau, *Le Siège*, p. 149.

[33] Pietri, *Christiana respublica*, pp. 1052–3, also thinks that we should not reduce too quickly the papal election of 530 to a struggle between pro-Ostrogoths and pro-Byzantines.

[34] Jordanes, *Getica* 59.304–5 (F. Giunta and A. Grillone [eds], *Jordanis De origine actibusque Getarum*, Fonti per la storia d'Italia, vol. 117 [Rome, 1991], p. 125); V.A. Sirago, *Amalasunta. La regina (ca. 495–535)*, Donne d'Oriente e d'Occidente, vol. 9 (Milan, 1999), p. 57; A. Amici, *Iordanes e la storia gotica*, Quaderni della Rivista di bizantinisca, vol. 6 (Spoleto, 2002), p. 101; G. Pilara, *La città di Roma fra Chiesa e Impero durante il conflitto gotico-bizantino*, Scienze storiche, filosofiche, pedagogiche e psicologiche, vol. 194 (Rome, 2006), pp. 22 and 61, n. 3; and Goltz, *Barbar*, p. 297.

separates the attitude of the Amals towards the empire from the Ostrogothic military aristocracy (which cannot have been, at this time, responsible for Boniface's nomination).³⁵

If only we had some additional information on this *pristina contentio* that Theodoric wanted to avoid by choosing Felix IV (III) in 526, because it was surely part of the reason that led Felix to appoint his successor. Perhaps it is related to the Laurentian-Symmachian schism, which recently led the king to believe that the disorders could reoccur? The problem here is the succession of John I, who had angered Theodoric for having secretly negotiated with the imperial authorities on an unknown subject. Were these negotiations political, religious or both? Is it an invasion project of the Ostrogothic kingdom, in complicity with the Roman bishop? Nothing can be totally excluded, but there is absolutely no indication in the sources that allows such a conclusion.

As the problem seems to be linked to the schism of 498/501–506/7, the nature of the negotiations might be found in John I's possible involvement in it. The 'Laurentian' that he would have been, theoretically should have been in favour of some theological concessions for the resolution of Acacian schism. Is there a similar issue in 526? In fact, yes! The reunion of Chalcedonians and Miaphysites/Monophysites under the Theopaschite formula *unus de/ex Trinitate cruxifixus/incarnatus/passus est* was already a real preoccupation for the imperial power at this date, in particular because this formula had been officially condemned by the Roman church since 520.³⁶ It is therefore not impossible that the discussion with John focused on neo-Chalcedonian theology and its acceptance by the apostolic see. For Theodoric, the religious aspect of the problem surely mattered little. The fact that the central protagonists of the schism were still engaged in such dealings, while some of their fiercest opponents were still alive, might have encouraged the old Ostrogothic ruler to take drastic measures against the pope and his other ambassadors.³⁷ Among the former adversaries who were still alive, we find the

---

³⁵ Procopius, *B.Goth.* 1.2.1–1.4.4 (Veh, *Gotenkriege*, pp. 14–31).

³⁶ Hormisdas, *Ep.* 124 (CCL 85A.115-121) = JK 850. On the Theopaschite controversy see A. Grillmeier, *Jesus der Christus im Glauben der Kirche*, Bd. 2/2. *Die Kirche von Konstantinopel im 6. Jahrhundert*, ed. Th. Hainthaler (Freiburg im Breisgau, Basel and Vienna, 2004 [rev. edn]), p. 333–63, in the light of Blaudeau, *Le Siège*.

³⁷ As the Theopaschite formula is presented as one of compromise, it is important to remember that many Roman aristocrats showed a real interest in it. One of the first was the 'Symmachian' Flavius Anicius Probus Faustus Junior Niger, to whom a Roman (?) priest named Trifolius asserted that he must not follow it. This was at the time of the papal condemnation of the formula by Hormisdas. See Trifolius, *Epistula ad beatum Faustum senatorem contra Joannem [Maxentium] Scytham monachum* (CCL 85.135–141); and

person who had convinced the bishop of Rome to condemn the Theopaschite formula: Dioscorus.[38] Thus, it seems very difficult to imagine him as the candidate of the pro-Constantinople camp, either in 526 or in 530.[39]

So, a party presumably linked to the Laurentian-Symmachian schism tried to elect one of their own in the first of the two papal elections, with the risk of causing serious disturbances in Rome. The candidate is unknown to us. Maybe he was a supporter of John I's initiative. Maybe he was an opponent, i.e. a rigid

---

Blaudeau, *Le Siège*, pp. 41, 53, 83, 188–190 and 216–7. In contrast, the possible 'Laurentian' Boethius would have been favourable to the formula, at least at the time of the writing of his *opuscula sacra*. See V. Schurr, *Die Trinitätslehre des Boethius im Lichte der 'skythischen Kontroversen'*, Forschungen zur Christlichen Literatur- und Dogmengeschichte, vol. 18/1 (Paderborn, 1935); Chadwick, *Boethius*, pp. 185–222; G. Zizza, 'Il De Trinitate di Boezio e polemica antiariana', in CISAM, *Teoderico*, pp. 819–49 (where we see that Boethius might have 'killed two birds with one stone', by condemning tacitly at the same time Ostrogothic Arianism [one of the breaking point with Theodoric?]); and Blaudeau, *Le Siège*, p. 191, n. 141. Finally, the position of Cassiodorus is less clear. All that one knows is that he was part of the group of 11 aristocrats – among whom we find former 'Symmachians', as well as former 'Laurentians' – who reproached Pope John II (533–5) for not having informed them of his acceptance of the formula. Were they against it or were they simply complaining that the Roman bishop committed himself without informing Ravenna? See John II, *Ep.* 3 (Schwartz, *ACO*, 4/2.206–10) = JK 885; and Blaudeau, *Le Siège*, pp. 193–4. The subject was very perilous. It is therefore perhaps not insignificant that Procopius, *B.Goth.* 1.3.6–9 (Veh, *Gotenkriege*, pp. 22–4), opens a parenthesis on the danger for both priest and layman in investigating the nature of God, not long before beginning his narrative on the Gothic War.

[38] See Dioscorus, *Suggestiones* (*Verum est*) (*Collectio Avellana, Ep.* 216) (CSEL 35.675–6); and (*Per Eulogium*) (*Collectio Avellana, Ep.* 224) (CSEL 35.685–7); Germanus of Capua (and others Roman legates), *Suggestio* (*Cum Dei*) (*Collectio Avellana, Ep.* 217) (CSEL 35.677–9); John Maxentius, *Responsio adu. ep.* [*CXXIV*] 1.1 (7).81 (CCL 85A.125); 4 (20).276 and (21).283 (CCL 85A.132); 8 (26).350 (CCL 85A.134); and 9 (35).487, 492 and 495 (CCL 85A.138–9); and many passages of Blaudeau, *Le Siège*.

[39] Schwartz, *ACO*, 4/2.xviii; and Blaudeau, *Le Siège*, p. 149, n. 86. Justinian's opinion about Dioscorus is probably perceptible in the use of his excommunication, by the emperor himself before the fifth ecumenical council, at Constantinople in 553 and by some prelates during it, to support the validity of the post-mortem condemnations of the authors of the Three Chapters. Dioscorus is indeed presented as a true *papa*, but his rehabilitation by Pope Agapitus I (535–6) is totally ignored. Maybe Constantinople had never officially accepted Agapitus' initiative. See Justinian, *Ep. contra Tria Capitula* 78 (E. Schwartz et al. [eds], *Drei dogmatische Schriften Iustinians*, Legum Iustiniani imperatoris vocabularium. Subsidia, vol. 2 [Milan, 1973 (2nd edn)], pp. 124 [68]–5 [68*]; where Lawrence is also mentioned!); Justinian, *Edictum de recta fidei (uel Confessio fidei)* 55 (Schwartz, *Drei dogmatische Schriften*, pp. 168–9); Second Council of Constantinople, *Actiones* 5.64 and 8.4.17 (J. Straub [ed.], *ACO*, t. 4: *Concilium universale Constantinopolitanum sub Iustiniano habitatum*, vol. 1: *Concilii actiones VIII – appendices Graecae – indices* [Berlin, 1971], pp. 104 and 212).

Roman Chalcedonian, perfectly able to resist the theological innovations proposed by the imperial authorities, as was the case in 530 with Dioscorus and the Theopaschite formula. The only solution found by the Ostrogothic monarchy to counter both threats to public order was to overcome its usual reserve in religious matters by appointing the Roman bishop. With neither Felix IV (III) nor Boniface II being remembered as ambitious, they were chosen to prevent stances that could provoke confrontations between eastern and western Romans, which could force the king to pronounce on questions that might endanger harmony with the empire.[40] If there was a pro-Gothic aspect to their nominations, it was surely not conducted against someone or something, but rather to favour the 'non-intervention in religious affairs' policy established by Theodoric. In 530, Boniface appeared as a non-interventionist against Dioscorus, a fierce opponent of the Theopaschite formula, and therefore a more acceptable candidate, even though events would prove the next year that Boniface was quite prepared to defend Roman prerogatives when challenged by Constantinople.

Such a reconstruction of the 530 papal election gives sense to the positioning of the Felix-Boniface dossier discovered by Guerrino Amelli – the instructions of Felix IV (III) for his succession, its contestation by the Senate and Boniface's post-mortem condemnation of Dioscorus allegedly signed by 60 priests. This compilation was presumably composed in Rome, around 25 March 534, to justify the acceptance by John II (formerly Mercurius, as he was the first Roman bishop to change his name) of the Theopaschite formula, which certainly constituted one of the major turning points, if not *the* major

---

[40] On Boniface's lack of religious ambition, Blaudeau, *Le Siège*, p. 180, writes: 'Il ne s'agit donc pas de classer Boniface comme le premier pape allemand mais bien de relever que la tendance qu'il représente est celle qui s'affiche comme la plus compatible avec un statu quo en fonction duquel Rome ne développe aucune politique religieuse d'envergure en direction de l'Orient.' This statement can also be applied to Felix. Thus, one might wonder if they were actually involved in church affairs before their pontificates. The quality/title of 'Caelius' (it is not a name!) which could be attributed to Felix in a document indicates that he was once a notorious 'Symmachian' or that he was an important 'Laurentian' formally reconciled with Symmachus. See Felix IV (III), *Constitutum de ecclesia Rauennatensi* = Agnellus of Ravenna, *Lib. pont. ecclesiae Rauennatis* 60 (CCM 199.230) = JK 877; the passage must, however, be read in the light of Mommsen's comments on it, like the one on MGH.AA 12.490 (Caelius). Considering that Dioscorus could have been the other candidate for the papacy in 526, it would make more sense that he was a former 'Symmachian', since it is difficult to imagine that Theodoric had opposed someone who held the same opinion as Caelius Johannes/John I. What better way to revive the *pristina contentio*? Felix could only have been an unaligned man or a moderate former 'Symmachian' and this also applies to Boniface.

turning point, of Justinian's reign, at least in the context of the re-conquest of Italy.[41] Even if it is quite clear that Boniface II did not condemn Dioscorus for his opposition to John I's possible initiative, the reasons why the author of the *Novariensis* has placed in parallel the justification of John II's decisions in theological matters and the formal conviction of the most important opponent to such choices seems now perfectly logical.[42]

Conclusion

The double election of 530 was the consequence of an attempt by part of the Roman clergy to counter the solution found by the Gothic king and his Roman ministers such as Cassiodorus to avoid a new clash between Roman citizens (and not between Romans and Goths) this time around the question of the acceptance of the Theopaschite formula. Boniface II seemed to be a man who would not stir up trouble on this issue while Dioscorus would. Given John II's acceptance of the formula and the fact that no other Roman bishop revisited that decision – neither Agapitus I (535–6), who was the son of a 'Symmachian' priest beaten to death by the 'Laurentians' and who

---

[41] On this *collectio* see Schwartz, *ACO*, 4/2.xvi–xx; Schurr, *Die Trinitätslehre*, pp. 185–97; Grillmeier, *Jesus*, p. 30; and Blaudeau, *Le Siège*, p. 219. As a proof that the recognition of the neo-Chalcedonian theology by the Italian clergy was a major issue of the negotiations conducted just before the beginning of the Gothic war, the Byzantine ambassadors of 533 (Demetrius of Philippi and Hypathius of Ephesus) and 534 (the same, together with the senator Alexander) took care of both ratification of the Theopaschite formula and secret negotiations with Theodahad and Amalasuintha. See John II, *Ep.* 2 (*Collectio Avellana, Ep.* 84) (CSEL 35.320–8) = JK 884; Agapitus I, *Ep. ad Iustinianum* (*Gratulamur*) (*Collectio Avellana, Ep.* 91) (CSEL 35.342–7) = JK 898; Procopius, *B.Goth*. 1.3.5–9 and 13–29 (Veh, *Gotenkriege*, pp. 22–9); Liberatus of Carthage, *Breu. causae Nest. et Eutych*. 19.2 (E. Schwartz [ed.], *ACO*, t. 2: *Concilium universale Chalcedonense*, vol. 5: *Collectio Sangermanensis* [Berlin, 1936], p. 134); and Stein, *Histoire*, pp. 335–7.

[42] Is there a link between the fact that John II recognised the Theopaschite formula and that he took the name of one of his predecessors who was possibly the first to be open to the neo-Chalcedonian theology? Cassiodorus, *Variae* 9.15–7 (MGH.AA 12.279–82), informs us that the end of 533 and the very beginning of 534 were times of simony, violence and arrests in Rome. Since this was the eve of the Gothic War, one might think that the Ostrogothic monarchy tried to play a last card by allowing the election of a character truly favourable to the empire, a man ready for a real compromise in religious matters. Of John II's possible links with the 'Laurentian' party, perhaps we must also mention his use of the *versio prima* of Dionysius Exiguus' *Collectio canonum* in his letter to Caesarius of Arles.

rehabilitated the memory of Dioscorus[43], nor Silverius (536–7), who was the son of the pope who officially condemned Theopaschism, i.e. Hormisdas, nor Vigilius (537–55), who was the man initially chosen by Boniface II as his successor[44] – the effort was ultimately in vain.

---

[43] It is interesting to note that Cassiodorus was a good friend of both Agapitus, unequivocally a 'Dioscorian' (and a 'Symmachian'?), and of Dionysius Exiguus, a very active 'Laurentian' at the time of the Laurentian-Symmachian schism. This situation confuses even more our understanding of his position during the events of 498/501–6/7 and his attitude toward the Theopaschite formula. Blaudeau's portrayal (*Le Siège*, p. 45), of the author of the *Collectio Avellana*, who wanted to celebrate Dioscorus, while being careful not to cast aspersions on Dionysius Exiguus, could almost apply to Cassiodorus. Cassiodorus' religious position is however much clearer after his *conversio*, as he seems to have become an opponent to Justinian's policy in this matter. See Cassiodorus, *Institutiones* 1.11 (R.A.B. Mynors, *Cassiodori Senatoris Institutiones*, [Oxford, 1961 (2nd edn)],pp. 35–6); F. Troncarelli, *Vivarium: I libri, il destino*, Instrumenta Patristica, vol. 33 (Turnhout, 1998), pp. 20–21.

[44] We do not know anything about the involvement of Vigilius' family in the Laurentian-Symmachian schism. As he belonged to the Milanese aristocracy on his father's side, one might think that it was closer to Symmachus' party than to Lawrence's because the bishop of Milan of that time, (Caelius?) Laurentius I, was a moderate 'Symmachian' (as were Felix IV [III] and Boniface II?).

Chapter 11

Gregory the Great and Sicily: An Example of Continuity and Change in the Late Sixth Century

Christopher Hanlon

Introduction

It is a well-known fact that the pontificate of Gregory the Great (590–604) stands at a time of transition between Late Antiquity and the Early Middle Ages.[1] Above all things, Gregory sought to preserve the proper ordering of creation with its associated trinitarian understandings. In practice, his activity as pope may be examined from a number of perspectives. In choosing that of Sicily, one is presented with a world in microcosm in which certain social groupings emerge as being of particular significance.[2] These, in turn, became the source of several priorities within the papal administrative system as it developed under Gregory. His relations with and shaping of the local Sicilian bench of bishops is of major significance for his activity elsewhere in the church. His use

---

[1] The source for much of the material in this paper is the *Registrum Epistolarum* of Gregory the Great himself. As regards the numbering of these letters, this is the numbering system adopted in J.R.C. Martyn (trans.), *The Letters of Gregory the Great*, Medieval Sources in Translation, vol. 40, 3 vols (Toronto, 2004). This in turn was based on the numbering adopted by D. Norberg (ed.), *S. Gregorii Magni Registrum epistolarum*, CCL, vols 140 and 140A (Turnhout, 1982).

[2] General understandings of the world in which Gregory the Great lived have been influenced by the magisterial work of scholars such as R.A. Markus, *The End of Ancient Christianity* (Cambridge, 1990); R.A. Markus, *Gregory the Great and His World* (Cambridge, 1997); and P.R.L. Brown, *The Rise of Western Christendom* (Oxford, 2003 [2nd edn]). The present work has a far more limited scope, the state of the province of Sicily. On Gregory's involvement in Malta see H. Scerri, 'Gregory the Great Deposes a Disobedient Bishop', in J. Baun, A. Cameron, M. Edwards and M. Vinzent (eds), *Studia Patristica*, vol. 48, papers presented at the Fifteenth International Conference on Patristic Studies held in Oxford 2007 (Leuven, 2010), pp. 321–6.

of administrators (*rectores*, *defensores*, etc.) to manage the affairs of the Sicilian patrimony of the Roman church gave expression to what was to become a recognisable system of Roman church governance throughout the Middle Ages. His relations with Byzantine officials charged with the imperial government of the island (the *praetor Siciliae* and his retinue) provide a glimpse into the association between church *auctoritas* and state *potestas* within the context of a wider world in Late Antiquity.

Gregory the Great's Thought

In seeking to understand the priorities of papal administration at the end of the sixth century under Gregory the Great, it is necessary to first make some comments about the theoretical basis upon which that administration was built. Fundamental to its operation was the notion of 'order' (*ordo*),[3] which was established and preserved through the exercise of 'authority' (*auctoritas*) and 'power' (*potestas*) in a number of ways. The concept is a difficult one to pin down, largely because of the vagueness resulting from the sheer scope of its field of operations. Even Gregory himself did not attempt to systematise the elements of his thought on the subject. Rather, his thoughts are found scattered throughout his various works. Yet, any study of Gregory's activity must attempt to grapple with its enormity.

The concept is important everywhere in Gregory's thinking, whether it be the universe at large, the world of angels and men, the life of the ecclesial community or the ordering that takes place within the souls of individual human beings. According to this concept, the whole of existent reality is stretched out in one colossal order of being; from its summit and source, God, through to the lowest inanimate created object. In brief, then, Gregory's understanding of the world in which he lived was based on the perception of a hierarchy of authority and power operating within that world, which was, as Robert Markus reminds us, broader than the merely visible and imbued with the divine presence, manifested in clerics who represented and implemented that divine *ordo*.[4]

---

[3] G.R. Evans, *The Thought of Gregory the Great* (Cambridge, 1986), p.117, noticed this characteristic, but her observation needs correction on one vital point. She described Gregory's theoretical basis as lying in his notion of 'right order' (*rectus ordo*). For Gregory, such a description would have been tautologous: all 'order' is right; its opposite would have been disorder or chaos.

[4] Markus, *The End of Ancient Christianity*, pp. 22–3.

Gregory's thought is shot through with Greek philosophical assumptions, as mediated largely through the works of St Augustine. But there are also differences between the two churchmen. These reflect changes that had taken place in literary tastes and intellectual activity from one century to the next. It is not that Gregory never mastered the philosophical process of classical thinking, as much as evidence that Gregory did not have Augustine's love for philosophical abstractions and Neoplatonic dialectic. This change of emphasis was something that Gregory appears to have shared with some of his contemporaries, such as Cassiodorus. Augustine's style was almost too rich and florid for his liking; the sixth century required a more sober grandeur.[5] In his reworking of both Augustine and elements of classical philosophy, Gregory made the thought of an intellectual elite available to the masses in a popular form. To this he also added elements which had become part of popular piety, some might even say superstition; and gave them their first systematic and dogmatic treatment.[6] As well, Gregory's preaching was directed mainly towards those whose responsibility it was to preserve the divine order amongst their people.[7] It is little wonder that he was concerned in his letter writing with questions that involved the maintenance of that *ordo*.

These, then, are some of the elements which, together, made up the model of Gregorian thought. They exist, alongside Gregory's world of lived experience, and provided a synthesis of classical thinking which, in turn, became a springboard for the future debates and work of the medieval schoolmen.

The Byzantine World of Gregory's Lived Experience

Gregory the Great was born in Rome ca. 540 into an influential senatorial family. The family's residence was on the Caelian Hill in the vicinity of the old imperial palace. During his childhood, the Justinian reconquests in Italy and North Africa would have been contemporary events. Gregory himself relates that his great-great-grandfather was Felix III (II) (483–92),[8] and he may also

---

[5] Evans, *The Thought of Gregory the Great*, pp. 13 and 34; and F. Homes Dudden, *Gregory the Great, His Place in History and Thought*, vol. 2 (London, 1905), p. 310.

[6] Evans, *The Thought of Gregory the Great*, p. 15; and Homes Dudden, *Gregory the Great*, p. 358.

[7] Markus, *Gregory the Great*, pp. 31–3.

[8] Gregory I, *Dial.* 4.17.1 (SC 265.68); and Gregory I, *Hom. xl in euang.* 38.15 (SC 522.482). See J. Moorhead, 'On Becoming Pope in Late Antiquity', *JRH*, 3 (2006): pp. 279–93.

have been related to Pope Agapetus I (535–36).⁹ Gregory would have been well acquainted with the state of affairs in Sicily, despite it not being recorded as to whether he ever visited the island in person. His family had considerable land holdings there; after he became a monk, he established six monasteries on his Sicilian estates.¹⁰

Gregory was well educated in both Roman law and other secular learning, something which was both recognised by his contemporaries and attested to, on numerous occasions, in the collection of letters which make up his *Register*. Under emperors Justin II and Tiberius II, he held office in the restored imperial regime which followed Justinian's successful Gothic War, ultimately attaining, ca. 573, the rank of *praefectus urbi* of Rome.¹¹ When his father died, Gregory abandoned his secular career to become a monk in the newly established monastery of St Andrew. He was not allowed to remain in monastic seclusion for long, however; ca. 578, he was ordained deacon and sent by Pope Pelagius II as his personal representative (*apocrisarius*) at the imperial court of Emperor Tiberius II in Constantinople.

Gregory's arrival in Constantinople coincided more or less with Tiberius II becoming sole emperor. Tiberius had risen to prominence amongst the imperial troops pursuing the war against the Persians under Justin II, nephew and successor of the great Justinian. They had ruled together from 574, but in 578 Justin died, leaving Tiberius to rule on alone until 582. During his time in the imperial city, he made many powerful friends in both secular and religious walks of life. These were to remain amongst his correspondents after he became pope. Notable amongst them was the future emperor Maurice, then commander of the

---

⁹ If the reference to Gordian, a cleric of the church of Saints John and Paul, in *Lib. pont.*59.1 (L. Duchesne and C. Vogel [eds], *Le* Liber pontificalis; *Texte, introduction et commentaire*, BEFAR, vol. 1 [Paris, 1955 (2nd edn)], p. x, is reliable.

¹⁰ Gregory of Tours, *Historia Francorum* 10.1 (MGH.SRM 1.478). It has been possible to identify some of them: (i) S. Georgio 'in massa ... Maradotis' – see Gregory I, *Ep.* 2.29 (CCL 140.115–16) = JE 1183; and S. Borsari, *Il monarchesimo Bizantino nella Sicilia e nell'Italia meridionale prenormanne*, (Naples, 1963), p.28; (ii) 'il monastero Lucuscano, dedicato ai SS Massimo ed Agata a Palermo' (the 'monasterium nostrum' of *Ep.* 9.20 [CCL 140A.580] = JE 1544) – see Borsari, *Il monarchesimo*, p.29, n.27; (iii) S. Ermete [Hermes] at Palermo 'monasterium meum' where Urbicus was abbot (*Ep.* 6.39 [CCL 140.412–13] = JE 1419) – see Borsari, *Il monarchesimo*, p.30; J. Richards, *Consul of God. The Life and Times of Pope Gregory the Great* (London, 1980), p.153; and Abbazia di San Martino delle Scale (7 km out of Monreale) – see R. Andrews and J. Brown, *Sicily. The Rough Guide* (London, 1977), p. 74.

¹¹ Alternatively, he could have been *praetor urbanus*; opinions are divided. See *Ep.* 4.2 (CCL 140.218–9) = JE 1273, from September 593. See Martyn, *The Letters of Gregory the Great*, vol.1, p. 288, n. 7.

imperial bodyguard (*excubitores*) and son-in-law to the old emperor, Tiberius. Like Tiberius II, Maurice had come to prominence during the Persian Wars. About 574 Maurice was named Caesar, along with another *patricus*, Germanos. When Gregory became godfather to Maurice's first-born son, Theodosius, the two men bound themselves together with the most solemn ties of kinship.[12]

Gregory was to remain in Constantinople until 585 or 586, when he was recalled to Rome to assist the pope in dealing with the more difficult problems that faced the western church. By that time, Maurice had been emperor some four years. When Pelagius II died, Gregory succeeded him as pope, being consecrated bishop of Rome on 3 September 590.[13] Events had ensured that he had become both an intimate and an expert in the governmental processes of the late Roman empire administered from the East.

Gregory the Great and Imperial Officials in Sicily

Gregory's relationship with the empire's administrators in Sicily is an illustration of how well he understood the system of government at large. As a loyal citizen of the empire, Gregory retained the highest respect for its administrators, maintaining that the stature of their office must always transcend questions of personalities. The displeasing conduct of a particular official, or officials, must not be allowed to alter a subject's respect for the office occupied by that official.[14] Yet, as a pastor, Gregory also had the duty of reproving and correcting the violence and corruption so often found in public life of any age.

Under Justinian's solution for the government of the island, following the end of the Gothic War, the senior administrative official was known as the *praetor Siciliae*. This *praetor* was appointed directly from Constantinople, and was of proconsular rank, enjoying almost unlimited power.[15] His role and duties were

---

[12] M. Whitby, *The Emperor Maurice and his Historian: Theophylact Simocatta on Persian and Balkan Warfare*, OHM (Oxford, 1988), p.215.

[13] He remained in office until his death on 12 March 604. Buried in St Peter's, his epitaph acclaimed him as 'consul of God'.

[14] Gregory I, *Moralia in Job* 25.16.37 (CCL 143B.1262). Gregory uses Gen. 9:23 to illustrate his point. There, the sons of Noah covered the nakedness of their drunken father to conceal their father's sin.

[15] Justinian, *Nouellae* 75 and 104 (R. Schöll and W. Kroll [eds], *Corpus Iuris Civilis*, vol. 3: *Novellae* [Hildesheim: Weidmann, 1963 (13th edn)], pp. 378 and 500), issued 536 or 537; A.H.M. Jones, *The Later Roman Empire 284–602: A Social, Economic and Administrative Survey*, 2 vols (Oxford, 1964), p. 283; and E. Stein, *Histoire du Bas-Empire de la disparition de l'Empire d'Occident à la mort de Justinien (476–565)* (Paris, 1949), p. 425.

based on regulations imposed by Rome during the Punic Wars. Under Augustus a further development took place. The island became a senatorial appointment, the first of Rome's *coloniae*.

The *praetor Siciliae* exercised his authority through various subordinates. His financial officers were two *quaestores*, one, based at Syracuse, for the eastern part of the island, the other, based at Lilybaeum, for the west.[16] Part of their duties involved collection of 10 per cent of the annual harvest, as well as the purchase at a fixed price of supplementary quantities of grain as required. In addition, the various imperial estates on the island were under the supervision and care of a *procurator* who reported directly to Constantinople.

There appear to have been three holders of the office of *praetor Siciliae* during the pontificate of Gregory the Great. At its beginning, the incumbent was Justin.[17] His corrupt practices while in office led to his removal and the installation of Libertinus as successor in 593.[18] Despite his moving against the abuses of his predecessor, it appears that Libertinus was guilty of similar offences, for, between August and October 598, Libertinus himself was called to render an account of his behaviour before ex-consul Leontius, who had been sent from Constantinople to rectify matters.[19]

---

[16] Gregory I, *Ep.* 3.49 (CCL 140.195) = JE 1254, provides evidence of the presence of one such subordinate (*loci seruatore*), at Lilybaeum in July 593. See also Stein, *Histoire du Bas-Empire*, p. 468, n. 1.

[17] For Justin see Gregory I, *Epp.* 1.2 (CCL 140.2–3) = JE 1068; 2.29 (CCL 140.115–16); 2.50 (CCL 140.141–5) = JE 1186; and 3.37 (CCL 140.182–3) = JE 1242; and *PLRE* 3.756–7.

[18] For Libertinus see ibid., 3.37 (CCL 140.182–3); 5.32 (CCL 140.299–300) = JE 1347; 7.19 (CCL 140.470) = JE 1465; 9.5 (CCL 140A.567) = JE 1529; 10.12 (CCL 140A.838–9) = JE 1780; and 11.4 (CCL 140A.862–5) = JE 1794; and *PLRE* 3.776–7.

[19] For Leontius see ibid., 8.33 (CCL 140A.557–9) = JE 1522; 9.4 (CCL 140A.565–6) = JE 1528; 9.32 (CCL 140A.592–3) = JE 1556; 9.34 (CCL 140A.594) = JE 1558; 9.46 (CCL 140A.605) = JE 1570; 9.50 (CCL 140A.608–9) = JE 1576; 9.55 (CCL 140A.613) = JE 1577; 9.56 (CCL 140A.614) = JE 1578; 9.57 (CCL 140A.614–15) = JE 1579; 9.63 (CCL 140A.619–20) = JE 1588; 9.77 (CCL 140A.632) = JE 1601; note also 9.207 (CCL 140A.766–7) = JE 1733; 9.107 (CCL 140A.659–60) = JE 1631; 9.131 (CCL 140A.681–2) = JE 1655 ; 9.183 (CCL 140A.739–40) = JE 1709; and 11.4 (CCL 140A.862–5); *PLRE* 3.776–7; and P. Goubert, *Byzance avant l'Islam*, vol. 2: *Byzance et l'Occident sous les successeurs de Justinien* (Paris, 1956), pp. 243–4. Leontius was appointed to the Sicilian post at about the same time as Gennadius was appointed exarch of Africa and Callinicus as exarch of Italy. One may speculate whether the appointments were linked in any way. Further, it has been suggested that Leontius may have been a descendant of the patrician Leontius, who was a contemporary and rival of Emperor Zeno. See Goubert, *Byzance avant l'Islam*, p.242; Evagrius, *Hist eccl.* 3.16 and 27 (J. Bidez and L. Parmentier [eds], *The Ecclesiastical History of*

Whatever the shortcomings on the part of individual imperial administrators, Gregory retained the highest respect for them and sought to promote a collaborative relationship between church and state. In May 593, he asked Libertinus to move against the Jew Nasas, for owning Christian slaves in contravention of the law, and for setting up a shrine that was not a Christian one. He also urged Libertinus to devote his energy to seeking out and punishing heathens and Manichees and so to recall them to the Catholic faith.[20]

The collaborative relationship extended to ecclesiastical processes as well. In April 595, Deacon Cyprian was instructed by the pope to join with Libertinus in investigating several wayward clerics in the Syracuse region.[21] When the will of Theodore, late bishop of Lilybaeum, was called into question, in September 595, Cyprian was called to join with the ex-consul Leontius in examining the actions of Theodore's successor, Bishop Decius. Defender Romanus was instructed to work with Leontius in investigating Bishop Leo of Catania, in October 598.[22] In July 599, Leontius and Bishop John of Syracuse judged the case of Crescentius who had been accused of theft.[23]

Yet, Gregory, unlike the *praetor Siciliae*, was more than a mere administrator. As pope, he had been entrusted with an office of pastoral care (*curatio*) and, when circumstances required it, he was not slow to express displeasure with government officials. In March 591, he urged his sub-deacon, Peter, to seek to correct without fail cases that come to his attention, where people have suffered

---

Evagrius with the Scholia [London, 1898], pp. 114 and 123–4); and Martyn, *The Letters of Gregory the Great*, p. 579, n. 160.

[20] Gregory I, *Ep.* 3.37 (CCL 140.182–3). For other letters of Gregory concerning Jews and Samaritans see *Epp.* 5.7 (CCL 140.273–4) = JE 1323, to Deacon Cyprian; and 8.21 (CCL 140A.540–541) = JE 1509, to Bishop John at Syracuse; R.A.Markus, 'The Legacy of Pelagius: Orthodoxy, Heresy and Conciliation', in R.D. Williams (ed.), *The Making of Orthodoxy: Essays in Honour of Henry Chadwick,* (Cambridge, 1989), pp. 214–34, at p. 231; and P. Maymó i Capdevila, 'Gregory the Great and the Religious Otherness: Pagans in a Christian Italy' in J. Baun, A. Cameron, M. Edwards and M. Vinzent (eds), *Studia Patristica*, vol. 48, papers presented at the Fifteenth International Conference on Patristic Studies held in Oxford 2007 (Leuven, 2010), pp. 327–32.

[21] Gregory I, *Ep.* 5.32 (CCL 140.299–300).

[22] For Decius see ibid., 6.13 (CCL 140.382) = JE 1392; and for Leo see 2.29 (CCL 140.115–16); 5.32 (CCL 140.299–300); 6.20 (CCL 140.390) = JE 1399; 8.7 (CCL 140A.524) = JE 1494. The cases were followed with interest in Constantinople, as witnessed by 9.4 (CCL 140A.565–6), to Decius; and 9.32 (CCL 140A.592–3), to Leo, informing the court-bishop Domitian of Melitene of proceedings. It is worth noting that Bishop Domitian was the other godparent, alongside Gregory, of Emperor Maurice's eldest son, Theodosius.

[23] Ibid., 9.183 (CCL 140A.688–9).

violence and deprivation of what is rightfully theirs.[24] He expressed regret that Justin, the praetor, had prevented Sicily's bishops from making their *ad limina* visit to Rome in August 591,[25] and was concerned that Libertinus might also do likewise in May 597.[26] When Libertinus fell from office in June 600, he provided for his household out of the church's resources.[27]

Ex-consul Leontius' purge of corrupt officials in 598 produced a series of interventions from Gregory. To some he provided sanctuary and sought their safe-conduct to appear before the tribunal: Gregory, ex-praetorian prefect of Italy;[28] *magister militum*, Apollonius;[29] and the *uir clarissimus*, Laurence,[30] are examples of this. The ex-praetor Libertinus he could not save; but his imprisonment and subsequent flogging brought forth a passionate censure from the pope:

> I have learnt this one thing well and truly, that even if he committed some fraud in public affairs, his property should be curtailed, not his freedom. For the times of our most pious emperor are being totally blackened by the fact that free men are being killed, not to mention the offence to almighty God, not to mention the grievous damage to your reputation. For there is this difference between peoples' kings and a Roman emperor, the kings of peoples are masters of slaves, but a Roman emperor is the master of free men.[31]

Gregory reminded Leontius of a commonly assumed political ideal at the time: that the Roman empire was a political organisation charged with the

---

[24] Ibid., 1.38a (CCL 140A.1092–4) = JE 1102.
[25] Ibid., 1.70 (CCL 140.78–9) = JE 1139.
[26] Ibid., 7.19 (CCL 140.470).
[27] Ibid., 10.12 (CCL 140A.838–9).
[28] Ibid., 8.33 (CCL 140A.557–8); 9.4 (CCL 140A.565–6); 9.50 (CCL 140A.608–9); 9.55 (CCL 140A.613); and 9.78 (CCL 140A.633) = JE 1602. Goubert, *Byzance avant l'Islam*, pp.243–4, uses this case as proof that the powers of Leontius' commission extended beyond Sicily.
[29] Gregory I, *Epp.* 9.16 (CCL 140A.577); and 9.34 (CCL 140A.594).
[30] Ibid., 9.63 (CCL 140A.619–20); and 9.131 (CCL 140A.681–2).
[31] Ibid., 11.4 (CCL 140A.862–5). This comment, based on an original by Themistus, *Oratio* 11, was later reused in *Ep.* 13.32 (CCL 140A.1033–4) = JE 1899, as part of Gregory's first response to the overthrow of Emperor Maurice by the brutal Phocas in May 603. There is one difference in this latter case: the letter to Phocas begins with the stylistic *Gloria in excelsis Deo*, which was customary at the beginning of every imperial reign. But examination of the similarity of circumstances in which the words of *Epp.* 11.4 and 13 32 were written reveals Gregory's true feelings, beneath the language of diplomatic speech. His Sicilian experience with Leontius may have prepared him for the horrors to come.

Gregory the Great and the Sicilian Bishops

If, in the mind of the pope, the conduct of the imperial administrators left much to be desired, what can be said of church administration on the island? Sicily had been spared much of the destruction visited upon mainland Italy during Justinian's Gothic War, and it had escaped the fresh turmoil of the Lombard invasions. A number of people had fled as refugees to the relative safety that the island offered; others had seen their property violently stolen from them, while still others, including some bishops, had become comfortable and fat on the proceeds of prosperity. Several of the 13 sees on the island had fallen vacant. In a word, the life of the church in Sicily appeared to be in a state of stagnation. Under such circumstances, the tasks of civic oversight and pastoral care often fell to the bishops.

Gregory the Great rose to meet the challenge. During the early years of his pontificate he intervened more in the affairs of the Sicilian bishops than he did elsewhere. Indeed, the first letter of his *Register*, dated September 590,[32] was addressed to the bishops of Sicily, informing them of the appointment of a Roman sub-deacon, Peter, as his administrator (*rector*) of the papal patrimony on the island as well as papal vicar. In doing this he was mimicking in ecclesiastical affairs the order of civil affairs, where, as has been seen, the *praetor Siciliae* was a direct appointment from Constantinople.

Sub-deacon Peter was one of Gregory's close confidants. He knew the pope's mind well, sharing with him his explorations of Scripture and his desire for contemplation of the eternal truths. When Gregory wrote *Dialogorum* (between 593–94), he chose Peter as his interlocutor. After this date little is known of him.[33] Peter filled the office of papal vicar and administered the patrimony of the Roman church from September 590 until July/August 592. During that time 13 letters were addressed to him by Gregory.[34]

---

[32] Ibid., 1.1 (CCL 140.1–2) = JE 1067.

[33] It may be tempting to try to associate him with the Peter who administered the Campanian patrimony from September 592 to June 593, or to the Peter who was defender in Ravenna in 596; but the name is a common one and one should proceed with caution.

[34] Gregory, *Epp.* 1.9 (CCL 140.11) = JE 1076; 1.18 (CCL 140.17–18) = JE 1086; 1.38a (CCL 140. 1092–4); 1.39 (CCL 140.45) = JE 1109; 1.42 (CCL 140.49–56) = JE 1112; 1.44 (CCL 140.58) = JE 1114; 1.54 (CCL 140.67) = JE 1124; 1.65 (CCL 140.74–5)

As Sub-deacon Peter set out for Sicily on 16 March 591, the pope urged him to investigate the situation in which the Sicilian church found itself. He was to see to it that the bishops were not to become embroiled in secular law suits, except in so far as their duty of pastoral care was involved. People under the care of the Roman church needed to be protected from the violence of others who sought to steal from them. He was to urge the bishops to gather for 'the birthday of St Peter' (29 June).[35]

Gregory's appointment of Peter paved the way for future church reform. This began in August the same year, with a purification of the bench of bishops. Bishops Gregory of Agrigentum, Leo of Catania and Victor of Palermo were to present themselves in Rome for investigation, and the remainder were encouraged to come for the feast of St Peter.[36]

A comprehensive pattern of ecclesiastical patronage emerged, involving the nomination of hand-picked candidates for the task that presented itself. This approach appears to be at variance with Gregory's ideas, expressed in other contexts: of episcopal collegiality and due process taking its course before a consensus was reached. Sicilian conditions at the time obliged Gregory to change his approach in order to achieve his ends.[37]

The linchpin of the Gregorian reform of the Sicilian hierarchy was the archbishop of Syracuse. To fill this position, in October 591, Gregory chose one of his close friends, Maximian.[38] Maximian had been the abbot of St Andrew's, the monastery Gregory had set up in his family home on the Caelian Hill. Along with some other monks, he accompanied Gregory to Constantinople in 579. In Constantinople, he would have been one of the group of monks who attended Gregory's instructions on Job, which after 595 would emerge as *Moralia*. He would have been party to Gregory's many friendships with people at court. When Gregory became pope in 590, Maximian moved in with him to the papal palace; one presumes on similar terms to those which had seen him journey to

---

= JE 1134; 1.67 (CCL 140.76) = JE 1136; 1.69 (CCL 140.77–8) = JE 1138; 1.70 (CCL 140.78–9); 1.71 (CCL 140.79–80) = JE 1140; and 2.50 (CCL 140.141–5).

[35] Ibid., 1.38a (CCL 140. 1092–4).

[36] Ibid., 1.70 (CCL 140.78–9). Getting the Sicilian bishops to come to Rome remained problematic (see *Ep.* 7.19 [CCL 140.470]). On Gregory's concept of his Petrine authority in general see G. Demacopoulos, 'Gregory the Great and the Appeal to Petrine Authority', in J. Baun, A. Cameron, M. Edwards and M. Vinzent (eds), *Studia Patristica*, vol.48, papers presented at the Fifteenth International Conference on Patristic Studies held in Oxford 2007 (Leuven, 2010), pp. 333–46.

[37] In the process, the Sicilian bench was heavily Latinised; but this may have been an unlooked-for side effect, rather than any conscious proceeding against local Greek clergy.

[38] Gregory I, *Ep.* 2.5 (CCL 140.93) = JE 1159.

Constantinople. Later, he consulted Maximian over a story about Nonnosus, for inclusion in *Dialogues*, which were then being written.[39]

From this, it can be concluded that Maximian knew Gregory's mind as well as anyone. It is some measure of the importance that Gregory placed on Sicilian affairs that he should appoint him archbishop of Syracuse and papal vicar – in succession to Sub-deacon Peter – in October 591.[40] To him fell the oversight of ecclesiastical concerns on the island: to correct abuses where they might occur, to see to the removal of corrupt bishops and to replace them with more suitable successors, to administer the collection of church revenues justly, without appearing harsh in the manner of their collection, and to protect the values of clerical and monastic discipline.[41]

But, in November 594, Maximian died[42] and all was once again placed in jeopardy. Gregory needed a man in Sicily whom he could trust. He found him in John, archdeacon of Catania; and, in October 595, raised him to the episcopate, with the use of the pallium.[43] Under his guidance, the reforms begun by Peter and Maximian were able to achieve the necessary quality of permanence. This is demonstrated by the fact that, after 595, episcopal elections in Sicily proceeded in a fashion which was more regular and closer to the theoretical model, outlined by Gregory, for the conduct of such events. The Sicilian bishops were now able to operate as a recognisable unit within the church.

This was a major achievement which had been managed with subtlety and skill and a great measure of success. In January 603, it was possible for Gregory to address the bishops of the principal sees both collectively and by name: Gregory of Agrigentum, Leo of Catania, Secundinus of Taormina, Donus of Messina,

---

[39] Ibid., 3.50 (CCL 140.195–6) = JE 1255. The story appeared as *Dial.* 3.36 (SC 260.408).

[40] Ibid., 2.5 (CCL 140.93). In this letter of appointment, Gregory made it clear that this was a personal one, not one attached to the appointment as archbishop of Syracuse. It would lapse on Maximian's death. Maximian was the recipient of at least 12 letters from Gregory: 2.5 (CCL 140.93); 2.15 (CCL 140.101) = JE 1171; 2.21 (CCL 140.108) = JE 1177; 2.48 (CCL 140.139–40) = JE 1185; 3.12 (CCL 140.159) = JE 1216; 3.50 (CCL 140.195–6); 3.53 (CCL 140.199–200) = JE 1258; 4.11 (CCL 140.228–30) = JE 1282; 4.12 (CCL 140.230) = JE 1283; 4.14 (CCL 140.232) = JE 1285; 4.36 (CCL 140.256–7) = JE 1307; and 4.42 (CCL 140.263) = JE 1314.

[41] For bishops see ibid., 2.15 (CCL 140.101); 2.21 (CCL 140.108); 3.12 (CCL 140.159); 3.53 (CCL 140.199–200). For the collection of revenue see ibid., 4.11 (CCL 140.228–30); and 4.36 (CCL 140.256–7). For monastic and clerical lifestyle-protection see ibid., 4.11 (CCL 140.228–30); and 4.42 (CCL 140.263).

[42] Ibid., 5.20 (CCL 140.288–9) = JE 1339.

[43] Ibid., 6.18 (CCL 140.388) = JE 1397. In all, Gregory wrote 35 letters to Archbishop John of Syracuse.

Lucidus of Leontino and Trajan exiled from Malta.[44] All had been his nominees, and to them may be added the dioceses of Palermo, Triocala and Lipari. Where before the Sicilian bishops had appeared a disorganised lot with some corrupt individuals, now, thanks to Gregory's vigilance in oversight, an ordered bench of bishops emerged. How things fared after Gregory's death is unclear, however, as evidence for the remainder of the seventh century is fragmentary. This only serves to highlight even further the significance of the work of Gregory the Great.

Monastic Life in Sicily

A third group on the island was also the object of Gregory's particular supervision: those men and women who, like himself, had embraced the monastic life. At the time that he did so, he endowed six monasteries on his family's Sicilian estates.[45] His was not an isolated example, as other letters of Gregory reveal. There was Adeodata, who founded a women's monastery in her home at Lilybaeum,[46] Ianuaria, who established an oratory on Massa Furiana in the diocese of Tindari,[47] Isidore, who provided in his will for the establishment of a hospice at Palermo,[48] Julian, who founded a monastery at Catania,[49] as well as others whose names have been lost in the mist of history.

Whenever he heard of abuses and disputes amongst monks and nuns, Gregory was not slow to act. As in the case of wayward bishops, investigators were appointed to examine the circumstances. Sub-deacon Peter was instructed to employ ex-praetor Romanus to manage the business affairs of Abbot John's monastery (St. Lucy's, Syracuse?),[50] while surveyor John was appointed to determine boundaries disputed between the same monastery and that of St Peter's, Baiae (Abbot Caesarius).[51] Notary Stephen was sent to investigate two fugitive monks in Maratodis,[52] Deacon Cyprian is to judge the case of Petronella, a nun who has been seduced by Agnellus, son of Bishop Agnellus, who has made her pregnant and is now claiming the property Petronella has bestowed on her

---

[44] Ibid., 13.32 (CCL 140A.1033–4).
[45] See above, n. 7.
[46] Gregory I, *Ep*. 9.233 (CCL 140A.815) = JE 1760.
[47] Ibid., 9.181 (CCL 140A.738) = JE 1708.
[48] Ibid., 9.35 (CCL 140A.594–5) = JE 1559.
[49] Ibid., 13.21 (CCL 140A.1022) = JE 1888; and 13.35 (CCL 140A.1037–9) = JE 1902.
[50] Ibid., 1.67 (CCL 140.76).
[51] Ibid., 7.36 (CCL 140.499–500).
[52] Ibid., 2.26 (CCL 140.112–13) = JE 1182.

convent.⁵³ Bishop Leo of Catania and notary Hadrian were sent to enforce a proper monastic lifestyle in the monastery of St Vitus on Mount Etna.⁵⁴

Where the final outcome was likely to prove a contentious one, the pope was in the habit of making the final decision himself. Such instances were his restoration of the penitent monk Cicero to his former status,⁵⁵ his outlining the circumstances under which Agatho may be received as a monk in St Hermas' monastery, Palermo (Abbot Urbicus),⁵⁶ and his settlement of deciding a property dispute between the monastery of Sts Maximus and Agatha, Palermo (Abbot Domitius) and the Valerii hospice, Rome.⁵⁷

To guarantee the monks' life of prayerful contemplation Gregory sought to ensure that the traditional distinction between clerics and monks be maintained.⁵⁸ While he acknowledged the general principle that bishops had spiritual jurisdiction over monks and nuns living in their dioceses – including the right to punish those who failed to live by their monastic rule – he was reluctant to allow the bishop the right to interfere in the internal life of the establishment. Over-zealous bishops could find themselves faced with no less an opponent than the pope himself.⁵⁹ Bishops who wished to use monasteries as places for the celebration of public masses or as places for the establishment of their episcopal sees were expressly forbidden to do so.⁶⁰

If the occasion required it, however, Gregory was quite prepared to remove monks from their monastic seclusion, so that needs of the wider church might be met. At the beginning of his pontificate, he authorised Sub-deacon Peter to select monks from Sicilian monasteries to work in places without a priest.⁶¹ One individual appears right across the whole range of Gregorian missionary activity, providing a common thread through each of them; he is the monk and abbot Cyriacus (†600).⁶² He appears first in Sicily, and then successively in Sardinia

---

⁵³ Ibid., 4.6 (CCL 140.222–3) = JE 1277.
⁵⁴ Ibid., 14.16 (CCL 140A.1089–90) = JE 1993; and 14.17 (CCL 140.1090–1) = JE 1994 – Gregory's last two letters.
⁵⁵ Ibid., 5.28 (CCL 140.295) = JE 1345.
⁵⁶ Ibid., 6.49 (CCL 140.422) = JE 1429.
⁵⁷ Ibid., 9.67 (CCL 140A.622–3) = JE 1607.
⁵⁸ Ibid., 4.11 (CCL 140.228–30).
⁵⁹ Ibid., 14.16-7 (CCL 140A.1089–91).
⁶⁰ U. Berlière, 'L'Exercice du ministère paroissial par les moines dans le Haut Moyen-Age', *RB*, 39 (1927): pp. 227–50, at pp. 231–2.
⁶¹ Gregory I, *Ep.* 1.18 (CCL 140.17–18).
⁶² Ibid., 2.50 (CCL 140.141–5); 4.23 (CCL 140.241–2) = JE 1295; 4.25 (CCL 140.244) = JE 1297; 4.26 (CCL 140.244–6) = JE 1298; 4.27 (CCL 140.246) = JE 1299; 5.2 (CCL 140.267) = JE 1318; 9.1 (CCL 140A.562–3) = JE 1525; 9.11 (CCL 140A.572–3)

(with Bishop Felix), Gaul and finally in Visigothic Spain. Gregory must have trusted him very much to have used his talents so widely. The combined effect of Gregory's monastic reforms was to provide the church with personnel who could be deployed on various ecclesiastical ventures. The pope's continued and constant patronage ensured that monasticism took its place within the fabric of western Christian society.

The Papal Patrimony in Sicily

Sicily was a significant part of the Roman empire's granary, particularly in the time after the fall of Africa to the Vandals, although even this should not be exaggerated.[63] Huge plantations (*latifundia*) produced grain that was exported to Rome. Field work was done by large numbers of slaves, who were often prisoners-of-war. When corn was required for shipment to Rome, it was bought from the *coloni* at market prices. The payment of rental on these properties seems to have been frequently made in gold.[64]

This state of affairs continued during the sixth century, but to grain was added exports in wool, timber and wine. Considerable investment was made in buildings in the coastal cities at this time, while settlements in the interior were converted into large villas, occupied by senators whose presence was no longer required in Rome.

In examining the system of imperial government in Sicily it has already been noted that the various imperial estates on the island were under the supervision and care of a *procurator* who reported directly to Constantinople. Here too, Gregory the Great imitated the order of civil administration in his arrangement of the lands of papal patrimony.

= JE 1535; 9.209 (CCL 140A.768) = JE 1736; 9.214 (CCL 140A.772–5) = JE 1743; 9.219 (CCL 140A.782–90) = JE 1747; 9.220 (CCL 140A.790–2) = JE 1748; 9.230 (CCL 140A.811–12) = JE 1758; and 11.10 (CCL 140A.873–6) = JE 1800.

[63] A.H. Merrills, 'Introduction – Vandals, Romans and Berbers: Understanding Late Antique North Africa', in A.H. Merrills (ed.), *Vandals, Romans and Berbers: New Perspectives on Late Antique North Africa* (Aldershot, 2004), pp. 3–28, at p. 11; and Jonathan Conant, *Staying Roman: Conquest and Identity in Africa and the Mediterranean, 439–700*, Cambridge Studies in Medieval Life and Thought 4th series, vol. 82 (Cambridge, 2012), 90–95.

[64] Jones, *Later Roman Empire*, p. 804: for the purchase of corn from *coloni* (Gregory I, *Ep.* 1.42 [CCL 140.49–56]); and for gold rents (5.7 [CCL 140.273–4]). On slavery see A. Serfass, 'Slavery and Pope Gregory the Great', *JECS*, 14 (2006): pp. 77–103.

The papal patrimony in Sicily was huge. Estimates are that it contained 400 *massae* covering about one-nineteenth of the island's surface.[65] The importance of these lands to the papacy may be understood from the 74 letters that Pope Gregory addressed to his administrators there, a number far in excess of those addressed to patrimonial officials elsewhere.[66] Yet there were other large landholdings on Sicily besides those of the emperor and the pope. Ecclesiastical landowners included the churches of Milan and Ravenna; even the name of one of the administrators is known: the Ravennese deacon, John. The private landholdings of Gregory's family were sufficient to endow six monasteries.[67]

Pope Gregory's *Register* of letters provides a detailed source of data for an analysis of the business of the Sicilian patrimony. The names of its administrators (*rectores*) and their staff are known, together with their approximate terms of office. At the beginning of the pontificate, it appears that the whole administration was placed under the care of Sub-deacon Peter (September 590–August 592). After his departure, Gregory chose to divide responsibilities – following the model of the secular government – with Syracuse and Palermo becoming bases for the eastern and western parts of the island. *Rectores* at Syracuse were Deacon Cyprian (July 593–October 598), defender Romanus (October 598–August 601) and notary (*chartularius*) Hadrian (January 603–March 604).[68] Members of the staff of the Syracusan patrimony at one time or another included defenders (*defensores*) Peter and Vitus (October 598) and notary Pantaleon (June 603). *Rectores* at Palermo were defenders Candidus (June 594–October 598) and Fantinus (September/October 598–September 603),[69] while staff members

---

[65] So Jones, *Later Roman Empire*, p. 769; Brown, *The Rise of Western Christendom*, p. 206; and V. Recchia, *Gregorio Magno e la società Agricola* (Rome, 1978), p. 16, basing their calculations on a reading of Gregory, *Ep.* 2.50 (CCL 140.141–5). But this assessment may not be an accurate one. For the discussion on the issue see Martyn, *The Letters of Gregory the Great*, p. 229, n. 161, with which K. Sessa, *The Formation of Papal Authority in Late Antique Italy: Roman Bishops and the Domestic Sphere* (Cambridge, 2012), p. 117, n. 145, agrees. V. Prigent, 'La Sicile byzantine, entre Papes et Empereurs', in D. Engels, L. Geis and M. Kleu (eds), *Zwischen Ideal und Wirklichkeit* (Stuttgart, 2010), pp. 202–30, at pp. 213–4, n. 72, estimates the extent of the patrimony to be 80,000 hectares, rather than the 800,000 hectares, which Jones and the others would suggest.

[66] E. and E. Spearing, *The Patrimony of the Roman Church in the time of Gregory the Great* (Cambridge, 1918), p. 7.

[67] For Milan see Gregory I, *Ep.* 1.80 (CCL 140.87–8) = JE 1149; for Ravenna see *Ep.* 13.25 (CCL 140A.1026) = JE 1892; and for Gregory's family see n. 7 above.

[68] From February 599, Hadrian had been on the staff of the Palermo patrimony.

[69] Fantinus had been on the staff of the patrimony from the days of Sub-deacon Peter (May 591). On Candidus' retirement (October 598), he succeeded him in office.

included notaries Beneatus (April 593–March 595) and Hadrian (February 599–June 601).[70]

The duties of the patrimonial administrators were far reaching. As might be expected, they included decision-making in property disputes,[71] matters relating to the price of corn,[72] the collection of rents[73] and the sale of unprofitable herds.[74] But they also included matters more wide ranging in nature, concerning all levels of Sicilian society. They were to protect the field workers (*rustici*) on the farms from anyone who would do them violence,[75] to care for widows and orphans,[76] to superintend the operation of church hospices, as well as provide benefits and pensions for the needy.[77] They were to act as executors for wills and legacies[78] and to oversee the construction of oratories and monasteries.[79] The enforcement of clerical celibacy[80] and of monastic discipline[81] was entrusted to them, as was the pursuit of heresy and its eradication.[82] It was part of their duties to see to it that

---

[70] This was before his transfer to Syracuse. The cases of Hadrian and Fantinus provide tantalising hints at the career-paths that were possible within the patrimonial administration.

[71] Gregory I, *Epp.* 1.1 (CCL 140.1–2); 1.36 (CCL 140.43) = JE 1106; 1.42 (CCL 140.49–56); 2.30 (CCL 140.116–17) = JE 1184; 2.50 (CCL 140.141–5); see also 1.9 (CCL 140.11); 1.71 (CCL 140.79–80); 5.33 (CCL 140.300–301) = JE 1348; 9.10 (CCL 140A.571) = JE 1534; 9.33 (CCL 140A.593) = JE 1557; 9.48 (CCL 140A.607) = JE 1574; 9.75 (CCL 140A.630) = JE 1599; 9.89 (CCL 140A.643) = JE 1613; and 9.171 (CCL 140A.729) = JE 1697.

[72] Ibid., 1.42 (CCL 140.49–56); and 1.70 (CCL 140.78–9).

[73] Ibid., 9.107 (CCL 140A.569–60).

[74] Ibid., 2.50 (CCL 140.141–5).

[75] Ibid., 1.42 (CCL 140.49–56); 9.46 (CCL 140A.605); and 9.210 (CCL 140A.769) = JE 1737.

[76] Ibid., 7.41 (CCL 140.505) = JE 1487; 9.39 (CCL 140A.598) = JE 1563; 9.46 (CCL 140A.605); and 9.48 (CCL 140A.607).

[77] Ibid., 1.18 (CCL 140.17–18); 1.44 (CCL 140.58); 1.65 (CCL 140.74–5); 1.69 (CCL 140.77–8); 3.55 (CCL 140.204) = JE 1260; 4.28 (CCL 140.247) = JE 1300; 5.7 (CCL 140.273–4); 6.4 (CCL 140.372) = JE 1383; 6.38 (CCL 140.412) = JE 1418; 9.37 (CCL 140A.596) = JE 1561; 9.43 (CCL 140A.601) = JE 1567; 9.110 (CCL 140A.662) = JE 1635; 9.145 (CCL 140A.696) = JE 1669; 9.151 (CCL 140A.706–7) = JE 1676.

[78] Ibid., 1.42 (CCL 140.49–56); 9.8 (CCL 140A.569–70) = JE 1532; 9.10 (CCL 140A.571); 9.35 (CCL 140A.594–5); 9.75 (CCL 140A.630).

[79] Ibid., 9.35 (CCL 140A.594–5); and 9.165 (CCL 140A.723–4) = JE 1691; oratory: 1.54 (CCL 140.67).

[80] Ibid., 1.42 (CCL 140.49–56); and 9.111 (CCL 140A.663–4) = JE 1636.

[81] Ibid., 1.67 (CCL 140.76); 2.50 (CCL 140.141–5); 4.6 (CCL 140.222–3); 5.28 (CCL 140.295); 5.33 (CCL 140.300–301); and 9.54 (CCL 140A.612–13) = JE 1575.

[82] Ibid., 3.27 (CCL 140.172–3) = JE 1231; 5.7 (CCL 140.273–4); and 5.32 (CCL 140.299–300).

the provisions enacted in Justinian's legal code concerning Jews were observed.[83] To them fell the obligation, at a local level of engineering harmonious relations between the papacy and both imperial officials[84] and Sicily's bishops.[85] Perhaps most importantly of all, these administrators were entrusted with the recruitment of staff[86] and with the responsibility of conducting episcopal elections whenever vacancies of this nature should occur.[87]

Between *rectores, chartularii, notarii* and the *rustici* was the class known as the overseers (*conductores*). Their existence is attested to in both the Theodosian and Justinianic legal codes.[88] Indeed, without them the patrimony would have ceased to function. The overseer lived on the home farm (*conduma*), which was surrounded by a number of tenancies (*colonicae*).[89] In this way the large landed estate was be divided into *massae*, which were, in turn, further subdivided into the basic unit of land ownership: farmsteads (*fundi*). The layout of these *fundi* was remarkably stable, as is illustrated by the fact that they were often named after some long-past owner.[90] *Conductores* were charged with the duty of collecting rents and passing them on to the papal agents. Unlike the tenant farmers, who were tied to the land, overseers usually leased their land on short-term contracts. The papacy regulated the terms of these leases by means of licences (*libelli*).[91]

---

[83] Ibid., 1.69 (CCL 140.77–8); 2.50 (CCL 140.141–5); 5.7 (CCL 140.273–4); 7.41 (CCL 140.505); 8.23 (CCL 140A.543–4) = JE 1511; 9.38 (CCL 140A.597) = JE 1562; and 9.40 (CCL 140A.598–9) = JE 1564.

[84] Ibid., 9.28 (CCL 140A.589) = JE 1552; 9.32 (CCL 140A.592–3); and 9.79 (CCL 140A.633–4) = JE 1603.

[85] Ibid., 1.70 (CCL 140.78–9); 6.20 (CCL 140.390); 7.19 (CCL 140.470);and 9.32 (CCL 140A.592–3).

[86] Ibid., 1.18 (CCL 140.17–18); 9.119 (CCL 140A.671–2) = JE 1644.

[87] Ibid., 5.20 (CCL 140.288–9); 5.23 (CCL 140.290) = JE 1340; 6.13 (CCL 140.382); and 7.38 (CCL 140.502–3) = JE 1484.

[88] *CTh* 10.4.3 (Th. Mommsen and P. Krüger [eds], *Codex Theodosianus*, vol. 1: *Theodosiani Libri XVI cum constitutionibus Sirmondinis* [Hildesheim, 1990], p. 535); and 10.26.2 (Mommsen and Krüger, *Codex Theodosianus*, p. 570); and *CI* 11.72.1 (Th. Mommsen and P. Krüger [eds], *Corpus Iuris Civilis*, vol. 2: *Codex Justinianus* [Hildesheim, 1989 [11th edn]), p. 452); and 11.74.1 (Mommsen and Krüger, *Codex Justinianus*, p. 452). See Recchia, *Gregorio Magno e la società Agricola*, p. 48.

[89] Recchia, *Gregorio Magno e la società Agricola*, p. 51.

[90] E.g., Gregory I, *Epp.* 1.9 (CCL 140.11) – Fullionacum; 1.42 (CCL 140.49–56) – Varronianum and Cinci; 7.38 (CCL 140.502–3) – Largia; 9.23 (CCL 140A.583) = JE 1547 – Leucas and Samanteria; 9.37 (CCL 140A.596) – Disteria; 9.120 (CCL 140A.672) = JE 1645 – Getina; 9.165 (CCL 140A.723–4) – Cosmas; 9.171 (CCL 140A.729) – Papyriana; 9.181 (CCL 140A.738) – Furia; and 9.236 (CCL 140A.819–20) = JE 1763– Gelas.

[91] See Cassiodorus, *Variae* 5.7 (CCL 96.MGH.AA 12.147–8).

Tenant farmers were, on the other hand, tied to the land they worked. The differences in their standard of living and that of the slaves is not known, but, if Gregory's letter addressed to defender Fantinus in September/October 598 is anything to go by, they were not very high. On that occasion, Gregory instructed Fantinus to ensure that they had enough to live on.[92]

The produce of the patrimony, whether destined to meet the demands of imperial taxation or to supply a dole for the urban poor in cities such as Rome, remained the responsibility of the landowner – in this case the papal administrators. To them also fell the twin responsibilities of shipping and storage of that produce.[93]

Conclusion

Gregory the Great's first and last letters were addressed to Sicily. The first – one might almost describe it as a mission statement – was addressed to the island's bishops, announcing the appointment of Sub-deacon Peter as administrator of the papal patrimony there. The last was addressed to one of Sub-deacon Peter's successors, the notary Hadrian, at Syracuse. In between, Gregory wrote some 143 letters concerning Sicilian affairs. In many ways, these present an abridged version of the concerns found in his complete *Register* of letters.

From them it is possible to discern the means used by the pope to both reconstitute and reform the Sicilian bench of bishops. Under the leadership of the archbishop of Syracuse – first Maximian and later John – corrupt bishops were replaced and their successors were encouraged to perform their duties of episcopal oversight and enthusiasm. By January 603, as has been seen, it was possible for Gregory to address them as a coherent body of church leaders.

Gregory the monk had an ongoing concern for monastic discipline as well as for the preservation of a life of prayerful contemplation within the monastic community. This concern never left him. It began with the endowment of six monasteries on his family's Sicilian holdings and remained until his very last letter, which concerned the quality of the monastic lifestyle in a monastery on Mount Etna. Yet, he was also able to harness the forces of monasticism for missionary purposes, as in the case of Abbot Cyriacus. The pope's continued

---

[92] Gregory I, *Ep.* 9.10 (CCL 140A.571).
[93] Recchia, *Gregorio Magno e la società Agricola*, pp. 66–7; and C. Pietri, 'La Rome de Grégoire', in *Gregorio Magno e il suo tempo*, XIX Incontro di studiosi dell'antichità cristiana, Roma, 9–12 maggio 1990, SEAug, vol. 33 (Rome: Institutum Patristicum Augustinianum, 1991), pp. 9–32, at p. 24.

and constant patronage ensured that monasticism prospered and took its place within the fabric of western Christian society.

Affairs of the papal patrimony were multifaceted and all-encompassing. *Epistula* 2.50 serves as an illustration of this. The letter treats subjects ranging from the protection of nuns, the pastoral care of Jews, the breeding of cattle, the maintenance of church plate, the rental of church lands, the administration of wills and legacies and payment of pensions for the poor, to the supply of a horse and mules for papal processions. This vigilance and attention to detail from both the pope and his local administrators was vital in an Italy beset by the trauma of the Lombard invasions. The produce of the Sicilian estates did much to off-set the effects of food shortages.

In his exercise of authority and power within the Sicilian context, Gregory drew much from the system of government adopted by the Byzantine administration. Indeed, imperial officials, such as the *praetor Siciliae* and his *quaestores*, must be treated with the greatest respect, despite their shortcomings, on account of the office they occupied. The respect was maintained through a succession of office-bearers: first Justin, then Libertinus and finally Leontius. Yet, at the same time he was able to exercise human rights and extend the office of pastoral care. He reminded ex-consul Leontius – as he was later to remind the brutal Emperor Phocas – 'There is this difference between peoples' kings and a Roman emperor, the kings of peoples are masters of slaves, but a Roman emperor is the master of free men.'[94]

These then are some features of Gregory the Great's Sicilian administration and the issues that he had to deal with. They appear as in the full light of day. By comparison, information for the rest of the seventh century is fragmentary. It stands in the shadows alongside the achievement of Gregory the Great.

---

[94] See n. 28.

Bibliography

Ancient Sources

Acta synodi Romani anno 502 (Theodor Mommsen, [ed.], *Cassiodori senatoris variae*, MGH.AA, vol. 12 [Berlin: Weidmann, 1894], 438–55).

Ado of Vienne, *Martyrologium* (Genevieve Renaud, and Jacques Dubois (eds), *Le martyrologe d'Adon: ses deux familles, ses trois recensions: texte et commentaire* [Paris: CNRS, 1984]).

Agapitus I, *Epistula ad Iustinianum (Gratulamur)* (Otto Günther [ed.], *Epistulae imperatorum pontificum aliorum inde ab a. CCCLXVII usque ad a. DLIII datae Avellana quae dicitur collectio*, CSEL, vol. 35 [Vienna: Tempsky, 1895], 342–7).

Agapitus I, *Epistula ad Iustinianum (Licet de)* (Otto Günther [ed.], *Epistulae imperatorum pontificum aliorum inde ab a. CCCLXVII usque ad a. DLIII datae Avellana quae dicitur collectio*, CSEL, vol. 35 [Vienna: Tempsky, 1895], 333–8).

Agnellus of Ravenna, *Liber pontificalis ecclesiai Ravennatis* (Deborah Mauskopf-Deliyannis [ed.], *Agnelli Ravennatis liber pontificalis ecclesiae Ravennatis*, CCM, vol. 199 [Turnhout: Brepols, 2006]).

Alberigo, Giuseppe, et al. (eds), *The Ecumenical Councils from Nicaea I to Nicaea II (325–787)*, CCCOGD, vol. 1 (Turnhout: Brepols, 2006).

Ambrose, *Epistulae* (Otto Faller and Michaela Zelzer [eds], *Sancti Ambrosii Opera*, part 10: *Epistulae et Acta*, CSEL, vols 82/1–4 [Vienna: Hölder-Pichler-Tempsky and Verlag der Österreichischen Akademie der Wissenschaften, 1968–96]).

Ambrose, *Hymni* (Jacques Fontaine [ed.], *Ambroise de Milan. Hymnes* [Paris: Cerf, 1992]).

Ambrosiaster, *In epistula ad Efesios* (Heinrich Josef Vogel [ed.], *Ambrosiastri qui dicitur commentaries in epistulas Paulinas*, part 3: *In epistulas ad Galatas, ad Efesios, ad Filippenses, ad Colosenses, ad Thesalonicenses, ad Timotheum, ad Titum, ad Filemonem*, CSEL, 81/3 [Vienna: Hoelder-Pichler-Tempsky, 1969]).

Amelli, Ambrogio Maria (Guerrino), *Spicilegium Casinense complectens analecta sacra et profana e codd. Casinensibus aliarumque bibliothecarum collecta atque edita*, t. 1 (Monte Cassino: Typi archicoenobii Montis Casini, 1888–93).

Ammianus Marcellinus, *Res gestae* (Guy Sabbah, *Ammien Marcellin. Histoires*, 6 vols, Collection des Universités de France [Paris: Les Belles Lettres, 1968–99]).

Athanasius, *Apologia secunda* (Hans Georg Opitz [ed.], *Athanasius Werke*, vol. 2/1: *Die "Apologien"* [Berlin: De Gruyter, 1938], 87–168).

Augustine, *Breuiculus collationis cum Donatistis libri tres* (Eugenio Cavallari, *Opere di Sant'Agostino*, part 1: *Opere polemiche*, NBA, vol. 16/2 [Rome: Città Nuova Editrice, 2000], 75–216).

Augustine, *De baptismo contra Donatistas* (Antonio Lombardi, *Opere di Sant'Agostino*, part 1: *Opere polemiche*, NBA, vol. 15/1 [Rome: Città Nuova Editrice, 1998], 266–606).

Augustine, *De ciuitate Dei* (Domenico Gentili, with Agostino Trapè, Robert Russell, and Sergio Conta, *Opere di Sant'Agostino*, part 1: *Opere filosofico-dommatiche*, NBA, vol. 5/1–3 [Rome: Città Nuova Editrice, 1990–91 (2nd edn)]).

Augustine, *Enerrationes in Psalmos* (Angelo Corticelli, Riccardo Minuti and Benedettine di S. Maria di Rosano, *Opere di Sant'Agostino*, part 3: *Discorsi*, NBA vols 25–28/2 [Rome: Città Nuova Editrice, 1967–93]).

Augustine, *Epistulae* (Terenzio Alimonti and Luigi Carrozzi, *Opere di Sant'Agostino*, part 2: *Le Lettere*, NBA, vols 20/1–23/A [Rome: Città Nuova Editrice, 1992]).

Augustine, *Sermones* (Michele Pellegrino et al., *Opere di Sant' Agostino*, part 3: *Discorsi*, NBA vols 29–35/2 [Rome: Città Nuova Editrice, 1979–2002]).

Basil, *Epistulae* (Yves Courtonne [ed.], *Saint Basile. Lettres*, 3 vols, Collection des Universités de France [Paris: Les Belles Lettres, 1957–66]).

Berlin-Brandenburg Academy of Sciences and Humanities (ed.), *Corpus Inscriptionum Latinarum*, 17 vols (Berlin: Berlin-Brandenburg Academy of Sciences and Humanities, 1893–986).

Canones in causa Apiarii (Charles Munier [ed.], *Concilia Africae A. 345–A. 525*, CCL, vol. 149 [Turnholt: Brepols, 1974], 95–148).

Cassian, (Michael Petschenig and Gottfried Kreuz [eds], *Cassianus*, CSEL, vols 13 and 17 [Vienna: Österreichischen Akademie der Wissenschaften, 2004 (rev. edn)]).

Cassiodorus, *Institutiones* (Roger A.B. Mynors [ed.], *Cassiodori Senatoris Institutiones* [Oxford: Clarendon Press, 1961 (2nd edn)]).

Cassiodorus, *Variae* (Theodor Mommsen [ed.], *Cassiodori senatoris Variae*, MGH.AA, vol. 12 [Berlin: Weidmann, 1894]).
Celestine I, *Epistulae* (PL 50.417–558 = Pierre Coustant, *Epistolae Romanorum Pontificum et quae ad eos scriptae sunt a S. Clemente I usque ad Innocentum III*, t. 1 [Paris: L.-D. Delatour, 1721], cols 1051–218).
Chavasse, Antoine (ed.), *Sancti Leonis magni Romani pontificis tractatus septem et nonaginta*, CCL, vol. 138–8A (Turnhout: Brepols, 1973).
Chronographus anni CCCLIIII (Theodor Mommsen [ed.], *Chronica Minora saec. IV. V. VI. VII*, vol. 1, MGH.AA, vol. 9 [Berlin: Weidmann, 1892], 13–148).
Clercq, Charles de (ed.), *Concilia Galliae a.511–a.695*, CCL, vol. 148A (Turnhout: Brepols, 1963).
Codex Iustinianus (Theodor Mommsen and Paul Krüger [eds], *Corpus Iuris Civilis*, vol. 2: *Codex Justinianus* [Hildesheim: Weidmann, 1989 (11th edn)]).
Codex Theodosianus (Theodor Mommsen and Paul Krüger [eds], *Codex Theodosianus*, vol. 1: *Theodosiani Libri XVI cum constitutionibus Sirmondinis* [Hildesheim: Weidmann, 1990]).
Collectio Avellana (Otto Günther [ed.], *Epistulae imperatorum pontificum aliorum inde ab a. CCCLXVII usque ad a. DLIII datae Avellana quae dicitur collectio*, CSEL, vol. 35 [Vienna: Tempsky, 1895]).
Constitutio Sirmondinis (Theodor Mommsen and Paul Krüger [eds], *Codex Theodosianus*, vol. 1: *Theodosiani Libri XVI cum constitutionibus Sirmondinis* [Hildesheim: Weidmann, 1990]).
Conti, Marco (ed.), *Priscillian of Avila: The Complete Works*, OECT (Oxford: Oxford University Press, 2010).
Council of Chalcedon, *Canones* (Giuseppe Albergio et al. [eds], *The Ecumenial Councils from Nicaea to Nicaea II (325–787)*, CCC OGD, vol 1 [Turnhout: Brepols, 2006]).
Council of Constantinople (553), (Johannes Straub [ed.], *ACO*, t. 4: *Concilium universale Constantinopolitanum sub Iustiniano habitatum*, vol. 1: *Concilii actiones VIII – appendices Graecae – indices* [Berlin: Walter de Gruyter, 1971]).
Council of Nicaea (325), *Expositio fidei* and *Canones* (Giuseppe Alberigo et al. [eds], *The Ecumenical Councils from Nicaea I to Nicaea II (325–787)*, CCCOGD, vol. 1 [Turnhout: Brepols, 2006], 19–34).
Coustant, Pierre (ed.), *Epistolae Romanorum Pontificum et quae ad eos scriptae sunt a S. Clement I usque ad Innocentum III*, t. 1 (Paris: L.-D. Delatour, 1721).
Cyprian, *Epistulae* (Gerard Frederik Diercks [ed.], *Sancti Cypriani Episcopi Epistularium*, CCL, vols 3B–C [Turnhout: Brepols, 1994–6]).

Damasus, *Epigrammata* (Antonio Ferrua [ed.], *Epigrammata Damasiana: Recensuit et adnotauit*, Sussidi allo studio delle antichità cristiana, vol. 2 [Vatican City: Pontificio Istituto di Archeologia Cristiana, 1942]).

[Damasus], *Epistula ad Gallos episcopos* (Yves-Marie Duval, *La décrétale* Ad Gallos Episcopos: *son texte et son auteur. Texte critique, traduction française et commentaire*, Supplements to Vigiliae Christianae, vol. 73 [Leiden and Boston: Brill, 2005]).

Dessau, Hermann (ed.), *Inscriptiones Latinae Selectae*, 3 vols (Berlin: Weidmann, 1892–1916).

Diehl, Ernest (ed.), *Inscriptiones Latinae Christianae Veteres*, 3 vols (Berlin: Weidmann, 1925–31).

Dioscorus, *Suggestiones ad Hormisdam* (Otto Günther [ed.], *Epistulae imperatorum pontificum aliorum inde ab a. CCCLXVII usque ad a. DLIII datae Avellana quae dicitur collectio*, CSEL, vol. 35 [Vienna: Tempsky, 1895], 618–21, 675–6, 682–3, 685–7, 694).

Ennodius of Pavia, *Epistulae* (Friedrich Vogel [ed.], *Magni Felicis Ennodii Opera. Vita Epiphanii*, MGH.AA, vol. 7 [Berlin: Weidmann, 1885], 1–326).

Ennodius of Pavia, *Vita Epiphanii* (Friedrich Vogel [ed.], *Magni Felicis Ennodii Opera. Vita Epiphanii*, MGH.AA, vol. 7 [Berlin: Weidmann, 1885], 84–109).

Epiphanius of Constantinople, *Epistula ad Hormisdam* (Otto Günther [ed.], *Epistulae imperatorum pontificum aliorum inde ab a. CCCLXVII usque ad a. DLIII datae Avellana quae dicitur collectio*, CSEL, vol. 35 [Vienna: Tempsky, 1895], 652–4).

Epitome Cononiana Libri pontificalis [usque ad LVI] (Theodor Mommsen [ed.], MGH.GPR, vol. 1 [Berlin: Weidmann, 1898], 229–63).

Epitome Feliciana Libri pontificalis (Theodor Mommsen [ed.], MGH.GPR, vol. 1 [Berlin: Weidmann, 1898], 229–63).

Epitome historiae ecclesiasticae Theodori Anagnostae (uel Letoris) et Iohannis Diocrinomeni (Günther Christian Hansen [ed.], *Theodorus Anagnostes. Kirchengeschichte*, GCS n.F., vol. 3 [Berlin: Brandenburgische Akademie der Wissenschaften, 1995 (2nd edn)]).

Excerpta Valesiana II (Ingemar König [ed.], *Aus der Zeit Theoderichs des Großen. Einleitung, Text, Übersetzung und Kommentar einer anonymen Quelle*, Texte zur Forschung, Bd 69 [Darmstadt: Wissenschaftliche Buchgesellschaft, 1997]).

Eusebius, *Historia ecclesiastica* (Eduard Schwartz [ed.] and Gustave Bardy [trans.], *Eusèbe de Césarée. Historique ecclésiastique*, SC, vols 31, 41, 55 and 73 [Paris: Les Éditions du Cerf, 1952–87]).

Evagrius, *Historia ecclesiastica* (Joseph Bidez and Léon Parmentier [eds], *The Ecclesiastical History of Evagrius* [London: Methuen and co., 1898]).

Ewald, Paul (ed.), 'Die Papstbriefe der Brittischen Sammlung, 2', *NA*, 5 (1880): 503–96.

Faustinus and Marcellinus, *Liber precum* (Otto Günther [ed.], *Epistulae imperatorum pontificum aliorum inde ab a. CCCLXVII usque ad a. DLIII datae Avellana quae dicitur collectio*, CSEL, vol. 35 [Vienna: Tempsky, 1895], 5–44).

Felix III (II), *Epistulae* (Andreas Thiel [ed.], *Epistolae Romanorum pontificum genuinae et quae ad eos scriptae sunt a S. Hilaro usque ad Pelagium II*, vol. 1 [Braunsberg: Eduard Peter, 1867], 221–84).

Felix IV (III), *Constitutum de ecclesia Ravennatensi* (Deborah Mauskopf-Deliyannis [ed.], *Agnelli Ravennatis Liber pontificalis ecclesiae Ravennatis*, CCM, vol. 199 [Turnhout: Brepols, 2006], 226–31).

Felix IV (III), *Praeceptum* (Eduard Schwartz ([ed.], *ACO*, t. 4: *Concilium universale Constantinopolitanum sub Iustiniano habitum*, vol. 2: *Iohannis Maxentii libelli – Collectio codicis Novariensis XXX – Collectio codicis Parisini 1682 – Procli Tomus ad Armenios – Iohannis Papae II Epistula ad uiros illustres* [Strasbourg: Carol J. Trübner, 1914], 96–7).

Fragmentum Laurentianum Libri pontificalis (Theodor Mommsen [ed.], MGH. GPR, vol. 1 [Berlin: Weidmann, 1898], ix–xi).

Gaudentius of Brescia, *Tractatus* (Ambrose Glück [ed.], *S. Gaudentii episcopi Brixiensis Tractatus*, CSEL, 68 [Vienna: Hoelder-Pichler-Tempsky, 1936]).

Gelasius I, *Epistulae* (Andreas Thiel [ed.], *Epistolae Romanorum pontificum genuinae et quae ad eos scriptae sunt a S. Hilaro usque ad Pelagium II*, vol. 1 [Braunsberg: Eduard Peter, 1867], 285–613).

Gennadius, *De uiris illustribus;* (Ernest Cushing Richardson [ed.], *Hieronymus. Liber de uiris inlustribus, Gennadius. Liber de uiris inlustribus*, TU, vol. 14/1 [Leipzig: J. C. Hinrich, 1896]).

Germanus of Capua et al., *Suggestiones ad Hormisdam* (Otto Günther [ed.], *Epistulae imperatorum pontificum aliorum inde ab a. CCCLXVII usque ad a. DLIII datae Avellana quae dicitur collectio*, CSEL, vol. 35 [Vienna: Tempsky, 1895], 641–2, 671–3, 677–80, 683–4, 688–90).

Gesta de nomine Acacii (Otto Günther [ed.], *Epistulae imperatorum pontificum aliorum inde ab a. CCCLXVII usque ad a. DLIII datae Avellana quae dicitur collectio*, CSEL, vol. 35 [Vienna: Tempsky, 1895], 440–53.

Gratian, *De rebaptizatoribus* (Otto Günther [ed.], *Epistulae imperatorum pontificum aliorum inde ab a. CCCLXVII usque ad a. DLIII datae Avellana quae dicitur collectio*, CSEL, vol. 35 [Vienna: Tempsky, 1895], 54–8).

Gregory I, *Dialogorum libri iv* (Adalbert de Vogüé [ed.] and Paul Antin [trans.], *Grégoire le Grand. Dialogues*, SC, vols 251, 260 and 265 [Paris: Les Éditions du Cerf, 1978–80]).

Gregory I, *Epistulae* (Dag Norberg [ed.], *S. Gregorii Magni Registrum Epistularum libri I–XIV*, CCL, vols 140 and 140A [Turnhout: Brepols, 1982]).

Gregory I, *Epistulae* (John R.C. Martyn [trans.], *The Letters of Gregory the Great*, Medieval Sources in Translation, vol. 40, 3 vols [Toronto: Pontifical Institute of Medieval Studies, 2004]).

Gregory I, *Homiliae xl in euangelia* (Raymond Étaix [ed.], Charles Morel [trans.] and Bruno Judic [notes], *Grégoire le Grand. Homélies sur l'Évangile*, SC, vols 485 and 522 [Paris: Les Éditions du Cerf, 2005–8]).

Gregory I, *Moralia in Iob* (Marc Adriaen [ed.], *S. Gregorii Magni. Moralia in Iob*, CCL, vols 143A–B [Turnhout: Brepols, 1979–85]).

Gregory of Tours, *Historia Francorum* (Bruno Krusch and Wilhelm Levison [eds], *Gregorii Episcopi Turonensis libri Historiarum X*, MGH.SRM, vol. 1, part 1 [Hannover: Hahn, 1937–51 (2nd edn)]).

Hormisdas, *Epistulae* (Otto Günther [ed.], *Epistulae imperatorum pontificum aliorum inde ab a. CCCLXVII usque ad a. DLIII datae Avellana quae dicitur collectio*, CSEL, vol. 35 [Vienna: Tempsky, 1895], 495–742).

Hormisdas, *Epistula* 124 (François Glorie [ed.], *Maxentii aliorumque Scytharum monachorum necnon Joannis Tomitanae urbis episcopi opuscula accedunt 'Capitula S. Augustini'*, CCL, 85A [Turnhout: Brepols, 1978], 115–21).

Hydatius, *Chronicon* (Alain Tranoy [ed. and trans.], *Hydace. Chronique*, SC, vols 218–19 [Paris: Les Éditions du Cerf, 1974]).

Innocent I, *Epistulae* (PL 20.463–612 = Pierre Coustant [ed.], *Epistolae Romanorum Pontificum et quae ad eos scriptae sunt a S. Clemente I usque ad Innocentum III*, t. 1 [Paris: L.-D. Delatour, 1721], cols 739–920).

Innocent I, *Epistula* 25 (Robert Cabié [ed.], *La lettre du pape Innocent Ier à Décentius de Gubbio [19 mars 416]. Texte critique, traduction et commentaire*, Bibliothèque de la Revue d'histoire ecclésiastique, vol. 58 [Louvain: Publications universitaires de Louvain, 1973]).

Isidore of Seville, *De uiris illustribus* (Carmen Codoñer Merino [ed.], *El "De Viris Illustribus" de Isidoro de Sevilla, estudio y edición crítica*, Theses et Studia Philologica Salamanticensia, vol. 12 [Salamanca: Universidad de Salamanca, 1964]).

Jerome, *Apologia contra Rufinum* (Pierre Lardet [ed.], *S. Hieronymi presbyteri opera*, part 3: *Opera polemica*, CCL, 79 [Turnhout: Brepols, 1982]).

Jerome, *De uiris illustribus* (Ernest Cushing Richardson [ed.], *Hieronymus. Liber de uiris inlustribus, Gennadius. Liber de uiris inlustribus*, TU, vol. 14 [Leipzig: J.C. Hinrich, 1896], 1–101).

Jerome, *Epistulae* (Isidorus Hilberg [ed.], *Sancti Eusebii Hieronymi Epistulae*, CSEL, vols 54–6 [Vienna: Österreichischen Akademie der Wissenschaften, 1996 (rev. edn)]).

Jerome, *Vita Malchi* ((PL 23.53–60)

John Chrysostom, *Epistula ad Innocentium* 1 (Anne-Marie Malingrey [ed.], *Palladios. Dialogue sur la vie de Jean Chrysostome*, SC, vol. 342 [Paris: Les Éditions du Cerf, 1988], 68–95).

John Chrysostom, *De Lazaro conciones 1–7* (PG 48.961–1054).

John II, *Epistula* 2 *(Inter claras)* (Otto Günther [ed.], *Epistulae imperatorum pontificum aliorum inde ab a. CCCLXVII usque ad a. DLIII datae Avellana quae dicitur collectio*, CSEL, vol. 35 [Vienna: Tempsky, 1895], 320–28).

John II, *Epistula* 3 *(Olim quidem)* (Eduard Schwartz ([ed.], *ACO*, t. 4: *Concilium universale Constantinopolitanum sub Iustiniano Habitum*, vol. 2: *Iohannis Maxentii libelli – Collectio codicis Novariensis XXX – Collectio codicis Parisini 1682 – Procli Tomus ad Armenios – Iohannis Papae II Epistula ad uiros illustres* [Strasbourg: Carol J. Trübner, 1914], 206–10).

John II the Cappadocian, *Epistula ad Hormisdam* (Otto Günther [ed.], *Epistulae imperatorum pontificum aliorum inde ab a. CCCLXVII usque ad a. DLIII datae Avellana quae dicitur collectio*, CSEL, vol. 35 [Vienna: Tempsky, 1895], 607–10).

John Maxentius, *Libellus fidei* (François Glorie [ed.], *Maxentii aliorumque Scytharum monachorum necnon Joannis Tomitanae urbis episcopi opuscula accedunt 'Capitula S. Augustini'*, CCL, 85A [Turnhout: Brepols, 1978], 3–25).

John Maxentius, *Responsio aduersus epistula [CXXIV] Hormisdae* (François Glorie [ed.], *Maxentii aliorumque Scytharum monachorum necnon Joannis Tomitanae urbis episcopi opuscula accedunt 'Capitula S. Augustini'*, CCL, 85A [Turnhout: Brepols, 1978], 123–53).

Jordanes, *Getica* (Francesco Giunta and Antonino Grillone [eds], *Jordanis De origine actibusque Getarum*, Fonti per la storia d'Italia, vol. 117 [Rome: Istituto storico italiano per il medio evo, 1991]).

Justin I, *Epistula ad Hormisdam* (Otto Günther [ed.], *Epistulae imperatorum pontificum aliorum inde ab a. CCCLXVII usque ad a. DLIII datae Avellana quae dicitur collectio*, CSEL, vol. 35 [Vienna: Tempsky, 1895], 636–7).

Justinian, *Digesta* (Theodor Mommsen and Paul Krüger [eds], *Corpus Iuris Civilis*, vol. 1: *Institutiones, Digesta* [Hildesheim: Weidmann, 1993 (25th edn)]).

Justinian, *Edictum de recta fidei (uel-Confessio fidei)* (Eduard Schwartz et al. [eds], *Drei dogmatische Schriften Iustinians*, Legum Justiniani imperatoris vocabularium. Subsidia, vol. 2 [Milan: Giufrè, 1973 (2nd edn)], 129–69).

Justinian, *Epistula contra Tria Capitula* (Eduard Schwartz et al. [eds], *Drei dogmatische Schriften Iustinians*, Legum Justiniani imperatoris vocabularium. Subsidia, vol. 2 [Milan: Giufrè, 1973 (2nd edn)], 45–69).

Justinian, *Nouellae* (Rudolf Schöll and Wilhelm Kroll [eds], *Corpus Iuris Civilis*, vol. 3: *Novellae* [Hildesheim: Weidmann, 1963 (13th edn)]).

Lactantius, *De mortibus persecutorum* (Jacques Moreau [ed. and trans.], *Lactance. De la mort des persécuteurs*, SC, vols 39, 2 parts [Paris: Les Éditions du Cerf, 2006]).

Leo I, *Epistulae* (PL 54.593–1213).

Leo I, *Epistula* 4 (Hubert Wurm [ed.], 'Decretales selectae ex antiquissimis Romanorum Pontificum epistulis decretalibus', *Apollinaris*, 12 [1939]: 40–93, at 79–93).

Leo I, *Epistula* 28 (Eduard Schwartz [ed.], *ACO*, t. 2: *Concilium vniversale Chalcedonense*, vol. 2: *Versiones particulares*, pars 1: *Collectio Novariensis de re Eutyches* [Berlin: Walter de Gruyter, 1932], 24–33).

Leo I, *Epistulae* 121 and 142 (Karl Silva-Tarouca [ed.], *S. Leonis Magni: Epistulae contra Eutyches haeresim*, pars 2: *Epistulae post Chalcedonense concilium missae (aa. 452–458)*, Textus et documenta. Series theologica, vol. 20 [Rome: Pontificia Universitas Gregoriana, 1935], 126–8 and 147–8).

Leo I, *Epistulae* 59 and 137 (Eduard Schwartz ([ed.], *ACO*, t. 2: *Concilium universale Chalcedonense*, vol. 4: *Leonis papae I epistularum collectiones* [Berlin: Walter de Gruyter, 1932], 34–7 and 89–90).

Leo I, *Sermones* (Antoine Chavasse [ed.], *Sancti Leonis magni Romani pontificis tractatus septem et nonaginta*, CCL, vol. 138–8A [Turnhout: Brepols, 1973]).

Liberatus of Carthage, *Breuiarium causae Nestorianorum et Eutychianorum* (E. Schwartz [ed.], *ACO*, t. 2: *Concilium universale Chalcedonense*, vol. 5: *Collectio Sangermanensis* [Berlin: Walter de Gruyter, 1936], 98–141).

Liberius, *Epistula ad Eusebium, Dionysium et Luciferum* (Alfred Leonhard Feder [ed.], *S. Hilarii episcopi Pictaviensis opera*, Pars Quarta: *Collectanea antiarianea parisina*, CSEL, vol. 65 [Vienna: F. Tempsky, 1916], 164–6).

Liber pontificalis (Louis Duchesne and Cyrille Vogel [eds], *Le* Liber pontificalis: *Texte, introduction et commentaire*, BEFAR, 3 vols [Paris: de Boccard, 1955–7 (2nd edn)]).

Liber pontificalis (Theodor Mommsen [ed.], *Libri pontificalis*, MGH.GPR, vol. 1 [Berlin: Weidmann, 1898]).

Loewenfeld, Samuel (ed.), *Epistolae pontificum Romanorum ineditae* (Leipzig: Veit, 1885).

Magnus Maximus, *Epistula ad Siricium* (Otto Günther [ed.], *Epistulae imperatorum pontificum aliorum inde ab a. CCCLXVII usque ad a. DLIII datae Avellana quae dicitur collectio*, CSEL, vol. 35 [Vienna: Tempsky, 1895], 90–91).

Martínez Díez, Gonzalo and Rodríguez, Félix (eds), *La colección canónica Hispana*, 6 vols, Monumenta Hispaniae Sacra, serie Canónica (Madrid: Consejo Superior de Investigaciones Cientificas, 1966–2002).

Martyrologium Hieronymianum (Giovanni Battista de Rossi and Louis Duchesne [eds], *Acta Sanctorum Novembris*, t.2/1 [Brussels: Socii Bollandiani, 1894], [1–194]).

Mommsen, Theodor and Krüger, Paul (eds), *Codex Theodosianus*, vol. 1: *Theodosiani Libri XVI cum constitutionibus Sirmondinis* (Hildesheim: Weidmann, 1990).

Munier, Charles (ed.), *Concilia Galliae a. 314 – a. 506*, CCL, vol. 148 (Turnhout: Brepols, 1963).

Musurillo, Herbert, *The Acts of the Christian Martyrs* (Oxford: Clarendon Press, 1972).

Optatus, *De schismate Donastistarum* (Mireille Labrousse [ed.], *Optat de Milève Traité contre les Donatiste*, SC, vols 412–3 [Paris: Les Éditions de Cerf, 1995–6])

Palladius, *Dialogus* (Anne-Marie Malingrey and Philippe Leclercq [eds], *Palladios. Dialogue sur la vie de Jean Chrysostome*, SC, vols 341–2 [Paris: Les Éditions du Cerf, 1988]).

Paschale Campanum (Theodor Mommsen [ed.], *Chronica Minora saec. IV. V. VI. VII*, vol. 1, MGH.AA, vol. 9 [Berlin: Weidmann, 1892], 744–50).

Paulinus of Milan, *Vita Ambrosii* (Gabriele Banterle [ed.], *Le fonti latine su Sant'Ambrogio*, Opera Omnia di Sant' Ambrogio, vol. 24/2 [Milano: Biblioteca Ambrosiana; Roma: Città Nuova, 1991], 28–85).

Paulinus of Nola, *Carmina* (Wilhelm de Hartel and Margit Kamptner [eds], *Sancti Pontii Meropii Paulini Nolani: Carmina*, CSEL, vol. 30 [Vienna: Verlag der Österreichischen Akademie der Wissenschaften, 1999 (rev. edn)]).

Paulinus of Nola, *Epistulae* (Wilhelm de Hartel and Margit Kamptner [eds], *Sancti Pontii Meropii Paulini Nolani Opera: Epistulae*, CSEL, vol. 29 [Vienna: Österreichischen Akademie der Wissenschaften, 1999 (rev. edn)]).

Pelagius, *Epistula ad Demetriadem* (PL 33.1099–120).

Pelagius I, *Epistulae* (Pius Maria Gassó and Columba Maria Batlle [eds], *Pelagii I Papae epistulae quae supersunt [556–561]*, Scripta et Documenta, vol. 8 [Montserrat: In Abbatia Montisserrati, 1956]).

Photius, *Bibliotheca* (René Henry [ed.], *Bibliothèque* [Paris: Les Belles Lettres, 1959–77]).

Pliny the Younger, *Epistulae* (Mauritius Schuster and Rudolphus Hanslik [eds], *C. Plini Caecili Secundi epistularum libri novem: Epistularum ad Traianum liber: Panegyricus*, Bibliotheca Scriptorum Graecorum et Romanorum Teubneriana [Stuttgart and Leipzig: Teubner, 1992 (3rd edn)]).

Praeceptum Theoderici Magni contra sacerdotes substantiae ecclesiarum alienatores (Theodor Mommsen [ed.], *Cassiodori Senatoris Variae*, MGH.AA, vol. 12 [Berlin: Weidmann, 1894], 392]).

Priscian of Caesarea, *Carmen in laudem Anastasii imperatoris* (Alain Chauvot [ed.], *Procope de Gaza, Priscien de Césarée. Panégyriques de l'empereur Anastase Ier*, Antiquitas. Reihe 1: Abhandlungen zur alten Geschichte, Bd 35 [Bonn: Dr Rudolf Habelt, 1986], 56–83).

Priscillian, *Tractate* (Marco Conti [ed.], *Priscillian of Avila: The Complete Works*, OECT [Oxford: Oxford University Press, 2010], 33–163).

Procopius, *De bello Gothico* (Otto Veh [ed.], *Prokopius von Caesarea*, vol. 2: *Gotenkriege* [Munich: Ernst Heinemann, 1970 (2nd edn)]).

Prosper of Aquitaine, *De gratia Dei et libero arbitrio contra Collatorem* (PL 51.213–76).

Prosper of Aquitaine, *De prouidentia Dei* (Miroslav Marcovich [ed.], *Prosper of Aquitaine: De providentia Dei. Text, Translation and Commentary*, Supplements to *Vigiliae Christianae*, vol. 10 [Leiden and New York: E.J. Brill, 1989]).

Prosper of Aquitaine, *De uocatione omnium gentium* (PL 51.647–722).

Prosper of Aquitaine, *Epitoma chronicon* (Theodor Mommsen [ed.], *Chronica Minora saec. IV. V. VI. VII*, vol. 1, MGH.AA, vol. 9 [Berlin: Weidmann, 1892], 341–85).

Pseudo-Damasus, *Epigrammata* (Maximilian Ihm [ed.], *Damasi epigrammata accedunt Pseudodamasiana aliaque ad Damasiana inlustranda idonea*, Anthologiae Latinae Supplementa, vol. 1 [Leipzig: Teubner, 1895]).

Pseudo-Zacharias of Mytilene, *Historia ecclesiastica* (Ernest W. Brooks [ed.], *Historia ecclesiastica Zachariae Rhetori vulgo adscripta*, 2 vols, CSCO, vols 83 and 84 = CSCO, Scriptores Syri. vols 38 and 39 [Louvain: L. Durbecq, 1919–1921]).

Quae gesta sunt inter Liberium et Felicem episcopos (Otto Günther [ed.], *Epistulae imperatorum pontificum aliorum inde ab a. CCCLXVII usque ad a.*

DLIII datae Avellana quae dicitur collectio, CSEL, vol. 35 [Vienna: Tempsky, 1895], 1–5).

Registri ecclesiae Carthaginensis excerpta (Charles Munier [ed.], *Concilia Africae A. 345–A. 525*, CCL, vol. 149 [Turnholt: Brepols, 1974], 173–228).

Rossi, Giovanni Battista de, rev. Angelo Silvagni et al. (eds), *Inscriptiones Christianae Urbis Romae septimo saeculo antiquores*, 10 vols, n.s. (Rome: Pontificio Istituto di Archeologia Cristiana, 1922–92); original 2 vols of de Rossi (Rome: Officina Libraria Pontificia, 1857–88).

Schwartz, Eduard (ed.), *Publizistische Sammlungen zum acacianischen Schisma*, Abhandlungen der Bayerischen Akademie der Wissenschaften. Philosophisch-historische Abteilung. Neue Folge, 10 (Munich: Bayerische Akademie der Wissenschaften, 1934).

Silva-Tarouca, Karl (ed.), *Epistularum Romanorum pontificum ad vicarios per Illyricum aliosque episcopos. Collectio Thessalonicensis ad fidem codicis Vat. Lat. 5751*, Textus et documenta. Series theologica, vol. 23 (Rome, Pontificia Universitas Gregoriana, 1937).

Simplicius, *Epistulae* (Andreas Thiel [ed.], *Epistolae Romanorum pontificum genuinae et quae ad eos scriptae sunt a S. Hilaro usque ad Pelagium II*, vol. 1 [Braunsberg: Eduard Peter, 1867], 174–220).

Siricius, *Epistulae* (PL 13.1131–94 = Pierre Coustant [ed.], *Epistolae Romanorum Pontificum et quae ad eos scriptae sunt a S. Clemente I usque ad Innocentum III*, t. 1 [Paris: L.-D. Delatour, 1721], cols 623–700).

Siricius, *Epistula* 4 (Karl Silva-Tarouca [ed.], *Epistularum Romanorum pontificum ad vicarios per Illyricum aliosque episcopos. Collectio Thessalonicensis ad fidem codicis Vat. Lat. 5751*, Textus et documenta. Series theologica, vol. 23 [Rome, Pontificia Universitas Gregoriana, 1937], 19).

Siricius, *Epistula* 5 (Charles Munier [ed.], *Concilia Africae a.345–a.525*, CCL, vol. 149 [Turnholt: Brepols, 1974], 59–63).

Sixtus III, *Epistulae* (PL 50.583–618 = Pierre Coustant [ed.], *Epistolae Romanorum Pontificum et quae ad eos scriptae sunt a S. Clemente I usque ad Innocentum III*, t. 1 [Paris: L.-D. Delatour, 1721], cols 1231–72).

Sozomen, *Historia ecclesiastica* (Günther Christian Hansen [ed.], *Sozomenus. Kirchengeschichte*, GCS n.F., vol. 4 [Berlin: Brandenburgische Akademie der Wissenschaften, 1995 (2nd edn)]).

Sulpicius Severus, *Chronica* (Ghislaine de Senneville-Grave [ed. and trans.], *Sulpice Sévère. Chroniques*, SC, vol. 441 [Paris: Les Éditions du Cerf, 1999]).

Sulpicius Severus, *Vita sancti Martini* (Jacques Fontaine [ed. and trans.], *Sulpice Sévère. Vie de saint Martin*, 3 vols, SC, vols 133–5 [Paris: Les Éditions du Cerf, 1967–9]).

Symmachus, *Epistulae* 2 and 3 (Wilhelm Gundlach [ed.], *Epistolae Merowingici et Karolini Aevi*, t. 1, MGH.Epp., vol. 3 [Berlin: Weidmann, 1892], 33–5).

Synod of Elvira (305?), *Canones* (Gonzalo Martínez Díez and Félix Rodríguez [eds.], *La colección canónica Hispana*, vol. 4, Monumenta Hispaniae Sacra, serie Canónica [Madrid: Consejo Superior de Investigaciones Cientificas, 1984], 233–68).

Synod of Arles (314), *Canones* (Charles Munier [ed.], *Concilia Galliae a.314–a.506*, CCL, vol. 148 [Turnhout: Brepols, 1963], 3–25).

Synod of Laodicea (320), *Canones* (Cuthbert Hamilton Turner [ed.], *Ecclesiae Occidentalis Monumenta Iusis Antiquissima*, t. 2 [Oxford: Clarendon Press, 1907], 323–400).

Synod of Gangra (328), *Canones* (Cuthbert Hamilton Turner [ed.], *Ecclesiae Occidentalis Monumenta Iuris Antiquissima*, t. 2 [Oxford: Clarendon Press, 1907], 147–214).

Synod of Carthage (390), *Canones* (Charles Munier [ed.], *Concilia Africae a.345–a.525*, CCL, vol. 149 [Turnholt: Brepols, 1974], 11–19).

Synod of Toledo (400), *Canones* (Gonzalo Martínez Díez and Félix Rodríguez [eds.], *La colección canónica Hispana*, vol. 4, Monumenta Hispaniae Sacra, serie Canónica [Madrid: Consejo Superior de Investigaciones Cientificas, 1984], 323–44).

Synod of Broga (561), *Canones* (José Vives et al., *Consilios Visigóticos e Hispano-Romanos*, España Cristiana, Textas, vol. 1 [Barcelona and Madrid: CSIC, 1963).

Theophanes, *Chronographia* (Carl de Boor [ed.], *Theophanis Chronographia*, vol. 1 [Leipzig: G. Teubner, 1883]).

Thiel, Andreas (ed.), *Epistolae Romanorum pontificum genuinae et quae ad eos scriptae sunt a S. Hilaro usque ad Pelagium II*, vol. 1 [Braunsberg: Eduard Peter, 1867].

Trifolius, *Epistula ad beatum Faustum senatorem contra Joannem [Maxentium] Scytham monachum* (François Glorie [ed.], *Scriptores 'Illyrici' minores*, CCL, vol. 85 [Turnhout: Brepols, 1972], 135–41)

Valentinian I, *Epistula ad Praetextatum* (Otto Günther [ed.], *Epistulae imperatorum pontificum aliorum inde ab a. CCCLXVII usque ad a. DLIII datae Avellana quae dicitur collectio*, CSEL, vol. 35 [Vienna: Tempsky, 1895], 49).

Valentinian II, *Epistula ad Pinianum* (Otto Günther [ed.], *Epistulae imperatorum pntificium aliorum inde ab a. CCCLXVII usque ad a. DLIII datae Avellana quae dicitur collectio*, CSEL, vol. 35 [Vienna: Tempsky, 1895], 47–8).

Valentinian II, Theodosius I and Arcadius, *Epistula ad Salustium* (Otto Günther [ed.], *Epistulae imperatorum pontificum aliorum inde ab a. CCCLXVII usque ad a. DLIII datae Avellana quae dicitur collectio*, CSEL, vol. 35 [Vienna: Tempsky, 1895], 46–7).

Valentinian III, *Nouella* (Theodor Mommsen and Paul M. Meyer [eds], *Codex Theodosianus*, vol. 2: *Leges Novellae ad Theodosianum pertinentes* [Hildesheim: Weidmann, 1990], 69–154).

Wurm, Hubert (ed.), 'Decretales selectae ex antiquissimis Romanorum Pontificum epistulis decretalibus', *Apollinaris*, 12 (1939): 40–93.

Zelzer, Michaela (ed.), *Sancti Ambrosi Opera*, part 10: *Epistulae et Acta*, t. 3: *Epistularum liber decimus, Epistulae extra collectionem, Gesta Concili Aquileiensis*, CSEL, vol. 82/3 (Vienna: Hoelder-Pichler-Tempsky, 1982).

Zosimus, *Epistulae* (PL 20.639–86 = Pierre Coustant [ed.], *Epistolae Romanorum Pontificum et quae ad eos scriptae sunt a S. Clemente I usque ad Innocentum* III, t. 1 [Paris: L.-D. Delatour, 1721], cols 935–86).

Modern Sources

Accorsi, Maria Letizia, 'Il complesso dei SS. Silvestro e Martino ai Monti dal III al IX secolo. Appunti di studio', in Federico Guidobaldi and Alessandra Guiglia Guidobaldi (eds), *Ecclesiae Urbis*, Atti del congresso internazionale di studi sulle chiese di Roma (IV–X Secolo), Roma, 4–10 Settembre 2000, SAC, vol. 59, 3 vols (Vatican City: Pontificio Istituto di Archeologia Cristiana, 2002), 1.533–63.

Adkin, Neil, 'Pope Siricius' "Simplicity" (Jerome, epist. 127, 9, 3)', *Vetera Christianorum*, 33 (1996): 25–8.

Allen, Pauline and Morgan, Edward, 'Augustine on Poverty', in Pauline Allen, Bronwen Neil and Wendy Mayer, *Preaching Poverty in Late Antiquity: Perceptions and Realities*, Arbeiten zur Kirchen- und Theologiegeschichte, Bd 28 (Leipzig: Evangelische Verlagsanstalt, 2009), 119–70.

Amelli, Ambrogio Maria (Guerrino), *Nuovi contributi alla teologia positiva. San Leone Magno e il primato del romano pontefice in Oriente* (Monte Cassino: Tipi di Montecassino, 1908 [repr. of *S. Leone Magno e l'Oriente*, with a new foreword]).

Amici, Angela, *Iordanes e la storia gotica*, Quaderni della Rivista di bizantinisca, vol. 6 (Spoleto: Fondazione CISAM, 2002).

Amory, Patrick, *People and Identity in Ostrogothic Italy, 489–554*, Cambridge Studies in Medieval Life and Thought, 4th series (Cambridge: Cambridge University Press, 1997).

Andrews, Robert and Brown, Jules, *Sicily. The Rough Guide* (London: Harrap Columbus, 1977).

Babut, Ernest-Charles, *Priscillien et le priscillianisme* (Paris: Librairie Honoré Champion, 1909).

Bagnall, Roger S., et al., *Consuls of the Later Roman Empire*, Philological Monographs of the American Philological Association, vol. 36 (Atlanta: Scholars Press, 1987).

Barclift, Philip, 'Shifting Tones of Pope Leo the Great's Christological Vocabulary', *CH*, 66 (1993): 221–39.

Bartolozzi Casti, Gabriele, 'Battisteri presbiteriali in Roma. Un nuovo intervento di Sisto III?', *Studi Romani* 48 (1999): 270–88.

Bautz, Friedrich Wilhelm (ed.), 'Gelasius I.', in *Biographisch-Bibliographisches Kirchenlexikon*, vol. 2 (Hamm: Traugott Bautz, 1990), 197–9.

Berger, Adolf, *Encyclopedic Dictionary of Roman Law* (Philadelphia: The American Philosophical Society, 1953).

Berlière, Ursmer., 'L'Exercice du ministère paroissial par les moines dans le Haut Moyen-Âge', *RB*, 39 (1927): 227–50.

Berschin, Walter, *Biographie und Epochenstil im lateinischen Mittelalter*, vol. 1: *Von der Passio Perpetuae zu den Dialogi Gregors des Großen*, Quellen und Untersuchungen zur lateinischen Philologie des Mittelalters, vol. 8 (Stuttgart : Hiersemann, 1986).

Birley, Anthony R., 'Magnus Maximus and the Persecution of Heresy', *BJRL*, 66 (1982–3): 13–43.

Blair-Dixon, Kate, 'Damasus and the Fiction of Unity', in Federico Guidobaldi and Alessandra Guilglia Guidobaldi (eds), *Ecclesiae Urbis*, Atti del congresso internazionale di studi sulle chiese di Roma (IV–X Secolo), Roma, 4–10 Settembre 2000, SAC, vol. 59, 3 vols (Vatican City: Pontificio Istituto di Archeologia Cristiana, 2002), vol. 1, 331–52.

Blair-Dixon, Kate, 'Memory and Authority in Sixth-Century Rome: The *Liber Pontificalis* and the *Collectio Avellana*', in Kate Cooper and J. Hillner (eds), *Religion, Dynasty, and Patronage in Early Christian Rome, 300–900* (Cambridge: Cambridge University Press, 2007), 59–76.

Blaudeau, Philippe, '*Vice mea*: Remarques sur les représentations pontificales auprès de l'empereur d'Orient dans la seconde moitié du Ve siècle (452–496)', *MEFRA*, 113 (2001): 1059–1123.

Blaudeau, Philippe, 'Condamnation et absolution synodales. Le cas du légat pontifical Misène de Cumes (483, 495)', in *I concili della cristianità occidentale secoli III–V*, XXX Incontro di studiosi dell'antichità cristiana, Roma 3–5 maggio 2001, SEAug, vol. 78 (Rome: Institutum Patristicum Augustinianum, 2002), 513–21.

Blaudeau, Philippe, 'Symbolique médicale et dénonciation de l'hérésie: le cas monophysite dans les sources pontificales de la seconde moitié du Ve siècle', in Véronique Boudon et Bernard Pouderon (eds), *Les Pères de l'Église face à la science médicale de leur temps*. Actes du 3e colloque d'études patristiques (Paris, 9–11 septembre 2004) organisé par l'Institut Catholique de Paris et l'Université de Tours avec la participation de l'UMR –CNRS 8062 'Médecine grecque', Théologie historique, vol. 117 (Paris: Beauchesne, 2005), 497–524.

Blaudeau, Philippe, *Alexandrie et Constantinople (451–491). De l'histoire à la géo-ecclésiologie*, BEFAR, vol. 327, (Rome: École française de Rome, 2006).

Blaudeau, Philippe, 'Rome contre Alexandrie? L'interprétation pontificale de l'enjeu monophysite (de l'émergence de la controverse eutychienne au schisme acacien 448–484)', *Adamantius*, 12 (2006): 140–216.

Blaudeau, Philippe, 'Motifs et structures de divisions ecclésiales. Le schisme acacien', *AHC*, 39, (2007): 65–98.

Blaudeau, Philippe, 'Between Petrine Ideology and Realpolitik: The See of Constantinople in Roman Geo-ecclesiology (449–536)', in Gavin Kelly and Lucy Grig (eds), *Two Romes: Rome and Constantinople in Late Antiquity* (Oxford: Oxford University Press, 2012), 364–86.

Blaudeau, Philippe, *Le Siège de Rome et l'Orient (448–536). Étude géo-ecclésiologique*, CEFR, vol. 460 (Rome: École française de Rome, 2012).

Blaudeau, Philippe, 'A propos des sections 3 et 4a de l'Avellana (n°51–78): comment documenter le rejet de Chalcédoine manifesté en Orient?', in Alexander Evers (ed.), *Emperors, Bishops, Senators: The Significance of the Collectio Avellana (367–553 AD)*, Rome, 1–2 April 2011 (Loyola University of Chicago John Felice Rome Center, Royal Netherlands Institute of Rome, Istituto Patristico Augustinianum) (forthcoming).

Blázquez Martínez, José María, 'Prisciliano, introductor del ascetismo en Hispania. Las Fuentes, Estudio de la investigación moderna', in Guilleromo Fatás Cabeza (ed.), *I Concilio Caesaraugustano MDC Aniversario* (Zaragoza: Institución 'Fernando el Católico', 1981), 65–121.

Borrell Viader, Agustí, 'Les tradicions sobre el viatge de sant Pau a Hispània en la Primera carta de Climent i en el Cànon de Muratori', in Josep Maria Gavaldà Ribot et al. (eds), *Pau, Fructuós i el cristianisme primitiu a Tarragona (segles I–VIII)*, Actes del Congres de Tarragona (19–21 de Juny de 2008), Biblioteca Tarraco d'Arqueologia, vol. 6 (Tarragona: Fundació Privada Liber, 2010), 157–66.

Borsari, Silvano, *Il monarchesimo Bizantino nella Sicilia e nell'Italia meridionale prenormanne*, (Naples: Istituto italiano per gli studi storici, 1963).

Bowes, Kim, '" ... Nec sedere in uillam". Villa-Churches, Rural Piety, and the Priscillianist Controversy', in Thomas S. Burns and John W. Eadie (eds), *Urban Centers and Rural Contexts in Late Antiquity* (East Lansing, MI: Michigan State University Press, 2001), 323–48.

Bowes, Kim, *Private Worship, Public Values, and Religious Change in Late Antiquity* (Cambridge: Cambridge University Press, 2008).

Brandenburg, Hugo, *Die frühchristlichen Kirchen in Rom vom 4. bis zum 7. Jahrhundert: Der Beginn der abendländischen Kirchenbaukunst* (Regensburg: Schnell and Steiner, 2005), translated into English by Andreas Kropp, as *Ancient Churches of Rome from the Fourth to the Seventh Century: The Dawn of Christian Architecture in the West*, Bibliothèque l'Antiquité Tardive, vol. 8 (Turnhout: Brepols, 2005 [Eng. edn]).

Brändle, Rupert, 'Petrus und Paulus als nova sidera', *Theologische Zeitschrift*, 48 (1992): 207–17.

Bratož, Rajko, 'Gelasio', *Enciclopedia dei Papi*, vol. 1 (Rome: Istituto della enciclopedia italiana, 2000), 458–62.

Bretone, Mario, *Geschichte des römischen Rechts. Von den Anfängen bis zu Justinian* (Munich: C.H. Beck, 1992).

Brown, Peter R.L., *The Cult of the Saints: Its Rise and Function in Latin Christianity*, The Haskell Lectures on History of Religions, new series, vol. 2 (Chicago: Chicago University Press, 1981).

Brown, Peter R.L., *Poverty and Leadership in the Later Roman Empire*, The Menahem Stern Jerusalem Lectures (Hanover, NH and London: University Press of New England, 2002).

Brown, Peter R.L., *The Rise of Western Christendom* (Oxford: Blackwell, 2003 [2nd edn]).

Brown, Peter R.L., *Through the Eye of a Needle: Wealth, the Fall of Rome and the Making of Christianity in the West, 350–550 AD* (Princeton: Princeton University Press, 2012).

Brown, Thomas S., 'Everyday Life in Ravenna under Theoderic: An Example of his "Tolerance" and "Prosperity"?', in CISAM, *Teoderico il Grande e i Goti d'Italia. Atti del XIII Congresso internazionale di studi sull'Alto Medioevo* (Milan, 2–6 November 1992), Atti dei Congressi, vol. 13 (Spoleto: CISAM, 1993), 77–99.

Browne, Millicent, 'The Three African Popes', *The Western Journal of Black Studies*, 22 (1998): 57–70.
Burrus, Virginia, *The Making of a Heretic: Gender, Authority, and the Priscillianist Controversy*, TCH, vol. 24 (Berkeley and Los Angeles: University of California Press, 1995).
Cain, Andrew, *The Letters of Jerome: Asceticism, Biblical Exegesis, and the Construction of Christian Identity in Late Antiquity*, OECS (Oxford: Oxford University Press, 2009).
Cameron, Averil, Ward-Perkins, Bryan and Whitby, Mary (eds), *The Cambridge Ancient History*, vol. 14: *Late Antiquity: Empire and Successors, A.D. 425–600* (Cambridge: Cambridge University Press, 2000 [2nd edn]).
Canella, Teresa, 'Gli *Actus Silvestri*: l'invenzione di un'identità statale cristiana', *Annali di storia dell'esegesi*, 21 (2004): 289–302.
Canella, Teresa, *Gli* Actus Silvestri. *Genesi di una leggenda su Costantino imperatore*, Uomini e mondi medievali. Collana del Centro italiano di studi sul Basso Medioevo – Accademia Tudertina, vol. 7 (Spoleto: CISAM, 2006), 135–77.
Capizzi, Carmelo, *L'imperatore Anastasio I [491–518]. Studio sulla sua vita, la sua opera e la sua personalità*, Orientalia Christiana Analecta, vol. 184 [Rome, 1969], 261–73.
Capo, Lidia, *Il* Liber pontificalis, *i Longobardi e la nascita del domino territoriale della Chiesa romana*, Istituzioni e società, vol. 12 (Spoleto: Fondazione CISAM, 2009).
Cappuyns, Maïeul, 'L'auteur du *De vocatione omnium gentium*', RB, 39 (1927): 198–226.
Cappuyns, Maïeul, 'Le premier représentant de l'augustinisme médiéval, Prosper d'Aquitaine', RTAM, 1 (1929): 309–37.
Carmassi, Patrizia, 'La prima redazione del *Liber Pontificalis* nel quadro delle fonti contemporanee: Osservazioni in margine alla vita di Simmaco', in *Atti del colloquio internazionale 'Il* Liber Pontificalis *e la storia materiale'* (Rome, 21–22 février 2002), Mededelingen van het Nederlands Instituut te Rome, Antiquity, vols 60–61 (Rome: Van Gorcum, 2003), 235–66.
Caspar, Erich, *Geschichte des Papsttums von den Anfängen bis zur Höhe der Weltherrschaft*, 2 vols (Tübingen: J.C.B. Mohr [Paul Siebeck], 1930–33).
Cavallera, Ferdinand, 'La lettre sur l'évêque Bonose est-elle de saint Sirice ou de saint Ambroise?', BLE, 21 (1920): 141–7.
Cerrito, Alessandra, 'Oratori ed edifici di culto minori di Roma tra il IV secolo ed I primi decenni del V', in Federico Guidobaldi and Alessandra Guiglia Guidobaldi (eds), *Ecclesiae Urbis*, Atti del congresso internazionale di studi

sulle chiese di Roma (IV–X Secolo), Roma, 4–10 Settembre 2000, SAC, vol. 59, 3 vols (Vatican City: Pontificio Istituto di Archeologia Cristiana, 2002), 1.397–418.

Chadwick, Henry, 'St. Peter and St. Paul in Rome: The Problem of the Memoria Apostolorum ad catacumbas', *JThS*, n.s. 8 (1957): 39–51.

Chadwick, Henry, *Priscillian of Avila: The Occult and the Charismatic in the Early Church* (Oxford: Clarendon Press, 1976).

Chadwick, Henry, *Boethius. The Consolations of Music, Logic, Theology, and Philosophy* (Oxford: Clarendon Press, 1981).

Christie, Neil, *From Constantine to Charlemagne: An Archaeology of Italy, AD 300–800* (Aldershot, England, and Burlington, VT: Ashgate, 2006).

Clark, Elizabeth A., 'Claims on the Bones of Saint Stephen: The Partisans of Melania and Eudocia', *CH*, 51 (1982): 141–56.

Classen, Peter, *Kaiserreskript und Königsurkunde: Diplomatische Studien zum Problem der Kontinuität zwischen Altertum und Mittelalter*, Byzantina keimena kai meletai, vol. 15 (Thessaloniki: Kentron, 1977).

Coarelli, Filippo, *Guida Archeologica di Roma* (Rome: Laterza, 1995 [3rd edn]).

Collins, Roger, *Early Medieval Spain: Unity in Diversity, 400–1000*, New Studies in Medieval History (New York: St. Martin's Press, 1995 [2nd edn]).

Collins, Roger, *Visigothic Spain 409–711*, A History of Spain (Oxford: Blackwell, 2004).

Conant, Jonathan, *Staying Roman: Conquest and Identity in Africa and the Mediterranean, 439–700*, Cambridge Studies in Medieval Life and Thought, 4th series, vol. 82 (Cambridge: Cambridge University Press, 2012).

Condurachi, Emil, 'Factions et jeux du cirque à Rome au début du VIe siècle', *Revue historique du Sud-Est européen*, 18 (1941): 95–102.

Cooper, Kate, 'The Martyr, the Matrona and the Bishop: The Matron Lucina and the Politics of Martyr Cult in Fifth- and Sixth-Century Rome', *EME*, 8 (1999): 297–317.

Cooper, Kate, 'Ventriloquism and the Miraculous: Conversion, Preaching and the Martyr Exemplum in Late Antiquity', in Kate Cooper and Jeremy Gregory (eds), *Signs, Wonders, Miracles: Representations of Divine Power in the Life of the Church*, Studies in Church History, vol. 41 (Chippenham: Boydell and Brewer, 2005), 22–45.

Cooper, Kate and Hillner, Julia (eds), *Religion, Dynasty, and Patronage in Early Christian Rome, 300–900* (Cambridge: Cambridge University Press, 2007).

Corcoran, Simon, *The Empire of the Tetrarchs: Imperial Pronouncements and Government AD 284–324* (Oxford: Clarendon Press, 1996).

Cosentino, Augusto, 'Il battesimo a Roma: edifici e liturgia', in Federico Guidobaldi and Alessandra Guiglia Guidobaldi (eds), *Ecclesiae Urbis*, Atti del congresso internazionale di studi sulle chiese di Roma (IV-X Secolo), Roma, 4-10 Settembre 2000, SAC, vol. 59, 3 vols (Vatican City: Pontificio Istituto di Archeologia Cristiana, 2002), 1.128-37.

Cosentino, Salvatore, *Prosopografia dell'Italia bizantina (493-804)*, 2 vols (Bologna: Lo Scarabeo, 1996-2000).

Coşkun, Altay, 'Der Praefect Maximinus, der Jude Isaak und der Strafprozeß gegen den Bischof Damasus', *JbAC*, 46 (2003): 17-44.

Croke, Brian, 'Justinian under Justin: Reconfiguring a Reign', *ByzZ*, 100 (2007): 13-56.

Curran, John, *Pagan City and Christian Capital: Rome in the Fourth Century*, OCM (Oxford: Clarendon Press, 2000).

Custodio Vega, Angel, *El Primado Romano y la Iglesia Española en los Siete Primeros Siglos* (El Escorial: Imprenta del Monasterio, 1942).

Davis, Raymond, *The Book of Pontiffs (*Liber Pontificalis*): The Ancient Biographies of the First Ninety Roman Bishops to AD 715*, TTH, vol. 6 (Liverpool: Liverpool University Press, 2000 [2nd edn]).

Decret, François and Fantar, Mhamed, *L'Afrique du Nord dans l'antiquité: histoire et civilisation, des origines au Ve siècle* (Paris: Payot, 1998 [2nd edn]).

Delmulle, Jérémy, 'Le *Liber epigrammatum* de Prosper d'Aquitaine, un petit catéchisme augustinien', in Marie-France Gineste-Guipponi and Céline Urlacher-Becht (eds), *La renaissance de l'épigramme dans la latinité tardive*, Actes du colloque de Mulhouse, 6-7 October 2011, Collections de l'Université de Strasbourg, Études d'archéologie et d'histoire ancienne (Paris: De Boccard, 2013), 193-209.

Demacopoulos, George, 'Gregory the Great and the Appeal to Petrine Authority', in J. Baun, A. Cameron, M. Edwards and M. Vinzent (eds), *Studia Patristica*, vol.48, papers presented at the Fifteenth International Conference on Patristic Studies held in Oxford 2007 (Leuven: Peeters, 2010), 333-46.

Demacopoulos, George, *The Invention of Peter: Apostolic Discourse and Papal Authority in Late Antiquity* (Philadelphia, PA: University of Pennsylvania Press, 2013).

Denzey, Nicola, *The Bone Gatherers: The Lost Worlds of Early Christian Women* (Boston: Beacon Press, 2007).

Di Berardino, Angelo, 'The Poor must be Supported by the Wealth of the Church (*Codex Theodosianus* 16.2.6)', in Geoffrey D. Dunn, David Luckensmeyer, and Lawrence Cross (eds), *Prayer and Spirituality in the Early Church*, vol. 5: *Poverty and Riches* (Strathfield, NSW: St Pauls Publications, 2009), 249-68.

Di Capua, Francesco, 'Leone Magno e Prospero de Aquitania', in Antonio Quacquarelli (ed.), *Scritti minori*, vol. 2 (Rome: Desclée, 1959), 184–90.

Diefenbach, Steffen, *Römische Erinnerungsräume: Heiligenmemoria und kollektive Identitäten im Rom des 3. bis 5. Jahrhunderts n. Chr.*, Millennium-Studien, vol. 11 (Berlin and New York: Walter de Gruyter, 2007).

Duchesne, Louis, 'La succession du pape Félix IV', *Mélanges d'archéologie et d'histoire*, 3 (1883): 239–66.

Duchesne, Louis, *Histoire ancienne de l'Église* (Paris: De Boccard, 1910).

Duchesne, Louis, *L'Église au VIe siècle* (Paris: Fontemoing, 1925).

Ducloux, Anne, *Ad ecclesiam confugere. Naissance du droit d'asile dans les églises (IVe – milieu du Ve s.)*, De l'archéologie à l'histoire (Paris: de Boccard, 1994).

Dunn, Geoffrey D., 'Cyprian of Carthage and the Episcopal Synod of Late 254', *REAug*, 48 (2002): 229–47.

Dunn, Geoffrey D., 'Roman Primacy in the Correspondence between Innocent I and John Chrysostom', in *Giovanii Crisostomo. Oriente e Occidente tra IV e V secolo*, XXXIII Incontro di studiosi dell'antichità cristiana, Roma, 6–8 maggio 2004, SEAug, vol. 93 (Rome: Institutum Patristicum Augustinianum, 2005), 687–98.

Dunn, Geoffrey D., 'The Elements of Ascetical Widowhood: Augustine's *De bono viduitatis* and *Epistula* 130', in Wendy Mayer, Pauline Allen and Lawrence Cross (eds), *Prayer and Spirituality in the Early Church*, vol. 4: *The Spiritual Life* (Strathfield, NSW, 2006), 247–56.

Dunn, Geoffrey D., *Cyprian and the Bishops of Rome: Questions of Papal Primacy in the Early Church*, ECS, vol. 11 (Strathfield, NSW: St Pauls Publications, 2007).

Dunn, Geoffrey D., 'The Validity of Marriage in Cases of Captivity: The Letter of Innocent I to Probus', *ETL*, 83 (2007): 107–21.

Dunn, Geoffrey D., 'Innocent I and the Illyrian Churches on the Question of Heretical Ordination', *JAEMA*, 4 (2008): 65–81.

Dunn, Geoffrey D., 'The Christian Networks of the Aniciae: The Example of the Letter of Innocent I to Anicia Juliana', *REAug*, 55 (2009): 53–72.

Dunn, Geoffrey D., 'Innocent I and the Suburbicarian Churches: The Letter to Florentinus of Tivoli', *JAEMA*, 6 (2010): 9–23.

Dunn, Geoffrey D., 'Canonical Legislation on the Ordination of Bishops: Innocent I's Letter to Victricius of Rouen', in Johann Leemans et al. (eds), *Episcopal Elections in Late Antiquity*, AKG, Bd 119 (Berlin: Walter de Gruyter, 2011), 145–66.

Dunn, Geoffrey D., 'The Development of Rome as Metropolitan of Suburbicarian Italy: Innocent I's *Letter to the Bruttians*', *Aug*, 51 (2011): 161–90.

Dunn, Geoffrey D., 'Innocent I's Letter to Lawrence: Photinians, Bonosians, and the *Defensores ecclesiae*', *JThS*, n.s., 33 (2012): 136–55.

Dunn, Geoffrey D., 'The Roman Response to the Ecclesiastical Crises in the Antiochene Church in the Late-Fourth and Early-Fifth Centuries', in David Sim and Pauline Allen (eds), *Ancient Jewish and Christian Texts as Crisis Management Literature: Thematic Studies from the Centre for Early Christian Studies*, Library of New Testament Studies, vol. 445 (London: T & T Clark, 2012), 112–28.

Dunn, Geoffrey D., 'The Letter of Innocent I to Marcian of Niš', in Dragiš Bojpvić (ed.), *Saint Emperor Constantine and Christianity*, International Conference Commemmorating the 1700th Anniversary of the Edict of Milan, 31 May–2 June 2013, 2 vols (Niš: ПУНТА, 2013), 1.319–38.

Dunn, Geoffrey D., 'The Clerical *cursus honorum* in Late Antique Rome', *Scrinium*, 9 (2013): 132–45.

Dunn, Geoffrey D. 'Innocent I's Letter to the Bishops of Apulia', *JECS*, 21 (2013): 27–41.

Dunn, Geoffrey D., 'Zosimus and the Gallic Churches', in Wendy Mayer and Bronwen Neil (eds), *Religious Conflict from Early Christianity to the Rise of Islam*, AKG, Bd 121 (Berlin: Walter de Gruyter, 2013), 169–85.

Dunn, Geoffrey D., 'The Emergence of Papal Decretals: The Evidence of Zosimus of Rome', in Geoffrey Greatrex and Hugh Elton with L. McMahon (eds), *Shifting Genres in Late Antiquity* (Farnham: Ashgate, 2015), 81–92.).

Duval, Yves-Marie, 'Jérôme et l'histoire de l'Église du IVe siècle', in Bernard Pouderon and Yves-Marie Duval (eds.), *L'historiographie de l'Église des premiers siècles*, Théologie historique, vol. 114 (Paris: Beauchesne, 2001), 381–408.

Duval, Yves-Marie, *La décrétale* Ad Gallos episcopos: *son texte et son auteur. Texte critique, traduction française et commentaire*, Supplements to Vigiliae Christianae, vol. 73 (Leiden and Boston: Brill, 2005).

Duval, Yvette, Loca sanctorum Africae: *Le culte des martyrs en Afrique du IVe au VIIe siècle*, Collection de l'École française de Rome, vol. 58 (Rome: École française de Rome, 1982).

Dvornik, Francis, 'Pope Gelasius and Emperor Anastasius I', *ByzZ*, 44 (1951): 111–16.

Eger, Otto, 'Relatio', *Real-Encyclopädie*, vol. 1A/1 (Stuttgart: J.B. Metzler, 1914): 563–4.

Elberti, Arturo, *Prospero d'Aquitania: teologo e discepolo* (Rome: Edizioni Dehoniane, 1999).

Enßlin, Wilhelm, 'Papst Johannes I. als Gesandter Theoderichs des Grossen bei Kaiser Justinus I', *ByzZ*, 44 (1951): 127–34.

Ertl, Nelly, 'Diktatoren frühmittelalterliche Papstbriefe', *Archiv für Urkundenforschung*, 15 (1938): 57–60.

Escribano, Victoria, 'Heresy and Orthodoxy in Fourth-Century Hispania: Arian and Priscillianism', in Kim Bowes and Michael Kulikowski (eds), *Hispania in Late Antiquity: Current Perspectives*, The Medieval and Early Modern Iberian World, vol. 24 (Leiden and Boston: Brill, 2005), 121–49.

Evans, Gillian R., *The Thought of Gregory the Great*, (Cambridge: Cambridge University Press, 1986).

Ewald, Paul, 'Acten zum Schisma des Jahres 530', *NA*, 10 (1885): 412–23.

Fatás Cabeza, Guillermo (ed.), *I Concilio Caesaraugustano MDC Aniversario*. (Zaragoza: Institución 'Fernando el Católico', 1981).

Fellermayr, Josef, *Tradition und Sukzession im Lichte des römisch-antiken Erbdenkens. Untersuchungen zu den lateinischen Kirchenvätern bis zu Leo dem Großen* (Munich: Minerva-Publikation, 1979).

Fellermayr, Josef, 'Hereditas', *Reallexikon für Antike und Christentum*, vol. 14 (Stuttgart: Anton Hiersemann, 1988): 626–48.

Ferreiro, Alberto, 'Jerome's Polemic against Priscillian in the *Letter* to Ctesiphon (133, 4)', *REAug*, 39 (1993): 309–32.

Ferreiro, Alberto 'Sexual Depravity, Doctrinal Error, and Character Assassination in the Fourth Century: Jerome against the Priscillianists', in Elizabeth A. Livingstone (ed.), *Studia Patristica*, vol. 28, papers presented at the Eleventh International Conference on Patristic Studies held in Oxford 1991 (Leuven: Peeters, 1993), 29–38.

Ferreiro, Alberto, 'Priscillian and Nicolaitism', *VChr*, 52 (1998): 382–92.

Ferreiro, Alberto, 'Petrine Primacy, Conciliar Authority, and Priscillian', in *I concili della cristianità occidentale secoli III–V*, XXX Incontro di studiosi dell'antichità cristiana, Roma, 3–5 maggio 2001, SEAug, vol. 78 (Rome: Institutum Patristicum Augustinianum, 2002), 631–45.

Ferreiro, Alberto, '"Petrine Primacy" and Gregory of Tours', *Francia*, 33 (2006): 1–16.

Finn, Richard D., *Almsgiving in the Later Roman Empire. Christian Promotion and Practice (313–450)*, OCM (Oxford: Oxford University Press, 2006).

Folliet, Georges, 'Le dossier de l'affaire Classicianus (Epist. 1* and 250)', in Claude Lepelley (ed.), *Les lettres de saint Augustin découvertes par Johannes Divjak*, Communications présentées au colloque des 20 et 21 Septembre 1982, EAA, vol. 98 (Paris: Études augustiniennes, 1983), 129–46.

Fournier, Eric, 'Exiled Bishops in the Christian Empire: Victims of Imperial Violence?', in Harold Drake (ed.), *Violence in Late Antiquity: Perceptions and Practices* (Aldershot: Ashgate, 2006), 157–66.

Frakes, Robert M., *Contra potentium iniurias: The Defensor Civitatis and Late Roman Justice*, Münchener Beiträge zur Papyrusforschung und antiken Rechtsgeschichte, vol. 90 (Munich: C.H. Beck, 2001).

Gadioz, Jean, 'Prosper d'Aquitaine et le Tome à Flavien', *RSR*, 23 (1949): 270–301.

Galonnier, Alain, *Boèce. Opuscula sacra*, vol. 1: Capita dogmatica *(Traités II, III, IV)*, Philosophes médiévaux, vol. 47 (Louvain: Peeters, 2007).

García Sánchez, Justo, 'El derecho romano en el concilio de Elvira (s. IV)', in *I concili della cristianità occidentale secoli III–V*, XXX Incontro di studiosi dell'antichità cristiana, Roma, 3–5 maggio 2001, SEAug, vol. 78 (Rome: Institutum Patristicum Augustinianum, 2002), 589–606.

García Villoslada, Ricardo et al., *Historia de la Iglesia en España*, vol. 1: *La Iglesia de la España romana y visigoda (siglos I–VIII)*, Biblioteca de Autores Cristianos, Maior, vol. 16 (Madrid: Biblioteca de Autores Cristianos, 1979).

Gavaldà Ribot, Josep Maria et al. (eds), *Pau, Fructuós i el cristianisme primitiu a Tarragona (segles I–VIII)*, Actes del Congres de Tarragona (19–21 de Juny de 2008), Biblioteca Tarraco d'Arqueologia, vol. 6 (Tarragona: Fundació Privada Liber, 2010).

Geertman, Herman, 'Forze centrifughe e centripete nella Roma cristiana: Il Laterano, la Basilica Iulia e la Basilica Liberiana', *Rendiconti della Pontificia Accademia Romana di Archeologia*, 59 (1986–7): 63–91.

Geertman, Herman (ed.), *Atti del colloquio internazionale 'Il Liber Pontificalis e la storia materiale' (Rome, 21–22 février 2002)*, Mededelingen van het Nederlands Instituut te Rome, Antiquity, vols 60–61 (Rome: Van Gorcum, 2003).

Geertman, Herman, *Hic fecit basilicam: Studi sul* Liber Pontificalis *e gli edifici ecclesiastici di Roma da Silvestro a Silverio* (Leuven: Peeters, 2004).

Geertman, Herman, 'La genesi del *Liber Pontificalis* romano. Un processo di organizzazione della memoria', in François Bougard et Michel Sot (eds.), *Liber, Gesta, histoire. Écrire l'histoire des évêques et des papes, de l'Antiquité au XXIe siècle* (Turnhout: Brepols, 2009), 37–107.

Giaro, Tomasz, 'Responsa', *Der Neue Pauly*, vol. 10 (Stuttgart: J.B. Metzler, 2001), 931–2.

Gillett, Andrew, 'Rome, Ravenna, and the Last Western Emperors', *PBSR*, 69 (2001): 131–67.

Giordani, Roberto, '*Novatiano beatissimo martyri Gaudentius diaconus fecit*: Contributo all'identificazione del martire Novaziano della catacomba anonima sulla Via Tiburtina', *Rivista di Archeologia Cristiana*, 68 (1992): 240–51.

Godoy Fernández C., 'Les tradicions del viatge de sant Pau a Hispània en la literature apòcrifa', in Josep Maria Gavaldà Ribot et al. (eds), *Pau, Fructuós i el cristianisme primitiu a Tarragona (segles I–VIII)*, Actes del Congres de Tarragona (19–21 de Juny de 2008), Biblioteca Tarraco d'Arqueologia, vol. 6 (Tarragona: Fundació Privada Liber, 2010), 167–80.

Goltz, Andreas, *Barbar – König – Tyrann. Das Bild Theoderichs des Großen in der Überlieferung des 5. bis 9. Jahrhunderts*, Millennium-Studien. Studien zu Kultur und Geschichte des ersten Jahrtausends n. Chr, Bd 12 (Berlin and New York: Walter de Gruyter, 2008).

Goubert, Paul, *Byzance avant l'Islam*, 2 vols (Paris: Picard, 1956).

Goubert, Paul, 'Autour du voyage à Byzance du pape S. Jean I. (523–526)', *OCP*, 24 (1958): 339–52.

Greatrex, Geoffrey, 'Justin I and the Arians', in Maurice F. Wiles and Edward J. Yarnold (eds), *Studia Patristica*, vol. 34, papers presented at the Thirteenth International Conference on Patristic Studies, Oxford 1999 (Leuven: Peeters, 2001), 72–81.

Green, Bernard, *The Soteriology of Leo the Great*, OTM (Oxford: Oxford University Press, 2008).

Green, Malcolm R., 'Pope Innocent I: The Church of Rome in the Early Fifth Century', (DPhil diss., Oxford 1973).

Grillmeier, Alois, *Jesus der Christus im Glauben der Kirche*, Bd 2/2: *Die Kirche von Konstantinopel im 6. Jahrhundert*, ed. Theresia Hainthaler (Freiburg im Breisgau, Basel and Vienna: Herder, 2004 [rev. edn]).

Grodzynski, Denise, 'Pauvres et indigents, vils et plebeians (Une étude terminologique sur le vocabulaire des petites gens dans le Code Théodosien)', *Studia et documenta historiae et iuris*, 53 (1987): 140–218.

Guerrini, Paola, 'Le chiese e i monasteri del trastevere', in Federico Guidobaldi and Alessandra Guiglia Guidobaldi (eds), *Ecclesiae Urbis*, Atti del congresso internazionale di studi sulle chiese di Roma (IV–X Secolo), Roma, 4–10 Settembre 2000, SAC, vol. 59, 3 vols (Vatican City: Pontificio Istituto di Archeologia Cristiana, 2002), 1.377–96.

Guyon, Jean, 'La vente des tombes à travers l'épigraphie de la Rome chrétienne (IIIe, VIIe siècles): le rôle des fossores, mansionarii, parepositi et prêtres', *MEFRA*, 86 (1974): 540–96.

Guyon, Jean, 'Les Quatre Couronnés et l'histoire de leur culte des origines à la fin du IXe siècle', *MEFRA*, 87 (1975): 505–61.

Guyon, Jean, *Le cimetière aux deux lauriers. Recherches sur les catacombes romaines*, BEFAR, vol. 264 (Rome: École française de Rome, 1987).

Guyon, Jean 'Cunctis solacia fletus ou le testament-épigraphe du pape Damase', in Quaeritur inventus colitur: *Miscellanea in onore di Padre Umberto Maria Fasola*, SAC, vol. 40/2 (Vatican City: Pontificio Istituto di Archeologia Cristiana, 1989), 423–38.

Harnack, Adolf von, 'Der erste deutsche Papst (Bonifatius II., 530/32) und die beiden letzten Dekreten des römischen Senats', *Sitzungsberichte der Preussischen Akademie der Wissenschaften. Philosophisch-historische Klasse* (1924): 24–42.

Heather, Peter, 'Merely an Ideology ? – Gothic Identity in Ostrogothic Italy', in S.J. Barnish and Federico Marazzi (eds), *The Ostrogoths from the Migration Period to the Sixth Century. An Ethnographic Perspective* (San Marino, 8–12 September 2000), Studies in Historical Archaeoethnology, vol. 7 (Woodbridge: The Boydell Press, 2007), 31–79.

Hess, Hamilton, *The Early Development of Canon Law and the Council of Serdica*, OECT (Oxford: Oxford University Press, 2002).

Hillner, Julia, 'Families, Patronage, and the Titular Churches of Rome, c. 300–c. 600', in Kate Cooper and Julia Hillner (eds), *Religion, Dynasty, and Patronage in Early Christian Rome, 300–900* (Cambridge: Cambridge University Press, 2007), 225–61.

Holum, Kenneth G. and Vikan, Gary, 'The Trier Ivory, *Adventus* Ceremonial and the Relics of Saint Stephen', *Dumbarton Oaks Papers*, 33 (1979): 113–33.

Homes Dudden, Frederick, *Gregory the Great, His Place in History and Thought*, 2 vols (London: Longmans, Green, 1905).

Hoogma, Robertus Petrus, *Der Einfluss Vergils auf die Carmina Latina Epigraphica* (Amsterdam: North-Holland Publishing Company, 1959).

Hornung, Christian, 'Die Sprache des römischen Rechts in Schreiben römischer Bischöfe des 4. und 5. Jahrhunderts', *JbAC*, 53 (2010): 20–80.

Hornung, Christian, *Directa ad decessorem: Ein kirchenhistorisch-philologischer Kommentar zur ersten Dekretale des Siricius von Rom*, Jahrbuch für Antike und Christentum Ergänzungsband Kleine Reihe, vol. 8 (Münster: Aschendorff Verlag, 2011).

Howard-Johnston, James and Hayward, Paul A. (eds), *The Cult of the Saints in Late Antiquity and the Early Middle Ages: Essays on the Contribution of Peter Brown* (Oxford: Oxford University Press, 1999).

Humfress, Caroline, 'A New Legal Cosmos: Late Roman Lawyers and the Early Medieval Church', in Peter Lineham and Janet L. Nelson (eds), *The Medieval World* (London and New York: Routledge, 2001), 557–75.

Humfress, Caroline, *Orthodoxy and the Courts in Late Antiquity* (Oxford: Oxford University Press, 2007).

Hunter, David G., 'The Raven Replies: Ambrose's *Letter to the Church at Vercelli* (*Ep.ex.coll. 14*) and the Criticisms of Jerome', in Andrew Cain and Josef Lössl (eds), *Jerome of Stridon: His Life, Writings and Legacy* (Farnham: Ashgate, 2009), 175–89.

Huskinson, Janet M., *Concordia Apostolorum. Christian Propaganda at Rome in the Fourth and Fifth Century: A Study in Early Christian Iconography and Iconology* (London: BAR, 1984).

Hwang, Alexander Y., *An Intrepid Lover of Perfect Grace: The Life and Thought of Prosper of Aquitaine* (Washington, DC: Catholic University of America Press, 2009).

Jacobs, Andrew, 'Writing Demetrias: Ascetic Logic in Ancient Christianity', *CH*, 69 (2000): 719–48.

Jacques, François, 'Le défenseur de cité d'après la Lettre 22* de saint Augustin', *REAug*, 32 (1986): 56–73.

Jaffé, Philippe, *Regesta Pontificum Romanorum ab condita ecclesia ad annum post Christum natum MCXCVIII*, 2 Bd., rev. Wilhelm Wattenbach (Leipzig: Veit, 1885 [rev. edn]).

James, Norman W., 'Leo the Great and Prosper of Aquitaine: A Fifth-Century Pope and his Adviser', *JThS*, n.s. 44 (1993): 554–84.

James, Norman W., 'Prosper of Aquitaine Revisited: Gallic Correspondent or Resident Papal Adviser', in M. Vizent (ed.), *Studia Patristica*, vol. 69, papers presented at the sixteenth International Conference on Patristic Studies, Oxford 2011 (Leuven, 2013), pp. 267–76.

Jasper, Detlev, 'The Beginning of the Decretal Tradition: Papal Letters from the Origin of the Genre through the Pontificate of Stephen V', in D. Jasper and H. Fuhrmann, *Papal Letters in the Early Middle Ages*, History of Medieval Canon Law (Washington DC: Catholic University of America Press, 2001), 1–133.

Jasper, Detlev and Fuhrmann, Horst, *Papal Letters in the Early Middle Ages*, History of Medieval Canon Law (Washington DC: Catholic University of America Press, 2001).

Jones, Arnold H.M., *The Later Roman Empire 284–602: A Social, Economic, and Administrative Survey*, 2 vols (Oxford: Basil Blackwell, 1964).

Kakridi, Christina, *Cassiodors* Variae. *Literatur und Politik im ostgotischen Italien*, Beiträge zur Altertumskunde, Bd 223 (Munich and Leipzig: K.G. Saur, 2005).

Kelly, John N.D., *The Oxford Dictionary of Popes* (Oxford and New York: Oxford University Press, 1986).
Kjaergaard, Jørgen, 'From Memoria Apostolorum to Basilica Apostolorum. On the Early Christian Cult Centre on the Via Appia', *Analecta Romana Instituti Danici*, 13 (1984): 59–76.
Klingshirn, William E., 'Charity and Power: Caesarius of Arles and the Ransoming of Captives in Sub-Roman Gaul', *JRS*, 75 (1985): 183–203.
Krabbe, Kathryn Clare, *Epistula ad Demetriadem De Vera Humilitate: A Critical Text and Translation with Introduction and Commentary*, Catholic University of America Patristic Studies, vol. 97 (Washington, DC: Catholic University of America Press, 1965).
Krautheimer, Richard, *Corpus Basilicarum Christianarum Romae*, 5 vols (Vatican City: Pontoficio Istituto di Archeologia Cristiana, 1937–77).
Kulikowski, Michael, *Late Roman Spain and its Cities* (Baltimore: Johns Hopkins University Press, 2004).
Kurdock, Anne, '*Demetrias ancilla dei*: Anicia Demetrias and the Problem of the Missing Patron', in Kate Cooper and Julia Hillner (eds), *Religion, Dynasty, and Patronage in Early Christian Rome, 300–900* (Cambridge: Cambridge University Press, 2007), 190–224.
Langen, Joseph, *Geschichte der römischen Kirche bis zum Pontifikate Leo's I. Quellenmäßig dargestellt* (Bonn: Max Cohen und Sohn, 1881).
Lécrivain, Charles, 'Relatio', *Dictionnaire des antiquités grecques et romaines*, vol. 4/2 (Paris: Hachette Livre, 1911), 830.
Lécrivain, Charles, 'Rescriptum', *Dictionnaire des antiquités grecques et romaines*, vol. 4/2 (Paris: Hachette Livre, 1911), 844–6.
Leone, Anne, 'Christianity and Paganism, IV: North Africa', in Augustine Casiday and Frederick W. Norris (eds), *Constantine to c. 600*, Cambridge History of Christianity, vol. 2 (Cambridge: Cambridge University Press, 2006), 231–47.
Leone, Anne, *Changing Townscapes in North Africa from Late Antiquity to the Arab Conquest*, Munera, vol. 28 (Bari: Edipuglia, 2007).
Lepelley, Claude, *Les Cités de l'Afrique romaine au Bas-Empire*, 2 vols, Collection des Études Augustiniennes: Antiquité, vols 80–81 (Paris: Études augustiniennes, 1979–81).
Lepelley, Claude, 'La crise de l'Afrique romaine au début du Ve siècle, d'après les Lettres nouvellement découvertes de saint Augustin', *Comptes rendus des séances de l'Académie des Inscriptions et Belles Lettres*, 125 (1981): 445–63.
Lepelley, Claude, 'La Cité africaine tardive, de l'apogée du IVe siècle à l'effondrement du VIIe siècle', in Jens-Uwe Krause and Christian Witschel

(eds), *Die Stadt in der Spätantike – Niedergang oder Wandel?*, Akten des internationalen Kolloquiums in München am 30. und 31. mai 2003, Historia Einzelschriften, Bd 190 (Stuttgart: Franz Steiner, 2006), 13–32.

Lepelley, Claude, 'Facing Wealth and Poverty: Defining Augustine's Social Doctrine', The Saint Augustine Lecture, 2006, *AugSt*, 38 (2007): 1–17.

L'Huillier, Peter, *The Church of the Ancient Councils: The Disciplinary Work of the First Four Ecumenical Councils* (Crestwood, NY: St. Vladimir's Seminary Press, 1996).

Liebeschuetz, J.H.W.G. and Hill, Carole, *Ambrose of Milan: Political Letters and Speeches*, TTH, vol. 43 (Liverpool: Liverpool University Press, 2005).

Lieu, Samuel N.C., *Manichaeism in the Later Roman Empire and Medieval China*, WUNT, vol. 63 (Tübingen: Mohr, 1992 [2nd edn]).

Lizzi Testa, Rita, *Senatori, popolo, papi: il governo di Roma al tempo dei Valentiniani* (Bari: Epipuglia, 2004).

Llewelyn, Peter A.B., 'The Roman clergy During the Laurentian Schism (498–506): A Preliminary Analysis', *Ancient Society*, 8 (1977): 245–75.

Logan, Alastair, 'Constantine, the *Liber Pontificalis* and the Christian Basilicas of Rome', in Allen Brent and Markus Vizent (eds), *Studia Patristica*, vol. 50, papers presented at the National Conference on Patristic Studies, Cambridge, 2009 (Leuven: Peeters, 2011), 31–53.

Luongo, Gennaro, 'Paolino testimone del culto dei santi', in Gennaro Luongo (ed.), *Anchora vitae*, Atti del II convengo paoliniano nel XVI centenario del ritiro di Paolino a Nola (Nola 18–20 maggio 1995) (Naples and Rome: LER, 1998), 295–347.

Maccarrone, Michele, '"Sedes Apostolica – Vicarius Petri". La perpetuità del primato di Pietro nella sede e nel vescovo di Roma (Secoli III–VIII)', in Michele Maccarrone (ed.), *Il primato del vescovo di Roma nel primo millennio. Richerche e testimonianze*, Atti del Symposium storico-teologico, Roma, 9–13 Ottobre 1989, Atti e Documenti, vol. 4 (Vatican City: Libreria Editrice Vaticana, 1991), 275–362.

McKitterick, Rosamond, 'Roman Texts and Roman History in the Early Middle Ages', in Claudia Bolgia, Rosamond McKitterick and John Osborne (eds) *Rome across Time and Space: Cultural Transmission and the Exchange of Ideas, c. 500–1400* (Cambridge: Cambridge University Press, 2011), 28–33.

McLynn, Neil B., *Ambrose of Milan: Church and Court in a Christian Capital*, TCH, vol. 22 (Berkeley and Los Angeles: University of California Press, 1994).

McLynn, Neil B., 'Crying Wolf: The Pope and the Lupercalia', *JRS*, 98 (2008): 161–75.

McLynn, Neil B., 'Damasus of Rome: A Fourth-Century Pope in Context', in Therese Fuhrer (ed.), *Rom und Mailand in der Spätantike: Repräsentationen städtischer Räume in Literatur, Architektur und Kunst*, Topoi Berlin Studies of the Ancient World, vol. 4 (Berlin: De Gruyter, 2012), 305–20.

MacMullen, Ramsay, *The Second Church: Popular Christianity A.D. 200–400* (Atlanta: Society of Biblical Literature, 2009).

McShane, Philip A., *La romanitas et le pape Léon le Great: L'apport culturel des institutions imperials à la formation des structures ecclésiastiques*, Recherches Théologie, vol. 24 (Tournai and Montreal: Desclée, 1979).

Maier, Harry O., 'The Topography of Heresy and Dissent in Late Fourth-Century Rome', *Historia: Zeitschrift für alte Geschichte*, 44 (1995): 232–49.

Manigk, Alfred, 'Hereditarium ius', *Real-Encyclopädie*, vol. 8/1 (Stuttgart: J.B. Metzler, 1912), 625–6.

Marcovich, Miroslav (ed.), *Prosper of Aquitaine: De providentia Dei. Text, Translation and Commentary*, Supplements to *Vigiliae Christianae*, vol. 10 (Leiden and New York: E.J. Brill, 1989).

Marin, Marcello and Moreschini, Claudio (eds), *Africa cristiana. Storia, religione, letteratura*, Letteratura Cristiana Antica (Brescia: Morcelliana, 2002).

Markus, Robert A., 'Chronicle and Theology: Prosper of Aquitaine', in Christopher Holdsworth and Timothy P. Wiseman (eds), *The Inheritance of Historiography 350–900* (Exeter, 1986), 31–43.

Markus, Robert A., 'The Legacy of Pelagius: Orthodoxy, Heresy and Conciliation', in R.D. Williams (ed.), *The Making of Orthodoxy: Essays in Honour of Henry Chadwick* (Cambridge: Cambridge University Press, 1989), 214–34.

Markus, Robert A., *The End of Ancient Christianity* (Cambridge: Cambridge University Press, 1990).

Markus, Robert A., *Gregory the Great and his World* (Cambridge: Cambridge University Press, 1997).

Martindale, John R., *The Prosopography of the Later Roman Empire*, vol. 3: *A.D. 527–641* (Cambridge: Cambridge University Press, 1992).

Mathisen, Ralph W., *Ecclesiastical Factionalism and Religious Controversy in Fifth-Century Gaul* (Washington, DC: Catholic University of America Press, 1989).

Mathisen, Ralph W., 'The Council of Turin (398/399) and the Reorganization of Gaul ca. 395/406', *Journal of Late Antiquity* 6 (2014): 264–307.

Matthews, John, *Western Aristocracies and Imperial Court A.D. 364–425* (Oxford: Clarendon Press, 1998 [2nd edn]).

Maymó i Capdevila, Pere, 'Gregory the Great and the Religious Otherness: Pagans in a Christian Italy' in J. Baun, A. Cameron, M. Edwards and

M. Vinzent (eds), *Studia Patristica*, vol. 48, papers presented at the Fifteenth International Conference on Patristic Studies held in Oxford 2007 (Leuven: Peeters, 2010), 327–32.

Merdinger, Jane E., *Rome and the African Church in the Time of Augustine* (Yale: Yale University Press, 1997).

Merrills, Andrew H., 'Introduction – Vandals, Romans and Berbers: Understanding Late Antique North Africa', in Andrew H. Merrills (ed.), *Vandals, Romans and Berbers: New Perspectives on Late Antique North Africa* (Aldershot: Ashgate, 2004), 3–28.

Mihoc, Vasile, 'The Tradition on St. Paul's Journey to Spain in the Church Fathers', in Josep Maria Gavaldà Ribot et al. (eds), *Pau, Fructuós i el cristianisme primitiu a Tarragona (segles I–VIII)*, Actes del Congres de Tarragona (19–21 de Juny de 2008), Biblioteca Tarraco d'Arqueologia, vol. 6 (Tarragona: Fundació Privada Liber, 2010), 181–92.

Minnerath, R., 'La tradition doctrinale de la primauté pétrinienne au premier millénaire', in *Il primato del succesore di Pietro*, Atti del Simposio teologico, Roma, 2–4 Dicembre 1996, Atti e Documenti, vol. 7 (Vatican City: Libreria Editrice Vaticana, 1998), 117–46.

Mommsen, Theodor, 'Actenstücke zur Kirchengeschichte aus dem Cod. Cap. Novar. 30', *NA*, 11 (1886): 367–8.

Mommsen, Theodor, *Gesammelte Schriften*, Bd 6: *Historische Schriften. Dritter Band* [Berlin: Weidmann, 1910], 605–9).

Mommsen, Theodor, *Römisches Staatsrecht*, vols 1–3/2 (Tübingen: Wissenschaftliche Buchgemeinschaft, 1952 [4th edn]).

Moorhead, John, 'The Laurentian Schism: East and West in the Roman Church', *CH*, 47 (1978): 125–36.

Moorhead, John, 'The Decii under Theoderic', *Historia*, 33 (1983): 107–15.

Moorhead, John, *Theodoric in Italy* (Oxford: Clarendon Press, 1992).

Moorhead, John, 'On Becoming Pope in Late Antiquity', *JRH*, 30 (2006): 279–93.

Muhlberger, Steven, *The Fifth-Century Chroniclers: Prosper, Hydatius, and the Gallic Chronicler of 452*, ARCA Classical and Medieval Texts, Papers and Monographs, vol. 27 (Leeds: Francis Cairns, 1990).

Neil, Bronwen, '*On True Humility*: An Anonymous Letter on Poverty and the Female Ascetic', in Wendy Mayer, Pauline Allen and Lawrence Cross (eds), *Prayer and Spirituality in the Early Church*, vol. 4: *The Spiritual Life* (Strathfield, NSW: St Pauls Publications, 2006), 233–46.

Neil, Bronwen, *Leo the Great*, The Early Church Fathers (London and New York: Routledge, 2009).

Neil, Bronwen, 'Leo I on Poverty', in Pauline Allen, Bronwen Neil and Wendy Mayer, *Preaching Poverty in the Later Roman Empire: Perceptions and Realities*, Arbeiten zur Kirchen- und Theologiegeschichte, Bd 28 (Leipzig, 2009), 171–208.

Neil, Bronwen, 'Conclusions', in Pauline Allen, Bronwen Neil and Wendy Mayer, *Preaching Poverty in the Later Roman Empire: Perceptions and Realities*, Arbeiten zur Kirchen- und Theologiegeschichte, Bd 28 (Leipzig, 2009), 209–31.

Neil, Bronwen, 'Imperial Benefactions to the Fifth-Century Roman Church', in G. Nathan and L. Garland (eds), Basileia: *Essays on Imperium and Culture in Honour of E.M. and M.J. Jeffreys*, Byzantina Australiensia, vol. 17 (Brisbane: Australian Association for Byzantine Studies, 2011), 55–66.

Neil, Bronwen, 'The Papacy in the Age of Gregory the Great', in Bronwen Neil and M. Dal Santo (eds), *Companion to Gregory the Great*, Brill's Companions to the Christian Tradition, vol. 47 (Leiden: Brill, 2013), 3–27.

Neil, Bronwen, '*De profundis*: The Letters and Archives of Pelagius I of Rome (556–561)', in Bronwen Neil and Pauline Allen (eds), *Collecting Early Christian Letters: From the Apostle Paul to Late Antiquity* (Cambridge: Cambridge University Press, forthcoming).

Neil, Bronwen, 'Papal Letter Collections', in Edward Watts, Cristiana Sogno and Brad Storin (eds), *A Critical Introduction and Reference Guide to Letter Collections in Late Antiquity* (Berkeley and Los Angeles: University of California Press, forthcoming).

Neil, Bronwen and Allen, Pauline (intro. and trans.), *The Letters of Gelasius I (492–496): Pastor and Micromanager of the Church of Rome*, Adnotationes, vol. 1 (Turnhout: Brepols, 2014).

Noble, Thomas F.X., 'Theodoric and the Papacy', in CISAM, *Teoderico il Grande e I Goti d'Italia. Atti del XIII Congresso internazionale di studi sull'Alto Mediaevo* (Milan, 2–6 November 1992), Atti dei Congressi, vol. 13 (Spoleto: CISAM, 1993), 395–423.

Norton, Peter, *Episcopal Elections 250–600: Hierarchy and Popular Will in Late Antiquity*, OCM (Oxford: Oxford University Press, 2007).

Ohme, Heinz, *Kanon ekklesiastikos: Die Bedeutung des altkirchlichen Kanonbegriffs*, AKG, Bd 67 (Berlin and New York: De Gruyter, 1998).

Orlandis, José, 'El Primado Romano en la España Visigoda', in Michele Maccarrone (ed.), *Il primato del vescovo di Roma nel primo millennio. Richerche e testimonianze*, Atti del Symposium storico-teologico, Roma, 9–13 Ottobre 1989, Atti e Documenti, vol. 4 (Vatican City: Libreria Editrice Vaticana, 1991), 453–72.

Orlandis, José and Ramos-Lissón, Domingo, *Historia de los Concilios de le España Romana y Visigoda* (Pamplona: Ediciones Universidad de Navarra, S.A., 1986).

Picard, Jean-Charles, *Évêques, saints et cités en Italie et en Gaule: Études d'archéologie et d'histoire*, Collection de l' École française de Rome, vol. 242 (Rome: École française de Rome, 1998).

Picotti, G.B., 'Osservazioni su alcuni punti della politica religiosa di Teoderico', in CISAM, *I Goti in Occidente. Problemi* (Spoleto, 29 March – 5 April 1955), Settimane di studio del CISAM, vol. 3 (Spoleto: CISAM, 1956), 173–226.

Pieler, Peter E., 'Die Rechtsliteratur', in L.J. Engels and H. Hofmann (eds), *Spätantike: Mit einem Panorama der byzantinischen Literatur*, Neues Handbuch der Literaturwissenschaft, vol. 4 (Wiesbaden: Aula-Verlag, 1997), 565–99.

Pietri, Charles, '*Concordia apostolorum et renovatio urbis* (Culte des martyrs et propagande pontificale)', *Mélanges d'archéologie et d'histoire*, 73 (1961): 275–322.

Pietri, Charles, *Roma Christiana. Recherches sur l'Église de Rome, son organisation, sa politique, son idéologie de Miltiade à Sixte III (311–440)*, BEFAR, vol. 224 (Rome: École française de Rome, 1976).

Pietri, Charles, 'Clercs et serviteurs laïcs de l'Église romaine au temps de Grégoire le Grand', in Jacques Fontaine, Robert Gillet and Stan Pellistrandi (eds), *Grégoire le Grand: Colloque international du Centre National de la Recherche Scientifique, Chantilly, 15–19 septembre 1982* (Paris, 1986), 107–22.

Pietri, Charles, 'Régions ecclésiastiques et paroisses romaines', in *Actes du XIe Congrès international d'archéologie chrétienne (1986)*, SAC, vol. 41/2 (Rome: École française de Rome, 1989), 1035–62.

Pietri, Charles, 'La Rome de Grégoire', in *Gregorio Magno e il suo tempo*, XIX Incontro di studiosi dell'antichità cristiana, Roma, 9–12 maggio 1990, SEAug, vol. 33 (Rome: Institutum Patristicum Augustinianum, 1991), 9–32.

Pietri, Charles *Christiana respublica. Éléments d'une enquête sur le christianisme antique*, CEFR, vol. 234 (Rome: École française de Rome, 1997).

Pietri, Charles and Luce (eds), *Prosopographie chrétienne du Bas-Empire*, t. 2: *Italie (313–604)* (Rome: École française de Rome, 2000).

Pilara, Gianluca, *La città di Roma fra Chiesa e Impero durante il conflitto gotico-bizantino*, Scienze storiche, filosofiche, pedagogiche e psicologiche, vol. 194 (Rome: Aracne, 2006).

Prigent, Vivien, 'La Sicile byzantine, entre Papes et Empereurs', in D. Engels, L. Geis and M. Kleu (eds), *Zwischen Ideal und Wirklichkeit* (Stuttgart: Franz Steiner Verlag, 2010), 202–30.

Purcell, Nicholas, 'The Populace of Rome in Late Antiquity: Problems of Classification and Historical Description', in William V. Harris (ed.), *The Transformations of* Urbs Roma *in Late Antiquity*, Journal of Roman Archaeology Supplementary Series, vol. 33 (Portsmouth, RI: Journal of Roman Archaeology, 1999), 135–61.

Ramos-Lissón, Domingo, 'El tratamiento de la mujer en los cánones del Concilio I de Toledo (a. 400)', in *I concili della cristianità occidentale secoli III–V*, XXX Incontro di studiosi dell'antichità cristiana, Roma, 3–5 maggio 2001, SEAug, vol. 78 (Rome: Institutum Patristicum Augustinianum, 2002), 607–18.

Rapp, Claudia, *Holy Bishops in Late Antiquity: The Nature of Christian Leadership in an Age of Transition*, TCH, vol. 37 (Berkeley: University of California Press, 2005).

Raven, Susan, *Rome in Africa* (London and New York: Routledge, 1993 [3rd edn]).

Rebillard, Éric, 'L'Église de Rome et le développement des catacombes: à propos de l'origine des cimetières chrétiens', *MEFRA*, 109 (1997): 741–63.

Recchia, Vincenzo, *Gregorio Magno e la società agricola* (Rome: Edizio Studium, 1978).

Reekmans, Louis, 'L'œuvre du pape Damase dans le complexe de Gaius à la catacombe de S. Callixte', in *Saecularia Damasiana*, Atti del convengo internazionale per il XVI centenario della morte di Papa Damaso I, 11–12–384, 10–12 dicembre 1984, SAC, vol. 39 (Vatican City: Pontificio Istituto di Archeologia Cristiana, 1986), 261–81.

Reekmans, Louis, 'Recherches récentes dans les cryptes des martyrs romains', in Mathijs Lamberigts and Peter Van Deun (eds), *Martyrium in Multidisciplinary Perspective: Memorial Louis Reekmans*, BETL, vol. 117 (Leuven: Peeters, 1995), 32–70.

Reutter, Ursula, *Damasus: Bischof von Rom (366–384): Leben und Werk*, Studien und Texte zu Antike und Christentum, vol. 55 (Tübingen: Mohr Siebeck, 2009).

Richards, Jeffrey, *Consul of God: The Life and Times of Pope Gregory the Great* (London: Routledge and Kegan Paul, 1980).

Richards, Jeffrey, *The Popes and the Papacy in the Early Middle Ages, 476–752* (London and New York: Routledge, 1979).

Richardson, Ernest Cushing, 'Jerome and Gennadius: Lives of Illustrious Men', in Philip Schaff and Henry Wace (eds), *Nicene and Post-Nicene Fathers*, second series, vol. 3: *Theodoret, Jerome, Gennadius, Rufinus: Historical Writings, etc.* (Edinburgh: T & T Clark, 1892), 349–402.

Robinson, James H., *Readings in European History* (Boston: Ginn and Co., MA: 1905), 72–3.
Rosi, M., 'L'ambasceria di papa Giovanni I a Constantinopoli secondo alcuni principali scrittori', *Archivio della R. Società romana di storia patria*, 21 (1898): 567–84.
Rossi, Giovanni Battista de, 'Dei marmi trovata entro l'area della basilica. Sue relazioni col titolo urbano appellato *Fasciolae*', *Bullettino di'archeologia cristiana*, ser. 2, vol. 6 (1875): 49–56.
Rossi, Giovanni Battista de, 'Scavi nelle catacombe romane, specialmente nel cimitero di Domitilla', *Bullettino di'archeologia cristiana*, ser. 3, vol. 4 (1879): 91–6.
Rouche, Michel, 'La Matricule des pauvres. Évolution d'une institution de charité du Bas Empire jusqu'à la fin du Haut Moyen Âge', in Michel Mollat (ed.), *Études sur l'histoire de la pauvreté (Moyen âge – XVIe siècle)*, vol. 1 (Paris: Publications de la Sorbonne, 1974), 83–110.
Rougé, Jean, 'Escroquerie et brigandage en Afrique romaine au temps de saint Augustin (Epist. 8* and 10*)', in Claude Lepelley (ed.), *Les Lettres de saint Augustin découvertes par Johannes Divjak*, Communications présentées au colloque des 20 et 21 Septembre 1982, EAA, vol. 98 (Paris: Etudes Augustiniennes, 1983), 177–88.
Saecularia Damasiana, Atti del vonvengo internazionale per il XVI centenario della morte di Papa Damaso I, 11-12-384, 10–12 dicembre 1984, SAC, vol. 39 (Vatican City: Pontificio Istituto di Archeologia Cristiana, 1986).
Sághy, Marianne, '*Scinditur in partes populus*: Pope Damasus and the Martyrs of Rome', *EME*, 9 (2000): 273–87.
Sághy, Marianne, 'Martyr Cult and Collective Identity in Fourth-Century Rome', in Ana Marinković and Trpimir Vedriš (eds), *Identity and Alterity in Hagiography and the Cult of Saints* (Zagreb: Hagiotheca, 2010), 17–35.
Sághy, Marianne, 'Martyr Bishops and the Bishop's Martyrs in Fourth-Century Rome', in Trpimir Vedriš and John Ott (eds), *Saintly Bishops and Bishops' Saints* (Zagreb: Hagiotheca, 2012), 31–45.
Sághy, Marianne, '*Renovatio memoriae*: Pope Damasus and the Martyrs of Rome', in Ralf Behrwald and Christian Witschel (eds), *Rome in der Spätantike: Historische Erinnerung im städtischen Raum* (Stuttgart: Franz Steiner Verlag, 2012), 251–67.
Saitta, B., *La civiltas di Teoderico. Rigore amministrativo, "tolleranza" religiosa e recupero dell'antico nell'Italia ostrogota*, Studia historica, vol. 128 (Rome: 'L'Erma' di Bretschneider, 1993), 63–99.

Salzman, Michele Renee, *On Roman Time: The Codex-Calendar of 354 and the Rhythms of Urban Life in Late Antiquity*, TCH, vol. 17 (Berkeley: University of California Press, 1990).

Salzman, Michele Renee, 'Leo in Rome: The Evolution of Episcopal Authority in the Fifth Century', in G. Bonamente and Rita Lizzi Testa (eds), *Istituzioni, carismi ed esercizio del potere (IV–VI secolo d.C.)* (Bari: Edipuglia Press, 2010), 343–56.

Sánchez, Sylvain Jean Gabriel, *Priscillien, un chrétien non conformiste. Doctrine et pratique du Priscillianisme du IVe au VIe siècle*, Théologie historique, vol. 120 (Paris: Beauchesne, 2009).

Santorelli, Paola, 'L'epigramma a Proiecta di Damaso (51 F.)', in Salvatore Pricoco, Francesca Rizzo Nervo and Teresa Sardella (eds), *Sicilia e Italia suburbicaria tra IV e VIII secolo*, Atti del convengo di Studi, Catania, 24–27 ottobre 1989 (Catania: Rubbettino, 1991), 327–36.

Sardella, Teresa, *Società, Chiesa e Stato nell'età di Teoderico. Papa Simmaco e lo scisma laurenziano*, Armarium. Biblioteca di storia e cultura religiosa, vol. 7 (Soveria Mannelli: Rubbertino, 1996).

Sardella, Teresa, 'Papa Siricio e i movimenti ereticale nella Spagna di Teodosio I', in Ramón Teja Casuso and Cesáreo Pérez González (eds), *La Hispania de Teodosio Congreso Internacional, Segovia 395–1995-Coca, Segovia*, Actas volumen 1, (Segovia: Universidad SEK, 1997), 247–54.

Scerri, Hector, 'Gregory the Great Deposes a Disobedient Bishop', in J. Baun, A. Cameron, M. Edwards and M. Vinzent (eds), *Studia Patristica*, vol. 48, papers presented at the Fifteenth International Conference on Patristic Studies held in Oxford 2007 (Leuven: Peeters, 2010), 321–6.

Schmidt, Kurt-Dietrich, 'Papa Petrus ipse', *ZKG*, 54 (1936): 267–75.

Schurr, Viktor, *Die Trinitätslehre des Boethius im Lichte der "skythischen Kontroversen"*, Forschungen zur Christlichen Literatur- und Dogmenschichte, vol. 18/1 (Paderborn: F. Schöningh, 1935).

Schwartz, Eduard, *Der Prozeß des Eutyches*, Sitzungsberichte der Bayerischen Akademie der Wissenschaften, Philosophisch-historische Abteilung, vol. 5 (Munich: Königlich Bayerische Akademie der Wissenschaften, 1929).

Selb, Walter, 'Erbrecht', *JbAC*, 14 (1971): 170–84.

Serfass, Adam, 'Slavery and Pope Gregory the Great', *JECS*, 14 (2006): 77–103.

Sessa, Kristina, 'Christianity and the *Cubiculum*: Spiritual Politics and Domestic Space in Late Antique Rome', *JECS*, 15 (2007): 171–204.

Sessa, Kristina, 'Domestic Conversions: Household and Bishops in the Late Antique "Papal Legends"', in Kate Cooper and Julia Hillner (eds), *Religion,*

Sessa, Kristina, *'Domus Ecclesiae*: Rethinking a Category of *Ante-Pacem* Christian Space', *JThS*, n.s. 60 (2009): 90–108.

Sessa, Kristina, 'Exceptionality and Invention: Silvester and the Late Antique "Papacy" at Rome', in J. Baun, A. Cameron, M. Edwards and M. Vinzent (eds), *Studia Patristica*, vol. 46, papers presented at the Fifteenth International Conference on Patristic Studies held in Oxford 2007 (Leuven: Peeters, 2010), 77–94.

Sessa, Kristina, 'Ursa's Return: Captivity, Remarriage, and the Domestic Authority of Roman Bishops in Fifth-Century Italy', *JECS*, 19 (2011): 401–32.

Sessa, Kristina, *The Formation of Papal Authority in Late Antique Italy: Roman Bishops and the Domestic Sphere* (Cambridge: Cambridge University Press, 2012).

Sirago, Vito Antonio, *Amalasunta. La regina (ca. 495–535)*, Donne d'Oriente e d'Occidente, vol. 9 (Milan: Jaca Books, 1999).

Somerville, Robert and Brasington, B. C., *Prefaces to Canon Law Books in Latin Christianity: Selected Translations 500–1245* (New Haven and London: Yale University Press, 1998).

Sotinel, Claire, 'Le personnel épiscopal. Enquête sur la puissance de l'évêque dans la cité', in Éric Rebillard and Claire Sotinel (eds), *L'Évêque dans la cité du IVe au Ve siècle. Image et autorité*, CEFR, vol. 248 (Rome: École française de Rome, 1998), 105–26.

Sotinel, Claire, 'Chronologie, topographie, histoire: Quelques hypothèses sur S. Felix in Pincis, église disparue', in Federico Guidobaldi and Alessandra Guiglia Guiodobaldi (eds), *Ecclesiae Urbis*, Atti del congresso internazionale di studi sulle chiese di Roma (IV–X Secolo), Roma, 4–10 Settembre 2000, SAC, vol. 59, 3 vols (Vatican City: Pontificio Istituto di Archeologia Cristiana, 2002), 1.449–71.

Spearing, Edward and Evelyn, *The Patrimony of the Roman Church in the time of Gregory the Great* (Cambridge: Cambridge University Press, 1918).

Speigl, Jakob, 'Die Päpste in der Reichskirche des 4. und frühen 5. Jahrhunderts: Von Silvester I. bis Sixtus III.', in Manfred Greschat (ed.), *Das Papsttum*, vol. 1: *Von den Anfängen bis zu den Päpsten in Avignon*, Gestalten der Kirchengeschichte, vol. 11 (Stuttgart: Kohlhammer, 1984), 43–55.

Spera, Lucrezia, 'Interventi di papa Damaso nei santuari delle catacombe romane: il ruolo della committenza privata', *Bessarione*, 11 (1994): 111–27.

Stark, Rodney, *The Rise of Christianity: A Sociologist Reconsiders History* (Princeton: Princeton University Press, 1996).

Stein, Ernst, *Histoire du Bas-Empire*, ed. Jean-Rémy Palanaque, 2 vols (Paris: Desclée de Brouwer, 1949–59).

Steinby, Eva Margareta, *Lexicon Topographicum Urbis Romae*, 6 vols (Rome: Quasar, 1993–2000).

Studer, Basil, *La riflessione teologica nella Chiesa imperiale (secoli IV e V)*, Sussidi Patristici, vol. 4 (Rome, Institutum Patristicum Augustinianum, 1989).

Taylor, Justin, 'The Early Papacy at Work: Gelasius I (492–496)', *JRH*, 4 (1975): 317–32.

Teillet, Suzanne, *Des Goths à la nation gothique. Les origines de l'idée de nation en Occident du Ve au VIIe siècle*, Histoire, vol. 108 (Paris: Les Belles Lettres, 2011 [2nd edn]).

Teitler, Hans C., *Notarii and Exceptores: An Inquiry into the Role and Significance of Shorthand Writers in the Imperial and Ecclesiastical Bureaucracy of the Roman Empire (from the Early Principate to c. 450 A.D.)* (Amsterdam: J.C. Gieben, 1985).

Thacker, Alan, 'Rome of the Martyrs: Saints, Cults and Relics, Fourth to Seven Centuries', in Éamonn Ó'Carragain and Carol Neuman de Vegvar (eds), *Roma felix: Formation and Reflections of Medieval Rome*, Church Faith and Culture in the Medieval West (Aldershot: Ashgate, 2007), 13–49.

Troncarelli, Fabio, *Vivarium: I libri, il destino*, Instrumenta Patristica, vol. 33 (Turnhout: Brepols, 1998).

Trout, Dennis E., *Paulinus of Nola: Life, Letters, and Poems*, TCH, vol. 27 (Berkeley and Los Angeles: University of California Press, 1999).

Trout, Dennis E., 'Damasus and the Invention of Early Christian Rome', *Journal of Medieval and Early Modern Studies*, 33 (2003): 517–36.

Trout, Dennis E., 'Saints, Identity and the City', in Virginia Burrus (ed.), *Late Ancient Christianity*, A People's History of Christianity (Minneapolis: Fortress Press, 2005), 165–87.

Ubric Rabaneda, Purificación, *La Iglesia en la Hispania del siglo V* (Granada: Universidad de Granada, 2004).

Ullmann, Walter, "Leo I and the Theme of Papal Primacy', *JThS*, n.s. 11 (1960): 25–51.

Ullmann, Walter, *A Short History of the Papacy in the Middle Ages* (London: Routledge, 2003 [2nd edn]).

Ullmann, Walter, *Growth of the Papal Government in the Middle Ages: A Study in the Ideological Relation of Clerical to Lay Power* (London: Methuen, 1970 [3rd edn]).

Ullmann, Walter, *Gelasius I. (492–496): Das Papsttum an der Wende der Spätantike zum Mittelalter*, Päpste und Papsttum, vol. 18 (Stuttgart: A. Hiersemann, 1981).

Van Dam, Raymond, *Leadership and Community in Late Antique Gaul*, TCH, vol. 7 (Berkeley and Los Angeles: University of California Press, 1985).

Viciano i Vives, Albert, 'La Decretal del Papa Sirici a Himeri de Tarragona', in Josep Maria Gavaldà Ribot et al. (eds), *Pau, Fructuós i el cristianisme primitiu a Tarragona (segles I–VIII)*, Actes del Congres de Tarragona (19–21 de Juny de 2008), Biblioteca Tarraco d'Arqueologia, vol. 6 (Tarragona: Fundació Privada Liber, 2010), 659–74.

Vilella Masana, Josep, 'La correspondencia entre los obispos Hispanos y el Papado durante el siglo V', in *Cristianesimo e specificità regionali nel Mediterraneo Latino (sec. IV–VI)*, XXII Incontro di studiosi dell'antichità cristiana, Roma, 6–8 maggio 1993, SEAug, vol. 46 (Rome: Institutum Patristicum Augustinianum, 1994), 457–81.

Vilella Masana, Josep, 'Priscilianismo Galaico y política antipriscilianista durante el siglo V', *AntTard*, 5 (1997): 177–85.

Vilella Masana, Josep, 'Las primacías eclesiásticas en *Hispania* durante el siglo IV', *Polis*, 10 (1998): 269–85.

Vilella Masana, Josep, 'Los concilios eclesiásticos de la Tarraconensis durante el siglo V', *Florentia Iliberritana*, 13 (2002): 327–44.

Vilella Masana, Josep, 'La *Epístola* 1 de Siricio: Estudio Prosopográfico de Himerio de Tarragona', *Aug*, 44 (2004): 337–69.

Vitiello, Massimiliano, '*Cui Iustinus Imperator venienti ita occurit ac si beato Petro*. Das Ritual beim ersten Papst-Kaiser Treffen in Konstantinopel : eine römische Auslegung ?', *ByzZ*, 98 (2005): 81–96.

Vives, José, et al., *Concilios Visigóticos e Hispano-Romanos*, España Cristiana, Textos, vol. 1 (Barcelona and Madrid: CSIC, 1963).

Walser, Gerold, *Die Einsiedler Inschriftensammlung und der Pilgerführer durch Rom (Codex Einsidlensis 326)*, Historia, Einzelschriften, vol. 53 (Stuttgart: Franz Steiner, 1987).

Watson, William Lee, 'The Epigrams of St Damasus: A Translation and Commentary' (MA diss., University of Texas, Austin 1958).

Weckwerth, Andreas, 'Aufbau und Struktur der *Constitutio* des ersten Konzils von Toledo (400)', in *I concili della cristianità occidentale secoli III–V*, XXX Incontro di studiosi dell'antichità cristiana, Roma, 3–5 maggio 2001, SEAug, vol. 78 (Rome: Institutum Patristicum Augustinianum, 2002), 619–30.

Weckwerth, Andreas, *Ablauf, Organisation und Selbstverständnis westlicher Synoden im Spiegel ihrer Akten*, JbAC Erg.-Bd. Kleine Reihe, vol. 5 (Münster: Aschendorff, 2010).

Weltin, E.G., *The Ancient Popes*, The Popes through History, vol. 2 (Westminster, MD: The Newman Press, 1964).

Wenger, Leopold, *Die Quellen des römischen Rechts*, Denkschriften der Gesamtakademie, vol. 2 (Vienna: Adolf Holzhausens, 1953).

Wessel, Susan, *Leo the Great and the Spiritual Rebuilding of Rome*, Supplements to Vigiliae Christianae, vol. 93 (Leiden: Brill, 2008).

Whitby, Michael, *The Emperor Maurice and his Historian: Theophylact Simocatta on Persian and Balkan Warfare*, OHM (Oxford: Oxford University Press, 1988).

Wieacker, Franz, *Römische Rechtsgeschichte. Zweiter Abschnitt*, Handbuck der Altertumswissenschaft, vol. 10/3/1/2 (Munich: C.H. Beck, 2006).

Williams, George Huntston, 'Christology and Church-State Relations in the Fourth Century', *Church History*, 20.3 (1951): 3–33 and 20.4 (1951): 3–26.

Wirbelauer, Eckhard, *Zwei Päpste in Rom: der Konflikt zwischen Laurentius und Symmachus (498–514): Studien und Texte*, Quellen und Forschungen zur antiken Welt, vol. 16 (Munich: Tuduv, 1993).

Wirbelauer, Eckhard, 'Die Nachfolgerbestimmung im römischen Bistum (3.–6. Jh.): Doppelwahlen und Absetzungen in ihrer herrschaftssoziologischen Bedeutung', *Klio*, 76 (1994): 388–437.

Wojda, Jacek, *Communion et foi. Les trois premiers voyages des papes de Rome à Constantinople (484–555). Étude historique et théologique* (Siedlce: P.P.H. Iwonex, 2006).

Woods, David, 'The Date of the *Translation* of the *Relics* of SS. Luke and Andrew to Constantinople', *VChr*, 45 (1991): 286–92.

Zecchini, Giuseppe, *Ricerche di storiografia latina tardoantica*, vol. 2: *Dall'Historia Augusta a Paolo Diacono*, Centro ricerche e documentazione sull'Antichità classica. Monografie, vol. 34 (Rome: L'Erma di Bretschneider, 2008).

Ziegler, Aloysius K., 'Pope Gelasius and His Teaching on the Relation of Church and State', *CHR*, 27 (1942): 412–47.

Zizza, Giuseppe, 'Il De trinitate di Boezio e polemica antiariana', in CISAM, *Teoderico il Grande e i Goti d'Italia. Atti del XIII Congresso internazionale di studi sull'Alto Medioevo* (Milan, 2–6 November 1992), Atti dei Congressi, vol. 13 (Spoleto: CISAM, 1993), 819–49.

Zwierlein, Otto, *Petrus in Rom: Die literarischen Zeugnisse: Mit einer kritischen Edition der Martyrien des Petrus und Paulus auf neuer handschriftlicher*

Grundlage, Untersuchungen zur antiken Literatur und Geschichte, vol. 96 (Berlin and New York: De Gruyter, 2010 [2nd edn]).

Index

Biblical Passages

Genesis
   9:23 201

Matthew
   16:18–19 64, 71, 83
   16: 19 83, 148

Romans
   15:24 75
   15:28 75

1 Timothy
   3:2 105
   5:8 124

Roman Bishops (including claimants)

Agapitus (535–6) 139–40, 192–4, 200
Anastasius I (399–402) 29, 97–8
Anastasius II (496–8) 130, 134–5, 181
Antherus (235–6) 52

Benedict XVI (2005–13) 1
Boniface I (418–22) 20, 132
Boniface II (530–32) 7, 11–12, 132–3, 177–9, 181–2, 186, 189–190, 192–5

Calixtus (217–22) 27, 51, 83
Celestine I (422–32) 109, 113, 118–19, 134
Cletus (76–88) 21
Cornelius (251–3) 40

Damasus (366–84) 5, 8, 19–20, 28, 30–31, 34–6, 38–55, 57–62, 73–4, 76, 78–9, 83, 90, 92–5, 102, 104, 106, 118, 130, 133
Dionysius (259–68) 52
Dioscorus (claimant 530) 11–12, 132–3, 136, 177–83, 186, 189–90, 192–4

Eulalius 20
Eusebius (309) 40
Eutychian (275–83) 52
Evaristus (97–105) 21

Fabian (236–50) 52
Felix I (269–74) 34, 52
Felix II (claimant 355–65) 20
Felix III (II) (483–92) 134, 137–9, 146–7, 151, 157, 159–60, 163, 199
Felix IV (III) (526–30) 12, 132–3, 177–80, 182, 186, 190, 192–3, 195
Francis (2013–) 1

Gelasius I (492–6) 7, 10–11, 63, 129–30, 134–5, 137–9, 141–53, 155–61, 163–74
Gregory I (the Great) (590–604) 5–7, 10, 12–13, 33, 159, 165, 174, 197–215

Hilary (461–8) 28, 134
Hippolytus (claimant) 41, 46
Hormisdas (514–23) 113, 130–2, 136, 138, 140, 179, 191, 195

Innocent I (402–17) 8–9, 13, 35, 60, 64, 69–71, 75, 84, 89–91, 94, 97–107, 123, 162–3, 171

John I (523–6) 131, 137–8, 178, 183, 185–9, 191–2, 194
John II (533–5) 131–2, 140, 192–4
John Paul II (1978–2005) 1
Julius I (337–52) 19, 27, 30, 34

Lawrence (claimant 498–506) 177, 180–5, 192, 195
Leo I (the Great) (440–61) 5–6, 9–11, 61, 63–4, 67, 71, 75, 79–80, 84, 109–22, 124–5, 129, 133–4, 136, 140, 158–60, 163, 165–6, 169, 171–2, 177
Liberius (352–66) 19–20, 27, 30, 36, 44, 47, 59, 66, 78, 132
Lucius I (253–4) 52

Marcellus (308–9) 21, 40
Mark (336) 17, 24, 27, 34, 40, 47
Miltiades (311–14) 17, 26, 131, 157

Novatian (claimant 251–8) 46, 100

Pelagius I (556–61) 146, 159, 173, 177, 200
Pelagius II (579–90) 201
Peter (–67) 2–3, 10, 38, 40, 43, 47–8, 53–4, 62, 64, 71, 76, 80, 83–5, 100, 106, 128–9, 131–2, 137, 139, 141, 144, 148, 150–153, 167, 171, 206
Pontian (230–5) 46, 52

Silverius (536–7) 132–3, 177, 194
Simplicius (468–83) 130 135, 137–8, 160
Siricius (384–99) 7–8, 19, 29, 57–85, 90–91, 95–9, 102, 104–106
Sixtus II (257–8) 40, 51–2
Sixtus III (432–40) 64, 158
Stephen I (254–7) 52, 74, 91
Symmachus (498–514) 11, 130, 132–3, 135, 158, 168, 173, 177, 179–85, 193, 195
Sylvester I (314–35) 3, 17

Urban (222–30) 21

Ursinus (claimant 366–7) 20, 28, 34, 44, 58

Victor (189–99) 157
Vigilius (537–55) 177–8, 195

Zephyrinus (199–217) 51
Zosimus (417–18) 4, 8, 64, 121

Ancient Names and Works

Acacius of Constantinople 134–5, 138, 146, 151, 167, 181, 184
Acurius (Spanish bishop) 96
Adeodata 208
Ado of Vienne 9, 110
    Martyrologium 116
Adria (confessor) 52
Aetius (*magister utriusque militiae*) 110, 113, 119
Agatho (Sicilian monk) 209
Agnellus (Sicilian bishop) 208
Agnellus (son of Sicilian bishop) 208
Agnellus of Ravenna 127, 193
Agnellus of Verulana 163
Agnes (Roman martyr) 40–1, 44, 50
Alaric 166
Albinus (praetorian prefect of Gaul) 110, 113
Albinus Junior, Faustus/Flavius 184
Alexander (Italian bishop) 166
Alexander of Antioch 101
Amalasuintha (mother of Athalaric) 180, 182, 187, 190, 193
Amandianus (nobleman) 164
Ambrose 3, 30, 32, 37, 48, 53, 58–9, 79–80, 90–1, 93, 95–7, 106
    Epistulae 93, 96
    Hymnus 53
Ammianus Marcellinus 58
Ampliatus (*conductor*) 163
Anastasia (Pannonian martyr) 39–41
Anastasius (Italian bishop) 166
Anastasius I (emperor) 135–6, 139, 141, 150, 156, 166, 183–4, 188

Andrew (apostle) 54
Andromachus (senator) 143–5
Anterius (Spanish bishop) 96–7
Antonina (widow) 166
Anulinus 26
Apollonius (martyr) 41
Apollonius (*magister militum*)
April (Italian bishop) 164
Arcadius (emperor) 34
Asellus (archdeacon) 169
Athalaric (Ostrogothic king) 180, 182, 190
Athanasius
    Apologia secunda 27
Attila 119, 166
Augustine 112–13, 120, 123, 129, 156–9,
    161–3, 165–6, 168, 171, 173, 199
    *Breuiculus collationis cum Donatistis
        libri tres* 26
    De baptismo contra Donatistas 97
    De ciuitate Dei 168
    Enarrationes in Psalmos 172
    Epistulae 97, 123, 162, 168, 171–2
    Sermones 172
    Augustus (emperor) 202
Aurelian 24
Aurelius of Carthage 158
Auxentius of Milan 81

Basil of Caesarea 48
Basilides 74
    Epistulae 31–2
Bassus (Italian bishop) 166
Beneatus 212
Boethius 184–6, 191
Brumarius (*uir spectabilis*) 170

Caesarius (Sicilian abbot) 208
Caesarius of Arles 82, 168, 194
Callinicus 168
Callinicus (exarch of Italy) 202
Candidus (*defensor*) 211
canones in causa Apiarii 172
Caracalla (emperor) 24
Cassian 110, 113, 115, 117, 160

*De incarnatione Domini contra
    Nestorium* 113
Cassiodorus 169
Cassiodorus (praetorian prefect of Italy)
    180, 183, 185, 187, 190–91, 194,
    199
    Institutiones 194
    Variae 180, 185, 194, 213
Catalogus Liberianus 27, 34, 41–2
Chromatius of Aquileia 97
Chronica Gallica ad annum 452 121
Chronographus anni CCCLIIII 27, 34,
    41–2
Chrysanthius and Daria 41
Cicero (monk) 209
Claudius (*uir spectabilis*) 164
Clovis 140
Codex Iustinianus 213
Codex Theodosianus 33, 63, 94, 104, 162,
    164, 169, 213
Codex Thuaneus 115
Coelestinus (presbyter) 169
Constans I (emperor) 33
Constantina 40, 44–5
Constantine I (emperor) 3, 8, 17, 21, 26,
    33–7, 40, 44–5
Constantius (Italian bishop) 165, 170
Constitutio Sirmondinis 94
Crescentius (deacon of Thabarka) 47
Crispinus (Italian bishop) 165
Cyriacus (Sicilian abbot) 209, 214
Cyprian of Carthage 21, 75, 91, 97, 157–8
Cyprian (sixth-century deacon) 203, 208,
    211
Cyril of Alexandria 134

[Damasus]
    Epistula ad Gallos episcopos 60, 102
David (king) 100
Decentius of Gubbio 35
Decius (emperor) 24
Decius of Lilybaeum 203
Demetrias 112, 122–5
Demetrius of Philippi 193
Dictinius (Spanish bishop) 97, 99

Diocletian (emperor) 3
Dionysius (notary) 117
Dionysius Exiguus 194
Dionysius Filocalus, Furius 42
Domitia Lucilla 30
Domitian of Melitene 203
Domitius (Sicilian abbot) 209
Donatus (Spanish bishop) 96
Donus of Messina 207

Elegabalus 24
Elpidius (Spanish presbyter) 89, 91, 99, 101, 106
Emilius (Spanish bishop) 96
Ennodius of Pavia
    Epistulae 179
    Vita Epiphanii 168
Epiphanius of Constantinople 140, 189
    Relatio ad Hormisdam 180
Epiphanius of Lyons 168
Epitome Cononiana Libri pontificalis 180, 183–4
Epitome Feliciana Libri pontificalis 179, 181, 183–4
Eusebius (Greek confessor) 52
Eusebius of Caesarea 128
    Historia ecclesiastica 20, 26, 122
Eutyches (martyr) 43
Eutyches (heretic) 109, 114, 134
Excerpta Valesianus 139, 184, 186, 190
Exemplar professionum habitarum in concilio Toletano contra sectam Priscilliani aera ccccxxxviii 80, 96–7
Exsuperius of Toulouse 103, 105

Fantinus (*defensor*) 211–12, 214
Faustinian of Grumentium 165
Faustinus (martyr) 40–1
Faustinus (presbyter) 115
Faustinus and Marcellinus
    Liber precum 26, 28
Faustus (*defensor*) 161
Faustus (senator) 152–3
Faustus Junior, Flavius Anicius Probus 191
Felicissimus and Agapitus (deacons) 41, 52

Felix (asylum seeker/slave) 169
Felix (bishop) 164
Felix (bishop in Sardinia) 210
Felix (*uir clarissimus*) 159
Felix and Adauctus 40–1
Felix and Philip 41
Felix of Nola (third-century martyr) 29, 40, 45
Felix of Nola (fifth-century cleric = Felix the asylum seeker?) 169–71
Firmina (noblewoman) 167
Flavian of Constantinople 114
Flavitas of Constantinople 157
Fortunatus (Italian bishop) 166
Four Crowned Saints (Quattro coronati) 39
Fragmentum Laurentianum Libri pontificalis 135, 179, 183

Gaius (jurist) 63
Galerius (emperor) 26
Galla Placidia (empress) 114
Gaudentius of Brescia 53
Geiseric 166, 168
Gennadius 9, 110
    De uiris illustribus 109, 114–15
Gennadius (exarch of Africa) 202
Gennarius (deacon) 52
Germnos (*patricus*) 201
Germanus of Capua
    Suggestiones ad Hormisdam 180, 192
Gerontius (Italian bishop) 172
Gesta de nomine Acacii 129
Gordian (Roman presbyter) 200
Gorgonius 41
Gratian (emperor) 29, 33, 93–5, 106
Gregory (praetorian prefect of Italy) 204
Gregory of Agrigentum 206–207
Gregory of Granada (Elvira) 100
Gregory of Mérida 103–104
Gregory of Nyssa 48
Gregory of Tours 82
    Historia Francorum 200

Hadrian (notary) 209, 211–12, 214
Helena 40

Henotikon 180–82
Heorthasius (*uir spectabilis*) 169
Herculentius (Italian bishop) 164–5
Hereleuva (mother of Theodoric) 166
Herenias (Spanish bishop) 96
Hermes (martyr) 41
Hilary (Gallic layman) 109, 112
Hilary (Spanish bishop) 89, 91, 99, 101–103, 105–106
Himerius of Tarragona 8, 60–2, 65–71, 73–8, 80–4, 95–7, 99, 102, 105–106
Hippolytus (Greek confessor) 52
Honorius of Salona 163
Hydatius of Chaves
    Chronicon 96
Hydatius of Mérida 92, 94–6, 103
Hypatius of Ephesus 193

Ianuaria 208
Ianuarius 41
Inoportunus, Falvius 185
Instantius (Spanish bishop) 77, 91, 94–5
Irene (sister of Damasus) 41, 48–9
Ireneus and Abundius 41
Isaac (converted Jew) 45
Isidore 208
Isidore of Seville 81
Isonius (Spanish bishop) 96

Januarius (cleric) 166
Januarius (nobleman) 166
Jerome 30, 59, 106, 118, 130, 133
    Apologia conta Rufinum 105
    De uiris illustribus 29, 79, 114
    Epistulae 59, 105, 123–4
    Vita Malchi 128
John (deacon of Ravenna) 211
John (Italian bishop) 166, 169
John (Spanish bishop) 102
John (surveyor) 208
John II the Cappadocian
    Epistula ad Hormisdam 180
John Chrysostom 101
    De Lazaro conciones 48

Epistula ad Innocentum 97
John Maxentius
    Libellus fidei 179
    Responsio aduersus epistula 179, 192
John of Spoleto 172
John of Syracuse 203, 207–208, 214
John Talaïa 138, 180
Jordanes
    iGetica *190*
Judas (slave) 165
Julian 208
Justin (archdeacon) 161
Justin I (emperor) 137–40, 179–80, 184, 186
Justin II (emperor) 200, 202
Justin (*praetor Siciliae*) 202, 204, 215
Justin and companions (martyrs) 41
Justinian I (emperor) 63, 140, 177, 179, 184, 186, 188, 192–4, 199–201, 205, 213
Justus (Italian bishop) 163–4, 170
Justus of Lerins 170

Lactantius 135
    De mortibus persecutorum 26
Laurence (Italian bishop) 165
Laurence (*uir clarissimus*)
Laurentia (mother of Damasus) 41, 47, 49
Laurentius of Milan 195
Lawrence (deacon and martyr) 41, 52
Lawrence (*defensor*) 163
Lawrence (of Siena?) 163
Leo (emperor) 169
Leo of Catania 203, 206–207, 209
Leontius (consul) 202, 215
Leontius (Italian bishop) 172
Leontius (*patricus*) 202
Liberatus of Carthage 194
Liber pontificalis 3, 11, 21, 24, 26–7, 29, 34, 85, 124, 127–8, 130–40, 142, 146–7, 156–7, 161, 163, 168, 178–9, 181, 200
Liber Siluestri 3
Libertinus (*praetor Siciliae*) 202–3, 215
Lucidus of Leontino 208

Lucifer of Cagliari 100
Lucilla 50

Macedonius (*magister officiorum*) 93
Macrina 48–9
Magnus (deacon) 52
Magnus Maximus (emperor) 79, 96
Majoricus (Italian bishop) 169
Marcella 124
Marcellina (sister of Ambrose) 48–9
Marcellus (Greek confessor) 52
Marcian (emperor) 118–19
Marcus and Marcellinus (martyrs) 47, 49
Martha (Greek confessor) 52
Martia (Greek confessor) 52
Martialis 74
Martin of Tours 79, 168
Martyrologium Hieronynianum 29
Matasuentha 187
Maurice (emperor) 200–201, 203–204
Maurus (martyr) 41
Maxentius (emperor) 17
Maxima (slave owner) 163–4
Maximian of Syracuse 12, 206–207, 214
Maximus (cleric) 166
Melior (Italian bishop) 173
Mercurius 172
Minicius (Spanish bishop) 101–102
Misenus of Cumae 143, 146–9

Nasas (Jew) 203
Neon (Greek confessor) 52
Nereus and Achilleus 40
Nestorius 134
Nicetas of Aquileia 171
Noah 201
Nonnosus 207

Odoacer 143, 160, 167
Olibula (nun) 172
Olympius (deacon) 166
Optatus 25–6

Palladius
    Dialogus 97

Palladius (Italian bishop) 170
Pantaleon (notary) 211
Paternus (Spanish bishop) 96
Patruinus of Mérida 96, 103
Paul (apostle) 40, 43, 47–8, 53–4, 75, 78
Paulina (Greek confessor) 52
Paulinus of Milan
    Vita Ambrosii 30
Paulinus of Nola 38, 59
    Carmen 39
    Epistulae 59
Pelagius 112, 123
Peter (Italian bishop) 172
Peter (sub-deacon and *rector*) 203, 205–209, 211, 214
Peter and Marcellinus 40–1
Peter and Vitus (*defensores*) 211
Peter Mongus of Alexandria 134 138
Peter of Nola (fifth-century cleric) 170–1
Petronella (Sicilian nun) 208
Philip 169
Phocas (emperor) 204, 215
Photinus (Thessalonian deacon) 181
Photius 9, 110, 116
Placidia (slave owner) 163–4
Pliny the Younger 62
Postumius Festus, Rufius (consul) 181
Praeceptum Theoderici Magni contra sacerdotes substantiae ecclesiarum alienatores 183
Priscian of Caesarea
    Carmen in laudem Anastasii imperatoris 184
Priscillian 77–81, 90, 92–4, 96, 106
Probus (Apulian bishop) 170
Procopius
    De bello Gothico 186–7, 190, 192, 194
Proficius of Salpina 170
Proiecta 41, 48–9
Prosper of Aquitaine 9, 58, 109–22, 124–5, 128
    De prouidentia Dei 111–12
    De gratia Dei et libero arbitrio contra Collatorem 113

De uocatione omnium gentium 111, 120, 122–3
Epistula ad Demetriadem 112, 122, 124
Epitaphium Nestorianae et Pelagianae haereseon 113
Epitoma chronicon 9, 96, 110, 113, 115, 118–21, 129
Protus and Hyacinthus (martyrs) 41
pseudo-Damasus 59
Ptolomeus and Lucius (martyrs) 41

Quae gesta sunt inter Liberium et Felicem episcopos 34
Quinigesius (Italian bishop) 166, 170, 172
Quirinus (Pannonian martyr) 39

Romanus (*defensor*) 203, 208, 211
Rufinus 128
Rufinus (Italian bishop) 163–4
Rufinus (Spanish bishop) 101–103
Rusticus of Limoges 168

Sabinus (bishop) 161, 163, 165
Sallust (urban prefect 386) 34
Salvian (Spanish bishop) 77, 91, 94–5
Sapaudus (Italian bishop) 174
Saturninus (martyr) 41
Secundinus of Taormina 207
Septimus (Italian bishop) 121
Septimus (slave) 165
Septimius Severus (emperor) 24
Serenus (Italian bishop) 169, 173
Serenus of Nola 170
Severus Alexander 24
Sigibuldus (father of Boniface II) 279
Simplician of Milan 97
Simplicius (martyr) 40–1
Siracusius (Italian bishop) 165
Sixtus (notary) 146
Sozomen
    Historia ecclesiastica 21
Stephan (Italian bishop) 164–5, 170
Stephan (presbyter) 170
Stephen (martyr) 52
Stephen (notary) 208

Stephen (protomartyr) 123–4
Stephen of Larissa 12, 189
Succonius (North African bishop) 167
Suetonius 128
Sulpicius Severus 91, 93
    Chronicon 72, 93, 95–6
    Vita sancti Martini 168
Sylloge Einsiedlensis 28
Sylloge Laureshamensis 27–8
Sylvester of Grumentium 165
Symmachus Junior, Quintus Aurelius Memmius 184, 186
Symphosius (Spanish bishop) 96, 99, 101

Telesinus (nobleman) 166
Terrentianus (papal legate) 159
Tertullian 157
Themistus
    Oratio 204
Theodahad 177, 187, 193
Theodora (slave owner) 163, 165
Theodore of Lilybaeum 203
Theodoric (the Great) 11, 133, 137, 139–40, 152, 166–7, 170–1, 177, 180–87, 190–91, 193
Theodorus, Flavius 185
Theodorus Lector
    Epitome historia ecclesiastica 135, 181
Theodosius I (emperor) 33–4, 55, 81
Theodosius (son of Maurice) 201, 203
Theodoulos (presbyter) 115
Theophanes
    Cronicon 184
Thomas (apostle) 100
Tiberius II (emperor) 200
Tiburtius (martyr) 41
Tibutrius (*notarius*) 117
Timothy (apostle) 54
Timothy Aelurus 135
Tityrus (deacon) 41
Trajan 62
Trajan of Malta 208
Trifolius

Epistula ad beatum Faustum senatorem contra Joannem [Maxentium] Scytham monachum 191

Urbicus (Sicilian abbot) 200, 209

Valentinian I (emperor) 162
Valentinian II (emperor) 33–4, 58, 81
Valentinian III (emperor) 164
Valeria (Greek confessor) 52
Vegetinus (Spanish bishop) 96
Venerius of Milan 97
Viatrix and Rufus 40–1
Victor (Italian bishop) 173
Victor of Palermo 206
Victor of Tonnona 135
Victorius of Aquitaine 115
Victricius of Rouen 69, 71, 84, 102, 104
Vincent (deacon) 52
Vitalis, Martialis and Alexander (martyrs) 41
Vito 27

Wittigis 187

Zacharias of Mytilene
 Historia ecclesiastica 184
Zeno (emperor) 137, 139, 159, 181, 184, 202

Modern Authors and Editors

Accorsi, Maria Letizia 26
Adkin, Neil 59
Allen, Pauline 101, 122–3, 156–7, 159–60, 165, 172
Amelli, Ambrogio Maria (Guerrino) 177, 193
Amici, Angela 190
Amory, Patrick 171, 179, 187–8
Andrews Robert 200

Babut, Ernest-Charles 93
Bagnall, Roger S. 183
Banterle, Gabriele 30
Barclift, Philip 114
Bartolozzi Cast, Gabriele 31
Batlle, Columba Maria 174
Bautz, Friedrich Wilhelm 155
Behrwald, Ralf 42
Berger, Adolf 68
Berlière, Ursmer 209
Berschin, Walter 127–8
Bidez, Joseph 202
Birley, Anthony R. 93
Blair-Dixon, Kate 28, 130, 134–5
Blaudeau, Philippe 7, 11–12, 121, 134–6, 138–9, 180, 188–94
Blázquez Martínez, José Maria 78
Bojpvić, Dragiš 100
Bonamente, G. 121
Borrell Vaider, Agusti 75
Borsari, Silvano 200
Bougard, François 128
Bowes, Kim 7–8, 26, 29–33, 38, 90, 95, 123–4, 144–5
Brandenburg, Hugo 27–9, 40
Brändle, Rupert 54
Brasington, B. 62, 75
Bratož, Rajko 156–7
Bretone, Mario 62
Brown, Jules 200
Brown, Peter R.L. 37, 40, 49, 162, 197, 211
Brown, Thomas S. 182
Browne, Millicent 157
Burns, Thomas S. 90
Burrus, Virginia 55, 89, 92–3, 95, 98, 101

Cain, Andrew 105, 118, 124
Cameron, Averil 2, 10, 17, 187, 197, 203, 206
Canella, Teresa 183
Capizzi, Carmelo 135
Capo, Lidia 183
Cappuyns, Maïeul 110, 113
Carmassi, Patrizia 133
Carragain, Éamonn Ó. 38
Caspar, Erich 5, 59–60, 70, 90, 98, 142, 181, 185

Cavallera, Ferdinand 58
Cerrito, Alessandra 30
Chadwick, Henry 53, 78, 80, 89–98, 101, 103, 181, 184, 191
Chauvot, Alain 184
Chavasse, Antoine 111, 116
Christie, Neil 21–2
Clark, Elizabeth A. 39
Classen, Peter 67
Coarelli, Filippo 27
Collins, Roger 91
Conant, Jonathan 210
Condurachi, Emil 185
Conti, Marco 78, 92–5
Cooper, Kate 23, 38, 122, 130, 145
Corcoran, Simon 67
Cosentino, Augusto 31
Cosentino, Salvatore 187
Coşkun, Altay 58
Courtonne, Yves 31–2
Coustant, Pierre 60, 73, 89, 95, 109
Croke, Brian 138
Curran, John 17, 24, 27
Custodio Vega, Angel 75–6, 81

Dal Santo, Matthew 127, 174
Davis, Raymond 85, 124
Decret, François 157
Delmulle, Jérémy 122
Demacopoulos, George
Denzey, Nicola 38, 40
Dessau, Hermann 124
Deun, Peter Van 51
DiBerardino, Angelo 104
Di Capua, Francesco 109, 113
Diefenbach, Steffen 38
Diehl Ernest 124
Dubois, Jacques 116
Duchesne, Louis 21, 26–7, 29, 34, 42, 85, 124, 127, 130–40, 142, 146–7, 156, 161, 163, 168, 178, 190, 200
Ducloux, Anne 168–9
Dunn, Geoffrey D. 4, 7–8, 13, 32, 69, 75, 90, 94, 97, 98, 100–102, 104–105, 123, 158, 163, 171

Duval, Yves-Marie 60, 102, 128
Duval, Yvette 47
Dvornik, Francis 150

Eadie, John W. 90
Eger, Otto 62
Elberti, Arturo 113–14
Engels, L.J. 67, 211
Enßlin, Wilhelm 139, 185
Ertl, Nelly 128
Escribano, Victoria 95
Evans, Gillian R. 6, 198–9
Ewald, Paul 159, 165, 178

Faller, Otto 58
Fantar, Mhamed 157
Fatás Cabeza, Guilleromo 77–8
Fellermayr, Josef 63
Ferreiro, Alberto 7–9, 79–80, 82, 85, 89–90, 92–3
Ferrua, Antonio 28, 40, 43–8, 50–1, 53–4
Finn, Richard D. 160, 162, 172
Folliet, Georges 168
Fontaine, Jacques 53
Fournier, Eric 93
Führer, Therese 49
Frakes, Robert M. 162

Gadioz, Jean 109–10
Galonnier, Alain
García Sánchez, Justo 97
García Villoslada, Ricardo 75
Garland, L. 158
Gassó, Pius Maria 174
Gavaldà Ribot, Josep Maria 75, 79
Geis, L. 211
Geertman, Herman 24, 27, 128, 130–2, 135–6, 140, 178–9, 181, 183–4
Giaro, Tomasz 62
Gillett, Andrew 155
Gineste-Guipponi, Marie-France 122
Giordani, Roberto 46
Giunta, Francesco 190
Godoy Fernández, C. 76
Goltz, Andreas 183, 185–6, 190

Goubert, Paul 137, 185, 202, 204
Greatrex, Geoffrey 8, 184
Green, Bernard 109–111, 113, 116–18
Green, Malcolm R. 90
Gregory, Jeremy 38
Greschat, Manfred 57
Grig, Lucy 121, 188
Grillmeier, Alois 191, 193
Grillone, Antonino 190
Grodzynski, Denise 162
Guerrini, Paola 27, 31
Guidobaldi, Alessandra Guiglia 27–31
Guidobaldi, Federico 27–31
Guyon, Jean 39–40, 50–1

Hansen, Günther Christian 135
Harnack, Adolf von 178–9
Harris, William V. 160
Hayward, Paul A. 37
Heather, Peter 188
Henry, René 116
Hess, Hamilton
Hill, Carole 94
Hillner, Julia 23, 38, 122, 130, 145
Hofmann, H. 67
Holdsworth, Christopher 113
Holum, Kenneth G. 39
Homes Dudden, Frederick 199
Hoogma, Robertus Petrus 50
Hornung, Christian 7–9, 57, 60, 67, 69, 71–2, 74
Howard-Johnston, James 37
Humfress, Caroline 162–3
Hunter, David G. 105
Huskinson, Janet M. 53
Hwang, Alexander Y. 109–10, 112–14, 117, 120, 124

Ihm, Maximilian 59

Jacobs, Andrew 123
Jacques, François 162
Jaffé, Philippe 179
James, Norman W. 110, 114–15
Jasper, Detlev 59–60, 73–4, 76–7, 81–5

Jones, Arnold H.M. 201, 210–11

Kakridi, Christina 187
Kelly, Gavin 121, 188
Kelly, John N.D. 74, 83–4, 147
Kjaergaard, Jørgen 53
Kleu, M. 211
Klingshirn, William E. 168
König, Ingemar 184, 186
Krabbe, Kathryn Clare 122–4
Kroll, Wilhelm 201
Krüger, Paul 33, 63, 94, 162, 164, 169, 213
Kulikowski, Michael 90, 92, 95
Kurdock, Anne 122

Lamberigts, Mathijs 51
Langen, Joseph 59
Lécrivain, Charles 63
Leemans, Johann 69, 102
Leone, Anne 157
Lepelley, Claude 157, 162, 168, 171
L'Huillier, Peter 20, 97
Liebeschuetz, J.H.W.G. 94
Lieu, Samuel N.C. 95
Lizzi Testa, Rita 109, 121
Llewelyn, Peter A.B. 147
Logan, Alastair 33–4
Lössl, Josef 105
Lowenfeld, Samuel 170
Luongo, Gennaro 38

Maccarrone, Michele 83, 90, 92
McKitterick, Rosamond 128
McLynn, Neil B. 38, 49, 93–5, 143, 155
MacMullen, Ramsay 22
McShane, Philip A. 67, 116
Maier, Harry O. 28, 32, 34
Manigk, Alfred 63
Marcovich, Miroslav 112
Marin, Marcello 158
Marinković, Ana 39
Markus, Robert A. 6, 113, 118, 197–8, 203
Martyn, John R.C. 197, 200, 203, 211
Mathisen, Ralph W. 93, 98–9, 112, 116
Matthews, John 92

Mauskopf-Deliyannis, Deborah 127
Mayer, Wendy 4, 122–3, 157, 160, 165
Maymó I Capdevila, Pere 203
Merdinger, Jane E. 158
Merrills, Andrew H. 210
Meyer, Paul M. 164
Mihoc, Vasile 76
Minnerath, R. 83–4
Mommsen, Theodor 33, 41, 62–3, 94, 127, 131, 162, 164, 169, 178, 193, 213
Moorhead, John 159, 181, 183–5, 199
Moreschini, Claudio 158
Morgan, Edward, 157, 165, 172
Muhlberger, Steven 96, 110, 113, 115, 118–19
Musurillo, Herbert 41
Mynors, Roger A.B. 194

Nathan, G. 158
Neil, Bronwen 4, 7, 10–12, 109, 111, 116, 122, 156–60, 165, 171, 174
Neuman de Vegvar, Carol 38
Noble, Thomas F.X. 181–4
Norberg, Dag 5, 197
Norton, Peter 101

Ohme, Heinz 70
Opitz, Hans Georg 27
Orlandis, José 89–90, 99
Ott, John 39

Parmentier, Léon 202
Pérez González, Cesáreo 78
Picard, Jean-Charles 47
Picotti, G.B. 182
Pieler, Peter E. 67
Pietri, Charles 5, 23–5, 32–3, 38, 43, 71, 90, 94–5, 97, 99–101, 185, 214
Pilara, Gianluca 190
Pricoco, Salvatore 50
Prigent, Vivien 211
Purcell, Nicholas 160

Ramos-Lissón, Domingo 89
Rapp, Claudia

Raven, Susan
Rebillard, Éric
Recchia, Vincenzo
Reekmans, Louis
Renaud, Genevieve 116
Reutter, Ursula 38, 58, 60
Richards, Jeffrey 6, 147, 159, 174, 200
Richardson, Ernest Cushing 29, 109, 114
Rizzi Nervo, Francesca 50
Robinson, James H. 142
Rosi, M. 185
Rossi, Giovanni Battista de 29
Rouche, Michel 160
Rougé, Jean 171

Sághy, Marianne 7–8, 39, 42, 55
Saitta, B. 182
Salzman, Michele Renee 7, 9, 41, 121
Sánchez, Sylvain Jean Gabriel 90
Santorelli, Paola 50
Sardella, Teresa 50, 78, 185
Scerri, Hector 197
Schmidt, Kurt-Dietrich 64
Schöll, Rudolf 201
Schurr, Viktor 191, 193
Schwartz, Eduard 117, 119, 134, 179–80, 183–4, 192–4
Selb, Walter 64
Serfass, Adam 165, 211
Sessa, Kristina 1–3, 7, 17, 22, 112, 121, 144–5, 169, 171, 211
Silva-Tarouca, Karl 58, 119
Sim, David 101
Sirago, Vito Antonio 190
Somerville, Robert 62, 75
Sot, Michel 128
Sotinel, Claire 29, 117
Spearing, Edward and Evelyn 211
Speigl, Jakob 57
Spera, Lucrezia 50
Stark, Rodney 22
Stein, Ernst 179, 185, 187, 194, 201–202
Steinby, Eva Margareta 27
Straub, Johannes 192
Studer, Basil 113

Taylor, Justin 148, 155
Teillet, Suzanne 187–8
Teitler, Hans C. 117
Teja Casuso, Ramón 78
Thacker, Alan 38, 42
Thiel, Andreas 141, 143–6, 148, 150–53, 156–7, 159–61, 163–73
Troncarelli, Fabio 195
Trout, Denis E. 38, 54–5
Turner, Cuthbert Hamilton 31

Ubric Rabaneda, Purificación 74
Ullmann, Walter 5, 63, 71, 142, 155
Urlacher-Becht, Céline 122

Van Dam, Raymond 89, 96
Vedriš, Trpimir 39
Veh, Otto 186–7, 190, 192, 194
Viciano i Vives, Albert 78–9, 84
Vikan Gary 39
Vilella Masana, Josep 73, 84, 89–90
Vitiello, Massimiliano 139
Vives, José 80
Vogel, Cyrille 21, 26–7, 29, 34, 85, 124, 127, 130, 132–40, 142, 146–7, 156, 161, 163, 168, 178, 200

Walser, Gerold 28
Ward-Perkins, Bryan 187
Watson, William Lee 43
Weckwerth, Andreas 71, 91
Weltin, E.G. 90
Wenger, Leopold 62
Wessel, Susan 6
Whitby, Mary 187
Whitby, Michael 201
Wieacker, Franz 63
Williams, George Huntston 43
Williams, R.D. 203
Wirbelauer, Eckhard 58, 130, 133, 135, 177–8, 180–1, 183–5
Wiseman, Timothy P. 113
Witschel, Christian 42
Wojda, Jacek 185
Woods, David 39

Wurm, Hubert 163, 172

Zecchini, Giuseppe 186
Zelzer, Michaela 58
Ziegler, Aloysius K. 155
Zizza, Giuseppe 191
Zwierlein, Otto 64

General

Acherontinus 164 acolytes 21
Africa (North Africa) 4, 9, 17, 58, 74–5, 123, 150, 156–8, 162, 165–7, 171, 173–4, 187, 199, 202, 210
Alexandria 9, 20–1, 24, 118–19, 134, 179–81
almsgiving 10, 124, 167
Altinum 121
Amals 182–3, 187, 190
amphitheatres 24, 104
Antioch 9, 19–20, 100, 179
apocrisarius, see legates
Apollinarians, see heresy
Aquileia 121
archdeacons, see deacons
Arians, see heresy
Arles 4, 17
Arles, Synod of (314) 17
Asia 20, 31
Astorga-León 75, 96
Aurelian Wall 33, 36

Baetica 82, 89, 100
baptism and initiation 21, 31, 46, 65–6, 76, 78–82, 103, 105
baptisteries 31
Baths of Alexander Severus (Thermae Alexandrinae = Thermae Neronis) 24
Bern 115
Braga, Synod of (561) 80, 85
Britain 5, 9
Bruttii 169
burial 2, 21, 36, 47, 49, 51

Calabria 169
Campania 205
Campus Martius 24
Carthage 4, 75, 157–8, 166
Carthage, Synod of (345) 172
Carthage, Synod of (390) 31
Carthage, Synod of (419) 172
Carthaginensis 82, 89
Castor and Pollux 54
catacombs 8, 34, 38–40, 44, 49–50
    catacomb of Cyriaca 46
    catacomb of San Callisto 47, 51–2
    catacomb of San Sebastiano 47
Catania 208
cathedraticum 161
celibacy and sexual misconduct 76, 79–80, 82, 98, 143, 172, 212
cemeteries 33–5, 39–40, 51
census matriculorum 160
Chalcedon, Council of (451) 31, 134, 140, 164
chalice 140
children 21, 163, 171–2
circus 24, 33, 185
Codex Bambergensis 115
Codex Bernensis 115
Codex Novariensis 177
Collectio Avellana 26, 28, 34, 58, 93–4, 96, 129–30, 137–8, 143, 162, 180, 189, 192–4
Collectio Dionysio-Hadriana 157
Collectio Thessalonicensis 12, 58, 177
Constantinople 2, 5, 9, 12–13, 54, 117, 121, 129, 132–40, 146–7, 149–50, 152–3, 155, 163, 167, 177, 180–2, 184–90, 192–3, 200–203, 205–207, 210
Constantinople, First Council of (381) 2
Constantinople, Second Council of (553) 192
Crypt of the Popes, see catacomb of San Callisto
cup 140, 169
cura annonae 24, 158
curiales 103–104

cursus honorum 32–3, 67, 105

Dacia 187
Dalmatia 163
Dardania 137, 159
deacons 12, 20–1, 32–3, 46–7, 51–2, 59, 69, 104–105, 109, 113, 155, 157, 160–1, 163–4, 166, 169, 172–3, 179, 181, 186, 200, 203, 205–209, 211, 214
decretal 8, 59–61, 64–77, 79–85, 95, 134
defensor ecclesiae 158, 161–3, 166, 198, 211
defensor plebis, *defensor ciuitatis* 162–3
domus ecclesiae 21–3, 144–5
Donatists, see schism
doorkeepers 21

Easter 115, 118–129, 170
Edict of Milan 26
Elvira, Synod of (305?) 25, 33, 83, 97
Ephesus, Council of (431) 117, 134
equites singulares 24
Egypt 31
eucharist 31–2, 43, 146, 169–70
excommunication 91, 96–7, 100–102, 143–4, 146, 192
exorcists 21

fermentum 31, 35
Frumenta 163

Gallaecia 82, 96
Gallia, see Gaul
Gangra, Synod of (390) 31
Gaul 4–5, 7–9, 69, 74–5, 77–8, 81–4, 94, 96, 109–10, 112–14, 118, 120, 122, 124, 167, 210
Gepids 187
Girona 102
Gothic War 187, 193–4, 200–201, 205
Goths (see also Ostrogoths, Visigoths) 4, 165, 169, 183–4, 188, 190, 193–4
Gratiana 187

haeres 62–4, 71

heresy and heretics 65–6, 212
   Apollinarians 42
   Arians 38, 42–4, 76, 81–2, 85, 100, 137, 167, 169, 184–7, 191
   Dionysians 169
   Diophysites 184
   Eutychianism 116, 118, 134, 136
   Jovinianists 30, 34, 81
   Manichees 85, 95, 166, 169, 203
   Miaphysites/Monophysites 140, 183, 191
   Nestorians 134
   Nicolaitists 80
   Paulianists 82
   Pelagians 109, 112–13, 116, 119, 121, 156
   Photinians 163
   Priscillianists 8, 74, 77–81, 89–90, 96, 99, 101, 103
   Sabellianists 42
   Theopaschitism and Theopaschite formula 191–5
Hispania, see Spain
horrea publica 24
hortus 30
house-churches, see *domus ecclesiae*

Illyricum 9, 188
Illyricum Occidentale 4
Illyricum Orientale 4, 58, 189
Isis 24

Jews 45, 165–6, 169, 173, 203, 213, 215
Julian of Cos 121
Jupiter Ultor 24

Laodicea, Synod of (320) 31
latifundia 210
legates 102, 132–3, 136, 138–9, 159, 163, 186, 192, 200
Liguria 168
Lilybaeum 202, 208
Lipari 208
Lodi 39
Lombards 177, 205, 215

Luceria 170
Lupercalia 10–11, 143–4, 146, 149
Lusitania 82, 91–2, 94, 96, 103, 105

Macedonia 20
Maratodis
marriage 76, 105, 171, 187
Marseille 109, 112, 121
martyria 33
martyrs 28, 33–5, 37–47, 49–52, 54–5, 64, 139, 186
Massa Furiana 208
mausoleum 33, 44, 46–7
Mérida 74, 95
metropolitan 3–4, 9, 92–4, 96, 101–104, 121
Milan 3–4, 17, 26, 39, 58, 90–1, 93, 95, 97–8, 106, 168, 195, 211
military service and soldiers 52, 103–104, 163
Moesia Prima 187
monks 67–8, 76, 161, 200, 206, 208–210, 212, 214

Narbonensis Secunda 121
Neoplatonism 199
Nicaea, First Council of (325) 3, 20, 32, 68, 81–2, 92, 97, 101–102, 104, 106, 134
Nola 11, 38
notaries 112, 117–18, 121, 124, 146, 208–209, 211–14
Numidia 171
Nuremberg 115

ordination 32, 58, 91, 97–8, 100–105, 131, 133, 146–7, 163–4, 164, 170
orphans 21, 160–1, 172, 212
Ostrogoths 5, 12–13, 149, 155, 160, 177–80, 182, 185–92

Palermo 208, 211
pallium 207
Pannonia 39
patens 21, 140

patriarch 2, 147, 189
penance 21, 68–9, 77, 97–8, 100, 105
peregrini 161
Persia 187, 200
Persian War 200–201
poor 10, 160–3, 166–7, 214–15
praefectus urbi 200
praetorian prefect 3–4, 94, 113, 205, 208
praetor Siliciae 198, 201–204, 215
praetor urbanus 200
presbyters 20–1, 25, 32–3, 35, 99, 149, 209
priests, see presbyters
primate 2, 4
Priscillianists, see heresy
property 10, 17, 26, 35, 63, 161–3, 166, 172–3, 204–205, 208209, 212
Punic Wars 202

Ravenna 3, 5, 12–13, 132, 149, 155, 182, 192, 205, 211
readers (lectors) 21, 24, 32, 59, 76, 105
refugees 10, 156, 166–7, 205
relics 33, 39–40, 53, 123–4
Rhône river (Rhodanus) 168
Rimini, Synod of (359) 66, 78
Rome, churches and monasteries of
    basilica Apostolorum 34
    basilica Julii (iuxta Forum Traiani) 19, 27
    basilica Julii (iuxta Callistum) 19, 27, 34
    basilica Liberiana 19, 26, 28
    basilica Sessoriana (S. Croce in Gerusalemme) 19, 27, 31
    basilica Salvatoris in Laterano (Lateran) 17, 19, 26, 30–1
    ecclesia Clementis (S. Clemente) 19, 29, 31
    ecclesia Crescentiana (S. Sisto Vecchio) 19, 29
    ecclesia Equitii (S. Silvestro, S. Martino al Monte) 19, 26
    ecclesia Felicis 19
    ecclesia in Lucina (S. Lorenzo in Lucina) 19, 28, 31
    ecclesia Marcelli 19, 29
    monastery of St Andrew 200, 206
    Pammachius et Vizantis (SS Giovanni e Paolo) 19, 28, 30, 200
    S. Agnese fuori le Mura 34, 44
    S. Anastasia 19, 28, 31
    S. Caecilia 19, 29, 31
    S. Crisogono 19, 29, 31
    St Felix of Nola 29
    S. Lorenzo fuori le Mura 34
    SS Marcellinus and Paul 34
    S. Marcello 31
    S. Marco 19, 24, 27, 31, 34
    S. Maria Maggiore 28
    S. Paolo fuori le Mura 33–4
    S. Pietro 31, 33–4, 41, 53, 201
    S. Pudenziana 19, 29
    S. Sabina 31
    S. Stefano 31
    S. Stefano (Via Latina) 123
    S. Valentino 34
    S. Vito 27–8
    titulus Byzanti 28
    titulus Damasi (S. Lorenzo in Damaso) 19, 28, 41
    titusus Fasciolae (SS Nereo ed Achilleo) 19, 28
Rome, hills of
    Arx 24
    Aventine 24, 30, 48
    Caelian 199, 206
    Capitoline 24
    Esquiline 27–8
    Palatine 24, 28
    Pincian 29
    Quirinal 24
    Vatican 33, 53
Rome, streets
    Via Appia 47, 53
    Via Ardeatina 24, 34, 47
    Via Aurelia 34
    Via Flaminia 34
    Via Lata 24, 29
    Via Latina 31, 123
    Via Nova 24

Via Ostensis 33–4, 53
Via Portuensis 34
Via Tiburtina 46
Rome, Synod of (mid-third century) 20
Rome, Synod of (378) 32, 45, 93–4, 106
Rome, Synod of (382) 53
Rome, Synod of (386) 58, 102
Rome, Synod of (502) 168
Rome, Synod of (531) 189
Romulus and Remus 54
Rouen 38

Sabellianists, see heresy
Sardinia 46, 100, 209
schism and schismatics 3, 11–12, 35, 42,
    44–6, 55, 70, 97, 99–100, 102, 130,
    132, 150
  Acacian schism 12, 132, 135, 137–8,
    140, 147, 152, 155–6, 163, 168,
    179–80, 182, 184, 191
  Dioscoran schism 178
  Donatist schism 17, 26, 34, 42, 45, 97,
    166
  Laurentian schism 11, 130, 135–6, 178,
    180–2, 184–6, 188–92, 194–5
  Luciferian schism 26, 115
  Melitian schism 42
  Novatianist schism 42, 45–6, 79, 85, 97
  Ursinian schism 45
scrinia and archives 20, 41, 85, 117, 134,
    136, 146
Scyllaceum 169
Senate 3, 135, 148, 150, 152, 168, 190, 193
Septizodium 24
Serapeum 24
Serapis 24
Serbia 187
Serdica, Synod of (343) 25, 32, 95
Sicily 7, 12, 161, 173, 197, 200–201,
    204–11, 213–14
Sicily, monasteries of
  Abbazia di San Martino delle Scale 200
  Lucuscano (SS Massimo et Agata a
    Palermo) 200, 209
  S. Borsari 200

S. Ermete 200
S. Georgio 200
St Hermas, Palermo 209
St Lucy, Syracuse 208
St Peter, Baiae 208
St Vitus, Mt Etna 209, 214
Sirmium 187
slaves 10, 33, 161, 163–5, 168–9, 171–3,
    203–204, 210, 214–15
Spain 5, 7–9, 60, 73–5, 77–9, 81–5, 90–2,
    94–6, 100, 104, 106, 210
subdeacons, see deacons
suburbia 33–6, 39–40
Syracuse 12, 202–203, 207–208, 211–12,
    214

Tarraconensus 91, 95, 102
Tarragona 75, 78
Terracina 164
theatres 103
Thelepte (Zelle), Synod of (418) 58, 102
Thessalia 189
Thessaloniki 58
Tindari 208
titulus 21–3, 25, 30, 36
Toledo, Synod of (400) 80, 85, 89, 96–105
Toledo, Synod of (589) 85
Trastevere 27, 29–30, 32
Trier 4, 77
Triocala 208

usury 172

Valerii hospice, Rome 209
Vandals 4, 166, 187, 210
vases 21
Vatican, First Council of (1870) 2
Venefrana 165, 169
Venice 121
Venus Caelestis 24
Vibo 169
Vienne 4
virgins 48, 51, 105, 123
Visigoths 91, 210
Volaterra 161

widows 21, 47–8, 105, 123, 160–1, 166, 172, 212

zaja 165

Zaragoza, Synod of (380) 77–9, 90, 92, 94, 96